POCKET *A*DVENTURES

THE ALPS

Krista Dana

HUNTER

HUNTER PUBLISHING, INC,
130 Campus Drive, Edison, NJ 08818
732-225-1900; 800-255-0343; fax 732-417-1744
www.hunterpublishing.com

Ulysses Travel Publications
4176 Saint-Denis, Montréal, Québec
Canada H2W 2M5
514-843-9882, ext. 2232; fax 514-843-9448

Windsor Books International
5, Castle End Park, Castle End Rd, Ruscombe
Berkshire, RG10 9XQ England, ☎ 01189-346-367/fax 01189-346-368

ISBN 978-1-58843-630-6
© 2007 Hunter Publishing, Inc.

Photographs throughout the book are used courtesy of picswiss.ch, swiss-image.ch, Tourismus Salzburg, Tourismusverband Neustift im Stubaital, Nationalpark Hohe Tauern, Tourismusverband Sölden-Ötztal, Lech Tourismus, Silvretta Galtür, Tourismusverband Ischgl, Val Thorens Office de Tourisme, Tourismusverband St. Johan in Tirol, Office du Tourisme de Méribel, Tourist Board Mayrhofen, Office du Tourisme Val d'Isère, Füssen Tourismus, A.P.T. del Comasco, Oberammergau Tourismus, Verbier/Bagnes Tourism, Swiss Travel System, Luzern Tourismus, Interlaken Tourismus and the author.

Cover photo: *Italian Dolomites* (© ImageState/Alamy)
Index: Nancy Wolff

1 2 3 4

Table of Contents

INTRODUCTION   **1**
About This Book   2
How To Use It   2
Quick-Start Planning   3
The Alps   8
  Prehistory   8
  Climate   10
  Flora   12
    Vegetation Belts   12
    Alpine Flowers   13
  Fauna   15
Travel Basics   20
  When To Go   20
  Transportation   21
    Getting Here   21
    Getting Around   22
            By Car   22
            By Train & Bus   26
            By Cableway & Mountain Train   26
  Currency   27
  Where to Sleep   28
  Dining   29
  Connections   32
    Language   32
    Telephone   33
    Internet   33
    Time Zone   33
    Electricity   33
  Health & Safety   34
  Getting More Information   35

AUSTRIA   **37**
People & Culture   37
The Arlberg   41
  St. Anton am Arlberg   43
    History & Overview   43
    The Town   44
    Getting Here & Around   45
    Getting More Info   46
    The Sights   46
    The Adventures   47
    Where to Sleep   51

Where to Eat	52
Where to Party	53
Where to Play	54
Festivals & Events	55
St. Christoph	56
Lech	58
Ischgl	61
Bregenz	65
Feldkirch	71
Innsbruck & the Tyrol	73
Innsbruck	75
History & Overview	75
The Town	76
Getting Here & Around	76
Getting More Info	77
The Sights	77
The Adventures	82
On Innsbruck's Doorstep	84
Nordpark-Seegrube	84
Igls	84
Mutterer Alm	85
Azamer Lizum	86
Where to Sleep	86
Where to Eat	87
Where to Party	88
Where to Play	89
Festivals & Events	89
Seefeld	90
The Ötztal	92
The Stubaital	98
The Zillertal	100
Kitzbühel	104
History & Overview	104
The Town	105
Getting Here & Around	106
Getting Connected	107
The Sights	107
The Adventures	109
Where to Sleep	113
Where to Eat	114
Where to Party	114
Where to Play	115
Festivals & Events	115
St. Johann	116
Söll	119
Salzburg & the Salzburgerland	123
Salzburg	123

History & Overview 123
The Town 127
Getting Here & Around 127
Getting More Info 128
The Sights 128
     The Von Trapp Story 129
The Adventures 135
Where to Sleep 137
Where to Eat 138
Where to Party 139
Festivals & Events 140
The Salzkammergut 140
Zell am See & Kaprun 144
  Höhe Tauern National Park 148
  Krimml 149

FRANCE **153**
People & Culture 154
Mont Blanc Region 156
  Chamonix 157
    History & Orientation 157
    The Town 158
    Getting Here & Around 159
    Getting More Info 160
    The Sights 160
    The Adventures 163
    Where to Sleep 167
    Where to Eat 168
    Where to Party 169
    Where to Play 170
    Festivals & Events 170
    Argentière 172

GERMANY **175**
People & Culture 176
Munich & The Bavarian Alps 180
  Munich 180
    History & Orientation 180
    The Town 181
    Getting Here & Around 182
    Getting More Info 183
    The Sights 184
      Tours 189
    The Adventures 190
    Where to Sleep 192
    Where to Eat 193
    Where to Party 195
    Where to Play 196

Festivals & Events	196
Dachau	200
Chiemsee	202
Garmisch-Partenkirchen	205
History & Orientation	205
The Town	207
Getting Here & Around	207
Getting More Info	208
The Sights	209
The Adventures	211
Where to Sleep	218
Where to Eat	219
Where to Party	220
Where to Play	220
Festivals & Events	220
Oberammergau	221
Füssen	227
Berchtesgaden	231
History & Overview	231
The Town	232
Getting Here & Around	232
Getting More Info	233
The Sights	233
The Adventures	235
Where to Sleep	239
Where to Eat	240
Where to Party	240
Where to Play	241
Festivals & Events	241
Berchtesgaden National Park	242
Königsee	244
ITALY	**247**
Overview & Government	247
People & Culture	249
Milan & Northwest Italy	252
Milan	252
History & Overview	252
The Town	254
Getting Here & Around	255
Getting More Info	255
The Sights	256
Where to Sleep	259
Where to Eat	260
Where to Party	260
Festivals & Events	261
Lake Como	262
Turin	266

Courmayeur   270
  History & Orientation   270
  The Town   271
  Getting Here & Around   272
  Getting More Info   273
  The Sights   273
  The Adventures   274
  Where to Sleep   278
  Where to Eat   279
  Where to Party   280
  Where to Play   281
  Aosta   283
  Gran Paradiso National Park   286
Venice & Northeast Italy   288
  Venice   290
    History & Orientation   290
    The Town   292
    Getting Here & Around   293
    Getting More Info   294
    The Sights   294
    The Adventures   302
    Where to Sleep   306
    Where to Eat   308
    Where to Party   309
    Where to Play   310
    Festivals & Events   310
  Cortina d'Ampezzo   311
    History & Orientation   311
    The Town   312
    Getting Here & Around   313
    Getting More Info   315
    The Sights   315
    The Adventures   316
    Where to Sleep   321
    Where to Eat   322
    Where to Party   323
    Where to Play   323
    Festivals & Events   324
    The Val Gardena   324

LIECHTENSTEIN   **329**
History & Government   329
People & Culture   331
Vaduz   333
  The Town   333
  Getting Here & Around   334
  Getting More Info   335
  The Sights   335

Where to Sleep	338
Where to Eat	339
Where to Party	340
Where to Play	340
Festivals & Events	340
Malbun	342
Steg	344
SWITZERLAND	**347**
People & Culture	350
Geneva & The Valais	352
Geneva	353
History & Orientation	353
The Town	354
Getting Here & Around	354
Getting More Info	355
The Sights	355
The Adventures	359
Where to Sleep	359
Where to Eat	360
Where to Party	361
Festivals & Events	362
Lausanne	364
Zermatt	365
History & Orientation	368
The Town	369
Getting Here & Around	370
Getting More Info	371
The Sights	371
The Adventures	373
Where to Sleep	377
Where to Eat	379
Where to Party	379
Where to Play	380
Festivals & Events	380
Saas-Fee	381
Interlaken & the Jungfrau	384
Interlaken	385
History & Orientation	386
The Town	386
Getting Here & Around	387
Getting More Info	387
The Sights	387
The Adventures	388
Where to Sleep	400
Where to Eat	401
Where to Party	402
Where to Play	403

Festivals & Events	403
Lauterbrunnen	404
Grindelwald	406
Wengen	409
Mürren	411
Zürich & Central Switzerland	415
Zürich	416
History & Orientation	417
The Town	417
Getting Here & Around	418
Getting More Info	419
The Sights	420
The Adventures	422
Where to Sleep	423
Where to Eat	425
Where to Party	426
Where to Play	426
Festivals & Events	427
Rheinfall	428
Lucerne	429
History & Orientation	430
The Town	431
Getting Here & Around	431
Getting More Info	432
The Sights	433
The Adventures	435
Where to Sleep	439
Where to Eat	442
Where to Party	443
Where to Play	443
Festivals & Events	444
Engelberg	444
The Graubünden Region	449
St. Moritz	450
History & Orientation	450
The Town	451
Getting Here & Around	452
Getting More Info	453
The Sights	453
The Adventures	454
Where to Sleep	460
Where to Eat	462
Where to Party	463
Where to Play	463
Festivals & Events	463
Silvaplana	465
The Swiss National Park	467

Language Primer   469
Index   473

MAPS
Alpine Europe   inside cover
Alpine Austria   38
Bregenz & the Arlberg   42
Innsbruck & the Tyrol   74
Salzburg & Salzburgerland   126
Alpine France   152
Mont Blanc Region   157
Alpine Germany   177
Alpine Italy   248
Milan & Northwest Italy   253
Venice & Northeast Italy   289
Venice   291
Liechtenstein   330
Alpine Switzerland   349
Geneva & the Valais   358
The Jungfrau Region   389
Central Switzerland   416
The Graubünden Region   449

Acknowledgements

Although there is only one author's name listed on the front cover, this book is the result of a great many contributions. First thanks go to my outlandishly supportive family and friends, who allowed me to neglect real-world responsibilities during the many months I spent researching this project. I am blessed to call you mine.

Particular thanks go to my dad and mom, Bob and Mary Lou Smith; to Tom and Mitzi Smith, Lee and Jacqueline Collins, Roger and Deanne Wagner, Carol Barker, and the Sooners of Cohort 3; and to my husband, both for his unending support and his expertise in European history. Thanks go, as well, to editor and publisher Michael Hunter and the many publishing, editing, and tourism professionals who made this project click.

Finally, recognition goes to those countless strangers on mountain trails, ferry crossings, and ski slopes that offered their opinions and advice – some of it solicited, some of it not. Much of their insight is represented here.

Finally, and most forcefully, I thank Jethro: Life with him turns out to be the best adventure of all.

About the Author

A native of southern California, Krista Dana has lived and worked in Europe, Asia, and the Rocky Mountains. Along the way she's wrestled cocktails from thieving primates in Kenya, drifted on a broken-down boat among the Indonesian Islands, and raced Chinese school children to the top of The Great Wall. An avid skier and hiker, she has explored terrain ranging from Switzerland's Matterhorn to South Korea's Muju Mountain. Today, when not basking in the glow of her computer monitor, Krista plays in the dirt and snow near her current home in northern Utah.

Krista has written over 800 travel features, hotel reviews, and destination guides. Her first book, *The Alps Adventure Guide*, was published in 2004. She holds a master's degree in Human Relations and a doctorate in Organizations and Leadership.

Introduction

If castles, cuckoo clocks, and bell-laden cows dominate your image of the Alps, you are – like most travelers – missing out on one of Mother Nature's greatest gifts. It's a secret Europeans like to keep to themselves.

IN THIS CHAPTER

■ About this Book   2
■ How to Use It   2
■ Quick-Start Planning   3
■ The Alps   8
　■ Prehistory   8
　■ Climate   10
　■ Flora   12
　■ Fauna   15
■ Travel Basics   20

In addition to its wealth of cultural sights, the European Alps offer a wider range of outdoor recreation than any other similarly sized region in the world. Adventurers of all ages hike hut-to-hut on multi-day treks, skiers slide year-round on glacial slopes, and Sunday walkers stroll forested trails. Bikers loop icy blue lakes, and mountaineers scale up waterfalls and down canyon cliffs.

Europeans cherish their wilderness areas, and none more so than the pristine forests of the Alps. Modern adventurers run the gamut from rich to poor, young to old, and native to transient foreigner. So take a look around. That bus driver. . . This tour guide. . . Your hotel concierge. . . They may just be showing you the Europe they think you want to see. Take a moment to ask how they spend their own free time – odds are that each will spend a day outdoors this weekend.

Want to know where they go?

We did, too.

This project took flight after a personal search for information on Alpine recreation proved painstaking and, in the end, not terribly productive. Some information does exist, but mainly on scattered websites, and frequently only in local languages. As far as we can tell, European tourism offices still insist that foreigners want prettily packaged displays of stereotyped culture – and maybe some do. What we're after, however, are the richer rewards that come from getting down and dirty, cold and wet, out in the wonderfully wild outdoors.

Opposite: Gsteigwiler-Wildersil, in the Jungfrau, Switzerland

About This Book

Pocket Adventures: The Alps is just that – a pocket-sized guide to the best sights and adventures in the mountainous regions of Austria, France, Germany, Italy, Liechtenstein, and Switzerland. Based on experience gained through more than a decade of living in, traveling around, and writing about the Alps, we spotlight the best gateway cities, the best sightseeing bases, and the best outdoor adventures.

The precursor to this book, *The Alps Adventure Guide*, is a hefty tome that includes detailed information about sights and recreation in even the remotest Alpine regions. *Pocket Adventures: The Alps* distills that information into a portable guide that's ideally suited to on-the-go travelers who seek the best of the Alps – those sights and adventures most worthwhile, most easily reached, and most indicative of the Alpine experience.

Here, we cover the places where you're likely to end up when crossing the European Alps and the places that you shouldn't miss in-between, even if you have only a few days or a week to spend.

This book is written with three reader groups in mind:

- Students, couples, and families who want to add some adventure to a standard sightseeing tour
- Experienced travelers already familiar with the region and who now want something more from their travels
- Outdoor enthusiasts seeking new ways to play

In short, what all our readers have in common is this: the desire to *experience* rather than simply *look at* the Alps.

How To Use It

This guide features 13 recreational regions in six countries: Austria, France, Germany, Italy, Liechtenstein, and Switzerland. For each region, we've selected a handful of bases – villages, towns, national parks, and resorts – and highlighted the sights and adventures convenient to each.

Ringgenberg-Goldswill on Lake Brienz, Switzerland

In all, 58 destinations are covered here. Nineteen are spotlighted in detail, with in-depth information about what to see and where to sleep, eat, play, and party. In selecting these bases, we've weighed popularity, practicality, and convenience: Spotlighted destinations, then, include gateway cities (common fly-in entry points), towns particularly popular with Alpine travelers, and smaller recreational resorts easily reached via major transit routes. In addition, 39 more destinations are covered in brief snippets, profiling bases well worth a somewhat longer stay or a diversion from a pre-planned route. Often smaller or more remote than our spotlighted destinations, these memorable villages, valleys, and resorts are, in fact, some of our favorite places to play in the Alps.

Quick-Start Planning

Planning an adventure vacation is for many a daunting task. Selecting a destination is, of course, a critical part of that process and a particularly difficult decision for both those unaccustomed to international travel and those wishing to venture away from the tourist-trod path. The most straightforward planning method suits travelers with a particular culture, country, or route in mind – simply look at a map and peruse the this book's chapter intros to hunt down an ideal base.

For readers who want a bit more guidance, we make it easy with a quick-start strategy: three lists, each highlighting the best Alpine destinations by theme, vibe, and adventure.

- **Pick-A-Theme** – For those seeking the best of the Alps, we offer Pick-A-Theme lists. Here, round-ups assist in planning travel based on features such as Olympic resorts, best old-town centers, historic hotels, and dramatic drives.

- **Pick-A-Vibe** – For those weighing less tangible considerations, we suggest the Pick-A-Vibe list. For example, travelers can choose a destination for its village charm, big-name clout, or party-hearty frame of mind.

- **Pick-An-Adventure** – Travelers seeking a specific type of recreation should consult the Pick-An-Adventure list. The list boils down the best of our featured destinations for each activity.

PICK-A-THEME	
TOP OLD-TOWNS	**NATIONAL PARKS**
Historic towns with shops, cafés, and quaint hotels	The Alps' most pristine wilderness
■ Feldkirch	■ Berchtesgaden National Park
■ Kitzbühel	■ Gran Paradiso National Park
■ Oberammergau	■ Hohe Tauern National Park
■ Salzburg	■ Swiss National Park
■ Zurich	
MUSEUM TOWNS	**HISTORIC HOTELS**
An art-and-history buff's dream – towns with multiple museums	Elegant, creaky old dames from centuries gone by
■ Innsbruck	■ Badrutt's Palace (St. Moritz)
■ Lucerne	■ Gritti Palace (Venice)
■ Munich	■ Hospiz Alm (St. Christoph)
■ Salzburg	■ Kulm (St. Moritz)
■ Venice	■ Miramonti Majestic (Cortina)

Zurich	Villa d'Este (Como Cernobbio)
	Villa Serbelloni (Como Bellagio)
PEAK EXPERIENCES	**OLYMPIC LEGACIES**
The Alps' most spectacular mountains, each easily accessed by year-round cableway or train	Veterans of the world stage, these Olympic hosts still put on a good show
Jungfrau (Interlaken)	Chamonix (1924)
Matterhorn (Zermatt)	Cortina d'Ampezzo (1956)
Mont Blanc (Chamonix or Courmayeur)	Garmisch-Part. (1936)
Titlis (Engelberg)	Innsbruck (1964, 1976)
Valluga (St. Anton)	Lausanne (IOC Headqtrs.)
Zugspitze (Garmisch-Partenkirchen)	Meribel & Val d'Isere (1992)
	Munich (1972)
	St. Moritz (1928)
	Turin (2006)
DRAMATIC DRIVES	**THE SIGHTSEER**
These roads venture into the high Alps, skirting glaciers and traversing barren terrain	Must-see sights – check out Peak Experiences, too
Gerlos Pass (Zillertal- Krimml)	Eagle's Nest (Berchtesgaden)
Great St. Bernard Pass (Val d'Aosta - Valais)	Grand Canal (Venice)
Grossglockner Hochalpenstrasse (Hohe Tauern Nat'l Park)	Hofbrauhaus (Munich)
Silvretta Hochalpenstrasse (Arlberg)	Linderhof Castle (Oberammergau)
Timmeljoch Hochalpenstrasse (Ötztal – Italy)	Milan's Cathedral
	Neuschwanstein Castle (Fussen)
	Salzburg's Old Town
	St. Mark's Square (Venice)

PICK-A-VIBE

ALPINE CHARMERS	PARTY-HEARTY WINTER RESORTS
Traditional mountain hamlets exuding allure	Where the revelry starts early and lasts long
■ Lech, Austria	■ Chamonix, France
■ Mürren, Switz	■ Ischgl, Austria
■ Oberammergau, Germany	■ Kitzbühel, Austria
■ Saas-Fee, Switz	■ Ötztal (Solden, Austria)
■ Wengen, Switz	■ St. Anton, Austria
	■ Zermatt, Switz

FAMILY-FRIENDLY PLAYGROUNDS	GLAMOUR GIRLS
Fun destinations for parents and kids	Expensive, fur-lined resorts where socialites show up just to show off
■ Interlaken, Switz	■ Cortina, Italy
■ Lech, Austria	■ Courmayeur, Italy
■ Malbun/Steg, Liechtenstein	■ Kitzbühel, Austria
■ Meribel, France	■ St. Moritz, Switz
■ St. Johann, Austria	■ Zermatt, Switz
■ Zermatt, Switz	

CITY-SPORTSTER	CITY-SHOPPER
The best of both worlds – big-town conveniences with big mountains nearby	Havens of hedonism for shopping, dining, and entertainment
■ Geneva, Switz	■ Milan, Italy
■ Innsbruck, Austria	■ Munich, Germany
■ Lucerne, Switz	■ Salzburg, Austria
■ Salzburg, Austria	■ Venice, Italy
■ Vaduz, Liechtenstein	■ Zürich, Switz

GENTEEL HIDEAWAYS	SCENIC SPLENDOR
No paparazzi here – try these discreet retreats for a refined holiday	Mother Nature's best work. See also, National Parks, below
■ Lech, Austria	■ Cortina d'Ampezzo, Italy
■ Mürren, Switz	■ Jungfrau Region
■ Seefeld, Austria	■ Königsee, Germany
■ St. Christoph, Austria	■ Bellagio (Lake Como, Italy)
	■ Venice, Italy

PICK-AN-ADVENTURE

MOUNTAINEERING CLASSICS	WALKING & HIKING
The historical towns where alpinism got its start	Long, short, shallow, and steep – these resorts please with a variety of trails
■ Chamonix	■ Cortina
■ Cortina	■ Jungfrau Region
■ Courmayeur	■ Seefeld
■ Jungfrau Region	■ St. Moritz
■ St. Anton	■ Val Gardena
■ Zermatt	■ Zermatt

MOUNTAIN BIKING	ODDBALL EXTREMES
Put wheel to trail at these resorts	Europe's adventure sport outfitters bring on the adrenaline rush
■ Chamonix	■ Cortina
■ Garmisch-Partenkirchen	■ Engelberg
■ Innsbruck	■ Interlaken
■ Interlaken	■ Zillertal
■ Ischgl	
■ Zell am See	

LAKE SPORTS	WHITEWATER SPORTS
Sailors, swimmers, water-skiers, and kite-surfers head for these Alpine waters	Wild rides on Alpine rapids – get set to get wet
■ Chiemsee	■ Interlaken
■ Geneva	■ Lucerne
■ Interlaken	■ Ötztal
■ Silvaplana	■ Zell am See
■ Zell am See	■ Zillertal

AIRBORNE SPORTS	SUMMER GLACIER PLAY
Parasailing, sightseeing flights, helicopter rides, and ballooning – take a flying leap at these destinations	With skiing, tubing, dog-sledding, and ice caves, these glacier resorts stay cool in summer, too
■ Chamonix	■ Hintertux (Zillertal)
■ Interlaken	■ Jungfrau
■ Silvaplana	■ Kaprun

Introduction

■ St. Moritz	■ Saas-Fee
■ Zermatt	■ Stubaital
	■ Zermatt

SNOW-SLIDING FOR DISTANCE	SNOW-SLIDING FOR SPEED
With extensive lift networks and moderate slopes, these resorts please intermediate-level cruisers	Experts go steep and deep with high-gradient slopes, heli-skiing drops, and extreme off-piste opportunities
■ Cortina	■ Argentière
■ Ischgl	■ Chamonix
■ Kitzbühel	■ St. Anton
■ Sella Ronda (Val Gardena)	■ Zermatt
■ Söll	

SNOW-SLIDING FOR FAMILIES	SNOW FOR THOSE WHO DON'T SKI
Homey resorts with mild slopes and good ski-school programs	Ice-skating, tobogganing, sleigh rides, and more. There's a lot to do at these resort off-boards, too
■ Lech	■ Cortina
■ Saas-Fee	■ Jungfrau Region
■ Seefeld	■ Saas-Fee
■ St. Johann	■ St. Moritz
■ Wengen	■ Zermatt

The Alps

◆ Prehistory

Hundreds of millions of years ago, the Alps began their formation with the upward surge of the earth's crust. Over the course of millions of years more, limestone forced up along the Alpine axis, granite thrust into the western Alps, and – some 20 million years ago — the African continent collided with the Eurasian landmass, pushing, folding, and rippling the Alps to their current height. Nonetheless, the shape of the Alps has forever been in flux, as ever-present glaciers grow and recede, whittling valleys and ravines as they go. Additionally, these glaciers serve as the headwaters for many Alpine streams and rivers –

Aletsch Glacier, Switzerland

forces of water that shift and erode the land, changing the lay-
out of the mountains as they go. Together, the prehistoric subterranean collisions and glacial processes have sculpted one of
the world's great mountain ranges.

Sculptors of The Alps:
Glaciers & Their Lifecycles

Glaciers play a significant role in sculpting Alpine
geology as they progress through their three-stage
lifecycle. During the first phase, the *growth* period,
snow accumulates, turns to ice, and begins to flow
outwards and downwards under the pressure of its
own weight. As the process continues through
many seasons, the pressure from overlying snow
compacts the underlying layers, forming ever-
larger ice crystals – crystals that together take on
that chilling blue tint.

During the second phase of the glacial life cycle,
the *motion* period, the glacier begins to crawl. Valley glaciers flow down slopes, while continental
glaciers flow outward in all directions from a central
point. This movement can dramatically impact the
surrounding environment through both erosion

and deposition. In this manner, glaciers carve out valleys as they creep, wearing away rocks and soil and pushing that sediment ahead of the ice flow.

As the earth's climate gradually changes, glaciers begin the third and final phase of their life cycle, the *retreat*. Retreat is measured from the front of the glacier, and is said to occur when more ice is melted or ablated than is deposited each year. As the glacier retreats, it reveals the scars and valleys created during the moving phase. Alpine glaciers, generally smaller and less stable than polar glaciers, are particularly susceptible to glacial retreat and variation and, as such, the Alps harbor many examples of dramatic glacial sculpting.

Today, the Alps span some 1,000 km/600 miles from east to west. Starting in France, the range forms a crescent that arches through Switzerland, Liechtenstein, Austria, Germany, and Italy, and then drops down into Slovenia and the former Yugoslavia. The range includes several hundred peaks over 4,000 m/ 13,120 feet, with the tallest peak, Mont Blanc, reaching 4,810 m/15,777 feet.

◆ Climate

 The Alps harbor a variety of localized micro-climates, with climatic zones stacking up along the long, narrow wall of mountains at steep gradients. To the south, for example, travelers go from just above sea level at the foot of the Alps to over 2,500 m/8,200 feet above sea level with just a short drive. Further complicating the matter, the range runs east to west, dividing northern and southern Europe, so sides of the mountain range see very different amounts of precipitation and sunlight through the course of the seasons.

On the facing page are weather statistics from a representative sample of Alpine destinations. For comparison purposes, I've included Denver, Colorado, too.

☼ = summer season   ❅ = winter season
♦ = normal town activity   blank = closing period

	Berchtesg. GE	Bregenz AU	Chamonix FR	Cortina IT	Courmayeur IT	Engelberg SW	Garm.-Part. GE	Geneva SW	Innsbruck AU	Interlaken SW	Ischgl AU	Kitzbuhel AU	Lucerne SW	Milan IT	Munich GE	Salzburg AU	St. Anton AU	St. Moritz SW	Turin IT	Vaduz LI	Venice IT	Zermatt SW	Zürich SW
DEC	❅	♦	❅	❅	❅	❅	❅	♦	♦	❅	❅	❅	♦	♦	♦	♦	❅	❅	♦	♦	♦	❅	♦
	♦	♦	❅	❅	❅	❅	❅	♦	♦	♦	❅	♦	♦	♦	♦	♦	❅	❅	♦	♦	♦	❅	♦
	♦	♦	♦	♦			♦	♦	♦	♦	❅	♦	♦	♦	♦	♦			♦	♦	♦	❅	♦
NOV	♦	♦	♦	♦			♦	♦	♦	♦		♦	♦	♦	♦	♦			♦	♦	♦	♦	♦
	♦	♦	♦	♦			♦	♦	♦	♦		♦	♦	♦	♦	♦			♦	♦	♦	♦	♦
	♦	♦	♦	♦			♦	♦	♦	♦		♦	♦	♦	♦	♦			♦	♦	♦	♦	♦
OCT	♦	♦	♦	♦			♦	♦	♦	♦		♦	♦	♦	♦	♦			♦	♦	♦	☼	♦
	☼	♦	☼	☼			☼	♦	♦	☼		♦	♦	♦	♦	♦			♦	♦	♦	☼	♦
SEP	☼	♦	☼	☼	☼	☼	☼	♦	♦	☼		☼	♦	♦	♦	♦	☼		♦	♦	♦	☼	♦
	☼	♦	☼	☼	☼	☼	☼	♦	♦	☼	☼	☼	♦	♦	♦	♦	☼	☼	♦	♦	♦	☼	♦
	☼	♦	☼	☼	☼	☼	☼	♦	♦	☼	☼	☼	♦	♦	♦	♦	☼	☼	♦	♦	♦	☼	♦
AUG	☼	♦	☼	☼	☼	☼	☼	♦	♦	☼	☼	☼	♦	♦	♦	♦	☼	☼	♦	♦	♦	☼	♦
	☼	♦	☼	☼	☼	☼	☼	♦	♦	☼	☼	☼	♦	♦	♦	♦	☼	☼	♦	♦	♦	☼	♦
	☼	♦	☼	☼	☼	☼	☼	♦	♦	☼	☼	☼	♦	♦	♦	♦	☼	☼	♦	♦	♦	☼	♦
JUL	☼	♦	☼	☼	☼	☼	☼	♦	♦	☼	☼	☼	♦	♦	♦	♦	☼	☼	♦	♦	♦	☼	♦
	☼	♦	☼	☼	☼	☼	☼	♦	♦	☼	☼	☼	♦	♦	♦	♦	☼	☼	♦	♦	♦	☼	♦
	☼	♦	☼	☼	☼	☼	☼	♦	♦	☼		☼	♦	♦	♦	♦	☼	☼	♦	♦	♦	☼	♦
JUN	☼	♦	☼	☼	☼		☼	♦	♦	☼		☼	♦	♦	♦	♦	☼	☼	♦	♦	♦	♦	♦
	☼	♦	♦	♦			☼	♦	♦	☼		♦	♦	♦	♦	♦			♦	♦	♦	♦	♦
	☼	♦	♦	♦			♦	♦	♦	♦		♦	♦	♦	♦	♦			♦	♦	♦	♦	♦
MAY	♦	♦	♦	♦			♦	♦	♦	♦		♦	♦	♦	♦	♦			♦	♦	♦	♦	♦
	♦	♦	♦	♦			♦	♦	♦	♦		♦	♦	♦	♦	♦			♦	♦	♦	♦	♦
APR	♦	♦	♦	♦		❅	♦	♦	♦	♦	❅	♦	♦	♦	♦	♦			♦	♦	♦	❅	♦
	♦	♦	❅	❅		❅	♦	♦	♦	♦	❅	♦	♦	♦	♦	♦			♦	♦	♦	❅	♦
	♦	♦	❅	❅	❅	❅	❅	♦	♦	❅	❅	♦	♦	♦	♦	♦	❅	❅	♦	♦	♦	❅	♦
MAR	❅	♦	❅	❅	❅	❅	❅	♦	♦	❅	❅	❅	♦	♦	♦	♦	❅	❅	♦	♦	♦	❅	♦
	❅	♦	❅	❅	❅	❅	❅	♦	♦	❅	❅	❅	♦	♦	♦	♦	❅	❅	♦	♦	♦	❅	♦
FEB	❅	♦	❅	❅	❅	❅	❅	♦	♦	❅	❅	❅	♦	♦	♦	♦	❅	❅	♦	♦	♦	❅	♦
	❅	♦	❅	❅	❅	❅	❅	♦	♦	❅	❅	❅	♦	♦	♦	♦	❅	❅	♦	♦	♦	❅	♦
JAN	❅	♦	❅	❅	❅	❅	❅	♦	♦	❅	❅	❅	♦	♦	♦	♦	❅	❅	♦	♦	♦	❅	♦
	❅	♦	❅	❅	❅	❅	❅	♦	♦	❅	❅	❅	♦	♦	♦	♦	❅	❅	♦	♦	♦	❅	♦
	❅	♦	❅	❅	❅	❅	❅	♦	♦	❅	❅	❅	♦	♦	♦	♦	❅	❅	♦	♦	♦	❅	♦

◆ Flora

Nowhere on the globe has such an ecologically rich region been developed so thoughtfully. It's an admirable accomplishment. Tens of thousands of visitors venture to the Alpine wilderness each weekend but, even after centuries of use, much of this pristine wilderness remains intact. Preservation efforts continue, particularly in the national parks, and travelers are apt to witness a memorable display of plant and animal life.

Botanists categorize habitats into several vegetation belts, each delineating the types of flora that thrive there. The span of each categorical belt, however, can vary considerably among regions and even from one side to the other of a single mountain peak. (Some glaciers, in fact, sit at lower altitudes than do neighboring mountains' tree lines.) Thus, the altitude approximations offered below can be no more than estimations. In any case, Alpine travelers will witness a vast array of vegetation clinging to rock crevices, peeking through springtime snowbanks, and padding high-altitude pasturelands in a mat of lush grasses and flowers.

Vegetation Belts

Plants in the Alpine Belt

The first and lowest of the Alpine vegetation zones are the lowland **Planar** and **Collin belts**. These include much of the Alpine region surrounding Italy's lakes. The region produces olives, oaks, evergreens, and lemons. In addition, vines crawl up the sunny hillsides of the interior Alps' deep valleys. The Planar and Collin belts extend up to approximately 700 m/2,200 feet. Above, the **Mountain Belt** shows a mix of deciduous trees — primarily larch, oak, beech, and sycamore – a region similar in climate to that of lower Canada or the American northeast.

Above 1,500 m/4,900 feet or so, the terrain gives way to the **Subalpine Belt**, home of the lush high pasturelands that have for centuries drawn farmers and their herds during the summer months. A fertile blend of grasses enriches the herd's diet, infusing the dairy products with a delicious, herby tang. Trees here include spruce, fir, and larch, gradually changing to low-lying berries and dwarf shrubbery at higher altitudes.

The **Alpine Belt** lies above approximately 2,300 m/7,544 feet, encompassing the terrain between the tree line and the lowest permanent snowcaps. Despite its high altitude and lack of trees, there is a tremendous variety of plant life in this region, as shrubs and juniper give way to Alpine grasslands. Beyond, above approximately 2,800 m, the **Nival Belt** embraces the upper glacial regions, nurturing a still varied mix of plant life, including mosses, lichen, and algae.

Alpine Flowers

Although Alpine slopes offer a rich variety of flora year-round, the most vivid display of wildflower color comes between May and August, as the prime blooming season works its way up from the valley floors to the glaciers above. Fall colors are at their most spectacular in late September through early November. Still-green valleys rise gradually to bright gold larch fields, dark coniferous forests, red algae-covered slopes, and white snowcaps high above – all, if you're lucky, set against a deep blue sky swept clear by an autumn breeze.

> ✔ Much of the Alpine flora here are protected by law, and the look-but-don't-pick policies are well-respected by European adventurers. I hope you'll do the same.

Most common among the Alpine blooms are a variety of buttercup, bellflower, and gentian families. The spring **pasque flower**, or *Pulsatilla vernalis*, is a buttercup derivative with tough leaves and petals purple on the outside and white within. The small flower blooms from April through July in dry grasslands and stony soils at altitudes up to 3,500 m/11,480 feet. Look for the hairy, light-blue petals of the down-turned bearded

Pasque flower

bellflower, or *Campanula barbata*, throughout the summer in high-altitude pastures up to 3,000 m/10,000 feet.

Several species of **gentian** thrive all over the Alps, running the gamut from the yellow gentian, or *Gentiana lutea*, which grows up to three feet high, to the more typical trumpet gentian, or *Gentiana acaulis*, which grows just a few inches from the earth. Several gentian species are appreciated, too, for their medicinal properties – and monks have for centuries used the plant to make a potent schnapps.

Gentian

Among the showiest of the early Alpine blooms is the **white**

White crocus

crocus, or *Crocus vernus*, its sturdy lavender petals pushing up through the melting snow. The bright orange **fire lily**, or *Lilium bulbiferum*, draws attention, too. Look for its eye-catching blooms from June through July in woodland pastures and grasslands between 300 and 2,000 m/ 1,000-6,600 feet. Less extravagant and ever so dainty, the **lady's slipper**, or *Cypripedium calceolus*, is a lucky find. Legend dictates that whoever finds one of these little orchids will enjoy true love – but adds that whoever purposely looks for the flower will never find one.

Finally, the **edelweiss**, or *Leontopodium alpinum*, remains the most venerated of the Alpine flowers – a fame due in no small part to the popularity of

Fire lilies (Scott Bauer)

the movie *The Sound of Music*. Look for the little woolly gray stars in sunny beds of limestone rock and grasslands, normally

Edelweiss

between 1,700 and 3,500 m (5,600-11,500 feet) and blooming from July through September.

◆ Fauna

Although several majestic species such as brown bears and wolves have long disappeared from the European Alps, the mountains still play home to an extensive array of animals. Many are difficult to spot, however. To up your odds, visit in autumn, when animals move into the valleys to escape the coming snows. Keep watch, too, in the evenings and early mornings, when animals are active and foraging. (Feeding wild animals is, of course, always a bad idea – both for their health and your safety.) To further increase your chances of spotting wildlife, head for one of the national parks, where a wide range of birds and mammals are protected. Below, I list some favorites:

- **Berchtesgaden National Park**, Germany, www.nationalpark-berchtesgaden.de
- **Gran Paradiso National Park**, Italy, www.granparadiso.net
- **Höhe Tauern National Park**, Austria, www.nationalpark.at
- **La Vanoise National Park**, France, www.vanoise.com
- **Swiss National Park**, Switzerland, www.nationalpark.ch

Alpine ibex pair

If all else fails, head for the **Alpine Zoo** in Innsbruck. All the animals listed here are represented in the zoo – along with a few species now extinct in their natural habitats. The zoo actively participates in preservation, research, and rehabilitation projects, so your entrance fee is actually doing Alpine wildlife some good.

The **Alpine ibex**, or *Capra ibex*, is recognizable first for its enormous horns. It's almost twice the size of the chamois, and both males and female have horns – although the male's are much more grand. The highly maneuverable bovid prefers a habitat of rocky outcroppings at high altitude. Look for the ibex in La Vanoise National Park, which was created for its protection.

The **chamois**, or *Rupicapra rupicapra*, delights onlookers with Alpine acrobatics, leaping nimbly among rocks and along cliffs using its non-slip hooves. Male chamois mark tree branches with a musky scent secreted out of glands from just behind their horns. Look for these mountain goats in high Alpine terrain, especially the Gran Paradiso and Vanoise national parks.

Chamois

The **Alpine marmot**, or *Marmota marmota*, proves the favorite animal of many visitors. These big, beaver-like fur-balls live in large family groups, occupying extensive interconnecting bur-

Alpine marmot

Red fox (Malene Thyssen)

rows that provide both summer and winter homes – upper rooms for playful summer days and lower rooms to be sealed off during the winter hibernation. Marmots live throughout the Alps, and sightings from cableways and mountain trails are frequent. Look for them on sunny slopes. Listen, too – marmots whistle to warn others of danger.

The **red fox**, or *Vulpes vulpes*, disperses widely throughout the region. As it is usually the largest mammalian predator in its habitat, it rarely goes wanting for food. The omnivorous fox pre-

Snowhare

fers to feed on mice, marmots, and carcasses and inhabits a wide range of climatic zones. Look throughout the Alps for its rusty coat, black tail, and slinky, cat-like movements.

The **snowhare**, or *Lepus timidus*, ranks low on the food chain and is the favored prey of the golden eagle. Nonetheless, it's a clever little thing, camouflaging its coat with white in winter and brown in summer. Look for the mountain hare all across the Alps.

Bearded vulture

The white-headed **bearded vulture**, or *Gypaetus barbatus*, is enormous – with a wingspan of almost 10 feet, it is, in fact, Europe's largest bird of prey. Although extinct in parts of the Alps, the birds have made a feeble comeback in the high mountain terrain. Look for the paired mates nesting on cliffs and feeding on rabbits and marmots around the Höhe Tauern National Park in Austria.

The **golden eagle**, or *Aquila chrysaetos*, remains king of the peaks, and their numbers have increased dramatically since near-extinction in the late 19th century. The grand bird prefers to feed on hares and marmots in summer and carcasses in winter – much of the meat salvaged from avalanche kill. Eagles create huge nests at altitude, but hover in forested areas to hunt for

Golden eagle

food. Look for the bird around the high-pine pastures that serve as their hunting grounds.

Finally, we draw attention to the much less glamorous **Alpine chough**, or *Pyrrhocorax graculus*. This little black bird ranks among the heartiest of the Alps' feathered fauna, nesting at extreme elevations and toting food up from far below. A member of the Corvid family, the crow-like chough is glossy black with a yellow beak and red legs. It's a sociable breed. You will see them soaring on the updrafts around high-mountain lift stations.

Alpine chough

Travel Basics

◆ When To Go

Setting a date to visit involves all the normal travel concerns – temperature, weather, holidays, festivals. In other parts of the world, I like to go when few others do, enjoying lower rates and fewer crowds. But it doesn't work out that way in the Alps.

Many of the destinations shut down almost entirely between seasons. Local residents go on their own vacations or spend closure days completing maintenance and renovation tasks – and in some villages you'll be hard-pressed to find an open hotel, bakery, or café. So, when planning, first consider opening and closing periods in the destinations you hope to visit.

However, opening and closing dates are rarely definite and, although most resorts throw big opening and closing bashes, many hotels, restaurants, and cable networks gradually spin up to full operations. So, if you plan to travel along the edges of the opening season, do check in with the tourist office first.

SCHEDULING TIPS

■ In **August**, many European countries take vacations *en masse*, crowding tourist destinations, jamming roads, and pumping up hotel rates. That said, August is the balmiest month of the calendar. Its festivals are frequent, and the villages are fully open.

■ The same effect comes around in **February**, when the ski season hits its high point for the midwinter school breaks.

■ **January** is the least crowded month of the European ski season, as tourists head home after the holidays. It's cold on the slopes – but if you can take it, bargains abound.

◆ Transportation

Getting Here

Visitors who come to Europe specifically to visit the Alps can book flights into the gateway cities below. From the US, non-stop flights are in general most frequent to and from Zürich, Milan, and Munich. (Direct and connecting flights make connections into the other gateway cities as well.) A mind-boggling array of airlines offer flights to and from Europe. We suggest consulting both the airlines' direct reservation lines and the bargain-hunting search engines online. For gateway airport information, see the guide below:

PASSPORTS

International travelers to Europe must carry a passport – and getting one can take several months. Aside from the strict passport controls at airports, however, visitors will find that most countries here no longer check passports at borders. However, they can reinstate passport control at any time, so keep yours handy. You may be asked for your passport upon arrival at your hotel, where it's still common practice for the front desk to keep it overnight so as to record registration information.

GATEWAY AIRPORTS

Gateway	More Info	Location	City Transfers
Geneva, Switz	www.gva.ch	4 km west of Geneva	Bus, train
Innsbruck, Austria	www.innsbruck-airport.com	3 km west of center	Bus
Milan, Italy Malpensa Airport	www.sea-aeropimilano.it	45 km northwest of the center	Bus, train
Milan, Italy Linate Airport	www.sea-aeropimilano.it	7 km east of the center	Bus
Munich, Germany	www.munich-airport.de	28 km northeast of the center	Train, bus
Zürich, Switz	www.uniqueairport.com	In Kloten, 10 km north of the center	Train, bus

Getting Around

● BY CAR

Private autos remain the most convenient way to get around the Alps. Adventurers traveling in pairs or groups will find that renting a car is not expensive.

Most nations accept US drivers' licenses in lieu of an international permit – check with your rental agency upon reservation. Major US and European car rental agencies serve the Alps gateway cities – try Alamo, Avis, Budget, Europcar, Hertz, and Sixt. Several online search engines offer discounted rates too.

✔ For good deals on car rentals, check AutoEurope's search engine at www.autoeurope.com.

DRIVING TIPS

All cars are required by law to carry a first-aid kit, a warning triangle, and registration information. These should be provided by your rental agency. In addition, those planning to travel in Alpine areas between October and early spring should carry tire chains. Car rental agencies rent out these too, but most require prior arrangements – confirm your request when you reserve a car.

European roads – even the superhighways – frequently come to a standstill during holiday travel periods. Transalpine routes prove particularly painful during the winter season on Saturdays, when the ski resorts' weekly guests swap out. It's extremely frustrating (and I try to schedule around it), but Europeans have come to expect and accept the traffic as part of the ski holiday tradition.

Expect gas prices to run approximately three times more than in the United States. Some cars run on unleaded fuel, while others use diesel – something to know before you drive out of the rental agency's lot.

GASOLINE LINGO			
English	German	French	Italian
Diesel	Diesel	Diesel	Diesel
Gasoline	Benzin	Essence	Benzina
Unleaded gasoline	Bleifrei	Essence sans plomb	Senza piombo

International Road Signs

Steep Upgrade

Steep Downgrade

Hazardous Crosswinds

Right of Way on Priority Road

Bicylces Only

Cyclists and Pedestrians Only

Expressway Begins

Expressway Ends

Alternate Route for Express Traffic

300 Meters to Exit
Number of Bars Decreases with Distance, Each Bar Represents 100 Meters

Access to Expressway

International Route

Minimum Speed

One Way

Keep Left
(Keep Right on Right Arrow)

Turn Left
(Turn Right on Right Arrow)

No Passing Zone Ends

Speed Limit Zone Ends

Derestriction Sign
(Multiple Diagonal Lines)

National Speed Limit Applies
(Single Diagonal Line)

Danger

Yield

Curve

S-Curve

Uneven Road

Crossroads or Junction
Yield to Traffic from the Right

Two-Way Traffic

Railroad Crossing with Barriers

Stop

Speed Limit
Kilometers per hour
or miles per hour in U.K.

No Passing

Trucks Forbidden
to Pass

Yield to
Oncoming Vehicles

Closed to
Vehicles

Closed to Trucks
Heavier than
2.8 metric tons

Closed to
Automobiles

Closed to
Motor Vehicles

No Entry

No Parking

No Stopping

Customs Station:
Stop

Automobiles Only
Zone Ends

Dead End

Recommended
Maximum Speed

Parking

Europeans rely heavily on public transportation, and central parking facilities are in short supply. Parking spaces are often either time-limited short-term spots or in public garages. For short-term spaces with posted time limits, you'll need a parking disk placard. Most cars will come with one in the dash compartment. Spin the time wheel on the placard so it indicates the time you arrived and place it on the dash. Most public garages operate on an automated payment system. Grab a ticket on your way in, park your car, and carry the ticket with you. On departure, pay your fee either at the window or at the automated machine before returning to your car. A second variation on lot parking requires you to log your parking spot number at a central machine, pay for the needed time in advance, and then place the receipt on the dashboard.

● BY TRAIN & BUS

 Train travel remains one of the joys of European tourism. Systems are modern, fast, and timely, though not always inexpensive. Most Alpine destinations – right down to the smallest villages – are well served by rail or, at a minimum, by a convenient bus connection from the nearest rail station. A wide range of services is available, most available through the websites listed below; look for information on trip planning, baggage services, bike rentals, theme trips, and combination itineraries via rail, bus, boat, and cableway. If you go by rail, I recommend traveling with little baggage and, for longer rides during high season, paying the small fee to reserve a seat. (You don't have to sit there, but it's nice to know you can.) Ticketing procedures vary by country and rail line; for more information check the websites below.

EUROPEAN TRAIN TRAVEL
Austria . . . . www.oebb.at
France . . . . www.voyages-sncf.com
Germany . . . . www.bahn.de
Italy . . . . www.fs-on-line.com
Switzerland . . . . www.rail.ch

✔ **Rail Europe** offers one-stop shopping and a host of information regarding European rail passes. Check in at www.raileurope.com. For international bus transportation, inquire with **Eurolines** at www.eurolines.com.

● BY CABLEWAY & MOUNTAIN TRAIN

We hope that every European visitor experiences the thrill of ascending the Alps via one of the region's extensive uplift networks. Lifts serve pedestrians, paragliders, and snow-sport fans through the winter, and most resorts operate lifts in summer, too. Hikers and mountain-bikers (and their dogs) head for the hills via cable car, gondola, chairlift, funiculars, and mountain trains. The variety in engineering is astounding in itself – let alone the views once you reach the top. For more information on mountain transportation, see the *Getting Around* detail listed for each destination.

Introduction

Innsbruck cablecar

CAR-CARRYING TRAINS

One of the Alps' most interesting forms of transportation is the car-carrying train. Drivers load their cars onto a flatbed train, which then tugs the line of occupied autos through a mountain tunnel, saving motorists what in some cases would be a several-hour roundabout drive. Leaving a light on inside your car will make the bouncy ride a bit less bizarre, but beware the rookie mistake – when it comes time to disembark, a dead battery will make you the least popular traveler aboard. In the Swiss Alps, try the **Loetschberg Tunnel** between Kandersteg (near Interlaken) and the Valais region; the **Vereina Tunnel** between Klosters and Susch; or the **Furka Tunnel** between Realp and Oberwald.

◆ Currency

With the exception of Switzerland & Liechtenstein, the currency of the countries in this guide is the euro (€). There are 100 cents to €1 and coins are in denominations of 1, 2, 5, 10, 20 and 50 cents, as well as €1 and €2. Notes are in denominations of €5, 10, 20, 50, 100, 200 and 500.

Whereas the value of the US dollar was approximately €1.20 when work began on this guide, the dollar has slipped since that time and now stands at about €0.80. So, if you see an item priced at €1, the dollar equivalent would be $1.30, €10 would be $13, €100, $130.

Switzerland and Liechtenstein use the Swiss franc, abbreviated as CHF. The current value of 1 CHF is $0.82 or €0.65. It is divided into 100 cents. Coins come in denominations of 5, 10, 20 and 50 cents, as well as 1, 2 and 5 CHF. Banknotes come in values of 10, 20, 50, 100, 200 and 1,000 CHF.

◆ Where to Sleep

This guide rounds up hotels for each destination that have both a prime location and reasonable standards of comfort, narrowing coverage to those hostelries offering particularly memorable stays. Our hotel picks are categorized by price range – but you should be aware that seasonal fluctuations can be great, particularly in the resort areas. While luxury houses across Europe maintain similarly exquisite standards, hotels at lower ends of the scale tend to vary by region in comfort and cleanliness. In general, budget hotels in Italy and France offer less bang for your lodging buck than, say, Germany and Switzerland, where comfortable rooms and good service are common. The undisputed queen of Alpine hospitality is Austria. Here, cozy accommodations, duvet-topped beds, and family-style hospitality are the rule rather than the exception. Particularly in small towns and villages, Austria offers Europe's warmest welcome.

LODGING TIPS

- *If you enter town without a room, head for the tourist office or simply browse the streets for a vacancy sign – in German, zimmer frei; in French, chambre libre; in Italian, camera/stanza libera.*
- *Shared baths are common in budget hotels, hostels, B&B guesthouses, and mountain huts, so I recommend you pack a pair of shower flip-flops. In addition, traditional European towels are flimsy cotton affairs. While I've seen a lot more*

terrycloth in recent years, I still usually pack along a washcloth.

- *Breakfasts are normally included in budget and moderate room rates. Luxury hotels usually tack on a substantial charge. However, the meal is not an American-style feast, but a modest buffet spread of bread, meat, cheese, and jam, normally served with a choice of juices and coffee or tea.*

- *Bidets are a common European feature, a great little gadget intended for washing your nether regions. I've heard of some creative uses, too, ranging from a sock-soak to a baby bath. High-tech versions prove a real hoot, with water jets that have controls for pressure, temperature, and pattern; built-in blow dryers; and (requiring some imagination) portable remote controls.*

- *A wide range of accommodations are available, including youth hostels, private rooms, mountain huts, guesthouses, hotels, and spa resorts. I've included mostly hotels here When booking lodging at the lower end of the price range, expect to share a bath; at the upper end, expect to pay extra for breakfast.*

◆ Dining

 Alpine Europe offers a wide array of dining, and for each destination I've attempted to single out the most memorable dining experiences, whether pricey gourmet meals or freshly made picnic goods. Although our guide covers six countries, the region is home to three main culinary traditions: Italian, Germanic, and French. Italian cuisine permeates the Alps, just as it has the entire world: Diners enjoy fresh pastas and traditional *pizze* made with thin, cracker-like crusts, baked in a wood-fired oven, and served with a wonderful array of toppings – each pie hanging over the edges of a large plate. Even better, it's all yours. Traditional pizzas are intended as servings for one, even though most could easily provide a snack for three. Other culinary treats include fresh, homemade pastas – some varieties in northern Italy are stuffed with delicious meat, cheese, or squash concoctions and topped with rich sauces of butter, tomato, or walnuts. Grilled meats are popular in the Alpine regions, as are risotto (rice) dishes. Those unaccustomed to the art of Italian dining will be surprised to find that the main meal is served at midday and that it's often accompanied by copious quantities of red wine. Also notable: pasta dishes are served as a first (rather than main) course, and salads usually wrap up (rather than kick off) a full meal.

Wiener schnitzel (Rüdiger Wölk)

Austria and Germany are the strongholds of hearty Germanic fare. Germany offers the world its variety of sausages, or wurst, which come grilled and with bread, making a great afternoon snack, particularly when served with a liter-size mug of *bier*. Farther south, in Austria, delicious hearty meals run to a wide array of meat-and-potatoes fare – always a huge hit with both the men and the kids in our groups. Traditional *Wiener schnitzel* is a

solid choice, but I hope you'll branch out to try *gröstl*, a meat and potato pan fry, and *käsepatzle*, a Vorarlberg specialty of noodles and grated cheese, baked together and topped

Käsepatzle

with fried onions. Kids love *kaiserschmarrn*, a sweet mound of shredded pancake served with preserves, and adults love the *schnapps*, warm *gluhwein*, and potent *jagertee* – all three, drinks with a kick.

While Switzerland shares cuisines with each of its neighbors, its most intimate culinary relationship is with France. Along with the northwestern corner of Italy, Switzerland and France dish out an astounding array of cheese dishes. The *fondue Savoyarde* is the most famed of the cheese mixes here, a bubbling pot of *fromage* made tangy with white wine and a shot or two of *kirsche* liqueur. Raclette, too,

kaiserschmarrn

proves another oozy favorite: The traditional service involves a large block of cheese melted tableside over an open flame –

Raclette

and served with a mix of steamed potatoes and pickled vegetables. Other open-flame affairs include chunks of meat with fondues *bourguignonne*, a pot of hot oil; *chinoise*, a pot of boiling bouillon; and *Bacchus*, a pot of spiced local wine. Grilled specialties, mixed salads, and a variety of sweet and savory *crêpes* all prove popular, too.

DINING TIPS

■ *Unless there's a host posted at the door, European restaurants intend for you to come in and seat yourself. (Leave your coat and umbrella at the door.) In casual and traditional settings, it's not uncommon for strangers to share your table. Although it seems an oddly intimidating question to pose, you shouldn't be afraid to join a stranger's table, either. Just ask if the seats are free. You're not necessarily expected to chat – although it is a pleasant way to meet strangers.*

■ *Many cafés and mountain huts offer both self- and table-service. If you find a table without a cloth, menu, and such, it's a fairly good indicator that it's a cafeteria-style self-service arrangement. If there are menus on the table, stay put and you'll be served eventually. Also, if some tables are set with fine silver and others have just paper napkins, sit at a dressed table for a meal, at an undressed table for just a drink or snack.*

- *Many cafés also offer stand-up service. Pay for your drink and snack at the cashier, take your receipt to the barman, and he'll dispense the goods, which you then consume standing up at the bar.*

- *We hear many complaints about "poor" restaurant service, but I think the issue has less to do with quality than culture. In general, service is slow. Europeans dine out to relax and to enjoy – to rush you would be rude. Service is unobtrusive rather than obsequious, and so, to North Americans, the service may seem inattentive, too.*

- *Multi-course meals line up in varying orders depending on where you sit in the Alps. (Italians, for instance, often eat salad at the end of the meal.) In any case, don't be surprised to be asked in which order you'd like your meal. Also worth mentioning is the small glitch of timing. Lest food grow cold or stale, kitchens tend to serve individuals as their plates become ready rather than serving the table as a group.*

- *In most cases, you'll need to flag down your server to ask for the meal check. (Some cafés ask you to settle your bill immediately upon service.) A tip is not always expected in Europe. Ask if service is included in the check. If it is, you might still round up a euro or two when paying your bill. If not included, 10-15% is customary. Hand the extra to your server; leaving change on the table is considered overly impersonal.*

◆ Connections

Language

Three major languages and a host of minor dialects babble through the Alps. Visitors will find the "high" versions of German, French, and Italian most useful, although a fast-growing number of Europeans speak English. And, although even the feeblest linguistic attempts are appreciated, more often than not the reply will come back in English. I do suggest, of course, that every visitor learn some basic phrases. Give our *Language Primer* a quick study – it's in the appendix at the back of this book.

Telephone

Telephone numbers are changing rapidly in European countries as the old system has become inadequate. Area codes are changing, as are phone-number formats. In general, foreign phone numbers are dialed using *00 + country code* (see below) + the *phone number* without the 0 prefix. Domestic numbers are dialed using only the phone number with the 0 prefix. Tobacco shops, newsstands, post offices, and tourist offices sell two types of public phone cards: one with a scratch-to-see bar code; the other with a program chip or strip to be inserted into public phones. (We like the scratch-off variety, as it can be used from hotel rooms, too.)

INTERNATIONAL COUNTRY CODES	
Austria	+43
France	+33
Germany	+49
Italy	+39
Liechtenstein	+423
Switzerland	+41

Internet

Internet service is widely available, both in hotels and in a growing number of bars and cafés. Whenever possible, I've indicated surf stations for each spotlighted destination.

Time Zone

The Alpine nations lie in the Central European Time Zone, GMT + 1 hour, or, from the last weekend in March to the last weekend in October, GMT + 2 hours. Think Eastern Standard Time + 6 hours year-round.

Electricity

Electrical outlets in Europe supply 220-volt alternating current for a variety of plug shapes. Unless specifically designed for dual-voltage use, 110-volt electrical appliances will work only when connected to large, heavy, voltage transformers. (Common plug adapters – those lightweight kits found in travel shops – adapt only shape, not voltage.) That said, appliances designed for dual-voltage use work when fitted with these lightweight plug adapters. European plug shapes vary somewhat even within national borders. Your best bet is to pack along an adapter set; hotels have loaners if yours don't work.

✔ Consider leaving the blow-dryer at home; most hotels either loan hairdryers or stock them in rooms.

◆ Health & Safety

Europe has a modern medical infrastructure and, although some corners of the Alps lie far from urban centers, the emergency and airlift operations are well organized. The high Alpine terrain inspires many adventurers to stretch the limits of their physical and mental bounds. Done with reason, such challenges can land you triumphant amid some of the world's most spectacular scenery; done with haste, they can land you in a foreign hospital bed (or worse). Some tips for Alpine travelers:

 Emergency! Dial 112, Europe-wide.

SAFETY TIPS

- **Health insurance** *policies vary in their international coverage, and I advise that you check your own before you go. A plethora of companies specialize in additional travel and sports insurance, and you may even be asked upon purchasing your lift pass if you'd like rescue insurance tacked on.*

- **Sunburn** *threatens both skin and eyes, particularly at high altitudes and on snow. Spread on some sunscreen, take a hat and sleeves, and wear UV-protected sunglasses.*

- **Frostbite**, *or hypothermia, endangers Alpine adventurers as well. Dress warmly in layers whenever venturing out; wear a hat to prevent heat loss through your head; and don moisture-wicking under-layers and waterproof outerwear. Mild hypothermia causes fatigue, numbness, cramps, shivering, and slurred speech. Warm victims slowly without rubbing.*

- *All but the fittest will feel a bit winded when exercising at altitudes over 2,500 m/8,200 feet. The effect can be severe, however, and oxygen depletion can lead to **acute mountain sickness**. Headaches, dizziness, and breathlessness can lead to more extreme symptoms such as confusion, vomiting, and even death. Infants and children are particularly susceptible, and some experts recommend not taking youngsters to altitude at all.*
- *If you're heading out on a mountain trail, let someone know where you're heading and when you expect to return. (Your hotel's staff is a likely candidate; leave your key behind so they'll know when you return.) And, by the way, if you do end up needing helicopter assistance, get your signals right: Both arms up in a V means help is needed; one arm up waves them off.*
- ***Avalanches** can be a serious threat in many parts of the Alps, particularly to those who venture into the backcountry (which they should never do, of course, without a guide). Pay attention to avalanche warnings. The system rates danger on a scale from one to five, one being the lowest risk. Posted flags go from yellow to black, growing darker with graver avalanche danger. Local tourist offices and mountain guiding operators post notices, too.*

◆ Getting More Information

Throughout this guide, I have given web addresses for the various outfitters, hotels, tourist offices and other information sources. In some cases, these websites are in the local language only. If you do not speak the language, one solution is to go to www.google.com and insert the web address in the search box at the top. Then click on "Translate this page." Google will display the website in English.

For general information, check with the national tourism offices:

Austria	www.austria-tourism.at
France	www.franceguide.com
Germany	www.germany-tourism.de
Italy	www.italiantourism.com
Liechtenstein	www.tourismus.li
Switzerland	www.myswitzerland.com

Going Metric

GENERAL MEASUREMENTS

To make your travels a little easier, we have provided the following chart that shows metric equivalents for the measurements you are familiar with.

1 kilometer	=	.6124 miles
1 mile	=	1.6093 kilometers
1 foot	=	.304 meters
1 inch	=	2.54 centimeters
1 square mile	=	2.59 square kilometers
1 pound	=	.4536 kilograms
1 ounce	=	28.35 grams
1 imperial gallon	=	4.5459 liters
1 US gallon	=	3.7854 liters
1 quart	=	.94635 liters

TEMPERATURES

For Farenheit: Multiply centigrade figure by 1.8 and add 32
For Centigrade: Subtract 32 from Farenheit figure and divide by 1.8.

Centigrade		Farenheit
40°	=	104°
35°	=	95°
30°	=	86°
25°	=	77°
20°	=	64°
15°	=	59°
10°	=	50°

Austria

(Österreich)
Languages: German
Population: 8,169,929
Phone Country Code: +43
Currency: Euro

The Republic of Austria spans some 83,853 square km in south-central Europe. The entire western third of the nation lies in the Alps, and much of its central and southern territories are Alpine as well – some 75%

IN THIS CHAPTER

- People & Culture   4
- The Arlberg   9
- Innsbruck & the Tyrol   10
- Salzburg & the
      Salzburgerland   11

of the country is mountainous. The nation boasts a greater percentage of forested land than any other European nation – about 39% of its terrain is covered with trees. Austria shares its borders with eight other nations: Switzerland and Liechtenstein to the west, Germany and the Czech Republic to the north, Slovakia to the northeast, Hungary to the east, and Italy and Slovenia to the south.

Austria's government is partitioned into nine states and its capital is Vienna. It maintains a parliamentary democracy, with a strong central government. The president presides as the chief of state, and the head of government is the chancellor. From 1955, Austrian politics have vacillated between conservative and socialist policies. Recent issues include the influx of Yugoslav refugees and subsequent right-wing anti-immigration movements. Also controversial over the past decade have been growing unemployment levels, tax increases, and cuts in social services. Austria's unemployment rate hovers around 5.1%..

People & Culture

Austria's population is approximately 98% ethnic Austrian, with the remaining 2% split among several eastern European ethnicities, including Croat, Hungarian, Slovene, and Czech – mi-

Alpine Austria

norities that cluster along Austria's eastern border. Approximately 80% of the population claims a Roman Catholic religion, with 5% claiming some faction of the Protestant faith. Some 65% of all Austrians reside in urban settings, with 25% of the population living in the country's five largest cities: Vienna, Graz, Linz, Salzburg, and Innsbruck. The population density is approximately 97 people per square kilometer.

NATIONAL HOLIDAYS

1 January	New Year's Day
6 January	Epiphany
March/April	Easter; Easter Monday
1 May	Labor Day
10 days before Whit Sunday	Ascension Day
7th Sunday after Easter	Whit Sunday
Day after Whit Sunday	Whit Monday
Thursday after 8th Sunday after Easter	Corpus Christi
15 August	Assumption Day
26 October	National Day
1 November	All Saints Day
8 December	Immaculate Conception
25 December	Christmas Day
26 December	Boxing Day

TIMELINE

16 BC	Romans control Noricum Territory, including most of present-day Austria
9th Century AD	Ostmark is developed under French ruler Charlemagne
955 AD	Ostmark is annexed under the Holy Roman Empire
1278 AD	Rudolf I of Hapsburg, a German king, gains control and establishes the Hapsburg Dynasty, which maintained widespread power until 1918

1618-1648	Thirty Years' War
1740-1780	Reign of Maria Teresa
1756	Composer Wolfgang Amadeus Mozart born in Vienna
1756-1763	Prussian forces attack in 1756, bringing Austria into the Seven Years' War
1866	Austro-Prussian War ends with the defeat of Austria; an 1867 agreement with Hungary establishes the rule of Emperor Franz Josef
1914-1918	The assassination of Archduke Franz Ferdinand, heir to the throne, leads to the outbreak of World War I
1918	Austria established as a republic
1938	Hitler's "Anschluss" annexes Austria to Third Reich; renames the territory Ostmark
1938-1945	Under Hitler's command, Austrian forces fight on the eastern front
1945-1955	Allied forces occupy Austria until the Austrian State Treaty establishes an independent republic in 1955
1994	Austria joins European Union

MARIA THERESA

Maria Theresa in 1762

The only female ruler in the 650-year history of the Hapsburg Dynasty, Maria Theresa ascended the Austrian throne in 1740 as the daughter of Emperor Charles VI. She is often considered the "Savior of the Hapsburg State." It was under her reign that Austria developed into a modern state: government control was centralized, civil services were greatly expanded, public education was introduced, and reforms of the military were instituted. Almost immediately upon Maria Theresa's assumption of the throne, Prussia challenged her authority. Seeing that Austria had been weakened during the last years of Charles VI's rule, they invaded and occupied Silesia. Bavaria and France soon joined in and invaded Austria from the west. Maria Theresa did not falter. She strengthened the army, reorganized the tax structure, and centralized control efforts to build a force capable of reclaiming these lands. However, in 1756, with preparations nearly complete for a retaliatory campaign, Austria suffered a surprise attack from the Prussians – the onset of the Seven Years War. Despite these setbacks, Maria Theresa is credited with laying the groundwork for a resumption of Austria's eastward expansion. Maria Theresa reigned until her death in 1780.

✔ For additional tourist information, contact the Austrian National Tourist Office at www.austria-tourism.

The Arlberg

This chapter spans the westernmost region of Austria, that pointy piece of territory that juts along the borders of Germany, Switzerland, and Liechtenstein. The region covered here includes pieces of two Austrian provinces, the Vorarlberg to the west and, to the east, the westernmost fringes of the Tyrol. **Bregenz** is western Austria's cultural capital, an up-and-coming artsy town on the shore of Lake Constance. Medieval **Feldkirch** sits just south, the **Bregenzerwald forest** lies east, and the **Montafon Valley** stretches toward Silvaplana to the southeast. The terrain climbs its way east toward the high-altitude passes along the border of the Tyrol. Here, in the region known as the Arlberg, the **Lechtaler Alps** are home to **St. Anton**, **Lech**, and **St. Christoph**, while the **Paznaun Valley** to the south harbors **Ischgl** and neighboring **Galtür**. The area ranks among our fa-

Bregenz & the Arberg

Bodensee

GERMANY

Bregenz

Hittisau

Lustenau

Dornbirn

Silvretta
Hochalpenstrasse

Mellau

A14

Feldkirch

Damüls

200

Häselgehr

Lech

Steeg

Blundenz

Mt Valuga

St. Christoph

Vandans

Arlberg
Tunnel

Ischgl

188

Galtür

Reutte

Heiterwang

198

314

Nassereith

Imst

to
Innsbruck

186

Landeck

Jerzens

Pians

315

Pfunds

AUSTRIA

SWITZERLAND

ITALY

N

HUNTER PUBLISHING

25 MILES

25 KM

© 2007 HUNTER PUBLISHING, INC

vorite places in the Alps, home to both Austria's friendliest people and its most extreme mountain terrain.

◆ St. Anton am Arlberg

Population: 2,580

Base elevation: 1,300 m/4,264 feet

Mountain resort village

There's a lot to love about St. Anton. I adore it above all for its people, both its friendly residents and its spirited, hard-driving visitors. Although famed throughout the world as a winter resort, the village also has a respectable following among summertime hikers, bikers, and climbers. But St. Anton comes into its own as a superb playground for expert skiers. It's Austria's premier ski-bum resort – the rip-roaring bad boy of the Arlberg.

History & Overview

The Arlberg region occupies the western panhandle of Austria, the nation's most mountainous terrain. Once farmland, the region was opened to visitors in the 19th century by the arrival of the railway and the construction of the Flexen Pass road – basically a tunnel with an open gallery on one side. The now-famous Arlberg Ski Club was formed in St. Christoph in 1901. Member Hannes Schneider offered ski instruction here for the first time in 1907, assisted the Austrian military in the development of on-ski Al-

Skier above St. Anton

pine troops, and eventually developed the distinctive feet-together Arlberg style. Schneider also befriended British skier Sir Alfred Lunn, with whom he together coordinated the 1927 inaugural running of the Kandahar Race. Several local racers have gone on to great success and worldwide sporting fame in this and other World Cup competitions. World champions Karl Schranz and Marina Kiehl are just two of those. Today, the village enjoys a historical significance that spans an entire century – as home to Hannes Schneider, the father of modern skiing, and as host of the World Alpine Skiing Championships in 2001.

The Town

St. Anton's pedestrian zone

St. Anton sprawls along the Rosanna River, 30 km west of **Landeck**. The elongated town connects at its eastern edge with the neighboring villages of **Nasserein** and, farther down-valley, **St. Jakob**. The main valley road, the **Arlbergstrasse**, runs up from Innsbruck and into the center on its southern side. (Through traffic ducks into the Arlberg Tunnel, which empties out 14 km west of here.) The main train station sits on the hillside opposite town, across the main road and the river. St. Anton's action centers on its pedestrian zone and a long street called Dorfstrasse, which runs from the traffic circle at its western end downhill toward Nasserein. Paralleling Dorfstrasse just up the hill, Hannes Schneider Weg runs from the lifts to the wellness center along a lovely park, site of what was until just a few years ago an unsightly train yard. The main cable cars depart from just above the center, with other lift stations up the valley, above the wellness center, and at Nasserein.

Getting Here & Around

Visitors arriving by air will fly into Innsbruck, 100 km to the east; Zürich, 200 km to the west; or Munich, 250 km to the north. Airport transfers from Zürich are provided by **Arlberg Express**, ☎ 05582 226. The new, ultra-modern train station lies at the southern edge of the center, and train connections are frequent to both Innsbruck and Zürich.

Drivers will likely arrive via Landeck in the east or Feldkirch and the Arlberg Tunnel in the west. (Tunnel toll at last count was €8. 50). As the center of the village is a car-free zone, parking areas line the main road into town. Local and regional buses serve the area well. In winter, free shuttle buses operate day and night between the villages of St. Anton and St Jakob; between the bases of the Galzig and Rendl areas; and between Alpe Rauz and the nearby village of Zurs. Tickets must be purchased for travel between St. Anton and St. Christoph, Alpe Rauz, Zurs, and Lech. For taxi service, contact **Taxi Harry** at ☎ 0554 23 68 or **Taxi Griesser** at ☎ 0554 37 30.

Mountain transportation includes 44 local lifts, six of which run in summer for lift-served hiking and mountain biking. A variety of passes are available.

LIFT PASS PRICE SAMPLES
Winter
1-day adult Arlberg Pass €40.50
6-day adult Arlberg Pass €194
Summer
7-day all-mountain Wanderpass. €30
Pedestrian round-trip to the Valluga Summit . €18

Getting More Info

 The **tourist office** is in the center near the traffic circle, at the top of Dorfstrasse. New arrivals appreciate the electronic hotel map in the corridor outside; and skiers appreciate the resort Info Team, a group of multi-lingual folks that disperse across the mountain with the sole purpose of providing up-to-date information. Contact the tourist office at ☎ 05446 226 90, www.stantonamarlberg.com, info@stantonamarlberg.com.

The **post office** is along the main road into town, next door to the St. Antonerhof Hotel.

The **Mail Box Café** in the pedestrian zone offers Internet access. It's open 9 am-10 pm in season. **Jennewein Sport** also offers Internet access from its rental and sport shops.

The Sights

St. Anton is a sporting resort, and few sights stand out. Chief among them is the **St. Anton Ski Museum**, which documents the development of St. Anton, local cultural traditions, and the history of the local ski club. The museum is located in the Arlberg Kandahar Haus chalet – and its lovely interior is alone worth the price of admission.

St. Anton Ski Museum

It's open Sunday through Sunday, 3 pm to 6 pm in winter, less frequently in summer; ☎ 05446 24 75, www.museum-restaurant.at, €3. Also of interest to history buffs is the **Thöni**

Haus, dating from the Middle Ages and thereby among the region's oldest homes. The old wooden house is tucked inconspicuously away at Im Greis, and today remains in private hands.

✔ The tourist office offers guided village tours every Monday at 4 pm during the summer; the tours are free of charge.

The 360° view from 2,650-m/8,700-foot **Valluga Summit** offers one of the most spectacular panoramas of the Alps. From the small viewing platform at the top, views extend to the Lechtal Alps in the north, to the Zügspitze of Germany in the northwest, to the Silvretta and Switzerland's Bernina in the south, and to the Stubaital glaciers and Italy's Dolomites in the southeast.

The Adventures

● ON FOOT

Hikers enjoy 270 km of well-posted paths. Six summertime lifts access the local mountains, and 33 mountain huts offer refreshment. The tourist office runs a program of guided walking tours Tuesday through Friday in summer. Walks include an outing to an Alpine dairy farm, a walk through mountain flowers and a photo tour. Contact the tourist office for information and to make reservations, ☎ 05446 226 90, www.stantonamarlberg.com.

THE ARLBERG CLIMBERS' TRACK

Experienced climbers consider the Arlberg Climbing Track one of the Alps' most demanding and scenic fixed routes. The track stretches 2.8 km along the Lechtal Alps and takes around five hours to complete. To access the starting point, walk approximately 20 minutes east from the Valluga Grat cable car station toward the Einstieg or, from the Kapall chairlift, approximately 15 minutes west. Proper equipment, weather conditions, and expertise are required.

Austria

● IN WATER

Swimmers head year-round for the **ARLBERG-Well. com** and its pool facilities, which include an indoor pool, waterfalls, an outdoor river current, and excellent sauna area; contact ☎ 05446 4001, www.arlberg-well. com, for current open hours. In the summer, the **Waldschwimmbad** provides an outdoor pool in a forested locale. Watersport fans looking for more extreme action pair up with **H2O Adventures** (see *Sports Services, Outfitters & Guides* below, page 51) for canyoning, rafting, and such. Fishing is an option, too, both in the Rosanna River and at Lake Verwall. Make inquiries at the tourist office for permits and regulations.

● ON WHEELS

Summertime **mountain bikers** take advantage of 200 km of timber access road and designated trails. Routes run along the Rendlalpe, Tritschalpe, and Putzenalpe; one favorite 1.5-hour run climbs past the Verwallsee up to the Konstanzerhütte and, if you're game, another two hours up to the Heilbronnerhutte at 2,308 m/7,544 feet. The tourist office sells maps and guidebooks specifically for mountain bikers.

● IN THE AIR

Paragliding flights include training, trial course, and tandem jumps. For more information, contact Simon Penz at **Flight Connection Arlberg**, ☎ 0664 141 51 66, www.fca.at.

✔ The Summer Active Programme offers a gamut of recreational activities. Check in at local hotels and enjoy guided hikes, mountain bike rides, golf, archery, and children's fun-and-games with Hoppl the rabbit. A wide range of wellness courses is also on offer.

● ON SNOW & ICE

St. Anton is Austria's signature resort, a name well known throughout the **skiing** world. A mecca for on-ski experts, and a magnet for après-ski addicts. The ski region surrounding St. Anton includes 267 km of groomed runs served by 85 lifts in six resorts: St. Anton, St. Christoph, Stuben, Lech, Zurs, and Sonnenkopf. The 44 local lifts access the region's largest section of slopes, a 40-km network of steep, groomed pistes.

Recently, the resort invested €13 million in efforts to open up additional runs for beginning- and intermediate-level skiers. Improvements target the Rendl and Fang areas. Mid-level skiers can enjoy most of the mountain, including the area's longest run, a 10.2-km descent from the Vallugagrat down to the village. Experts head for the steep slopes at Schindlerkar or plunge off the Valluga peak for an exhilarating ride. (Certified guides must accompany you on the Valluga route. If you don't have a guide, the bouncer manning the cable car won't allow your skis on board.) Due to ecological concerns, helicopter skiing is no longer allowed.

St. Anton is predominately a skiing, rather than snowboarding, resort – up-and-comer Ischgl, just over the hill, has cornered that youthful niche market. Nonetheless, **free-style skiers** of all persuasions find funpark action, including a halfpipe and various jumps, on the Rendl. The lodge there, known as "Rendl Beach," proves popular on sunny afternoons. A total of 18 **mountain huts** stud the resort's slopes, offering food, drink, and high-altitude hospitality.

SKI SAFETY

St. Anton is one of the world's great resorts for expert skiers. If your skills do not fall into this category, take some care when on the local slopes. Piste difficulty is notoriously under-graded here, and I've encountered chopped up sections of "blue" piste that would easily qualify as black in a lesser resort. Avalanches are a very real threat – note the protective gates high above the village and heed all posted warnings. That said, there's no reason to fret, and there's always a way down – I just hope it's not with the services of St. Anton's 16 rescuers, here unnamed, and four avalanche dogs: Tasso, Dando, Arco, and Rambo.

Cross-country skiers enjoy 40 km of loipe (trails), including the lovely Verwall Trail, which tucks back into the Verwall Valley, looping around the lake and back to town. For **horse-drawn sleigh rides** along the same route, contact the tourist office or Martin Tschol, ☎ 05446 23 80. **Tobogganers** enjoy the four-km run at Gampen – rent sleds at the Rodelhütte below – and **ice-skating** and **curling** takes place on the small natural rink fronting the wellness center. Finally, some 70 km of cleared

winter walking paths wind around the village, including a nice hike up to the Rodelhütte restaurant.

Sports Services, Outfitters & Guides

■ **H20 Adventures** organizes a number of high-energy outings, including canyoning, tubing, rafting, ropes courses, and mountain biking tours. If what you've got in mind isn't on the list, they'll custom-tailor activities to your request. Contact ☎ 05446 39 37, www.events-more.at.

■ **Alber Sport** is my favorite among the 15 sports equipment and rental shops here. They have four outlets scattered around town. Contact ☎ 05446 34 00.

■ The **Arlberg Arena Mountain Hiking School** centralizes the expertise of several mountain guides. For treks throughout the Ferwall and Lechtal Alps, contact Ferdl Nöbl, ☎ 05446 28 66, www.Arlberg-arena.at.

■ The **Ski School Arlberg** and the **Ski and Snowboard School St. Anton**, the village's two ski schools, employ a total of 320 instructors and over 150 group courses at all ability levels. The Arlberg school is the older, traditional school, in operation since 1921, ☎ 05546 34 11, www.skischool-arlberg.com. The St. Anton school is at ☎ 05446 35 63, www.skistanton.com. Both are good.

Where to Sleep

St. Anton boasts a wide range of accommodations, some scattered into far-flung neighborhoods in Nasserein and St. Jakob – both of which are friendly, quiet villages but not what most visitors come here to experience. Most outlying accommodation re-

HOTEL PRICES	
€	Up to €80 per night
€€	€81 to €150
€€€	€151 to €250
€€€€	Over €250

Schwarzer Adler

mains closed through the summer. In-town rates soar at the height of winter.

The elegant **Schwarzer Adler** (€€€), a rambling old hotel with what must be St. Anton's most genteel staff. The rooms in the new wing are bright, the lounge has an open fire, and the new wellness center is an ideal place to rejuvenate; ☎ 05446 224 40, www.schwarzeradler.com. For on-mountain lodging near the Mooserwirt (and with an in-house après-ski scene to boot), book the Kössler Family's cozy **Kaminstube**; ☎ 05446 26 81, www.kaminstube.com.

In the center, try the **Angelika** (€€), ☎ 05446 22 54; or the newly remodelled **Hotel Garni Montana** (€€) in the pedestrian area, ☎ 05446 32 53. A short walk uphill from the center, near the lifts in the vicinity of the racing stadium, the **Haus am Fang** (€€), ☎ 05546 35 43, offers cozy residential accommodations at the slopes.

Where to Eat

One of the village's most elegant dining venues is, oddly, the **Museum Restaurant and Café** (€€). The restaurant occupies the ground floor of a forest-ensconced fairytale chalet, its cozy rooms surrounding a massive fireplace and each decked out in old-world chalet décor. Reserve a table at ☎ 0556 24 75. On the mountain at St. Christoph, don't miss the **Hospiz Alm** (see *St. Christoph* below).

Museum Restaurant

Across from the tourist office, try the **Hax'n Stub'n** (€€) – it's cozier inside than it might first appear, and there's upstairs seating, too. The simple **'S Wirtshaus am Alten Bahnhof** restaurant (€€) in the old train

station offers good traditional food as well.

The **Rodelstall** (€-€€), at the foot of the tobogganing run, boasts an open fireplace, regional cuisine and, on advance request, delicious spareribs; ☎ 0699 178 588 55. For less expensive fare, **Pomodoro Pizzeria** (€) at Dorfstrasse 5 is popular for its good selection of pizzas and convivial ambiance.

At the Moosewirt

Where to Party

St. Anton's reputation as a party town is well deserved, at least in winter, when adult crowds descend upon the village with revelry in mind. In summer, the village is a great deal quieter.

If you love après-ski parties, don't miss the afternoon action at the **Mooserwirt** mountain lodge in the hamlet of Moos, just above town. A deck full of picnic tables fills up early, as skis pile up outside. Inside, a DJ plays music to a house packed from dance floor, to stairway, to balcony – where a cross-cultural mix of international visitors drinks beer and dances on tables, ski boots and all. Beware, however, when the party slows down around dinnertime; you must then navigate the dark, icy slope down to the village on skis. The cries of tumbling drunks oft echo through the village center.

The **Krazy Kangaroo** just across the slope shares an equally renowned reputation and a lively – if younger and poorer – après-ski crowd. Down the hill at village center, après-ski action congregates at several scattered locales, although most places quiet down during the dinner hour before picking up again late (after everyone's had a shower and a nap). At the base of the slopes, near the ski school, the **Base Camp** gazebo bar offers a heated deck and a long list of warm drinks. Favorite afternoon-and-evening attractions include the **Underground,** a two-story bar with a dark basement and an upstairs pub; **Jacksy's** next door, for low-key conversation; the **Bar Cuba** for self-service beer; and the **Funky Chicken** for big, cheap beers and young, rollicking fun. For late-night dancing, try the **Piccadilly Pub** or the **Post Keller**, both in the Hotel Post. My favorite late-night bar, however, remains the **Platzl**, a dark, smoky dive with a fireplace and occasional live music.

Where to Play

 Although St. Anton wholeheartedly welcomes children in all seasons, the difficulty of the local ski slopes and the raucousness of the clientele here makes it less than ideal for families in winter. That said, many improvements have been made, particularly in the Nasserein area. Look for continued development here. In the summer, St. Anton's lively festival calendar and village ambiance makes for a great family atmosphere. The **kindergarten** accepts potty-trained children, the tourist office can help arrange **childcare**, and two great **playgrounds** entertain. The first, near the wellness center, on the site of the old train yard, offers water play, a fountain, and several toys. The second, up Rudi Matt Weg, at the foot of the town museum, delights with a good collection of wooden toys and – the kicker – a small fishing pond. A third playground is a 10-minute walk outside of the center, next to the lake at Verwall.

Festivals & Events

 St. Anton opens its winter season in early December with the **Radio 7 Ski Opening** party and pop concert for which fans bus in from Germany, Italy, and Switzerland. **Holiday season festivities** follow, including a torch-lit race and musical fireworks, a mountain celebration at St. Jakob's church, and the **Arlberg New Year Concert**. In January, the **Powder 8** event graces the local slopes, as pairs of skiers compete to carve the most perfect figure-eights as they descend. July brings traditional folklore and the **St. Anton Festival**, while August features the **Tent Feast**, during which local and visiting folklore bands parade through town in traditional costumes. Mountain bikers flock to town for the **Arlberg Mountain Bike Trophy** in August, when some 200 bikers race on the 20-km extreme downhill run. The **St. Anton Film Festival** takes center stage in mid September, showing international and regional takes on mostly mountain-related themes; and, later in September, the **Almabtrieb Harvest Festival** celebrates the return of the cattle from their summer Alpine pastures.

LANDECK CASTLE

Landeck sits 30 km east of St. Anton, on the way to Innsbruck. On a hill above the town perches Schloss Landeck, a 13th-century fortress that today houses the local museum. Inside the castle is a good collection of costumes and art and a cultural center that mounts a variety of events and exhibitions. For more information, contact ☎ 05442 632 02, www.schlosslandeck.at.

St. Christoph

St. Christoph

Population: 50

Base Elevation: 1,800 m/5,904 feet

Mountain resort village

Just 17 buildings comprise the hamlet of St. Christoph, a se-
clude, exclusive satellite resort of St. Anton that boasts a history all its own.

The settlement of St. Christoph lies at the top of the barren
Arlberg Pass, a six-km climb above St. Anton along a dramatic
tunnel road that's avalanche-protected with an opening on one

side. It is home to a ski
school, six expensive hotels,
and a national ski team training center. If you're not staying here – and given local
room rates, the odds are
good you're not – St.
Christoph provides little
more than a lunch stop on a
day-tripping ski route. If you
head for the Hospiz Alm,
however, St. Christoph is a
stop well worth making.

Hospiz Alm

The **Hospiz Alm** (€€) restaurant is owned and operated by the same family that runs the swanky Arlberg Hospiz Hotel down the road. The atmosphere in this old farmhouse, however, is much more fun. Rough-hewn wood, lots of stone, and a roaring fire create a cozy ambiance – and don't miss the stairway slide down to the bathrooms. (One of the region's best wine cellars lurks downstairs as well.) Excellent traditional cuisine makes this a favorite on-slope lunch stop for skiers, and the restaurant remains *the* place in the Arlberg for a romantically rustic dinner; ☎ 05446 36 25, www.hospiz.com, open winter only.

● THE BROTHERHOOD OF ST. CHRISTOPH

As was the custom in medieval times, the Christian men's order *Johanniter* maintained a network of high-altitude chapels en route to the holy land, offering shelter, food, and drink to travelers in need. So, although a chapel may have existed along the path prior his time, Heinrich Findelkind, a St. Anton pig herdsman, is attributed with founding the first hostel on this site in 1387. Findelkind was known to serve far beyond the duties expected of a hostel host, actively seeking out stranded travelers and bringing them to safety, even in the harshest winter weather. The Pope took note in 1386, and the Brotherhood of St. Christoph was officially established. After extensive recruiting throughout Italy, Bohemia, Poland, Germany, the Netherlands, and Switzerland, Heinrich Findelkind and the Brotherhood of St. Christoph had the financial and prayerful support of some 2,000 members by the time of the man's death around 1415.

Emperor Joseph II disbanded the brotherhood in 1780, and the hostel passed through several private ownerships before falling into ruin by the 19th century, when the new Arlberg railway line largely eliminated traffic over the pass. Government preservation efforts kicked in during 1898, and the hostel and its chapel found new life as a ski lodge for early sportsmen. On January 3rd of 1901, the legendary Arlberg Ski Club was founded here, a moment documented on a Hospiz tablecloth. Sadly, in January 1957, a fire destroyed all but the exterior walls of the structures – an event that, tragic as it was, resulted in the reestablishment of the ancient brotherhood, which was enacted in an effort to rebuild the historical site. Today, the Arlberg Hospiz Hotel stands on the site of the original hostel, and the Brotherhood of St. Christoph numbers over 13,000 members worldwide. Funds raised through membership fees pay for the upkeep of the chapel and donations to varied charities, including the sponsorship of children orphaned in mountain accidents.

 Want to stay? Well, unfortunately, a night at St. Christoph's famed hostel is these days far from free. If you've got the change to spare, however, by all means book accommodations at the **Arlberg Hospiz Hotel** (€€€€). Its rooms, suites, and apartments vary in décor, but all are luxurious; its private ski instructors rank among the region's best; and the sofa fronting its enormous fireplace is the mountain's

Arlberg Hospiz Hotel

most perfect place for a nightcap. Reserve at ☎ 05546 26 11, www.hospiz.com; hotel open winter only. If you'd prefer a less extravagant stay, the least expensive of the hotels here is the **Gasthof Valluga** (€€€), a cozy but still pricey place; ☎ 05446 28 23, www.arlberg.com/gasthof-valluga; gasthof-valluga@ arlberg.com. The hotel is open in winter only.

St. Christoph shares the St. Anton tourist information office. Contact ☎ 05446 226 90, www.stantonamarlberg.com.

Lech

Population: 1,466
Base Elevation: 1,450 m/4,756 feet
Mountain resort village

Lech is the quintessential Alpine holiday village: Chalets dot forested hillsides, a crystal-clear river runs through the center, and horse-drawn carriages await fares next to a covered bridge. First and foremost, Lech is loved by families, many of whom have been coming here for years.

This traditional village lies up the Flexen Pass, on the northern side of the Valluga mountain, approximately 20 km north of St. Anton. Although it is one of the Alps' more expensive resorts, the village is less pretentiously exclusive than St. Christoph, and a country-style gentility prevails.

Austria

Stuben

Some 300 m/1,000 feet up the hill from the village center perches the hamlet of **Oberlech**, a car-free village served by a lift that runs late into the night. Also near Lech are the satellite hamlets of **Stuben** and **Zug**, quiet hideaways perfect for walking, cross-country skiing, and horse-drawn sleigh and carriage rides. Between Lech and St. Christoph is **Zürs**, a treeless ski resort that largely closes up in summer.

LECH FOR KIDS

 Lech's children's programs are some of the best in the Alps. Its Mini and Junior Club adventure day programs entertain kids from three to 12 years old with a wide range of age-appropriate activities, including river rafting, pool swimming, fishing, picnicking, skating at the local fun park. For kids staying in Lech, the program (except for lunch) is free of charge. In winter, the Mini Club and the Oberlech kindergarten take kids three years and up. For guests staying in Oberlech, kindergarten childcare is free. The tourist office can help arrange babysitting year-round.

Zürs

From late November through April, Lech is a snowy wonderland. For skiers, the village partners up with nearby resorts to offer the **Arlberg Ski Pass**, which includes 85 lifts and 267 km of groomed runs and 185 km of ungroomed routes at resorts including St. Anton, St. Christoph, and Zurs, among others. The 110 km of groomed skiing above Lech is less extreme than that above St. Anton – another feature attractive to families. Other winter attractions include many sporting activities for non-skiers, such as a lighted tobogganing run, 19 km of cross-country runs, 25 km of cleared walking trails, and sleigh rides day and night. Now here, too, are the world's first heated chair lifts.

In summer, the valley's low-key relaxation brings loyal guests from all over Europe. From late June through late September, visitors hike on 250 km of trails, head into the hills on four lifts, enjoy a large forest pool, fish in mountain lakes, and mountain bike on a variety of trails. The local mountaineering school organizes classes and outings for a variety of sports across a full range of ability levels. In addition, free hikers' buses serve outlying trails, including the fascinating **Sea of Stone Trail**. Beginning near the crater-like Formarinsee, this four-hour, geology-themed loop encircles the Formaletsch peak, passing through a limestone treasure trove of fossils – some up to 200 million years old. Stone markers indicate fossil sites.

 Want to stay? It's neither the quietest nor the quaintest place in town, but the **Hotel Tannbergerhof** (€€-€€€)offers a good array of services directly in the village center – and at relatively reasonable rates. Post-flood renovations to the cellar, disco, and wellness facilities make this an even better day. It's at house number 111, just across from the river, and it welcomes guests for both the summer and winter seasons. In winter, the hotel's sidewalk café is a popular après-ski hangout. For reservations, dial

Hotel Tannbergerhof

☎ 05583 220 20, www.tannbergerhof.com.

 The local tourist office is along the main road in the center of town. For more information, contact ☎ 054483 31 55, www.lech-zuers.at.

◆ Ischgl

Population: 1,500

Base elevation: 1,377 m/4,517 feet

Mountain resort village

Once a mildly prosperous mining town, Ischgl is a place where both "hard rock" and "gold" have taken on entirely different meanings. I love wintertime Ischgl for its young, party-hearty spirit, its famed on-mountain concerts, and its trendy, pricey façade. The town lies largely dormant during its summer recuperation, although expanded summer lift service and a growing

Ischgl

following among hard-core mountain bikers promise to change all that.

The old settlement of "Yscla" first hit the maps as Rhaeto-Romans ventured over the Fimberpass in search of summer pasturelands. Today, the hopping holiday village of Ischgl is 100 km west of Innsbruck, a long way up the long Paznaun Valley. The resort village occupies a 1.5-kilometer stretch of the southern bank of the Trisanna River and boasts a lovely setting smack dab among the Silvretta, the Samnaun, and the Verwall mountains.

Although the village has a lengthy history, little of Ischgl's historical core remains today. Restaurants line the narrow streets, sporting goods shops flaunt the latest in high-tech equipment, and glossy hotels stretch out along the southern foothills, each vying for a coveted "ski-in" lot. All that said, Ischgl does not have the pretensions of such highbrow resorts as Kitzbühel and St. Moritz, but instead adopts a welcoming friends-and-fun atmosphere suitable for its young clientele.

Lift-served **mountain biking** is Ischgl's reason-for-being from mid-June through early October. The region's Silvretta Bike Arena maintains at least 35 marked tours between five and 55 km in length and with a vertical drop of over 2,000 meters/6,560 feet. In-the-know riders will appreciate the local influence of su-

Ski lift in Ischgl

perstar biker Hans Rey, who oversees the trail network here. For walkers, the village boasts 300 km of **hiking** trails and 18 Alpine huts in its immediate vicinity. The cable uplift network runs throughout the summer season, and numerous themed and guided walks are offered. In addition to many hotel-based programs, Ischgl Reservations runs daily guided hikes, including nature walks, high peak excursions, Alpine pasture walks, and low-intensity family itineraries. Our favorite outing, however, is a lift-assisted trek to Samnaun, Switzerland – see the *Smugglers' Run* info box below.

In winter, Ischgl's continually improving **skiing** facilities include 205 km of groomed trails. The downhill runs here suit intermediates best, but advanced skiers hire guides and head off-piste, and beginners take to the Idalp's sunny runs. Europe's **snowboarding** set loves Ischgl as much for its partying as for its on-slope attractions, which include an extensive funpark and a competition schedule featuring FIS World Cup events. **Cross-country skiers** enjoy 48 km of valley trails looping from Ischgl up to Galtur, and **winter walking trails** line the river bank and loop at altitude near Trida Sattel and Idalp.

Austria

THE SMUGGLERS' RUN

The Smugglers' Run is a cross-border route from Ischgl to Samnaun, Switzerland. The attractions? Duty-free shopping and the enduring thrill of crossing an international border on ski, foot, or bike. Although the most direct route between the two villages is via ski and lift, pedestrians can make this run year-round with the purchase of the Schmugglerticket lift pass (€19-27 for adults). The pass is good for a round-trip journey on the four lifts en route to Samnaun, and bikes can tag along, too, for no additional charge.

Finally, it must be said: Ischgl knows how to throw a party. In addition to its wild winter après-ski scene, the resort is renowned for its **mountain concerts,** held at the open and close of each season and during the Christmas and Easter holidays. But, these are not your run-of-the-mill *oompa* affairs. This little village brings in the crowds with big-name pop artists, performers that in the past few years have included Pink, Bon Jovi, Bob Dylan, Tina Turner, Rod Stewart, and Sting. Other festivals include the mid-January Shapes in White **snow-sculpting competition** and its summer-time cousin, the late-June European **fire-sculpting competition**, during which flame artists build elaborate frames before setting them afire over a small lake.

 Want to stay? The **Hotel Yscla** (€€-€€€) boasts a central location near the gondola and offers year-round biking, skiing, hiking, and dining packages. Reserve at ☎ 05444 5275, www.yscla.at .

 For more information, dial ☎ 0544 5266 or click www.ischgl.com. For further information regarding the opening status of Silvretta area cableways, check with www.silvretta.at.

The Silvretta Hochalpenstrasse

Built in 1953 to connect the Paznaun and Montafon valleys, the Silvretta Hochalpenstrasse offers an awe-inspiring look at western Austria's high Alpine landscape. The 22-km road winds its way through rugged terrain above Galtür to Bielerhöhe and the Silvretta Reservoir, interesting for its blue glacial waters, boat tours, and hiking opportunities. The reservoir is dammed at both ends, and the Ill River sheds its waters toward both the Rhein and Danube rivers. Past the lake, the road labors down into the forested Montafon Valley toward Bregenz. Be prepared for a hefty toll (€10.90 at last count) and boulder-colored cows along (and in) the road. The pass closes for snow from November through May. Simple accommodations are available at the roadside-yet-remote **Berggästhof Piz Buin** (€), ☎ 5558 4231, www.pizbuin-silvretta.at.

◆ Bregenz

Population: 28,000
Base Elevation: 398 m/1,305 feet
Tourist city
When writer Alexandre Dumas first entered Bregenz, he portrayed Lake Constance as "a piece of heaven framed in earth to

Bregenz

serve God as a mirror." Although you might utter a somewhat less poetic phrase, it is undeniably a lovely lake. Your personal assessment of central Bregenz, however, will likely hinge on your taste for contemporary architecture, small-city bustle, and modern art.

Bregenz lies amid hilly terrain on the easternmost shore of the Bodensee or, in English, Lake Constance. It's the third-largest lake in central Europe, spanning 540 square km, plunging to a depth of 252 m/826 feet, and running a shoreline circumference of 273 km. The city lies at the junction of Austria, Switzerland, Liechtenstein, and Germany, 120 km east of Zurich, 190 km southwest of Munich, and 200 km west of Innsbruck. It serves as the capital of the Vorarlberg region, and is the most culturally active city in the province.

The town stretches along the eastern edge of the lake, separated from the shore and its Seepromenade park by train tracks and a busy road. The lakefront attractions here are anchored to the west by the Strandbad beach facilities and the Seebuhne floating stage and, to the east, by the jetty and the Mili swimming pool. The city center lies in between, extending back toward the hills and up toward Oberstadt, the walled old town. Mt. Pfander rises a modest 1,064 m/3,300 feet to the east of the town center, its cable car departing from a valley station on the northeastern edge of town.

VORARLBERG ARCHITECTURE

The region has long honored an architectural allegiance to its traditional architecture, a style employing grayed, untreated wood, scale-like shingle siding, and light balconies. However, changes are afoot, and the cities of the Voralberg – particularly those clustered at the eastern edge of Lake Constance – now make much of their contemporary architecture. With aesthetic ideas based on traditional Vorarlberg methods, the designs focus on simplicity and economic functionality, using primarily glass, steel, concrete, and raw local wood. Both Bregenz and Dornbirn have good examples – locally, check out the Festival and Conference Center and the Bregenz Art Galley cube.

Bregenz's **old town** lies uphill from the center and is here
AUTHOR'S
CHOICE
known as the *Oberstadt*. Although it can be reached by car via Kirchstrasse, the most scenic route up is by foot along the Maurachgasse and the old-world Stadtsteig road, which leads up to the fortified old town. When you reach the walls at Martintor, don't miss the petrified sea creature dangling above the gate – a delightfully scary sight during a midnight thunderstorm. If conditions are such, it's worth a wet walk up. The Oberstadt remains largely residential, but at the northern corner of the walled complex rises the **Martinsturm**, Bregenz's signature landmark. Built in 1601, the tower boasts central Europe's largest onion-dome, and the

Martinskappelle chapel next door is home to some interesting 14th-century frescoes.

Of Bregenz's adventures, **ferryboat rides** on Lake Constance prove the most popular with kids. The *Weisse Flotte* ferry fleet plies between several Bodensee ports in Austria, Germany, and Switzerland. These include the island of Lindau, the town of Friedrichshafen with its Zeppelin Museum, the wine-producing town of Meersburg, and the flower-happy island of Mainau. In addition to regular ferry service, several theme cruises and package tours are offered; ☎ 05574 428 68, www.bodenseeschifffahrt.at. Boats depart Bregenz from the harbor just east of the jetty.

 Want to stay? Bregenz hotels cater to business-oriented folks, and rather characterless establishments are the norm. The exception here is the enchanting **Hotel Deuring Schlossle** (€€€€). The only hotel within the Oberstadt's walls, the Deuring Schlossle boasts lake views, a homey castle atmosphere, and one of the region's best restaurants. If you're splurging on a room here, don't miss dinner: The restaurant oc-

Hotel Deuring Schlossle

cupies one corner of the old town's ancient wall, its dining rooms decked out in elegant residential décor. Guests dine on light, creative cuisine and fine wines – and a brandy by the massive fireplace is an ideal way to end the evening. Reserve a table and room at ☎ 05574 478 00, www.deuring-schloessle.at.

HOTEL PRICES	
€	Up to €80 per night
€€	€81 to €150
€€€	€151 to €250
€€€€	Over €250

 The tourist office is in the Tourismushaus at Bahnhofstrasse 14, in the western corner of the pedestrian area. Its very helpful staff offers room reservation assistance, good sightseeing advice, and the informative *Discover Bregenz* pamphlets. For more information, check www.vorarlberg.cc.

◆ Feldkirch

Population: 31,005
Base Elevation: 460 m/1,509 feet
Tourist town

Feldkirch (Hans Wiesenhofer)

A small, charming city on the western border of Austria, halfway between Bregenz and Vaduz, Feldkirch is a seldom-visited place loaded with medieval ambiance.

The city got its start as a market and university town, developing its central network of alleys and squares along the Ill River by late in the 13th century. Today, much of the town's action continues to revolve around the old center's pedestrian marketplace.

Day tourists will enjoy a simple wander through the **old town** along its cobblestone alleys, which link two long, parallel squares, the **Neustadtplatz** to the east and the **Marktplatz** to the west. The Neustadt is now a bustling ring street with cramped parking; the Marktplatz remains a narrow market area encircled by elegant arcades. The **St. Johanneskirche** anchors the southern edge of the old town, and the 15th-century

Feldkirch in 1550 *(© Hebrew University of Jerusalem)*

cathedral **St. Nikolaus** and the nearby **Katzenturm** bell tower rise to the north. At the northwestern corner of town, the 14th-century **Churertor** still guards the city gates. Outside of the center, on a hill south of town, is **Schattenberg Castle**. First built in the 12th century, the **Montfort castle** has 13-foot-thick walls that alone make the steep hike or drive worthwhile. To get there, drive up Burgasse or follow the footpath up the Schlosssteig steps. Inside are a restaurant and museum, the latter open Tuesday through Sunday from 9 am-noon and 1-5 pm; December through January, 11 am-4 pm; closed November.

Several medieval **festivals** highlight the Feldkirch calendar and, if you can catch one, it's likely to be one of your trip's most memorable events. The **Montfort Markt**, the city's famous old-

Shattenberg Castle

world festival, comes each May to the foot of the Schattenburg Castle. The **Feldkircher Weinfest** fills the Marktplatz in early July and, later in the month, the **Gauklerfestival**, or Jugglers' Festival, brings 100 street artists to the Feldkirch, delightfully crowding the old medieval center with clowns, mimes, comedians, and, of course, jugglers. Finally, the Christmas season enlivens the old town with the **Blosengelmarkt**, **Advent singing**, and the **Feldkirch Christmas Market**.

Want to stay? The coziest place in town – and it has the best restaurant, too – is the lovely **Hotel Alpenrose** (€€), with a gracious staff, antique-heavy décor, and a 450-year-old history. The hotel is in the old center at Rosengasse 4. Reserve at ☎ 05522 721 75, www.alpen-rose.net.

The Feldkirch tourist office is at Schlossergasse 8. For more information, contact ☎ 05522 734 67, www.feldkirch.at.

Innsbruck & the Tyrol

Austria's Tyrol draws travelers year-round for its picturesque villages and its warm hospitality. The region squeezes between Germany and Italy, stretching the length of the Inn Valley along a wide river. At the region's center is the lively university city of Innsbruck. All around **Innsbruck**, within an hour's drive, valleys jut off into high-Alpine glacial terrain. It's into these valleys – the **Ötztal**, the **Stubaital**, and the **Zillertal** – that adventurers escape the city each weekend. The charming resort of **Seefeld** rests just south of the Zügspitze and the German border, and chic **Kitzbühel** puts on a good show to the east. Unlike the more extreme steeps of the Arlberg to the west, the rolling pastures here prove a family-friendly place to play. Catering to sightseers and adventurers of all ages and abilities, the Tyrol greets visitors with an ambiance of rustic coziness here called *gemutlichkeit*.

Innsbruck &
The Tyrol

N

25 MILES
25 KM

GERMANY

AUSTRIA

ITALY

Waidring
Lofer
312
St Johann
Kitzbühel
172
Kufstein
161
Söll
Westendorf
Mittersill
Wörgl
165
Krimml
Gerlos Pass
Achenkirch
A12
Mayrhofen
ZILLERTAL
181
Jenbach
169
Uderns
Achensee
Schwaz
Zell am Ziller
Hintertux
Schönberg
Innsbruck
A13
Seefeld
Sellrain
183
177
Neustift
STUBAITAL
Zugspitze
Telfs
Rombo Pass
189
Oetz
A12
136
Reutte
Jerzens
OTZTAL
Sölden-
Hochsölden
314
Nasereith
Imst
Obergurgl-
Hochgurgl

to Bischofshofen

© 2007 HUNTER PUBLISHING, INC

◆ Innsbruck

Population: 128,000

Base elevation: 575 m/1,886 feet

Gateway tourist city

Innsbruck is both the political capital and the cultural core of the Tyrol – a dynamic university town at once stirred by student energy and entrenched in traditional conservatism. With 25 holiday villages on its doorstep and two Olympic Winter Games under its belt, it's also the most athletically active city in the Alps. More than any other city I know, Innsbruck offers an ideal combination of city sightseeing and Alpine adventure.

History & Overview

Innsbruck sits on a site inhabited by Stone Age settlers as early as 4000 BC. The area's position at the intersection of the Inn and Wipp valleys made it a coveted stop along the early trade routes through the Alps, a convenient locale that continues to enrich the city today. The region saw stints under both Roman and Bavarian rule during the first millennium, and mention is first made of "Insprucke," or "a bridge over the Inn River," in the 12th century. The new town flourished from the 14th through the 19th centuries, enjoying booming growth as a cultural, administrative, and mining center. The ruling Hapsburg Family adored Innsbruck, making it their official residence and thereby attracting to the city the greatest artists, musicians, and writers of the time. The two world wars in the early 20th century brought the city's rise to an abrupt halt; but, even though extensive damage befell the city during World War II, it rebounded quickly, taking the world stage once more as host of the Olympic Winter Games both in 1964 and again in 1976.

Innsbruck lies in western Austria, along the Inn River at the crossroads of the Inntal and Wipptal valleys. The Nordkette mountain range rises dramatically to the north, and the Ötztal, Stubaital, and Zillertal Alps stretch out to the south. Two autobahns, the A12 and the A13, converge just south of town – the A12 running east toward Salzburg and west toward Landeck, and the A13 running south over the Brenner Pass into Italy.

Austria

The Town

Central Innsbruck fills a triangular chunk of land bordered by a kink in the wide Inn River and the autobahns to the south. The old town, or *altstadt*, lies at the western edge of the center and remains the focus of the city's tourism. The nucleus of the *altstadt* district is a pedestrian area along Herzog Friedrich Strasse, a cobblestone road lined with shops, arcades, and cafés. The university and most of the churches and museums of note sit on the old town's northeastern edge. **Markt Graben** and **Burg Graben** loop around the southern edge of the *altstadt*, perpendicular to Maria Theresienstrasse, the inner city's wide boulevard and its shopping district. The main town station – now under dramatic reconstruction – sits at the southern side of town, a 10-minute walk southeast of the *altstadt*.

Getting Here & Around

Visitors arriving by air will land at the Innsbruck Airport just west of town or transfer from Munich, 146 km north, or from Salzburg, 190 km northeast. Zürich is 250 km west, but direct train service makes Zürich a more convenient option than this distance suggests. For local transportation, Innsbruck operates a complicated network of buses and trams, most of which hub at the main train station on the southeastern edge of old town. (In addition to its modern trams, the city operates nostalgic streetcars with original wood-paneled interiors from June through September – look for them along the tramline to Igls.) For taxi service, ☎ 0512 53 11.

✔ The free **Club Innsbruck Card** is issued to hotel guests upon check-in. Guests receive discounts on sightseeing, activities, and transportation and an invitation to participate in free guided hiking tours. Your hotel can issue and validate a card upon your arrival. **The Innsbruck Card** is not free, but includes cable car rides, museum admissions, and use of The Sightseer tourist bus. Cards come in 24- , 48- , and 72-hour increments and are sold at the tourist office, attraction ticket counters, and many hotels. 24-hour cards run €23, which you'll make back after one round-trip ascent to the Seegrube; www.innsbruck-ticket-service.at.

Getting More Info

 The main tourist office is at Burg Graben 3, near the junction of Herzog Friedrich Strasse and Maria Theresienstrasse. For more information, contact ☎ 0512 598 50, www.innsbruck-tourismus.at. The tourist office can help with accommodations, sell you maps or event tickets, and sign you up for one of its one-hour guided city walks, which depart daily at 11 am, for €8 per person.

The main post office is at Maximilianstrasse 2. A second post office is at Bruneckerstrasse, just north of the train station.

The Sights

Innsbruck's small but charming **old town** is the center of the city's tourist action. Here, visitors wander back alleys, shop in the boutiques, and dine in outdoor cafés. Additionally, Innsbruck boasts 18 museums on topics ranging from alpinism to bells, running second only to Vienna among Austria's museum cities. At Herzog Friedrich Strasse 15, beneath the landmark **Goldenes Dachl**, or Golden Roof, is the **Maximilianeum**

The Goldenes Dachl

Museum. The museum memorializes the life of Emperor Maximilian I, great patron of Austrian art, music, and architecture. Visit May through September daily from 10 am-6 pm, and October through April, Tuesday through Sunday from 10 am-5 pm; ☎ 0512 58 11 11; €4. The **Tiroler Volkskunst Museum**, or Tyrolean Regional Heritage Museum, documents the Tyrol's history with fascinating displays of interior design and artistic craftsmanship. It's at Universitatsstrasse 2, near the Hofkirche, and is open Monday through Saturday from 9 am-5 pm; ☎ 0512

Emperor Maximilian I (by Dürer)

In the Hofkirche

58 43 02. The nearby **Hofkirche** houses the tomb of Emperor Maximilian I and is open to visitors daily from 9 am-5 pm when services are not in session.

At the Alpenzoo

A visit to the **Innsbruck Alpenzoo** is a hit with kids, and involves a ride up the Hungerburgbahn funicular at the base of the Seegrube and a pleasant stroll through the woods. The zoo is home to more than 2,000 Alpine animals – 150 species are represented. The park can also be reached by car. It's open daily from 9 am; ☎ 0512 29 23 23, www.alpenzoo.at.

Just south of town, the new **Bergisel Ski Jump** offers tours of its 47-m/

The Bergisel Ski Jump

154-foot tower. The sports stadium below was the site of the
Olympic Winter Games ski jumping events and today hosts
training and competitions throughout the year. Visit daily, 6 am-
5 pm, €6. Also south of town, near a stop along the Igls tram
route, **Schloss Ambras** offers a nice collection of historical art,
armor, and artifacts, all housed within the splendid surround-

ings of the 16th-century palace grounds. It's open daily, December through October, from 10 am-5 pm; ☎ 05252 47 45, www.khm.at/ambras.

Schloss Ambras

Austria

Swarovski Crystal World

Discerning shoppers will recognize the Austrian Swarovski name as one of the great manufacturers of precision-cut crystal. It all started here, just east of Innsbruck, when in 1895 Daniel Swarovski founded the company's first mill. Today, Swarovski Crystal World is a complex gleaming with water, glass, and crystal – more avant-garde exposition than museum. It's in Wattens, 20 km east of Innsbruck along the A12 Autobahn. It's open daily except Christmas and Easter 9 am-6 pm; entry is €8. For more information, contact ☎ 05224 510 80, www.swarovski-crystalworlds.com.

At Swarovski Crystal World

The Adventures

● ON WHEELS

 Innsbruck remains one of Europe's most outdoorsy cities, and its adventures span all seasonal sports. In summer, **mountain bikers** take to over 115 km of designated trails along the Nordkette range, and the **Nordparktrail** free-ride run drops 1,040 m/3,400 feet between the Seegrube and Hungerburg mountains – a huge hit with technical riders.

● ON FOOT

 Innsbruck's popular panoramic **climbing route** surmounts seven summits from Hafelekar to the Frau-Hitt-Sattel along a 3,000-m secured climbing route. It's not a particularly difficult climb, but newcomers should ask the advice and services of the **Alpinschule Innsbruck** in Natters at ☎ 0512 546 000, www.asi.at. Climbing gardens are at Axamer Lizum and Igls. **Walkers** enjoy trails through all 15 holiday resorts, along the river at city center, and the scenic Zirbenweg at Patscherkofel.

Hiking Azamer Lizum, near Innsbruck

✔ The **Innsbruck Alpine School**, in conjunction with the tourist office, organizes a program of free guided hikes offered daily between early June and late September.

The program utilizes over 40 different hiking trails, includes lantern-lit walks, sunrise hikes, and music-accompanied pasture strolls. Other services include a free hiking bus, equipment loans, and guiding arrangements. Inquire and make reservations at the tourist office.

● ON WATER

Floss rafting

New in Innsbruck is the rare opportunity to hop aboard a *Floss* raft, here a modern take on an old Alpine tradition. Each of the modern floats incorporates umbrella tables, beer service, and lots of convivial fun. ***Floss* rafting trips** set sail each Thursday from May through October, launching from the Kranebitten district on the western outskirts of town and finishing at the Löwenhaus Inn. €22 includes the ride and bus transfer. For reservations and information, ☎ 052 6355 83, www.flossfahrt.at.

● ON SNOW & ICE

In winter, Innsbruck's 25 resort villages – jointly marketed under the name Olympia Skiworld Innsbruck – offer a full spectrum of slopes and snow sports. In all, 80 lifts access 285 km of **skiing** pistes. **Ice sports** play in the city's Olympic halls, natural **toboggan runs** drop 60 km down local hills, and **cross-country skiers** head out on 300 km of trails. In Igls, daredevils can sample high-speed **bobsledding** on the Olympic run. Ride in an original competition sled accompanied by an expert pilot and brakeman (€85, by arrangement), or take the shorter layman's ride offered January through February each Tuesday from 10 am and Thursday from 7 pm (€30, reservations required). Sliders must be 14 years old to take the short ride; 16 for the long. Inquire and reserve at ☎ 0512 338 38. From May through September, the bob run is made on wheels each Thursday and Friday from 4-

Austria

6 pm; info and reservations, ☎ 0664 357 86 07, www.
sommerbobrunning.at.

On Innsbruck's Doorstep

Innsbruck counts 25 resort villages with its encircling Alpine terrain, each offering an array of summer and winter trails and a
wide range of sporting opportunities. Below, I highlight four of
the most popular resorts on Innsbruck's doorstep.

● NORDPARK-SEEGRUBE

All visitors should
scale the ridgeline of
Innsbruck's northern
mountain wall. The
freshly refurbished
Hungerburgerbahn
funicular chugs its
way from the north-
ern edge of town,
over the river, past
the zoo, and up to
the settlement of

Nordpark-Seegrube

Hoch-Innsbruck Hungerburg at 868 m/2,847 feet. From
there, the Nordkettenbahn cable car rises to Seegrube at 1,905
m/6,245 feet, whence a short cable-car ride delivers guests to
the area's highest peak, the **Hafelekarspitze** at 2,334 m/7,655
feet. From here, views stretch out to the **Zillertal**, the **Stubaital**,
and the **Ötztal Alps**. For more information, contact the
Innsbrücker Nordkettenbahnen at ☎ 0512 293 344, www.
nordpark.at.

✔ Every Friday from 5 to 11:30 pm, the Nordkettenbahn
   cable car brings guests to the Seegrube peak for a romantic dinner at the mountain restaurant and spectacular nighttime views over the city lights.

● IGLS

An hour's tram ride south from the center of Innsbruck, Igls is
the city's favorite forest playground. The quaint resort village
draws recreational hikers, bikers, and skiers, as well as the
world's best ice-sliding athletes, who come here to practice and

Austria

Igls and Patscherkofel Mountain

compete on the Olympic bobsled run. The **Patscherkofel** cable car climbs up to the local peak, passing over the bobsled tube and one of Europe's largest stands of stone pines. At the top, summertime visitors enjoy the continent's largest Alpine botanical garden, a plot harboring over 400 plants, and the hike down to the valley is pleasant and not fearfully steep. Between the village and the tram station, a tiny riverside park offers a **Kneipp water trail** – remove your shoes, and find relief for sore feet. For more information, contact www.patscherkofelbahnen.at.

✔ Igls has a number of hotels, and visitors preferring rural recreation over city sightseeing should consider basing here and day-tripping into Innsbruck.

● **MUTTERER ALM**

This small-time resort on the southwestern edge of Innsbruck offers gentle slopes for family hiking, biking, and skiing. It's also the starting point for the hike and bike trek that runs south to the Stubai Valley. Reopened in 2006 after a complete overhaul, the resort is a new favorite with families. Modern lifts, a lovely little village, and a free ski bus link to Axamer Lizum are draws here.

Azamer Lizum in summer

● AZAMER LIZUM

The most remote of the resorts highlighted here, Axamer Lizum lies 25 km west of Innsbruck. Its **Kalkkögel** peak affords splendid views over the **Inn Valley**, and a handful of hotels here offer slope-side accommodations. Although famed for its Olympic-caliber ski runs, the resort is popular as well with local snowboarders and summertime hikers. For more information, contact www.axamer-lizum.at.

Where to Sleep

The **Hotel Europa** (€€€€) is the choice of visiting dignitaries, but it's closer to the train station than it is to the city's sights. Elegant service, modern amenities, and the city's best restaurant are the draws here. Reserve at

Hotel Europa Tyrol

☎ 0512 59 31, www.europatyrol.com.

Hotel Innsbruck

The **Hotel Innsbruck** (€€-€€€) occupies a rambling old townhouse, just steps from either the old town or the Inn River, a location that makes it popular with bus tours that are overnighting. Its décor is contemporary, there's a small, basement pool, and the accommodations are comfortable enough. Inquire at ☎ 0512 59 86 80, www.hotelinnsbruck.com.

Goldener Adler (€€) is the most famous of the *altstadt*'s traditional inns; it's directly in the center and boasts a long list of distinguished patrons, of which King Ludwig, Goethe, and Mozart are just a few.

Goldener Adler

Reserve at ☎ 0512 571 11 10, www.goldeneradler.com.

The **Weisses Rössl** (€€), or "white stallion," has welcomed guests since 1410. The simple, traditional inn sits on a snug little alley in the *altstadt* – and is one of my favorite stays in town, both for its hospitable hosts and its delicious food; ☎ 0512 58 30 57, www.roessl.at.

HOTEL PRICES	
€.....	Up to €80 per night
€€	€81 to €150
€€€.....	€151 to €250
€€€€......	Over €250

The **Jungendherberge St. Nikolaus** (€) is the most central of the youth hostels here. Simple dorm-bedded rooms are the norm; ☎ 0512 28 65 15.

Where to Eat

Directly in the center, the **Goldenes Dachl** (€€) has traditional food, lots of beer, and a terrace beer garden at Hofgasse 1; and the cozy **Stiftskeller** (€€)

boasts an old-world setting, outdoor seating, and both Austrian and Italian food. It's at Stiftsgasse 1.

The **Weisses Rössl** (€€) at Kiebachgasse 8 serves up good regional specialties in a cheery atmosphere, or try the Gästhaus Gruber's **Das Wirtshaus am Markt** (€€), near the river at Innrain 22. The **Löwenhaus** (€€) has riverside dining on the banks of the Inn and a good selection of traditional dishes. It's at Rennweg 5, along the river walk approximately one kilometer north of the old town; ☎ 0512 58 54 79.

For a romantic meal out and the best traditional food in town, head for the **Europastüberl** (€€€) in the Hotel Europa, directly across from the train station.

For snacks, **Peter's TeaHouse** (€), in an ideal, upstairs location within view of the Goldene Dachl, offers over 250 kinds of tea accompanied by snacks and classical music.

RESTAURANT COSTS	
€	Less than €10
€€	€10 to €25
€€€	Over €25

Where to Party

Being both an Austrian city and a university town, Innsbruck has more than its share of watering holes. In the center, try the **Elferhaus**, in English "11th house," at Herzog Friedrich Strasse 11. The pub features beer, snacks, and, on the 11th day of each month, live music .

Theresienbräu, at Maria Theresienstrasse 51, was the first *wirtshaus* and brewery in Innsbruck, and today it's a favorite beer-hall hangout.

For disco dancing and DJ'd entertainment, head for the **Innkeller**, at Innstrasse 1, the **Café Bar Down Under** at Bogen 24, or the **Hafen** on the outskirts of town – all three stay lively till the wee hours. Live music kicks up frequently at a variety of late-night venues throughout town. Check with the tourist office (or the posters around the university) to see what's playing.

The **Casino Innsbruck** is a dressy affair with blackjack, roulette, slots, and popular dinner packages; it's at Salurnerstrasse in the Hilton Hotel; ☎ 0512 587 040, www.casinos.at.

The Tyrolean Evening Show

For more traditional evening entertainment, consider the **Tyrolean Evening Show** at the Gästhaus Sandwirt; it runs daily from April through October; ☎ 0512 263 263, www.tiroleralpenbuehne.com.

Where to Play

Children enjoy many of Innsbruck's activities, including **cable car rides**, **outdoor recreation**, and visits to the **Alpine zoo**. In Natters, between the resorts of Igls and Mutters, the **Natterser Lake Children's Program** offers a popular service that's free to holders of the Club Innsbruck Card. Organizers oversee activities such as adventure games, mini-golf, swimming, handicrafts, painting, and pony rides. The program operates from mid-May through mid-October, Monday through Friday, 10 am-5 pm; a shuttle service runs between Natters and the village of Igls. For more information, contact the tourist office.

Festivals & Events

Innsbruck celebrates the warmer months with the **Innsbruck Summer Festival**, a program of cultural festivals revolving more around art, music, and dance than folkloric tradition. From late June through early July, the **Summer Dance Festival** draws classical, modern, and

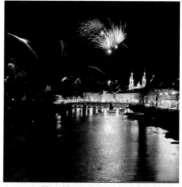

New Years in Innsbruck

ethnic dancers to the city's stages; and the **Innsbruck Festival**

Weeks, held from early July through late August, features a wide range of classical music concerts staged at various venues, including Ambras Castle and the Imperial Palace. Advent brings the city's **Christmas markets**, the most popular of which crowds the *altstadt* with stalls selling food, gifts, and the hot, mulled wine called *gluhwein*.

New Year's rings in with a party in old town and fireworks on the mountains above, and the **Mullerlaufen Parades** march through the *altstadt* streets each Saturday during the Carnival season. The winter sees world-class **athletic competitions** on Innsbruck's Olympic winter sports venues.

Innsbruck celebrates the spring thaw with the **Solstice in the Mountains Festival**, during which traditional fires are set all across the Nordkette mountain range.

Seefeld

Seefeld

Population: 3,100
Base Elevation: 1,200 m/3,936 feet
Mountain resort village

The Seefeld Holiday Region – a conglomerate comprised of Seefeld and four neighboring villages – enjoys a Europe-wide reputation as one of Austria's best village resorts. However, the action here is not the turbo-charged, adrenaline-pumping sort found elsewhere. It is instead a low-key, highbrow hum of soothing relaxation. Visitors come here, above all, to *breathe*.

Tucked up in a forest-bordered valley 25 km northwest of Innsbruck, near the German frontier and its Zügspitze mountain, Seefeld – or *Sevelt*, as it was called in the 11th century – enjoys an enviable locale midway between Innsbruck and Garmisch-Partenkirchen. The village first became a place of pilgrimage after the "miracle of the host" incident on Easter of 1384, when in the parish church an arrogant knight ate a consecrated communion wafer, causing the ground to shake and his feet to sink. Today's pilgrims, however, come in pursuit of more hedonistic pleasures.

Walking, biking, horseback riding, golf, and fishing are the town's most popular summertime pursuits. In the winter, skiers come for easy downhill runs, winter walking paths, and cross-country trails that were twice a venue for the Olympic Winter Games. Active guests also enjoy an expansive sports center, blessed with multiple swimming pools and a lake-top ice rink out front. The elegant little Seekapl church lies across the lake. It was surrounded by water when first erected in 1666.

The Seefeld Big Adventure Package

This package is a good half-day outing. It includes round-trip cable car rides and a cup of tea or coffee and cake at a mountain restaurant. The excursion starts from town, heading by cable car to the Rosshütte Middle Station for a 20-minute walking loop on the Zirbenweg trail. A second cable car goes to the Harmelekopf, a favorite paragliding launch point. Walkers return via the Rosshütte at mid-mountain for a coffee-and-cake break. From there, the Jochbahn cable car leads up to the Seefelder Joch peak, where the one-hour Panoramic Trail loop offers sweeping views. You return to town on the lift or hike down the lumber road. If you walk, your unused return lift ticket is good for a drink at the Rosshütte on your way back to town.

Want to stay? Big, modern chalet-hotels dominate Seefeld's lodging scene. Most are expensive. The **Gästhof Batzenhäusl** (€€) has simple rooms, some with balcony, and a nice location at the edge of the pedestrian shopping street. Guests enjoy use of the extensive wellness facilities – including pool, outdoor hot tub, and sauna – at the **Ferienhotel Kaltschmid**. It's next to the Raabach river and near the sports center; ☎ 05212 22 92, www.kaltschmid.co.at.

The excellent tourist office is in the pedestrian center, just across from the church. For more information, contact ☎ 0508 800, www.seefeld.com.

The Ötztal

Population(Sölden): 3,166
Base Elevation (Sölden): 1,377 m/4,517 feet
Resort valley

The Ötz Valley, or Ötztal, opens up at its northern end near the town of Sautens, just off the A12 Autobahn, and finally peters out at Obergurgl some 41 slow-driving km south. Skiers come year-round to the gla-

Summer in the Ötztal

cial slopes, climbers head up the Klettersteig wall near Langenfeld, and mountain bikers take to a magnificent trail running 80 km along the length of the valley.

Although several stops along the Ötztal road merit year-round tourist attention, our favorite bases are **Sölden** – the region's largest, loudest, rowdiest winter resort – and **Obergurgl**, at valley's end, a quiet little hamlet with a life all its own.

✔ If you visit in summer, consider the **Ötztal Card**. It offers access to valley buses, cableways (one per day), toll roads, museums, and swimming pools, and discounts at many other attractions. It is sold in seven- and 10-day increments. The seven-day card costs €45. Buy yours at any tourist office or at many ticket desks.

Huts in the mountains above Sölden

First, moving south from the northern mouth of the Ötztal, I stop at Umhausen. The Tyrol region's largest waterfalls, the **Stuibenfalls**, rise 150 m/492 feet in height and are less than an hour's hike east of town. Nearby, the new **Ötzi Dorf** open-air museum takes you for an archeological stroll through the Stone Age. Several huts demonstrate long-dead methods of handicraft, fishing gear, and baking techniques; a herd of farm animals (alive and well) entertains kids; and much is made, of course, of Ötzi, the valley's favorite prehistoric son (see below). The park is open daily, May through September, 10 am-6 pm; ☎ 05255 500 22, www.oetzi-dorf.com, €6.

ÖTZI

In 1991, hikers at altitude near the Ötztal's southern end stumbled upon an interesting find – a man, frozen in ice, with curious tools and an outfit most unfashionable. The man was un-iced, and scientific tests showed that he'd died here during the Neolithic Age, sometime around the fourth millennium before Christ. The world's archeologists and all Austria celebrated the sensational discovery, and the mummified marvel was christened "Ötzi" by his beaming hometown fans. Soon thereafter, however, geological surveys showed that the mummy had actually fallen just across the national border, and Italy demanded his remains repatriated. Today, the mummy rests in a refrigerated box in the South Tyrol Museum of Archaeology in Bolzano, Italy. He still enjoys something of a cult following, however; and there are rumors, too, of women who've petitioned to bear Ötzi's children by means of artificial insemination. Exactly how *that* would work out, I don't pretend to know.

Farther up the valley at Langenfeld, the **Ötztaler Heimat-und Freilichtmuseum** shows off historical buildings, tools, and traditions from a more recent age. It's open June through September, Monday through Friday, 10 am-noon and 2 to 5 pm, Sundays from 2 to 4 pm; ☎ 05253 55 40, www.oetztal-museum.at, €3. An English-language guide to the park is available.

More popular with kids is the nearby **Ötztaler Fun Park**, a climbing, jumping, swinging, skating kind of place – a playground paradise open daily from July through late September, 9 am to 11 pm, on September weekdays closing at 6 pm; ☎ 05253 649 49, www.oetztaler-funpark.at; €4.

Sölden rocks with a party-hearty beat all winter – one that merely wanes during the summer months – and evenings feature après-ski action in all its forms. Whether you like to dance on tables in ski boots or watch table-dancers wearing little more than that, Sölden entertains. Its ski slopes rise immediately above the town toward Hochsölden, the village's high-altitude hamlet. The Tiefenbach and Rettenbach glaciers are connected to town by cableway and to each other via both road and ski tunnels. Glacier skiing is done year-round as conditions allow; access the glaciers by lift or via the toll road that runs the 15 km from town. (The €16.50 toll is waived if you've pre-purchased a ski pass.) Glacier runs here are more varied than most, boasting one fast run that each October stages the World Cup racing circuit's season opener. Winter runs here total 149 km; summer glacier runs, considerably less.

Hannibal crossing the Alps (1510 fresco)

If you hit town in mid-April, Sölden's annual production of **Hannibal** is worth the price of admission. Some 500 actors re-enact Hannibal's 218 BC Alpine crossing, when he came across with an ungainly army of 60,000 Africans, Celts, and Spaniards – and their 34 elephant steeds. The Rettenbach Glacier becomes the stage for an unforgettable (if bizarre) display of lights, video, and pyrotechnics alongside action scenes featuring 24 snowcats, numerous snowmobiles, and several paragliders, among others. Contact the tourist office for ticket information.

Obergurgl

Farther south, the valley road climbs steeply to valley end, where the quieter, more traditional hamlet of **Obergurgl** nestles in splendid seclusion. It's among our favorite early-season ski resorts, as its slopes are high enough to have good snow, and as the social ambiance here tends more toward convivial mingling than meat-market melée. The village largely shuts down in summer, with only solitude-seeking hikers in town; but Obergurgl proves lively in the winter months, with 110 km of high-altitude ski runs, lift links to nearby Hochgurgl, and lots of ski-in accommodations – much of it booked well in advance.

ÖZTAL EXREMISTS

Although we've stuck mainly to mainstream sights in our coverage of the Öztal, visitors wishing to take part in more adrenaline-pumping activities will find no shortage of company in the Ötztal. The valley's youthful clientele comes here for canyoning, bungee jumping, whitewater rafting and kayaking – and two main outfitters help them find the fun. In Sölden, look up **Vacancia Outdoor** at Hauptstrasse 438, ☎ 05254 29 39, www.vacancia.at; farther north, consult the **Kajak & Raftingschule Ötztal**, ☎ 05252 67 21, www.rafting-oetztal.at.

Want to stay? In Sölden, I'm a fan of the cheery **Hotel Alpina** (€€-€€€). It's near the church, off the busy main road, and a short walk from the Hochsölden lift; ☎ 05254 50 20, www.riml. com.

Hotel Alpina

The hospitable Riml family also runs a less expensive house, the **Montana** (€-€€), just across the river; ☎ 05254 50 30, www.riml.com. In Obergurgl, I like the modern chalet-style **Edelwiess & Gurgl** (€€€). Inside, it warms with traiditional hospitality; outside, it fronts the lifts and a popular après-ski café. Inquire at ☎ 05256 62 23, www.edelweiss-gurgl.com.

 Find valley tourist information at www.oetztal.at. For more information on Sölden, stop by the tourist office in the Freizeit sport center or inquire at ☎ 05254 51 00, www.soelden.com. For more info on Obergurgl, contact the tourist office at village center or dial ☎ 05256 64 66, www. obergurgl.com.

Scenic Drive

The Timmelsjoch Hochalpenstrasse (high Alpine road) leads south from Hochgurgl up through the Ötztal's glacier country, over the 8,230-foot Timmelsjoch Pass, then descending into Italy. The scenic route is open only in summer and only during daylight hours, from late May through September, and the current toll is €13; for road information in German, contact ☎ 0512 581 970, www. timmelsjoch-hochalpenstrasse. Farther into Italy along the same route is the town of Bolzano, home to Ötzi and the **South Tyrol Archaeological Museum**. For museum information, check ☎ +39 (0)471 320 100, www.archaeologiemuseum.it.

The Stubaital

The Stubaital

Population(Neustift): 4,000
Base Elevation (Neustift): 1,000 m/3,280 feet
Resort valley

While neither the most glamorous nor the most expansive resort center around Innsbruck, the long Stubai Valley draws guests for its good hiking and climbing opportunities, for the nearby glacier and its long-season slopes, and for the wide selection of inexpensive, family-friendly accommodations.

The Stubai Valley, or Stubaital, stretches southwest from Schönberg, which sits 27 km south of Innsbruck, north of the Brenner Pass on the A13 Autobahn. Four villages lie along the Stubaital road, or Route 183, and the parallel Ruetz River: **Mieders**, **Telfes**, **Fulpmes**, and **Neustift**. Each village offers accommodations and limited lift facilities, but Neustift, farthest along the valley, by far gets the most attention from tourists.

✔ The **Stubaital Card**, offers a five-day summer package including free bus transport throughout the valley, travel on the tram between Fulpmes and Innsbruck, admission to four local swimming pools, and pedestrian use of the lifts at the glacier, at Schlick, and at Neustift. Tourist offices throughout the valley dispense cards in exchange for €45, children half-price.

Neustift

Austria

Neustift centers on the intersection of the Stubaital road and Dorfstrasse, a cramped side-street that loops through the heart of the village. The church, with its lovely cemetery, stands on the corner, and après-ski, nightlife, and dining establishments line the nearby square. Neustift's sporting facilities, however, lie mostly in the pastures on the southeastern edge of town, just across the Stubaital road. Here, visitors take to riverside walking paths, cross-country ski slopes, a paragliding field, the Elfer mountain lift, and a lighted nighttime toboggan run.

Although Neustift is the closest developed village to the Stubai Glacier, it is still a 20-km drive south to the glacier base – a commute best made in winter by local bus.

✔ Because the lots fill up early, drivers who attempt the commute by private vehicle may well find themselves on a bus anyway, with their cars parked somewhere down valley in a muddy, makeshift parking field.

The glacier slopes offer skiers 60 km of mostly intermediate and beginner runs and a 4.5-km cross-country loop. Snow sports on the glacier run year-round when condition allow.

✔ Stubai mountain guides lead daily summertime walks along the Stubai Glacier Trail from the Eisgrat gondola top station to the **Jochdohle**, Austria's highest restaurant. The tour departs at 11 am and takes approximately an hour one-way.

 Want to stay? In a pastoral setting on the outskirts of Neustift, the **Hotel Alpenschlössl** (€€) offers modern chalet-style accommodations and family-style hospitality. Its location is peaceful yet it is central to all sorts of sporting venues: the ice rink, the Elfer lift and its sledding run,

Hotel Alpenschlössl

the cross-country ski trails, and a riverside walking path. Reserve at ☎ 005226 20 50, www.alpenschloessl.at.

 For more info, contact the Neustift Tourist Office. It's at Dorf 3 in the Stubaitalhaus, ☎ 05226 2228, www. neustift.com.

The Zillertal

Population (Mayerhofen): 3,679
Base Elevation (Mayerhofen): 630 m/2,066 feet
Resort valley

This magnificent valley (see picture on the following page) stretches 30 km into some of central Austria's most lovely landscape. Along the way, it links a dozen small villages, many with their own lifts, side-valleys, and lakes – and draws throngs of weekenders year-round.

✔ Summer visitors should consider purchasing the **Zillertal Card**. The all-inclusive arrangement includes a daily ride on one of the valley's cable cars, entry to all public swimming pools, a visit to the Königsleiten Observatory and Planetarium, and free bus transportation. The cards are sold from early June through early October with validities of six, nine, or 12 days – the six-day version runs €40. Purchase cards at any valley tourist office.

Mayrhofen

At the southernmost tip of the valley, above the hamlet of Tux, the **Hintertux Glacier** obliges snow-sport lovers with year-round skiing and snowboarding. It also offers some of Austria's best off-season racing camps.

The Zillertal's most happening action – particularly in winter – centers on the village resort of **Mayrhofen**. First settled as an Alpine faming community, the village is today the Zillertal's most popular tourist resort, enjoying a splendid location at the confluence of the Zemmbach and Ziller rivers and at the foot of a magnificent ring of peaks. Trains and the Penkenbahn gondola depart from town center, and attractions include, in winter, several cross-country skiing loops, easy access to local ski slopes, and a lively après-ski scene; in summer, hiking, biking, glacier skiing, watersports, a nice pool complex, and – of course – the extensive adventure opportunities of the extended Zillertal valley.

Zillertal Outfitters

The Zillertal sees frenetic sporting activity during winter and summer season, largely because of its proximity to the city of Innsbruck. Transportation and trail networks are well developed here, as is

Facing page: The Zillertal in summer.

the army of sports outfitters, which offer adventure tour packages of every imaginable sort. Below are some of the best.

■ **Action Club Zillertal** operates the Mayrhofen's most adrenaline-charged outings. Activities include rafting, hydrospeed, canyoning, mountaining, paragliding, a "flying fox" ropes course, and balloon rides. Make arrangements at the office on Hauptstrasse 100, near the Penkenbahn station; ☎ 05285 629 77.

■ For hikers and climbers, there's no better guide in the Zillertal than Peter Habeler and his **Mount Everest** mountain sports school. The Mayrhofen native and his friend Reinhold Messner were the first to scale the Mt. Everest summit without the aid of oxygen. Today, the expert guide shares his expertise with visitors to his home valley. Inquire at ☎ 05285 628 29.

■ In Tux, the **Bergsportschule Tux** offers instruction for serious outdoorsmen and guiding across an array of mountaineering disciplines. They also offer climbing courses for children – although I imagine that there are few mothers outside of Austria who wish to see their six-year-olds dangling from an ice wall by pick and crampon. For more info, contact ☎ 05287 873 72, www.bergsportschule-tux.at.

 Want to stay? Mayrhofen's most luxurious accommodations are at the five-star **E l i s a b e t h h o t e l** (€€€€), a modern chalet with an expansive wellness center, a busy activity program, and a cozy fireplace

Elisabethhotel

Austria

bar; ☎ 05285 67 60, www.elisabethhotel.com. For less expensive lodging, try the **Berghof** (€€-€€€). The rowdy, rambling old chalet sits directly at town center; ☎ 05285 622 54, www.berghof.cc.

 The **Zillertal valley tourist office** centralizes information for the local villages; contact ☎ 05288 87 187 or www.zillertal.at for more information. The Mayrhofen office is in the village center at the Europahaus; contact ☎ 05285 67 60, www.mayrhofen.at. For additional info regarding Hintertux, log in at www.hintertux.at.

Scenic Drive: The Gerlos Alpine Road

If you're headed east after visiting the Zillertal, enjoy a scenic drive over the **Gerlos Pass**. The mountain road departs from Zell am Ziller, winding its way up to the Durlassbodensee and the 1,531-m/5,021-foot pass, then descends to the Salzachtal and the spectacular **Krimmler Falls** (see pages 148-50). The road is open year-round.

◆ Kitzbühel

Population: 8,200

Base elevation: 762 m/2,499 feet

Mountain resort town

Kitzbühel's medieval old town seduces with a flourish of fairytale charm. Brightly painted façades front cobblestone alleys, elegant boutiques beckon, and ancient town walls give an air of seclusion. Cozy as it may be, however, it's also a snobby, hobnobing sort of place where furs prove more fashionable than ski wear. Nonetheless, stock your wallet well and join the promenading crowd. You'll soon discover the allure that makes Kitzbühel a place worth lingering.

History & Overview

Kitzbühel grew up along the trade route between Italy and Munich, growing larger and richer when the mining industry moved in and the village was granted market status in 1255. King Lud-

Kitzbühel

wig II blessed the village with a charter in 1271, officially founding the town. Several centuries later, in 1892, Mayor Franz Reisch imported a pair of skis from Norway and liked them so much he created several ski runs, converted a few friends, and launched what would became a winter sports resort phenomenon. Political, film, and military luminaries soon made Kitzbühel their exclusive retreat, and the resort remains the playground of Europe's high society (visitors will note the correspondingly high prices). Left unscathed by both of the 20th-century wars, the medieval center of town remains largely intact to this day.

Kitzbühel lies on the northern edge of central Austria's Kitzbüheler Alps. The town spreads along the Kitzbüheler Ache river in a valley flanked by the 1,655-m Hahnenkamm to the west and the 1,996-m Kitzbüheler Horn to the east. The region's small but popular lake, the Schwarzsee, lies just west of town. Train tracks encircle the old town center, running north toward St. Johann and Salzburg and west toward Kirchberg and Innsbruck. Access roads follow much the same routes, with an additional thoroughfare heading south over the Pass Thurn.

The Town

The town of Kitzbühel perches on a hillside terrace below the Hahnenkamm peak. The town's tourism industry banks on its medieval nucleus, where two wide streets, the **Hinterstadt** to the west and the **Vorstadt** to the east, run parallel between the ancient center's walls. From the town gates run **Bichlstrasse** to the southeast, **Josef Herold Strasse** up the mountain to the west, **Franz Reisch Strasse** to the northwest toward the Schwarzsee, and **Josef Pirchl Strasse** northeast toward the train station. On the western edge of the center, train tracks divide the old town from the ski slopes and lifts, eventually running north toward the main station and west past the Schwarsee.

For mountain access, hop aboard the **Hahnenkammbahn gondola**, which climbs from the western edge of town up to the Hahnenkamm peak; or, cross the valley to the base of the **Kitzbüheler Hornbahn**, which climbs in two stages to the Kitzbüheler Horn on the east side of town.

Getting Here & Around

 Kitzbühel is well located within reasonable driving distance from several air and train transportation hubs: **Innsbruck**, 100 km to the west; **Salzburg**, 80 km to the northeast; and **Munich**, 160 km to the northwest. Trains pull into the main station on the northern edge of town, a 10-minute walk to the old town center. Local and regional buses hub here, too. The use of local buses is free in both summer and winter to holders of regional lift passes. For taxi service, call ☎ 05356 626 17.

Mountain transportation runs in both summer and winter. The main lift access points are the Hahenkammbahn gondola just above town, the Kitzbüheler Hornbahn across the valley, and the Fleckalmbahn gondola, which departs from a station approximately four km west of town. For more information on area lift service, contact ☎ 05356 69 57 15, www.bergbahn-kitzbuehel.com.

LIFT PASS PRICE SAMPLES	
Winter	
1-day adult	€37.50
6-day adult	€175
Round-trip on Hahnenkammbahn	€15
Summer	
Round-trip on Hahnenkammbahn	€15
3-day pedestrian pass	€36

Getting Connected

 The **tourist office** is at Hinterstadt 18, next to the movie theater in old town. The office has lots of brochures and an electronic hotel reservation board. Contact the tourist office at ☎ 05356 777, www.kitzbuehel.at.

Kitzbühel's post office is at Josef-Pirchl-Strasse 11. It's open Monday through Friday from 8 am to noon and 2-5 pm.

For Internet access, try the **Grieserl** at Im Gries 1, www.grieserl.com; or the **Internet Café Videothek** at Schlossergasse 10, next to the Hotel Schwarzer Adler.

The Sights

Kitzbühel's tourist attractions are mostly of the sporting or shopping type, and visitors will spend most of their time here simply wandering the cobblestone streets of the charming walled center. That said, several local churches merit a look. The **Katharinenkirche**, now a war memorial, is tucked away in the old town center; the 15th-century **Pfarrkirche**, on a knoll just north of center, has an

Pfarrkirche and Liebfrauenkirche

interesting Baroque interior; and next door, the **Liebfrauenkirche** harbors a showy display of lace-like stucco.

Situated in a 13th-century structure that's Kitzbühel's oldest house, the **Heimatmuseum** displays a collection of photos, crafts, and mining tools that tell the story of the town's history. It's open Monday through Saturday, 10 am-1 pm, at Hinterstadt 32; €6.50.

For those with mechanical interests, the **Bergahnmuseum**, or cable car museum, documents the history and technology of lift construction – and don't miss a simulated run down the Streif ski racecourse. The museum is appropriately located at the top station of the Hahnenkammbahn gondola lift; it's open daily 10 am-4 pm.

For fans of World Cup skiing, the blue house at Bichlstrasse 10 is the birthplace of **Toni Sailer** – who, in the 1950s, became a three-time Olympic champion, seven-time World Champion, and hometown Kitzbühel great.

TONI SAILER

Local boy Toni Sailer grew up on the slopes around Kitzbühel, honing his downhill skills and eventually securing fame as Austria's first skiing superstar. At age 17 he dominated the Tyrolean championships and, four years later, put on a similar show at the Olympic Winter Games at Cortina in 1956, winning three gold medals in the downhill, giant slalom, and slalom events – an Olympic record that today remains unchallenged. He retired at the ripe old age of 22 with an extraordinary career already under his belt. Today, Kitzbühel's favorite son serves as advisor to the local *Schischule Rote Teufel*, or Red Devil Ski School.

Owls in the Wildpark

Two attractions outside the town limits will please kids. The **Wildpark Tirol** is four km south of Kitzbühel along the road to Jochberg. A walking tour winds through enclosures housing deer, boars, yaks, lynx, marmots, ducks, and ibex, among others. It's open summer and winter from 9 am to 5 pm, with feedings (for the animals, not guests) at around 2:30 pm. Contact ☎ 05356 653 51 for more information. Just north of town along the Römerweg, the

Bauernhausmuseum Hinterobernau offers a look at a 16th-century traditional farmhouse, furnished, operated, and equipped as it would have been some 400 years ago. It's open daily from June through September, 1 to 5 pm, and in winter on request; ☎ 05356 642 15.

The Adventures

● ON FOOT

Hikers enjoy 187 km of marked **hiking trails** – and no less that 70 marked tour routes. In addition, the tourist office guides a wide selection of outings including our favorite, a hike with Olympic ski champion Ernst Hinterseer along the Streif ski-racing run (see *The Legendary Hahnenkamm* below). For an easy stroll, walkers and botany enthusiasts take the Hornbahn up to 1,800 m/5,900 feet for a wander through the **Alpine Flower Garden**. The garden harbors 120 varieties of flora, offers guided tours, and admission is free.

Although I don't usually consider golf and tennis to be Alpine adventures, this is what Kitzbühel's well-heeled clientele seems to do best. So, here goes: Four **golf courses** – two with 18 holes each, two with nine holes each – offer public play. The nine-hole **Golf & Landclub Rasmushof** is nearest the town center; ☎ 05356 652 520 for tee times. The town claims a total of 38 **tennis courts** – 14 of them at the **Tennis Club Kitzbühel**. For more information, ☎ 05356 643 20.

✔ Recreation opportunities are abundant here. The tourist office organizes guided hiking, biking, and skiing tours, free tennis and golf trials, nostalgic train rides, horseshoe tournaments, community concerts, folklore nights, and barbecues. Check in early during your stay to see what's in the works.

● ON HORSEBACK

The Gästeiger Family runs the **Henntalhof Reihalle** stable at Unterbrunnweg 21. Offerings include horseback riding and horse-drawn carriage and sleigh rides. Make arrangements in advance at ☎ 05356 646 24.

● IN WATER

The **Aquarena** indoor swimming complex offers several pools, sauna facilities, and spa treatments. The facility is just west of town near the Hahnenkammbahn valley station. Access is free to summer lift pass holders and greatly discounted to winter lift pass holders. For current hours, ☎ 05356 643 85.

Aquarena

Those preferring lake swimming can brave the crowds at the small **Schwarzsee** on the northwestern edge of town. All manner of water fun is available, including boat rentals, floating toys, slides, and swimming platforms. For more information, ☎ 05356 623 81. Fishing is an option at Schwarzsee, but licenses and fees must be squared away in advance with the police station in Kitzbühel. Those seeking whitewater action can make arrangements through **Adventure Club Kaiserwinkl** (see page 112).

● ON WHEELS

Several lifts offer free transport of **mountain bikes**, making high-altitude rides an option even for those who don't want to pedal up. Request a bike map at the tourist office. The tourist office also offers free **guided bike tours** from June through September. Several outfitters rent mountain bikes in the summer – the best is **Intersport Kitzsport** at Jochberger Strasse 7, ☎ 05356 622 04. A worthwhile **driving tour** explores the 7.5-km Panorama Road up to the Alpenhaus on the Kitzbüheler Horn. The €4 toll is redeemable at the Alpenhaus for food or drink. Get more information at www.kitzbuehelerhorn.com or www.alpenhaus.at.

Kitzbühel panorama

Austria

● IN THE AIR

For **tandem paragliding** flights, contact Manfred Hofer at the Hahnenkammbahn mountain station, ☎ 05356 671 94. A unique offering here, the Flight Safari package includes leaps from three mountains in one day. Private **balloon rides** can be arranged through **Ballooning Tyrol** in St. Johann; ☎ 05352 656 66.

● ON SNOW & ICE

Kitzbühel was a pioneer among European ski resorts, constructing Austria's first ski lift on the Hahnenkamm in 1928. Today's **skiing** facilities include 53 lifts and 145 km of groomed runs rated 50% easy, 42% intermedi-

ate, and 8% difficult. Five marked off-piste runs challenge advanced skiers, and mountain guides lead the way into the backcountry. Although local snow conditions are sometimes poor, the sheer extent of skiable terrain here means that decent snow can usually be found, and excellent mountain lodges mean that there's always a cozy place for a drink or snack.

Six local ski schools employ over 350 instructors each winter. We've heard good things about both the **Rote Teufel** and the **Skischule Total**.

Snowboarders head for the funpark and boarder-cross course on the Kitzbuhler Horn, and **cross-country skiers** enjoy four groomed loops in the immediate area and a total of 120 km of trails throughout the region. The 3.1-km trail at Schwarzsee has lights and snowmaking facilities. **Tobogganing** fans head for the two-km lighted run on the Gaisberg. Rent sleds at the valley station of the lift. **Winter walkers** take to 115 km of trails, joining the tourist office's guided theme, torch-lit, and moonlight hikes.

Ice-skaters head for Schwarzsee and the natural lake ice rink – it normally opens in mid-January and admission is free. An artificial rink at Lebenberg opens daily from 1 to 4 pm; admission charged. *Eisstockshiesen*, or **ice-stick shooting**, is offered both at the Schwarzsee Alpenhotel and at Lebenberg, and an indoor **curling** rink invites reservations at ☎ 05356 710 80; instruction and equipment rental can be arranged.

Sports Services, Outfitters & Guides

■ **Intersport Kitzsport** operates no fewer than six sporting good stores and equipment rental outlets. I had good luck at the Jochbergerstrasse store at house number 7, ☎ 05356 625 04 33, www.intersportrent.at.

■ **Adventure Club Kaiserwinkl** extends its service to guests of the Kitzbühel region. The outfitter offers a good range of adventuresome watersports, including rafting, canyoning, diving, and kayaking. Contact ☎ 05375 26 07 for more information.

■ The **Rote Teufel**, or "red devils," ski school has been in operation since 1926 and today offers a wide range of services, including racing, freestyle, and cross-country ski instruction. Contact the school at ☎ 05356 625 00, www.rote-teufel.at.

■ The **Skischule Total** offers a similar range of courses at comparable rates – but in addition features video analyses and a large proportion of British instructors. Contact the school at ☎ 05356 720 12, www.skischule-total.at.

Where to Sleep

Kitzbühel's accommodations are universally pricey, with soaring rate discrepancies between low season and the winter ski season.

HOTEL PRICES	
€.....	Up to €80 per night
€€........	€81 to €150
€€€......	€151 to €250
€€€€.......	Over €250

If you're in the mood to splurge, this is the place to do it – and several hotels will please guests who are willing to pay steep rates.

Directly in the old town center, the rustically luxurious **Hotel Goldener Greif** (€€€-€€€€) has been welcoming guests since 1271; reserve at ☎ 05356 643 11, www.hotel-goldener-greif.at.

Hotel Zur Tenne

My favorite town-center splurge, however, is the **Hotel Zur Tenne** (€€€-€€€€), a fetching townhouse hotel decked out in rustic country charm. Inquire at ☎ 05356 644 440, www.bayerischerhof.de/tenne/index_tenne.html. Sports-minded visitors like the **Hotel Rasmushof** (€€€€) for its private nine-hole golf course in summer and for its slopeside location in winter – and in all seasons for its excellent restaurant. Reserve at ☎ 05356 652 52, www.rasmushof.at.

The **Hotel Strasshofer** (€€-€€€) has comfy-enough rooms directly in the heart of old town on the Vorderstadt; ☎ 05356 622 85.

Those looking for budget accommodations

Hotel Strasshofer

Hotel Ehrenbachhöhe

will be hard-pressed in Kitzbühel. But a good deal by my estimation is the **Hotel Ehrenbachhöhe** (€€), a comfy old hotel at the top of the Hahnenkamm lift. It's directly on the ski slopes in winter, the starting point for numerous hikes in summer, and splendidly isolated year-round; ☎ 05356 62 15 10.

Where to Eat

For regional cuisine amid traditional surrounds, try the **Goldener Greif** (€€-€€€) at Hinterstadt 24, cozy up in the

RESTAURANT COSTS	
€	Less than €10
€€	€10 to €25
€€€	Over €25

Eggerwirt's Florian Room (€€), or – our favorite – head down the steps to Bichlstrasse 9 and the old-world gästhof, **Zum Zinnkrug** (€€), ☎ 05356 62613.

Several cafés dish out less expensive – but only rarely *in*expensive – meals. Try the **Adria Pizzeria** (€-€€) at Josef Pirchl Strasse 17 for good pizzas; the **Huberbräu Stüberl** (€-€€) at Vorderstadt 18 for to-the-point traditional dishes.

✔ The Hahnenkammbahn gondola runs late on Friday and Saturday nights in winter and Friday night in summer. Don't miss the opportunity for dinner at altitude in one of the candlelit mountain lodges. Reservations for the **Restaurant Hochkitzbuhel** can be secured at ☎ 05356 695 72 30.

Where to Party

Kitzbühel draws a mixed crowd to party places of varied persuasions. In the winter, for après-ski, The **Londoner Pub** at Franz-Reisch-Strasse is the

place to be for rowdy crowds and live music. Crowds gather, too, at the nearby **Stamperl** and, under the Hahnenkamm gondola, at the **Mockingstube**. Later, try the low-key **Highways** bar before hitting the dance floors at the **Olympia** and **Take Five** discos.

Kitzbühel's café culture huddles along the Vorstadt – and the **Café Praxmair** frequently draws a crowd. For elegant evenings out with pricey drinks and posh décor, try the **Gatto Bello**, the piano bar at the **Tenne**, or the bar at the **Goldener Greif**. The Kitzbühel **casino** proves popular as well; it's in the center near the Goldener Greif Hotel and is open daily from 7 pm, with blackjack, poker, roulette, and slot machines. Contact ☎ 05356 623 00, www.casinos.at.

Where to Play

Kids enjoy cable car rides, the **Aquarena** swimming complex, and visits to the **Wildpark Tirol** and the **Bauernmuseum**. **Playgrounds** are near the Mockingstube on Hahnenkammstrasse, northwest of the center at Pfarrau, and near the river at the corner of Jochbergerstrasse and Wagnerstrasse. In the summer, kids four years and up can join the Children's Paradise **day programs** offered by the tourist office. The tourist office also offers a list of local **babysitters**.

Festivals & Events

Kitzbühel's festival calendar is crowded with concerts, folk festivals, and sporting competitions. The winter kicks off in early December with the **Winterstart Party**. New Year's Day brings the **Fire & Music** on-slope show organized by the Rote Teufel, and late January ushers in Kitzbühel's famed **International Hahnenkamm Race**.

A **Gourmet Festival** highlights early February, and the **Kitzbühel Jazz Festival** swings around in mid-March. The summer season opens in mid-May with the **Alpine Vintage Car Rally**; continues through August with a number of **concerts**, **markets**, and **tennis** and **golf** competitions; and wraps up in late September with the **Alpine Cattle Drive**.

THE LEGENDARY HAHNENKAMM

Since its inception in 1931, the Hahnenkamm Ski Race has marked the height of the annual World Cup racing season. No other event draws more attention in Austria – and only the biannual World Championship and the quadrennial Winter Olympic Games come close. The world's finest skiers rip down the famed Streif Run each January – the men the last weekend of the month, the women a week prior.

Look easy? All but the most dangerous sections of the racecourse are open to the public after the race wraps up in late January. Give it a try, but the course does appear somewhat steeper when you're looking *down* it than when you're looking at it on TV. For additional race information and tickets, contact the **Kitzbüheler Skiclub** at ☎ 05356 735 55, www.hahnenkamm.com.

St. Johann

Population: 7,961
Base Elevation: 660 m/2,164 feet
Mountain resort town

Although just around the Kitzbühelerhorn Mountain from Kitzbühel, St. Johann seems a world away in terms of both atmosphere and cost. The people, prices, and attractions here

St. Johann ski lift, with Wilder Kaiser in background

Austria

are geared more towards family fun than the fashion-conscious.

The bustling village sits at the foot of the Kitzbühelerhorn, the mountain up which the local ski lifts climb. Rolling pasturelands stretch north toward the magnificent Wilder Kaiser, offering at once both Tyrolean village charm and striking Alpine scenery.

The village centers on its lovely parish church, a two-towered, onion-domed complex dating from 1723. The church and a wall of frescoed houses dominate the tiny market square, site of this

Ski lift Mittelstation

St. Johann in summer

town's many festivals. This pedestrian-only area sits adjacent to the busy Speckbacherstrasse, the narrow main drag that leads up to the mountain lift stations, and the main lift, the Harschbichl gondola, climbs the mountain from the residential area just across the tracks.

Activities in St. Johann run to outdoor recreation and festivals, all family-friendly and all deftly coordinated by the village's tourist office. Hiking, mountain biking, paragliding, ballooning, rafting, climbing, and canyoning – it's all available here. Check in with the **Adventure Center** at ☎ 05352 61422, www.mountain-high.at, to book a guide. In winter, over 100 km of groomed trails keep walkers walking, 60 km of easy and intermediate ski runs please downhill enthusiasts, and the excellent **St. Johann ski school** has a heart (and a great reputation) for serving families and beginning skiers. Book a lesson at ☎ 05352 64 777, www.ski-johann.at. Nighttime skiing and tobogganing are offered once or twice each week.

Après-ski and nightlife is rather subdued in St. Johann, but party-minded visitors can see what's on at **Bunny's Pub** or test the latest mix at the local brewery's pub, the **Huber-Bräu-Stüberl**.

Look for the brewery's control tower one block east of Speckbacherstrasse.

 Want to stay? The **Gästhof Post** (€€) is one of those few remaining gems – a historical old hotel in a prime location with budget rates. The friendly, family-run guesthouse is over 700 years old, and today offers small rooms decked out in a hodgepodge of furnishings, some antique and some just plain old. The frescoed façade faces the pedestrian square at Speckbacherstrasse 1, a quiet locale unless one of the village's fests is underway. Parking is free behind the hotel. Dial ☎ 05352 622 30 or click www.hotel-post.tv to book.

 St. Johann's central tourist office sits next to the post office along the rip-roaringly busy Poststrasse. Contact ☎ 05352 633 350 or www.st.johann.tirol.at for more information.

Söll

Population: 3,500
Base Elevation: 703 m/2,306 feet
Mountain resort village

Nestled between the craggy Wilder Kaiser and the Hohe Salve mountains, the charming village of Söll offers a wealth of recreation, an easily accessed locale, and loads of Tyrolean charm.

In the winter, the village is a favorite of British skiers and, in the summer, families flock here for the extensive network of hiking and biking trails. The village clusters around the 1765 landmark church, built on a central hill in Rococo style. A small but lively pedestrian area lies below, lined with hotels, shops, and restaurants.

Söll quite rightly advertises itself as a "walker's paradise." Over 700 km of walking paths wind through the area from village to village, valley to peak, and mountain hut to mountain hut. A favorite day out starts with a hike (or gondola ride) up past the boulder-topping **Stampfanger Chapel** to the mid-mountain hamlet of **Hochsöll**, where playgrounds and Hexenwasser (see box below) entertain kids and a handful of guesthouses serve up hearty fare. Farther up the mountain still, wanderers

ply through the **Hexenwald**, or Witch's Forest, to reach the peak of Höhe Salve. Here, visitors enjoy panoramic views of 70 Alpine peaks, take photos with cooperative, bell-laden cattle, and peek inside the **Salven Chapel** – at 1,829 m/6,000 feet, the highest chapel in Austria.

WITCHY WATERS

Kids of all ages can tickle their toes at Hochsöll, a 20-minute gondola ride up the mountain from Söll. **Hexenwasser**, a small water-themed park just below the gondola top station, invites visitors to take off their shoes and wander a 450-m barefoot trail – dipping into Kneipp-therapy basins, maneuvering a water labyrinth, and slip-sliding along wooden flues. But this is no fiberglass-and-chlorine contraption. The course is created of local stones, cut through an Alpine meadow, and irrigated with sparkling clear mountain water. It's a great way to cool off after a hot summer's hike, and German-only signs offer informative *wasser*-related facts. But be forewarned – on August weekends this quiet retreat feels more like an overcrowded city-park playground. (Open May through September; no entry fee; kids should pack their swimsuits, www.hexenwasser.at.)

Söll offers extensive biking opportunities, a full program of guided walks and activities, and an expansive swimming complex, the **Panoramabad**. Nearby villages are easily reached on foot, bike, snowshoe, or ski, and the Wilder Kaiser challenges climbers with one of the Alps' most difficult climbs. In winter, skiers explore the **SkiWelt**, Austria's largest interconnected ski area, on 250 km of groomed runs and with the help of 93 lifts. Söll enjoys an après-ski and nightlife scene that, for a village this size, is extraordinarily lively. Try **Pub 15**, the **Whisky Mühle**, and the **Salven Stadl**.

The Almabtrieb

✔ Traveling in mid-September? Don't miss Söll's traditional **Almabtrieb**, or mountain festival. The festival begins at Hochsöll with wood-carving, sheep-shearing, cheese- and bread-making, and lots of music and food. The height of the festival is the cattle parade, when farmers lead their highly adorned cows off the mountain pastures and through Söll's village center to their home stables for the winter.

Want to stay? The cheery **Hotel Tulpe** (€€) is up the hill from the main village, near the nursery slopes, pool complex, and gondola valley station; Stampfanger 17, ☎ 05333 52 23, www.hotel-tulpe.at. For lodging directly at village center, try the homey old **Postwirt Hotel** (€€), Dorf 83, ☎ 05333 50 81, www.hotel-postwirt.soell.at.

 The tourist information office is at Dorfstrasse 84 along the main pedestrian street. Contact ☎ 05333 52 16 or www.soell.at for more information.

Salzburg & the Salzburgerland

This section spans a wide chunk of central Austria, wrapping around the southeasternmost corner of Germany and taking in Austria's cultural capital, the city of Salzburg, and the region that shares its name. Known worldwide as home to both Mozart and *The Sound of Music*, conservative Salzburg remains Austria's most toured city. The nearby **Salzkammergut** region draws adventurers for its lovely lakes and forests. Just south, the Europa Sports Region – otherwise known as **Zell am See** and **Kaprun** – offers an admirable docket of year-round sports. Farther south rises the magnificent wilderness of the **Höhe Tauern National Park**, home to Austria's highest mountain, the **Grossglockner**, and the spectacular cascade of **Krimmler Falls**.

◆ Salzburg

Population: 146,000

Base elevation: 424 m/1,391 feet

Tourist city

The sound of music – Mozart's music – dances through the streets of this charming city, bouncing off onion-domed church towers and echoing off cobblestone streets. With its beautifully preserved old town, its numerous fine arts festivals, and its wealth of cultural history, sumptuous Salzburg should not be missed.

History & Overview

Although in ancient times Celtic and Roman settlers inhabited the valley, Salzburg's modern history begins with the Bishop St. Rupert, a crusading Franconian who in the late seventh century founded the Abbey of St. Peter, today the oldest Benedictine

Getreidegasse, the shopping street, Salzburg

cloister north of Italy. By the eighth century, Salzburg was promoted to an archbishopric, and its political and economic rise was underway, eventually affording the archbishops the title of Princes of the Holy Roman Empire. By mining and selling salt from the Salzkammergut and through their expansive land holdings, the prince-archbishops amassed the wealth reflected in the grand architecture that marks the *altstadt* today.

The height of Salzburg's development came in the 16th and 17th centuries, when Archbishop Wolf Dietrich von Raitenau employed his power, his Medici connections, and his Renaissance passion for all things Italian to set in motion a century-

Salzburg, seen from the Hohensalzburg Fortress (David Iliff)

Austria

long building spree that transformed Salzburg into an oddly Italianate city, complete with grand cathedrals, palace courtyards, and large squares. The city became part of Austria in 1816, and today it is the seat of government for the Austrian province that shares its name.

Salzburg occupies a valley in the north of the Salzburgerland, just a few km from the border of Germany. Beautifully sited along the Salzach River, the city lies just north of a magnificent stretch of Alps and just south of a region of rolling hills and small lakes. The Salzkammergut lake region stretches to the east. The region was the historical crossroads of several trade routes, and today is well-served by autobahns: the A10 toward Tauern, the A8 to Munich, and the A1 to Vienna converge just south of town.

Salzburg Altstadt, with the Fortress in the background (Thomas Pintaric)

Salzburg & Salzburgerland

GERMANY

AUSTRIA

ITALY

Vöcklabruck

Gmunden

Neumarkt

1

A1

Attersee

Haf

145

Salzburg

158

Hallein

Bad Ischl

Mandsee

Bad Aussee

Waidring

312

311

Wolfgang-see

Söll

164

Bischofshofen

Kitzbühel

Zellersee

164

161

Zell am See

311

Mittersill

Kaprun

168

167

A10

Grossglockner Hochalpenstrasse

Hohe Tauern National Park

▲ Mt Grossglockner

● Bad Gastein

■ Tauern Tunnel

108

107

Huben

106

Lienz

Lendorf

95

100

100

Spittal

111

Oberdrauburg

110

111

Villach

Arnoldstein

N

HUNTER PUBLISHING

25 MILES

25 KM

© 2007 HUNTER PUBLISHING, INC

The Town

The city of Salzburg unfolds along both banks of the Salzach River – the old town, or *altstadt*, on the left bank to the west; the new town, or *neustadt*, on the right bank to the east. (What's confusing about all this, however, is that the center of town lies along an east-west running bend of the Salzach – so that the old town is actually on the southern bank of the river.) Better landmarks, perhaps, are the center's two hills. The cliff-like **Mönchsberg** stretches to the west, running the length of old town and providing an elevated plot for the **Höhensalzburg Fortress** on its southern end; and, across the river to the east swells the **Kapuzinerberg**, a prominent hill topped off with the **Kupuzinkloster** monastery.

The old town's action revolves around the cathedral and its surrounding squares, which lie 120 m/394 feet below the cliff-top **Festung Höhensalzburg**. Picturesque, medieval alleys wind between the *altstadt*'s palaces and squares. The most famous of these, the Getreidegasse shopping street, runs roughly parallel to the river from Alter Markt to St. Blasius church. To the north, bridges across the Salzach River lead to the *neustadt* on the northern edge of the Kapuzinerberg hill. **Schloss Mirabell** and its expansive gardens spread out near the riverbank, and Rainerstrasse leads farther north to the main train station.

Getting Here & Around

On the western outskirts of the city, the **W. A. Mozart Airport** receives flights from all around Europe. The main train station is north of the town center, 1½ km from the *altstadt*. Bus hubs include the Südtirolerplatz directly in front of the train station, the Mirabellplatz in the *neustadt*, and Erzabt Klotz Strasse southwest of old town.

✔ If you're driving, finding your way into the vicinity of old town can prove quite a challenge; but in high-season, this irritation is a mere warm-up for the blood-boiling frustration brought on by the city's grossly inadequate parking. If your hotel offers valet parking, accept the service with gratitude – even at upwards of €25 per day, it's a bargain.

Once in the city center, visitors can reach most of Salzburg's attractions on foot or bike. Those wishing to use public transportation are limited to the local bus network; the service is free to holders of the Salzburg Card (see below).

Getting More Info

i The train station has a small information kiosk, but the main **tourist office** is in the old town at Mozartplatz. The office – jam-packed during the festival season – doles out a hodge-podge of pamphlets, sells a good town map, and provides a ticket sales service. It's open May through September, 9 am-8 pm, and from October through April, 9 am-6 pm; ☎ 0662 889 873 30, www.salzburginfo.at.

The city's most convenient post offices are in the old town at Residenzplatz and across the river at Dreifaltigasse near the Makartplatz.

For on-line access, head to the friendly **Internet Café Mozartplatz**. It's next to the tourist office and open daily from 10 am-10 pm.

The Sights

Today's Salzburg is one of the planet's most toured cities. Almost seven million visitors arrive each year – that's some 47 guests for every Salzburg resident.

THE SALZBURG CARD

This electronically programmed card offers unlimited transportation on the local bus system and entry to a long list of attractions. Purchase your card at the tourist office: 24-hour cards run €23; 48-hour cards, €29; and 72-hour cards, €34. Your card can be upgraded, either to Salzburg Plus Light, which includes a three-course meal and two beverages each day at a partner restaurant, or – for those who simply must have a plan – to Salzburg Plus, which includes pre-arranged accommodations, meals, coffee breaks, night caps, and concert or event tickets. Furthermore, any version of the Salzburg Card can be transferred to a Swatch Access wristwatch.

To see it all in a short time, hook up with one of the city's 100 certified city guides. The tourist office can help arrange **tours** by foot, van, bike, and horse-drawn carriage. The best of the organized bus tours is **Panorama Tours**, a Gray Line company that does a variety of regional outings, including the popular **Sound of Music** and **Kehlsteinhaus Eagle's Nest** tours. Reserve at ☎ 0662 88 32 11, toll-free in the US at 1-800-982-7969, or at www.panoramatours.com.

THE SOUND OF MUSIC

The charming story of the Von Trapp family gave the world its image of Austria: lush, rolling hills, elegant palaces, soaring Alpine peaks, and cities full of song. Rodgers and Hammerstein first put the tale to music when they wrote *The Sound of Music*, a musical production staged on Broadway in 1959. In 1964, a film starring Julie Andrews drew international acclaim and forever put Salzburg on the tourist map.

● THE VON TRAPP STORY

Baron von Trapp

Baron Georg von Trapp first distinguished himself as a submarine commander during his service with the Austrian Navy in World War I. By 1921, he and his wife, Agathe Whitehead, had seven children: Rupert, Agathe, Maria, Werner, Hedwig, Johanna, and Martina. Upon the mother's death in 1922, the Von Trapps moved from Vienna to Salzburg where, once settled, Georg von Trapp hired a young governess to care for his children. The governess, Maria Augusta von Kutschera, a novice from the Nonnberg Convent in old Salzburg, was soon adored by the children and, eventually, by Baron von Trapp as well.

They were married in the convent's church in 1927, and soon gave birth to two more daughters; but hard times were to follow. During the economic depression, the family lost its fortune, making only enough money to survive by giving family-style choral concerts throughout the region. In the face of Hilter's annexation of their beloved Austria, the Von Trapps defied the Nazi regime and emigrated to America in 1939. The family continued its choral pursuits and, even after their last son, Johannes, was born, made concert tours around the world. In 1941, the Von Trapp family settled in Stowe, Vermont, where they still own and operate the chalet-style Von Trapp Family Lodge.

The film version of *The Sound of Music* was largely filmed on location in and around Salzburg, and multiple tour operators here exploit the tourist appeal. The sites can be seen independently, of course, although pre-arranged bus tours do liberate you from transportation logistics. For fans, here's a rundown of the nearby film locations:

- **The Nonnberg Convent** – *Maria serves as a novice in this convent. It's here that the nuns sing Maria.*
- **Residenz Square** – *On her way to the Trapp Villa, Maria sings I Have Confidence.*
- **St. Peter's Cemetery** – *The Von Trapp family hides here behind the tombstones.*
- **The Festival Hall** – *The old riding school. Baron von Trapp here sings Edelweiss just before fleeing town.*
- **Mirabell Palace and Gardens** – *Maria and the children dance in the gardens, singing Do-Re-Mi and running up the rose hill steps.*
- **Leopoldskron Palace** – *This palace was used as the Trapp Villa; Maria and Baron dance and have cocktails on the terrace and balcony.*
- **Hellbrunn Palace** – *It's now home to the garden gazebo where Liesl and Rolf sing Sixteen Going on Seventeen.*
- **The Unterberg** – *This mountain was the location of both the opening and fleeing scenes.*

Mirabell Palace & Gardens (Skyguy414)

- **Mondsee Village** – *Maria runs across a local hill toward the convent. Several aerial shots were taken here.*
- **St. Michael's Church** – *This lovely church in Mondsee was the filming location for Maria and the Baron's wedding scene.*

Dominating the city from the southern end of the Mönchberg, the **Höhensalzburg Fortress**, or *festung*, should rank at the top of any visitor's must-see list. The site first saw construction in the 11th century, and that original castle underwent 600 years of reconstruction and expansion thereafter. The complex visitors tour today dates from 17th century, when local archbishops lost interest and began building palaces in the town below instead. Approach the imposing fortress from the trails atop the Mönchberg, from the steep Festungasse alley leading up from the *altstadt*, or via the Festungsbahn funicular, which departs from the cathedral's Kapitelplatz. (The train runs on electricity now, but an ingenious operation employing pumps, water-weight, and gravity did the trick when it first opened in 1892.) Funicular ride with fortress entrance costs €10; open daily, 9:30 am-7 pm; in summer, 9 am-6 pm.At the foot of the Höhensalzburg Fortress, a cluster of churches, squares, and palaces give the *altstadt* its distinctive skyline. Of greatest interest here are the enormous **Dom** cathedral, a 17th-century monument built after the site's original church finally succumbed to its eighth catastrophic fire. The squares surrounding the church are venues for many town festivals, markets, and performances; and the **Glockenspiel** atop the New Residence sounds its 35 bells three times each day: at 7 am, 11 am, and 6 pm. Nearby, **St. Peter's Cemetery** must rank among the world's most beautiful. If you can catch it at night, with candles flickering and an enormous full moon behind the fortress, it's also among the world's most haunting. Its cliff-side catacombs are open Tuesday through Sunday in summer, Wednesday through Sunday in winter; €1.

Mozart's Geburtshaus (Jonathan A White)

Winding through the center's alleys, visitors are bound to discover the **Getreidegasse**, a charming market street decked out with those gilt wrought-iron shop signs that figure prominently in any tourist guide. Fashion, food, and souvenirs – it's all here. Midway down this shopping street, at Getreidegasse 9, stands **Mozart's Geburtshaus**, or birthplace. The yellow house is recognizable for its tourist throngs, all awaiting their turns to visit the museum inside; open 9 am-6 pm, till 7 pm in July and August. Across the river, the Linzergasse makes an interesting shopping excursion – it's less expensive than the

Getreidegasse, too. Just north sits **Schloss Mirabell**, built in 1606 by the Archbishop Wolf Dietrich for Salome Alt and their children. Today, the palace serves government offices, but the garden and its Mozarteum and Marionettentheater are open to the public.

THE CITY OF MOZART

Salzburg's most famous son is Wolfgang Amadeus Mozart. Although born one of seven children, Wolfgang Amadeus, born 1756, and his sister, "Nannerl," were the only two who survived. Leopold Mozart, a vice-director of music for the archbishop, recognized his son's early talent and encouraged him toward music; the prodigy had learned piano at age three, violin at age five, and creative composition at age five. Mozart spent most of his childhood and teenage years touring and playing the courts of Europe. After his adult relationship with the archbishop deteriorated, Mozart moved to Vienna, married Constanze Weber as soon as he arrived, and gradually slid farther and farther into debt. In 1791, Mozart died in Vienna, a pauper. His body was buried there, in an unidentified mass grave at St. Mark's Cemetery. True fans will want to see all of Salzburg's Mozart memorials. In the *altstadt*, **Mozarts Gerburtshaus**, offers a look at the house in which the composer was born and the third-floor apartment in which he resided until he was 17. Near the cathedral, Mozartplatz square has as its focal point a **statue** of Mozart that was revealed in 1842 to kick off the city's first Mozart Festival. Finally, across town at Makartplatz 8, the **Mozart Wohnhaus**, or residence, is where Mozart resided between 1773 and 1780, composing 150 works during this time. Much of the house was destroyed during World War II, but the Dance Master's Hall, Mozart's concert hall, was salvaged and his apartment is now a museum. Fans of *The Magic Flute* will want to visit the **Mozarteum**, now an academy of music, for its gardens and the small **summer house** (transported there) in which Mozart composed this score. The grave of Mozart's sister Nannerl lies near that vault of Michael Haydn in **St. Peter's Cemetery**; his mother's grave lies near St. Sebastian's.

Schloss Hellbrunn

Several attractions draw tourists outside of the center. Most popular are day-trips out to **Schloss Hellbrunn**, a Renaissance palace famed for its aquatic gardens, which feature trick fountains, or *wasserspiele*. The fountains were installed by the humor-loving Markus Sittikus, a 17th-century archbishop who'd jovially startle his guests with water fun. (The picnic table's bench-mounted jets must have brought forth particular surprise.) Schloss Hellbrunn opens for castle and garden tours from April through October; in July and August, the gardens operate at night, too. Contact ☎ 0662 820 37 20, www.hellbrunn.

at, €8.50. Nearby, the **Salzburg Zoo** is open year-round, daily from 8:30 am; ☎ 0662 82 01 76, www.salzburg-zoo.at.

West of the city, the **Salzburg Freilicht Museum**, or outdoor museum, displays 60 original farm building, some of them 500 years old. Farmyards, handicraft demonstrations, and a great playground entertain. The park is open 9 am-6 pm, Tuesday through Sunday from April through November; ☎ 0662 85 00 11, www.freilichtmuseum.com, €6.

Farther north, Oberndorf's **Silent Night Chapel** – in German, the *Stille Nacht Kapelle* — and its museum pay homage to the site where the international Christmas carol of the same name was penned in 1818. Particularly popular for its Advent festivities, Oberndorf sits on the border of Germany, in a hilly region approximately 30 minutes from Salzburg; www.oberndorf.co.at.

The Adventures

 Salzburg is first and foremost a culture-oriented tourist city, but one that believes itself athletically inclined as well. The city embraces its natural setting – a surrounding wealth of lakes, forests, and mountains. Within the city limits, residents bike along riverside paths, through the city streets, and along the 410-km Mozart biking route. In fact, in this crowded old city, **biking** proves a more efficient means of transport than either private car or bus. Rent your wheels at **Top Bike Salzburg**, either at the main train station or on the old-town side of the Staatsbrücke; ☎ 06272 46 56, www.topbike.at.

Also in town, sportsters **hike** along the forested Mönchsberg, reached via cliff-side elevator at Museumplatz, and **climb** the "City Wall" cliff on the Kapuzinerberg. Outside of the city, the 1,288-m Gaisberg peak offers a lovely setting for **cycling, hiking,** and **paragliding. Cross-country skiers** enjoy 15 km of groomed trails and a 600-m nighttime loop.

THE UNTERSBERG LEGEND

South of the city near St. Leonhard rises the 6,078-foot Untersberg, Salzburg's highest peak. According to legend, Charlemagne and his armies have been asleep inside this magnificent mound for the

The Untersberg from the eastern side (TomK32)

past 1,200 years. Ravens keep watch around the peak; and rumblings within sound the waking grumbles of the great leader. When the time comes that the birds desert the mountain, evildoers beware: Charlemagne and his loyal followers will rise up and come to the aid of all honest men.

Want to check on those birds? A **cable car ride** (or a difficult climb) to the top affords magnificent views. Find more info at ☎ 06246 724 770, www. untersberg.net.

Although the city lost its bid for the 2010 Olympics, its **winter sports facilities** cannot be discounted. Most notably, the city lies within 90 km of several well-known Alpine resorts, including Zell am See, the Gastein Valley, Kitzbühel, Obertauern, Schladming, and Saalbach-Hinterglemm. In all, the Salzburgerland region encompasses some 25 ski resorts with over 600 lifts and 1,700 km of runs. (Keep in mind, however, that this is an enormous area and that many of the resorts here are small, scattered affairs.)

✔ If you want to ski but not drive, hop aboard the **Salzburg Snow Shuttle**. The bus departs Mirabell Square at 8:30 am each morning from late December to early March. Destinations vary by day, but include weekly excursions to Zell am See, Bad Gastein, and Kitzbühel. Your host will help arrange ski equipment rental, lift pass purchase, and activities for non-skiers. Bus tickets are €13; contact ☎ 0662 87 17 12 or the tourist office for more information.

Where to Sleep

 For traditional lodging in the center, our favorite is the **Goldener Hirsch** (€€€€), an elegant old house furnished in exquisite, country-style antiques – yes, you're supposed to *use* that 17th-century armoire. It's ideally situated, too; Getreide-

Goldener Hirsch lobby

gasse 37, ☎ 0662 808 40, www.goldenerhirsch.com.

What was once one of my favorite traditional inns is now one of my favorite artsy inns. In the center at Getreidegasse 41, the **Blaue Gans** (€€€) has undergone a dramatic overhaul, splashing bright colors and modern art throughout its ancient halls. Check in at ☎ 0662 84 24 91, www.blauegans.at.

Hotel Elefant

The **Käsererbräu** (€€€) has cozy traditional rooms at Kaigasse 33, ☎ 0662 84 24 45, www.kasererbraeu.at; and the family-run **Hotel Elefant** has been welcoming visitors for 400 years at Sigmund-Haffenergasse 4, just

off the Getreidegasee; ☎ 0662 84
33 97, www.elefant.at. The building itself is over 700 years old.

HOTEL PRICES	
€.....	Up to €80 per night
€€	€81 to €150
€€€......	€151 to €250
€€€€.......	Over €250

Tucked away on Kaigasse 7, the
Hotel Wolf (€€) offers basic
rooms in a prime *altstadt* locale, ☎ 0662 84 34 53, www.
hotelwolf.com; as does the small-and-simple **Trumer-Stube**
(€€) at Bergstrasse 6, ☎ 0662 87 47 76, www.trumer-stube.
at.

Where to Eat

For fish specialties and
a good wine selection,
try the romantic **Alt
Salzburg** (€€-€€€), at
Burgerspitalgasse 2, behind a

RESTAURANT COSTS	
€	Less than €10
€€..........	€10 to €25
€€€..........	Over €25

gated arch next to the Spielzeugmuseum; reservations at
☎ 0662 84 14 76.

The **Stiftskeller St. Peter** (€€) tucks up into the Mönchberg
cliff, a cave-like cellar drenched in old-world ambiance – an appropriate setting for the oldest restaurant in Europe. (It's been
in service for 1,200 years.) The food is traditional, and the tables line dark, vaulted halls and an ancient courtyard. The restaurant is behind St. Peter's church at Bezirk 4, ☎ 0662 841
268. Our other traditional favorite is the **s'Herzl** (€€-€€€),
the elegant Goldener Hirsch Hotel's stüberl. It's less formal
than the hotel's gourmet room, but still elegant, and the food
adheres to equally high standards. In fall, be sure to sample the
game specialties; reserve at ☎ 00662 808 48 89,
Getreidegasse 37.

The **Sternbräu** (€€) offers a collection of five courtyard restaurants, including an Italian bistro, an Austrian *stüberl*, and a
pleasant if busy beer garden. It's an upscale food court, really.
To find it, duck down the passage at Getreidegasse 23, ☎ 0662
840 717.

The city's first café, the lovely **Tomasselli** (€€), presides over
the Alte Markt, oozing with tradition and the gasps of those patrons who've just received their coffee bill. Another Salzburg
tradition, the **Augustiner Bräu** (€) beer garden offers *mass* of

Tomasselli Café

house-brewed beer. (Service is of the old-fashioned kind, however – wash off a mug, pay for your brew, then present the receipt at the beer counter.) The beer garden is 750 m/ 2,940 feet north of the old town along the river, at Augustiner-

gasse 4.

Where to Party

Salzburg's staid, sophisticated reputation is well deserved, and the biggest evening attractions here are musical concerts and, for tourists, a wide range of dinner shows. Check with the tourist office, ☎ 0662 889 873 30, www.salzburginfo.at, to see what **concerts** are in town – there will inevitably be at least a few, some of them in palaces, fortresses, and churches. The tourist office can also make reservations for any of the popular **dinner performances.** The ongoing but seasonal productions include a Mozart Dinner Concert in the Baroque Hall of the Stiftskeller; *Eine Kleine Nachtmusik* at the Höhensalzburg Fortress; and *The Sound of Music* at the Sternbräu.

That said, Salzburg is also a student city with several back-street bar scenes. For casual hangouts, head for the Rudolfskai along the Salzach, where the **Shamrock** flaunts frequent live music, the **Altstadtkeller** does jazz, and the **Barfly** spins up hard rock. Tucked between the river and the Mönchsberg at the northern tip of old town, the Gstättengasse is home to **The Club** disco and **JEXX**, a favorite for beer and chicken wings.

Across the river in *neustadt,* head for the charming Steingasse, where numerous bars, bistros, and cafés converge. Try **Pepe Gonzales** for Mexican snacks, and drink and dance till late at **Saitensprung**. Finally, Salzburg's favorite pop culture venue is the **Rockhouse**. The club books a range of live concerts, including pop, rock, jazz, blues, and metal – anything from punk to funk. It's out past the end of Linzergasse at Schallmooser Haupstrasse 46; dial ☎ 0662 848 78 40 to see what's on.

Festivals & Events

 Salzburg hosts 4,000 cultural events each year, so I won't be enumerating them all here, but odds are that you'll find some sort of festival in full swing upon your arrival. The city's festivals are, not surprisingly, almost exclusively musical events. During the last two weeks of January the **Mozart Weeks** take center stage, followed by the **Easter Festival** concerts and the **Pfingstfestspiele** Baroque music festival. The famous **Salzburger Festspiele** packs the town calendar with operas, plays, and concerts from late July through late August, with many performances held in the Festspielhauser, the archbishop's stables of yesteryear.

Kulturtage, or Culture Days, run from mid- to late October. Early November brings a change of key with the **International Jazz Fall Festival.** The Christmas season, too, brings a host of events, including three lovely **Christmas markets** – one at Mirabellplatz, one at Höhensalzburg fortress, and one, the largest, at the Domplatz in front of the Cathedral. The markets run from late November through Christmas Eve.

The Salzkammergut

Base Elevation: 385-2,000 m

Lake resort region

The Salzkammergut, sprawling east of Salzburg, is a hilly region best known for its 76 lakes. Between these lakes, however, are some of Austria's most beautiful forests – and lots and lots of salt.

In fact, it was the salt mining industry that once made the Salzkammergut the most contested region in Austria, a battle for wealth between the Hapsburgs of Vienna and the prince-archbishops of Salzburg. Today, the Salzkammergut's wealth lies not in salt but in tourism, and the region hosts guests year-round – in winter for the excellent, mostly easy, ski runs; in spring and summer for its lake sports and hiking and biking trails; and in fall, for Austria's most spectacular display of seasonal color.

Mondsee

This book and several others could be filled with only information on Salzkammergut's resorts and attractions. But we'll limit our coverage to a few of the best. Farthest west in the region, the lake closest to Salzburg, the **Mondsee** (and its village of the same name) boast *Sound of Music* connections and a fascinating archeological history. At the Marktplatz in the village, **St. Michael's Church** was the filming site for the Von Trapp wedding scene; and the village and its surrounding landscape feature in several aerial shots as well.

St. Wolfgang

More interesting to history buffs will be the **Heimatmuseum**, which documents the discovery of a local community dating from 2500 BC. Farther south, the **Wolfgangsee** lake runs 15 km and is flanked at its middle by the town of **St. Wolfgang**. The village is one of the region's most popular for both water and winter sports, and its parish church and tower museum prove reasonably interesting. Farther east at **Trunsee**, the peaceful Traunkirche gleams, surrounded by water. **Bad Ischl**, the region's most popular spa resort, lies in a valley to the southwest.

Halstatt (Candace Wintering)

The lovely little village of **Halstatt** may very well prove the highlight of any Austrian tour. Its old wooden houses stack up, wedged between the forested mountain and Halstättersee lake. Cars park in garages outside of town, and trains stop at a station across the lake. Passengers then are ferried into the village by boat. Most extraordinary here is a visit to the **Pfarrkirche** and its crowded cemetery – a cemetery so crowded, in fact, that burial there is only temporary. After 10 or so years of decomposition time, the bones are cleared out and – after the town gravedigger decoratively paints the skull – filed away in the Beinhaus. Have a look; it's open daily from 10 am-

6 pm, €1. If you're up for more, Halstatt also has an interesting history museum that lays out the village's Celtic ties.

The Salzkammergut Erlebnis-Card

Although you'd have to work hard to make the €400 savings it advertises, this card is nonetheless a good deal for those staying and playing awhile. The card offers discounts of up to 30% on rail, boat, and cable car transportation, as well as on admission to cave tours, salt mines, scenic toll road, wildlife parks, museums, and bathing facilities – among others. Cards are valid from May through October, and can be purchased at tourist offices, railway stations, and some hotels; €4.90.

Austria

For active visitors, sporting possibilities are ubiquitous throughout the region. Vacationers enjoy hiking and biking between the lakes, paragliding off pleasant peaks, scuba diving in clear Alpine waters, and swimming along grassy shores. Boat rental is offered at numerous outlets, water skiing proves popular at the Wolfgangsee, and sailors and windsurfers catch the breeze at Mondsee. In the winter, cross-country skiers hit lakeside trails, and downhillers enjoy the slopes around the Wolfgangsee and, to the south, in the more extreme Dachsteinguppe.

 Want to stay? Resort hotels, small inns, and cozy pensions abound throughout the Salzkammergut. In Hallstatt, try the **Gästhof Zauner-Seewirt** at Marktplatz 51, an old, family-run inn squeezed tight in the village center. Its excellent restaurant serves up regional and fish specialties. Reserve at ☎ 06134 82 46.

 Centralized tourist information for the Salzkammergut region is at ☎ 06132 269 09, www.salzkammergut.at. For more info on the Mondsee, contact www.mondsee.at; the Wolfgangsee, www.wolfgangsee.at; the Traunsee, www.traunsee.at; Bad Ischl, www.badischl.at; and for Halstatt, www.halstatt.net.

Zell am See, lakeside walkway

◆ Zell am See & Kaprun

Zell	*Kaprun*
Population: 9,900	Population: 3,100
Elevation: 757 m/2,483 ft	Elevation: 786 m/2,578 ft
Lake resort town	Mountain resort village

In the early 1970s, in a stroke of marketing genius, the lakeside health resort of Zell am See paired up with neighboring Kaprun, a glacier ski resort, to create the Europa Sports Region. Together, the pair offers a well-networked infrastructure and sporting opportunities for all seasons.

The Europa Sports Region sits in central Austria at the southern edge of the province of Salzburg, its two resorts, Zell am See and Kaprun, tucked into the foothills along the shores of the Zellersee. The town of Zell am See flanks the western edge of the lake at the base of the 6,455-foot Schmittenhohe. Across the Salzach Valley, 7 km to the south, the village of Kaprun huddles below the 9,935-foot Kitzsteinhorn and its Schmieding Glacier.

Zell am See grew up as a stop along the trade route from Italy to Germany – the route now followed by the Grossglockner Hochalpenstrasse through the Hohe Tauern National Park. The

Kaprun (Arpingstone)

town's population then worked at "Saumer", exporting salt to the south and importing wine to the north via the perilous transalpine route. In 1875, the railway came to town – gloriously entering along the banks of the lake, and toting tourism into the region. Nearby Kaprun got its start as a cattle-farming village and mountain-guiding center, reasons-for-being not far removed from those of today.

Austria

The focus of the Europa Sports Region falls on athletic rather than artistic or intellectual pursuits, and sightseeing runs secondary to sports here. Nonetheless, Zell's lakeside promenade and historical center – now almost entirely car-free – are certainly worth a stroll. Of historical note are the 11th-century **parish church** – peek inside at the 13th- through 15th-century frescoes – and the nearby medieval **Vogtturm**, which now houses the town's museum.

Visitors come year-round for lake and mountain play. In the summer, **hikers** and **bikers** enjoy the whopping 400 km of trails that wind through the Europa Sports Region. The Zellersee is the focus of the region's water-based activities. The large lake – four km long and over a kilometer wide – is filled by snow run-off rather than rivers and thus freezes quickly in winter and warms quickly in summer. From late April through October, swimmers enjoy **beaches** at six locations, three of which boast heated outdoor swimming pools. **Pedal-** and **row-boat rental, lake tours** by boat, **fishing, windsurfing,** and all other manner of lakeside play is on offer.

SUMMERTIME SNOW

The FunArea on the Kitzsteinhorn opens its glacial ice to summertime visitors who have an off-season hankering for snow sports. Oddball equipment, such as snowbikes, snowscoots, zipfelbobs, skifoxes, are up for rent, as are the more traditional skis, snowblades, and tubes. The Intersport Kitzsteinhorn does rentals right from the glacier plateau. The shop has snow-wear for hire as well. Check in at ☎ 06547 8621, www.kitzsteinhorn.at, for more information.

In the winter, the region's 57 lifts serve 130 km of groomed **ski trails**. **Cross-country skiers** head out on over 200 km of groomed loipe, and **winter walkers** step along 50 km of cleared hiking trails. Ice sports enthusiasts head for the ice stadium in Zell for **ice-skating, curling, and hockey** and to the

In Höhe Tauern National Park

natural rink on the Zellersee for ice-skating and such fun as **ice-surfing** and **ice-sailing**.

✔ If you're looking for evening fun, the **Crazy Daisy Restaurant, Bar, & So On** beckons, "You're always welcome! Don't eat yellow snow." The club is Zell's legendary place to party, especially during ski season, when an energetic young crowd fills the house. A beer garden and terrace accommodates summer crowds. See what's on at www.crazy-daisy.at, ☎ 06542 763 59.

Want to stay? As central as they come in Zell, the cheery **Sporthotel Lebzelter** (€€-€€€) has bright rooms and a cozy basement bar, ☎ 06542 776, .

The tourist office in Zell am See is on Brucker Bundesstrasse near the church. It's open 9 am-6 pm Monday through Friday and 9 am-noon and 2-6 pm on Saturday. Contact ☎ 06542 77 00 for more information. The tourist office in Kaprun is along the main road at village center. Contact ☎ 06547 864 30, www.kaprun.net, for more information. The resorts share a web site at www.europasportregion.at.

Höhe Tauern National Park

Base Elevation: 1,145 m-3,798 feet/3,755-12,316 feet

National Park

Central Europe's largest national park boasts as its centerpiece the 3,798-m/12,457-foot Grossglockner, Austria's highest peak. The immense territory appears positively primeval, with jutting bare mountain, murky glacial run-offs, and acres and acres of ice.

In fact, approximately one-tenth of the enormous park is covered year-round in ice, a glacier bed some 30 m/100 feet deep – and thickening at a rate of approximately one millimeter per year.

Visitors to this high-altitude wonderland are treated to what many consider Europe's finest nature preserve, and it's hard to argue. A habitat for Alpine species such as ibex, marmots, and the rare white-bearded vulture, the park also protects diverse flora that rebound each spring in a riot of color. Herds of mountain cattle call the park their summer home, too, and Alpine farmers use traditional techniques just as they have in centuries past. Two park attractions merit particular attention: First, the **Grossglockner Hochalpenstrasse**, covered here; second, lovely Krimmler Falls, covered below.

Although the Höhe Tauern National Park can be accessed via several roads – and via several hundred footpaths – the most popular route through the park remains the spectacular Grossglockner Hochalpenstrasse, or "Grossglockner High Alpine road" (otherwise labeled state road 107). The road runs south from Bruck and winds its way up past the lovely village of Fusch to the park entrance, where daytrippers pay an enormous fee for the privilege of driving in. (At last count, the fee was €26 per car per day; a fee as stunning as the landscape to which it opens access.)

Visitors zigzag upwards in the shadow of the glowering mountain. Along the road are visitors' centers, museums, lookout points, cafés, and nature trails – all worthwhile. Everyone should visit the **Pasterze Glacier** and heartier folk should venture backcountry to one of the park's high Alpine huts. (Consult a ranger for trail and weather conditions.) Once outside of the park's border, the road continues south toward Lienz and Italy.

✔ The Grossglockner Hochalpenstrasse is one of Austria's premier tourist destinations, and buses, bikes, and BMWs clog the road during August's high season. Your best bet? Go *early*. During high season, the gates open at 5 am. The next best thing? Park, get out, and walk – far, far from the madding crowds.

For more information, see www.nationalpark.at and www.grossglockner.at.

Krimml

Population: 866
Base Elevation: 1,067 m/3,500 feet
Tourist village

Huddled near the spectacular Krimmler Falls, this lovely village stacks up a pastoral foothill. Majestic peaks rise all around. Terrace cafes and cozy *stuberl* beckon, and in summer flowers spill off balconies blessed with magnificent mountain, valley, and waterfall views.

Krimmler Falls

Krimml is an extraordinarily lovely village and its falls are one of nature's most spectacular works. Visitors reach the tiny hamlet of Krimml through either the Salzach Valley (from Zell am See) or the Zillertal Valley and the Gerlos Pass (from Mayrhofen).

In addition to wintertime skiing, and in spite of direct access into the Höhe Tauern National Park, the primary focus in the village are the **Krimmler Falls**. At their finest on July afternoons, the roaring waterfalls dive a total of 380 m/1,246 feet through three segments of forest-ensconced chutes. A steep, asphalt trail hairpins alongside, allowing spectators – and there are many of them – refreshingly misty vantage points from which to experience this natural wonder. The trail continues past all three stages of the falls, eventually petering out into a gravel road and then a narrow dirt path.

Guesthouses serve up drinks, snacks, and souvenirs at prime points along the trail, and taxis ply a small road nearby, offering tired pedestrians an expensive ride back to base. (Check the info placard near Parking Area 3 for time-and-distance trail estimations.) Again, I recommend making the hike early in order to beat high-season crowds. One further note: Near the entrance to the falls trail splashes the **WasserWunderWelt**, an interesting exhibit that demonstrates the power of water through interactive (read, "wet") displays. Kids like it, and parents do, too. The park is open regularly in summer, 9:30 am-5 pm. Contact ☎ 06564 201 13, www.wawuwe.at, for more info.

Ferienhotel Krimmlerfälle

 Want to stay? I recommend staying the night – primarily to experience the charm of this valley without all the day-tourists. The most prestigious house in town is the **Ferienhotel Krimmlerfälle** (€€-€€€), ☎ 06564 72 03, www.krimmlerfaelle.at. But almost every house here offers rooms to rent, so newcomers need only look for the *zimmer frei* (room free) placards to find a vacation home.

 The tourist office is just below the church and next door to the post office. Contact ☎ 06564 723 90, www.krimml.at for more information.

Austria

Alpine France

N

GERMANY

SWITZERLAND

Dijon

FRANCE

Lausanne

Geneva

MONT BLANC

Chamonix

Lyon

Milan

Saint-Etienne

Grenoble

Torino
(Turin)

ITALY

Avignon

Monaco

Ligurian Sea

Nice

Marseille

Toulon

Golfe du Lion

Mediterranean Sea

100 MILES

100 KM

France

Language: French
Population: 59,765,983
Phone Country Code: +33
Currency: Euro

HANNIBAL

Hannibal was a third-century warmonger who had a bone to pick with the ruling Roman Empire. His father had died while fighting against the Romans in Spain – an event that motivated him to plan carefully and long toward the objective of completely destroying Roman power. Hannibal believed the Romans' most vulnerable spot was actually in Northern Italy, given the loose confederation of states and the continual turmoil between Rome and the neighboring Gauls. Hannibal and his army left Spain in 218 BC, trekking north up the Mediterranean coast, fighting much of the way. After securing the help of the Gauls, Hannibal crossed over the Alps somewhere between the Little St. Bernard and Mont Genèvre passes – an unlikely party of some 60,000 men and 34 elephants.

With his superior numbers, strategic tactics, and a little help from the Gauls, Hannibal won several battles, causing the Romans to withdraw the bulk of their army into central Italy. The war continued for several years until the Romans, in a surprise move, attacked and captured Spanish Carthagena, cutting Hannibal's main supply route. Hannibal continued to fight for several more years but, in 204 BC, the Romans finally attacked Carthage itself. The Roman success in Carthage led to a peace treaty between Carthage and Rome, and Hannibal withdrew. Still suspicious, however, the Romans pursued their nemesis; in 183 BC, unable to escape, Hannibal committed suicide rather than surrender.

Today, the French Republic spans 549,183 square km, making it western Europe's largest state. The geography

IN THIS CHAPTER
- People & Culture   154
- Mont Blanc Region   156

consists of flat plains and gently rolling hills in north and west, and mountainous terrain in the Pyrenees to the south and the Alps in the east. The Alps run almost the entire length of the eastern border, starting just north of the Mediterranean coast and extending up to the nation's border with Switzerland. The nation shares frontiers with Spain and Andorra to the south; Italy, Switzerland, and Monaco to the east; and Belgium, Luxembourg, and Germany to the north and northeast.

France is composed of 22 administrative regions, or states, and several dependent territories. Its capital is Paris. The republic maintains a multi-party system of government, with a president presiding as chief of state and a prime minister operating as head of government. Although the country has long pursued an active policy of integrating immigrants, recent unemployment rates remain among the highest in Europe – and frustration has led to a backlash of anti-immigration sentiment. Youth crime rates have risen dramatically as well, and gang violence is now problematic in the urban low-income housing developments. Unemployment rates now sit at 10%.

People & Culture

The population of France is a mix of ethnicities, just as it has been for the past millennium – but some 91% share a Celtic or Latin origin. Approximately 76% of the population claims the Roman Catholic faith; 5% are Muslims; and just 2% say they are Protestants. Three-quarters of France's people live in urban areas, the largest of which are Paris, Marseille, Lyon, Toulouse, Nice, and Strasbourg. The population density is approximately 110 people per square kilometer.

National Holidays

January 1	New Year's Day
	Good Friday

. . . . Easter
. . . . Easter Monday
May 1 . . . . Labor Day
May 8 . . . . Fête de la Victoire 1945
March/April . . . . Easter
. . . . Easter Monday
May1 . . . . Labor Day
10 days before Whit Sunday . . . . . Ascension Day
7th Sunday after Easter . . . . Whit Sunday
Day after Whit Sunday . . . . Whit Monday
July 14 . . . . Bastille Day
August 15 . . . . . . Assumption Day & National Day
November 1 . . . . All Saints Day
November 11 . . . . Armistice Day
December 25 . . . . Christmas Day

France

TIMELINE	
51 BC	Julius Cesar, a Roman emperor, conquers Gaul, the territory that is now France
218 BC	Hannibal, his army, and their elephants cross Alps
500 AD	Namesake tribes of France, the Franks, rule territory
1529	French troops led by Joan of Arc fight the English
1643-1715	Louis XIV, the Sun King, takes the throne at the age of five; under his long rule, France gains power across Europe
1789	French Revolution begins with citizens' attack on Bastille Prison
1803-1815	The Napoleonic Empire established as Napoleon Bonaparte promotes self from military leader to "First Consul for Life"; after several key losses (including Waterloo), Louis XVIII is restored as monarch
1914-1918	World War I; Germany's invasion of France ends with 1.3 million Frenchmen dead and twice that many injured; Treaty of Versailles officially ends war

1939-1945	World War II; With France's forces still largely depleted from World War I, Germany again invades; following the landing at Normandy, Allied forces liberate France in 1944 and defeat the Axis forces in 1945
1924	Chamonix hosts winter sporting events, considered the first staging of the Olympic Winter Games
1946-1954	French-Indochina War brings independence of Southeast Asian colonies
1959	De Gaulle established Fifth Republic; he is elected to a second term in 1965
1981	Francois Mitterand elected president and remains in office until 1995
1994	"The Chunnel," a tunnel under the English Channel, connects France and the United Kingdom
1995	Jacques Chirac elected president; he is elected to a second term in 2002

For more information, check the website for the French National Tourist Office at www.franceguide.com.

Mont Blanc Region

Soaring to Europe's loftiest heights, the majestic Mont Blanc nestles in eastern France, anchoring the borders between France, the southwestern corner of Switzerland, and the northwestern corner of Italy. The mountain provides a focal point for adventurers in all three countries. Although other Alpine regions in France certainly merit consideration, **Chamonix** is by far the most convenient for a quick introduction to the French Alps. The cheerful old town sees a steady, year-round stream of sporting tourists who come to enjoy its legendary mountaineering challenges and skiing terrain. The resort of **Courmayeur**, Italy, lies at the opposite end of the Mont Blanc Tunnel, and the **Valais** region of Switzerland nestles just over the Col des Montes pass. The region's vast wealth of natural sights and cultural diversity make it an outstanding option for a quick, looping tour of the Alps.

France

◆ Chamonix

Population: 10,109
Base elevation: 1,035 m/3,395 feet
Mountain resort town

To those who love it, it's simply "Cham" – a bustling mountain town beckoning to international adventurers of all persuasions. Here in the shadow of Mont Blanc, Europe's highest mountain, a dozen villages scatter up the Arve River, majestic peaks line up in rank, and glaciers lick the valley floor. In times past, it was the birthplace of mountaineering and the site of the first Olympic Games; today, few names garner such reverence among in-the-know adventurers.

History & Orientation

Chamonix popped up on the map in 1786 when Dr. Michel Paccard and Jacques Balmat became the first men to ascend Mont Blanc. Although already known as a center for alpinism, the village quickly became Europe's mountaineering capital, a

Mont Blanc, above Chamonix

reputation it maintains to this day. The town's hearty population took to skiing early in the 19th century, and the snow-sporting competitions they staged here in 1924 are considered the first running of the Olympic Winter Games. Today, Chamonix remains an international melting pot. Approximately half of its visitors each year come from foreign countries, and the town counts 40 nationalities among its permanent residents. The sporting tradition continues, and athletes across many mountaineering disciplines call Chamonix home.

Nestled in the shadow of the 15,778-foot Mont Blanc, in the Upper Arve Valley near the Swiss and Italian frontiers, Chamonix ranks among the most scenic resorts in the Alps. The town sprawls along a rushing river and a long, north-south hollow wedged between the Massif des Aiguilles Rouges to the west and the Mont Blanc Massif to the east. The valley's main roads, the N506 and N205, parallel the Arve River, connecting a dozen far-flung neighborhoods.

The Town

Town center revolves around its lively car-free old town and the Place Blamat, a riverside square memorializing the men who first conquered Mont blanc. From here, the Rue du Paccard

Chamonix town

heads south, the Rue Joseph Vallot heads north, and a network of smaller alleys web along the Arve's western shore. The tourist office lies on the western edge of the center; the train station, across the river down Avenue Michel Croz. A ring road diverts traffic from the center, and all around, majestic mountain peaks soar.

Getting Here & Around

Visitors arriving by air should fly into the international airport at Geneva, some 90 km northwest. Trains pull into the station on the center's eastern edge, and buses navigate through town and up-valley toward Argentière. Buses are free to ski-pass and guest-card holders. For taxi service, contact **Taxi Monard** at ☎ 0608 26 84 76, or **Taxi Rousseau** at ☎ 0607 67 88 85. Drivers will use two main roads, the N506 and N205. Past the neighborhoods of Argentière and Le Tour at the northern end of the valley, the N506 runs northeast over the Col de Montets and into Switzerland; past Les Houches at the southern end of the valley, the N205 turns west toward St. Gervais, hooking up with the A40 freeway to Geneva. The Mont Blanc Tunnel burrows into Italy; its entrance lies just south of town. For more info, check www.tunnelmb.com.

Three cable cars climb from the center's outskirts. On the western side of town, two lifts climb to Le Brevent; on the eastern side, a cableway climbs to l'Aiguille du Midi and Mont blanc.

LIFT PASS PRICE SAMPLES
Winter
1-day adult Cham'ski pass €46
6-day adult Cham'ski pass €220
Summer
Pedestrian weekly lift pass €98

Getting More Info

The Chamonix Mont-Blanc Tourist Office sits on the western edge of town center at 85 Place du Triangle de l'Amitie. For more info, contact them at ☎ 0450 53 00 24, www.chamonix.com.

The post office is directly in the center on the eastern side of the Place Balmat.

The Sights

Visitors to Chamonix should simply enjoy a stroll through the pedestrian center, perhaps stopping by the **Alpine Museum** at 89 Avenue Michel Croz. The museum houses a good collection of mountaineering artifacts as well as exhibits on winter sports history and regional culture. It's open from from 2 to 3 pm in the summer and 3 to 7 in winter; ☎ 0450 55 25 93; €4. Other than that, Chamonix's sights are all at altitude.

✔ The **Carte d'Hôte Guest Card** brings discounts on admission to a number of public services, including the Alpine museum, swimming pool, ice rink, and cross-country track – in addition to free ski-bus transportation. Cards are issued at check-in without charge to visitors lodging in area hotels.

Into the Mountains

Activities abound year-round in the mountains surrounding Chamonix. Footpaths, trains, and cableways lead back to adventures on glaciers, lakes, and mountain peaks – the options are overwhelming. Below I've rounded up a few favorite excursions by mountain transport.

L'Aiguille du Midi, north face

■ **L'Aiguille du Midi Cableway** – This is the classic tour of Mont Blanc. Cable cars depart the eastern edge of town for the breathtaking two-stage ride up to 3,842 m/12,602 feet. From there, visitors can cross into Italy via the Helbronner cableway. On either side of the border, views are spectacular, visitors standing eye-to-spire below Mont Blanc's glacial peak.

■ **Train du Montenvers** – First built in 1908, the rack railway chugs from Chamonix to Montenvers and the foot of the Mer de Glace, or "sea of ice." At the top, visitors enjoy views of the 14-km-long glacier, a crystal gallery exhibit, a museum of Alpine wildlife, and the Grotte de Glace, an ice grotto carved out from inside the glacier.

■ **Le Brevent and La Flegère Cableways** – These two tours depart the western edge of town for the 2,525-m Brevent Peak and the 2,385-m Index Peak. Rising on the western side of town, the peaks each enjoy spectacular big-picture views across the valley to the Mont Blanc Massif. Both are favorite areas for hiking and climbing; Le Brevent is a favorite paragliding launch site; and La Flegere offers good views of the Mer de Glace.

■ **The Grands Montets Cableway** – From the eastern edge of Argentière, a cable car climbs in two stages to 3,275 m/10,742 feet at Les Grands Montets. The peak offers a 360-degree panorama of the French, Italian, and Swiss Alps. In winter, the screamingly steep run off backside lures expert skiers from all around the globe.

The Mer de Glace glacier streaming slowly down the slopes of Mont Blanc (Zulu)

Upon arriving alongside the area's glaciers, you may well feel envy for those roping up and venturing out onto the ice. Although glaciers can be traversed by any visitor of reasonable fitness, a knowledgeable guide and appropriate gear are absolutely necessary. See guide listings below, and make arrangements before you go.

The Adventures

● ON FOOT

 Mountaineering is Chamonix's legacy and its passion. **Climbers** head for the Mont Blanc Massif and granite cliffs of Le Brevent and Les Aiguilles Rouges. In bad weather, they take to the **Richard Bozon Sports Center's** indoor climbing wall; ☎ 0450 53 23 70; entry €3.80, ages 14 and up. Chamonix offers 350 km of trails across a variety of terrain and altitudes – making it the most extensive **hiking** network in the Haute-Savoie region. One favorite walk starts at the mid-station of l'Aiguille du Midi cable car and heads three hours across the Gran Balcon Nord to Montenvers, its mountain restaurant, and the Mer de Glace. To return, walkers can take the Montenvers train or walk another two hours down to town.

France

The Mont Blanc Ascent

This is a difficult climb, not to be taken lightly. If climbing's your thing and you want to give it a shot, consult a qualified guiding service early on (see *Sports Services*, page 166). The climb is expensive – upwards of €1,500 – and reputable outfitters require that you arrive early in order to acclimatize and undertake preliminary training. The tourist office can help, too. Their booklet, *L'Ascension du Mont Blanc est Affaire d'Alpinisme,* can shed some light on local mountain protocol and safety.

The normal route takes climbers from Chamonix to Les Houches, Bellevue, Nid d'Aigle, the Tête Rousse Refuge and, finally, to the Aiguille du Gouter Refuge for the first night. The second day culminates with a summit ascent via Vallot; then a descent via Vallot, Grands Mulets, and Plan de l'Aiguille, where the cable car takes you back to town. Accommodations are in a mountain hut with half-board; lunches are packed in. Barring poor weather, the ascent can be attempted from mid-June through September.

● IN WATER

Chamonix's focus is on mountain sports rather than water, but swimmers enjoy the pool, whirlpool, waterslide, sauna, and hammam (Turkish bath) facilities at the **Richard Bozon Sports Center** at 214 Avenue de la Plage. The center is open daily in season; ☎ 0450 53 23 70, www.sports.chamonix.com, entry €5.

● ON WHEELS

Mountain bikers, like skiers, come to Chamonix for its varied terrain and extreme vertical drops. Several trails of varying difficulty line the valley floor, and steep runs descend from Planpraz near Le Brevent, from La Flegere, from Les Mottets, and above Argentière, from Lognan and Let Tour. The tourist office offers maps, and the excellent **Ecole de VTT** operates a rental and guiding service and can advise on trail conditions and closures. Check in at their hut just below the tourist office, open daily in summer 5-7 pm, or dial ☎ 0619 75 69 16.

● IN THE AIR

Paragliding is extremely popular here, and several outfitters arrange tandem flights. I like **Les Ailes du Mont Blanc** school, ☎ 0620 46 55 57. It's home to Sandie Cochepain, paragliding World Champion. For **balloon rides** out of Mégève, contact **Ballons du Mont Blanc**, ☎ 0450 21 03 07. **Chamonix Mont-Blanc Helicopters** offers rotor-propelled flights of varying lengths; ☎ 0450 54 13 82, www.helico.fr. And **Parachutisme** in Chambery extends its **parachuting** services to Chamonix guests; ☎ 0479 54 42 93.

● ON SNOW & ICE

Famed for its extensive off-piste and expert **skiing** and **snowboarding**, the Chamonix area offers over 150 km of marked runs (and many more off-piste routes), all served by some 50 lifts. Scattered across nine resort areas, the marked runs are graded 21% novice, 31% intermediate, 25% advanced, and 13% expert.

At the northern end of the valley, near Argentière, the Grand Montets area beckons to experts, who flock here for its famed vertical drops and snow-sure slopes. Below, Les Chosalets has good slopes for first-timers. Nearby, the hamlet of Le Tour enjoys a sunny position and mostly mild descents popular with intermediate-level skiers. Above the center of Chamonix, Le Brevent and La Flegère offer extensive slopes for skiers of all abilities, lots of sunshine, and spectacular views across the valley toward Mont blanc. Farther south at Les Bossons, Le Glacier du Mont-Blanc is a popular venue for nighttime skiing Wednesday through Saturday.

Skiing down La Vallée Blanche

LA VALLÉE BLANCHE

AUTHOR'S CHOICE For an up-close-and-personal view of glacial slopes, there's no better run than the Vallée Blanche, or white valley, ski route. Although technically an off-piste route, the run is one of the Alps' classic ski runs and it often attracts crowds. They come for the same reasons you should – spectacular mountain scenery, intimate glacier views, and a 24-km ski run of mostly intermediate difficulty.

✔ The slopes here are least crowded on weekday mornings – find a guide who'll head up the mountain early. The route descends from 3,842 m/12.600 feet at the top of the Aiguille du Midi cable car, from where there are stunning views of Mont Blanc. Adventurers navigate a steep, sporty ridgeline before stepping into their skis. Then, the long run loops down across the Mer de Glace glacier, passing crevasses, icefalls, and forests along the way. The Montenvers mountain restaurant at 1,913 m/6,275 feet offers hospitality and, if conditions are poor, a train ride back to Chamonix center. Every mountain guide in town knows the Vallée Blanche well – lest you fall of a cliff or into a glacial crevasse, don't venture onto the ice without one.

Chamonix is one of the few resorts offering visitors an opportunity to sample **dog-sledding**. **Huskydalen** offers an array of full- and half-day outings, including a popular "trapper evening"; ☎ 0450 47 77 24. **Cross-country skiers** enjoy 21 km of loipe, and **winter walkers** head out on 17 km of footpaths; the tourist office offers loipe and walking maps. The **Compagnie des Guides** arranges **snowshoeing** excursions, and **ice-skaters** hit the ice at indoor and outdoor rinks at the **Richard Bozon Sports Center**; ☎ 0450 53 12 36, €4.10 skate rental available.

Sports Services, Outfitters & Guides

16 guiding organizations and a whole mess of related tour operators take advantage of Chamonix's booming mountaineering market. As the resort is a long-time favorite among British visitors, English is widely spoken. I list some of the best services below:

■ Of the multi-sport outfitters in town, I like **Evolution 2**. The organization runs introductory alpinism courses, Mont Blanc excursions, mountain-bike outings, kids' programs, and rafting, hydrospeed, canyoning, and canoeing trips. In winter, the ski school and guiding program here are excellent, and dogsledding, helicopter flights, and snowshoeing are offered. For more info, contact ☎ 0450 55 90 22, www.evolution2.com.

■ With a similarly diverse array of services, the local chapter of the traditional **Compagnie des Guides** operates **Cham'Adventure**, a daily program of hiking, biking, paragliding, canyoning, hydrospeed, and rafting; ☎ 0450 53 55 70. In the winter and summer, the company arranges private guides; ☎ 0450 53 00 88, www.cieguides-chamonix.com.

■ The **High Mountain Office**, or OHM, is a free public service that documents all mountain activities available in the region and posts up-to-date information on mountain conditions. Check in with the OHM office at www.ohm-chamonix.com. The **Maison de la Montagne**, or Mountain Information Center, near the tourist office, posts weather and condition information as well. Know before you go.

Where to Sleep

Nearer the center, the rustic old **Hameau Albert 1er** (€€€€) has a gourmet restaurant, cozy rooms, and a new indoor-outdoor swimming pool; ☎ 0450 53 05 09, www.hameaualbert.fr. Directly in the center, try the grand old **Hotel Mont Blanc** (€€€€), a throwback from yesteryear that peers down on the pedestrian zone from the Allée du Majestic; ☎ 0450 53 05 64.

I liked the large **Park Hotel Suisse** (€€€) for its cozy décor,

Le Hameau Albert 1er

open fireplace, and view-blessed rooftop deck; ☎ 0450 53 07 58, www.chamonix-park-hotel.com.

The **Hotel Vallée Blanche** (€€-€€€) has long been a favorite for its central loca-

Park Hotel Suisse

tion on the river; ☎ 0450 53 04 50, www.vallee-blanche.com. Nearby, the **Gourmets & Italy** (€€) shares a similar position on the river but adds cheery color-coordinated

HOTEL PRICES	
€	Up to €80 per night
€€	€81 to €150
€€€	€151 to €250
€€€€	Over €250

prints and a good restaurant downstairs; ☎ 0450 50 53 01 38, www.hotelgourmets-chamonix.com.

✔ For an atmospheric stay outside the center, consider a room (€€) or dorm mattress (€) at the **Gîte Réfuge du Montenvers**. It's at the foot of the Mer de Glace glacier, and at the end of the Montenvers train line. A popular tourist outing during the day, the lodge takes on a cozier ambiance at night; ☎ 0450 53 87 70.

Where to Eat

 Le 3842 (€€€) restaurant is the highest gourmet house in Europe. It's at the top of the Aiguille du Midi cable car and, as you

RESTAURANT COSTS	
€	Less than €10
€€	€10 to €25
€€€	Over €25

might guess, enjoys spectacular views. Reserve at ☎ 0450 55 82 23.

The National (€€€) offers an elegant riverside dining room and traditional cuisine in the pedestrian zone at 3 Rue Paccard; ☎ 0450 53 02 23. And **Le Monchu** (€€) proves popular for its heated outdoor terrace – in addition, of course, to its grills, raclette, and fondue. It's in the center next to the casino, 1 Rue du Lyret, ☎ 0450 53 04 80.

✔ The winter-only **Cham'Gourmand** lift pass is a great deal for non-skiers who'd like to lunch at a mountain lodge. The €26 round-trip lift ticket also includes €26 worth of food at any participating restaurant. Check with the ticket office at the base of any area lift for more information.

L'M (€€), in the pedestrian zone on Rue Vallot, serves up delicious Savoyarde specialties on a torch-lit, terraced balcony; ☎ 0450 53 58 30. Also in the center, **Chez Nous** (€€) serves excellent fondues in a rustic dining room near the river; ☎ 0450

53 91 29. With great fondues as well, but up the valley in Argentière, **Le Carnotzet** (€€) proves itself worth the drive; ☎ 0450 54 19 43. For pizza, head for the **Casa Valerio** (€€).

The **Café La Terrasse** (€) boasts a riverside locale in the center and a charming Art Nouveau façade. Its side windows open to the sound of water, and it's open until 1 am.

La Poya (€), in the center at Rue du Lyret, serves up a long list of tasty crêpes until 11:30 pm.

Where to Party

Evenings in Chamonix revolve around a collection of low-key bars, four discos, and one casino. Afternoon après-ski and teatime is busy in Chamonix's center. Those looking for an early party should simply visit the pedestrian zone. Later, for nightclub action, head down the Rue Vallot and its tiny sidestreet, the Rue des Moulins. For a casual drink try **The Pub**, **Wild Wallaby's**, or **Queen Vic's**, a sports bar and pool hall with a popular happy hour. Nearby, the **Bar'd Up** is a good dive for pool and beer. Later, for music and dancing, head for the ever-thumping **Dick's Tea Bar** and **Choucas**, the popular après-ski hangout and late-night disco at 206 Rue Paccard. For a quiet, candlelit drink, try **Le Bourrique**

Casino Chamonix (Robert Bréda)

next to Dick's Tea Bar. The dressier **Casino Chamonix** at Place de Saussure spins roulette, slots, black jack, and poker. It's open every day from noon to 3 am; ☎ 0450 53 07 65; free entry.

Need a lift? (Robert Bréda)

Where to Play

 Chamonix is a resort crafted for Alpine extremists, and few families make this their vacation choice. That said, the standard children's activities, ski schools, and such are all in place. Kids enjoy the **mini-club activities** operating out of the Richard Bozon Sports Center in July and August, the **outdoor adventures** arranged by Cham'Adventure and Evolution 2 (see *Sports Services*, page 166), **miniature golf**, and the **video arcade** at 30 Rue des Moulins. In summer, there is a **skate park** near the cross-country ski building, a **trampoline** at Place du Mont Blanc, and **playgrounds** at the Mer de Glace, Les Planards, and Argentière.

Festivals & Events

 Like most of this athletic town's activity, Chamonix's festivals and events center on sporting pursuits. The winter kicks off with a **New Year's** celebration, and then the races begin – the biannual **Kandahar** race, the annual **FIS World Cup** events, and a wide range of cross-country, motor racing, and free-ride competitions. Spring brings **Carnaval**

and, in early March, the annual end-of-season **Cham' Jam** on-and-off-slope party.

The Mont Blanc Marathon

Summer ushers in a whole new schedule of warm-weather sporting competitions, including the **Mont Blanc Marathon** in June. **National Day** is celebrated with fireworks and music in mid-July, and the **Mineral Exchange** exhibition sets up in early August.

Each August 15th, Chamonix celebrates the **Fête des Guides**. The festival honors the region's hearty mountain guides with parties, light shows, street fairs, and finally, on Sunday, an outdoor mass that culminates with the blessing of the guides' ice picks and ropes.

For information on any of the above, contact the Tourist Board at ☎ 0450 53 00 24, www.chamonix.com.

La Route des Grandes Alpes

Those traveling from Chamonix to Geneva – or vice versa – should consider skipping the freeway and instead making the more scenic drive along the northernmost leg of the Route des Grandes

Alpes, or Grand Alps Route. In its entirety, the route runs the length of the French Alps – a total of some 700 km from Lake Geneva, or Lac Leman, in the north, to Nice on the Mediterranean Riviera in the south. Along the way, drivers pass through three national parks, two regional parks, and a number of smaller reserves. The road scales many high-altitude passes, necessitating the closure of much of the road from October through May.

Along the Route des Grandes Alpes, at the Col de l'Iseran

Argentière

Base Elevation: 1,252 m/4,107 feet

Mountain resort village

The village of Argentière is an oft-overlooked satellite of Chamonix, which lies eight km southwest. However, we find Argentière in some ways a better base than its more famous neighbor: Argentière is smaller and preserves a more traditional ambiance; Argentière is less expensive, both for food and for lodging; and Argentière is nearer to the Les Grands Montets, the legendary mountain experts come here to ski.

The village is based at the confluence of the Arve and Arveyron d'Argentière waterways amid the same spectacular mountain

Argentière (Robert Bréda)

scenery that blesses Chamonix. Lifts rise from its southeastern edge. Summertime guests enjoy hiking, biking, and climbing, while wintertime visitors ski on the Chamonix region's 150 km of groomed slopes. Cross-country skiers find some 16 km of marked trails; inexpensive *ski de fond* passes can be purchased at the tourist office. Shops, restaurants, and cafés line the main road, and small hotels and pensions duck off to the sides. Overall, it's a lovely little village, a quiet alternative for those looking to dodge Chamonix's bustling big-town scene.

✔ The **Argentière Guest Card**, issued by hotels at check-in, allows free unlimited travel on the Chamonix Bus shuttle, making day-trips down-valley an easy option.

 Want to stay? **Les Grands Montets** (€€€) has a lovely wood-paneled, fireside lounge. Although a short walk to town, the hotel is off the main road and is the closest lodging here to the lifts. Reserve at ☎ 0450 54 06 66, www.hotel-grands-montets.com.

 The tourist office is near the river at 24 Route du Village. Like the rest of the village, it's open from June through September and from December through early May. For more information, call ☎ 0450 54 02 14.

Le Col des Montets

Heading north from the village, drivers can make their way around Mount Blanc, entering Switzerland via Vallorcine after about 16 km. It's a lovely drive through the pass, Le Col des Montets, with spectacular terrain, emptying out along the steep hillside vineyard near Martigny, Switzerland. The road frequently closes in winter due to heavy snowfall, so wintertime drivers should have an alternate plan.

Germany

(Deutschland)
Language: German
Population: 83,251,851
Phone Country Code: +49
Currency: Euro

KING LUDWIG II

Bavaria's most fascinating character is Ludwig, the fairytale king. Born into the royal family as Prince Otto Ludwig Friedrich Wilhelm, the young boy spent his happiest days in his family's castle near Füssen at the Schwangau. At the age of 16, Ludwig heard his first opera, by Richard Wagner. Two years later, in 1864, Ludwig assumed the Bavarian throne and immediately sent for Wagner. Ludwig set Wagner up in a large villa, and erected the Bayreuth Opera House in his honor. For a time, the two were inseparable – a friendship that inspired much speculation.

However, Bavaria's strong ties to Austria forced Ludwig to support Austria in its 1866 war with Prussia. When Austria was defeated, control of the Bavarian army was ceded to the Prussian King. Then, in 1867, Ludwig became engaged to the sister of the Austrian Empress Sisi, but after several postponements and lots of strategic stiff-arming on Ludwig's part, the bride's father called off the match. Ludwig left Munich for his Alpine retreat, and it was there that he built his cluster of magnificent castles.

Two years later, Prussia went to war with France and, recalling the peace agreement from the 1866 war, called on Bavaria to supply arms. At the conclusion of the war, Wilhelm II "invited" Bavaria into the reestablished German Empire. Although Ludwig maintained the title of king, by 1871 he had lost all power. After a long decline into depression and bankruptcy, the fairytale king was deemed mentally unfit to rule and was removed to the lakeside Schloss Berg. Under mysterious circumstances, in June of 1886, he and his doctor were found drowned along the shallow shore. What happened there remains a mystery.

The Federal Republic of Germany covers 357,020 square km in north-central Europe. About 30% of its land is forested, and the Rhine, Danube, and Moselle are among its principal rivers. The terrain is a

IN THIS CHAPTER

■ People & Culture   176
■ Munich
  the Bavarian Alps   180

mixture of lowland plains in the north, highland plains in the central lands, and mountains in the South. Germany is bounded by Switzerland to the south, Austria to the southeast, Poland and the Czech Republic to the east, Denmark to the north, and France, Luxembourg, Belgium, and the Netherlands to the west.

Germany is composed of 16 states. Its capital is Berlin. The chief of state is the president; the head of government, the chancellor. Recent social issues stem from reunification and its costs, as wealth from the west continues to be sucked into modernization projects in the east. Unemployment rates have soared to 11%, only recently surpassing those of France. Furthermore, Germany's Basic Law provides for the unconditional citizenship of non-German speakers and for the acceptance of political refugees. Although new laws seek to regulate the influx, the country remains awash in social change, giving rise to racial violence and anti-immigration demonstrations.

People & Culture

Over 90% of Germany's population is of Germanic descent; the remainder is of foreign origin, including Danes, Turks, Italian,

Greeks, Slovaks, and Serbs. Approximately 50% of the population professes the Protestant faith – most of those follow the Lutheran sect. Some 45% are Roman Catholic , and 4% claim the Muslim religion. Over 84% of the population resides in urban settings, with a population density of 222 persons per square kilometer. The largest cities include Berlin, Hamburg, Munich, Cologne, and Frankfurt.

National Holidays

January1	New Year's Day
January6	Epiphany
January 7 through Shrove Tuesday	Carnival (Munich)
Friday before Easter	Good Friday
March/April	Easter
	Easter Monday
May 1	Labor Day
10 days before Whit Sunday	Ascension Day
7th Sunday after Easter	Whit Sunday
Day after Whit Sunday	Whit Monday
Thursday after 8th Sunday after Easter	Corpus Christi
August 15	Assumption Day
October 3	German Unity Day
October 31	Repentance Day
November 1	All Saints Day
November 14	Repentance Day
December 24	Christmas Eve
December 25	Christmas Day
December 26	2nd Christmas Day
December 31	New Year's Eve

TIMELINE	
2000-400 BC	Celtic tribes occupy the territory that is now Germany
936 AD	Otto the Great ascends to the throne of East Francia
1024-1125 AD	A succession of kingdoms gain power as the German Empire
1618-1648	Thirty Years' War destroys German Empire; by 1648, multiple principalities divide rule
1685	Composers George Frederic Handel and Johann Sebastian Bach are born
1864-1886	Age of King Ludwig II, Bavaria's "Fairytale King"
1864-1870	German principalities are unified; Prussian King Wilhelm I becomes emperor of the new German state
1914-1918	Germany invades Russia and France, leading to World War I and the defeat of Germany in 1918; the 1919 Treaty of Versailles imposes massive reparations
1933	Austrian Adolf Hitler becomes chancellor and the Nazi Party gains power
1936	Berlin hosts the Olympic Games
1939-1945	World War II; Germany annexes Austria in 1938 and invades Poland in 1939; Germany is finally defeated in 1945; Allies begin occupation
1949	Germany splits – the communist German Democratic Republic in the east under Soviet occupation, and the Federal Republic of Germany in the west under US, French, and British occupation
1961	Construction of the Berlin Wall
1989	The Berlin Wall torn down
1990-1991	Germany reunifies under Chancellor Helmut Kohl; in 1991, Berlin is established as the capital of the unified Germany
2005	Angela Merkel elected, becoming the nation's first female chancellor

For more information, visit the German National Tourist Office website at www.germany-tourism.de.

Munich & The Bavarian Alps

Land of fairy tales, fanciful castles, and fabulous Alpine terrain, Bavaria squeezes a wealth of attractions into a compact section of the Alps. The region centers on the bustling metropolis of Munich, a historical city famed for both its grand architecture and its great beer. To the southwest, plains stretch into Alpine foothills fronting Füssen and its famous castles. East of Füssen, mountain byways wind back to the quaint village of Oberammergau and to nearby Garmisch, home of the Zügspitze, Germany's highest peak. Farther east, the Berchtesgaden region towers into Austria, harboring the unspoiled landscape of Berchtesgaden National Park and its pristine Königsee.

◆ Munich

(München)
Population: 1.3 million
Base elevation: 530 m/1,738 feet
Gateway tourist city
Bavaria's capital bustles with energy, a student city bursting with art, industry, technology, and tourism. The city's tragic, war-torn past is studded with bright eras of royal glory and cultural achievement. Today, cosmopolitan Munich proves a fascinating place, indeed.

History & Orientation

Munich was officially founded by Henry the Lion on the 14th of June in the year 1158, and became the seat of Bavarian nobility in 1255. The city flourished in the 16th century as the German center of Renaissance culture,

Henry the Lion & Matilda of England (1188)

nurturing poets, writers, and artists under the rule of Duke Maximilian I. Munich burgeoned between the 18th and 19th centuries, as the population grew. Ludwig I, known as the "Prince of Muses", built the city into one of Europe's premier cultural centers by developing museums, theaters, and universities. King Max II commissioned several architectural gems, and King Ludwig II patronized music masters and craftsmen.

However, turbulent times rocked the early 20th century, as Hitler's National Socialists took control in 1933, and the World War that followed destroyed much of the city. American forces entered the city on April 30, 1945. Munich began to rebuild, and the city hosted the XX Olympic Summer Games in 1972. Sadly, however, the games were forever shadowed when Palestinian terrorists took hostages and killed 11 Israeli Olympic Team members. Today, Munich is Bavaria's political and cultural capital, drawing more domestic tourism than any other city in Germany.

Nymphenburg Palace (Gryffindor)

The Town

Munich presides over the southeastern corner of Germany, just west of Salzburg and just north of the Alps and Innsbruck. The Isar River cuts a 14-km swathe through the city center, and Munich's "rings" radiate from its banks – the outermost ring looping the city by beltway autobahn, the innermost encompassing the oldest part of the city. Anchoring the outskirts of this sprawling metropolis are several landmarks: **Nymphenburg Palace** to the west, the **Olympic Park** to the north, and the new **trade fair center** to the east.

Munich's tourism centers on the old city center loop and the **Marienplatz**, a pleasant one-km walk east from the main train station. Most of the city's attractions lie within a one-km radius of this square. From the center, the pedestrian shopping streets of Kaufingerstrasse and Neuhauserstrasse run west to Karlsplatz and the train station; Theatinerstrasse heads north to the Residenz, Ludwigstrasse, and the university district; and Sendlingerstrasse runs southwest toward Sendlinger Tor and the Theresienwiese festival grounds. Maximilianstrasse parades a long line of posh shops to the east.

Marienplatz with Neues Rathaus (Diliff)

Getting Here & Around

International travelers arriving by air will fly into **Munich Airport**, an ever-growing facility 28 km northeast of the city center. If you're stuck here awhile, the airport museum has a reasonable collection of historical airplanes, and the Visitors' Park and Visitors' Hill are relatively pleasant places to hang out. For more information, check www.

munich-airport.de. To reach the city center via public transportation, hop on the S-bahn train for the 40-minute ride into town.

Munich is Bavaria's main bus and train transportation hub. The city-center public transportation system is a tightly woven web of train, subway, tram, and bus routes.

✔ I heartily recommend the MVV *Hin unde Weg* brochure, a multilingual guide to sightseeing via Munich's public transportation system. Doled out by the tourist office, the guide offers a helpful description of the various types of public transport, the ticketing system, and the city's fare-determining zone rings.

A simpler way to clear up the issue, however, is to purchase a day pass or, if you plan to cover a few attractions, the München Welcome Card (see below).

✔ The **München Welcome Card** offers unlimited transport on all city buses, trams, and subways and discounts on various city tours, attractions, museums, and events. (But many discounted attractions don't advertise their discounted rates. Study your Welcome Card booklet and request discounts whenever purchasing tickets.) Welcome Cards can be purchased for one or three days; for one person or a group of up to five; and with or without a ride to and from the airport. (A one-day, one-person card without airport transfer costs €7.50). Buy yours at the airport, at your hotel, or at any tourist office.

Getting More Info

Tourist information outlets dole out brochures and maps – one office in the main train station and one in the Neues Rathaus at Marienplatz. The station office is open 9:30 am-6:30 pm, Monday through Saturday; 10 am-6 pm, Sundays; and the Marienplatz office is open 10 am-8 pm weekdays, 10 am-4 pm Saturdays. Get more information at ☎ 089 233 965 00, www.muenchen.de.

Two post offices are convenient to the city's tourist center. The first sits directly across the street from the front of the main train station. The second is at Max-Joseph Platz, just across the square from the National Theater.

For Internet access, try the massive **Easy Everything Internet Café** across from the main train station, the **Hard Rock Café** across from the Hofbräuhaus, the **Café Glockenspiel** at Marienplatz or, near the university, the student hang-out **CADU** at 10 Ludwigstrasse.

The Sights

Much of Munich's original architecture was destroyed during World War II, but some notable structures were either spared or have been rebuilt. In the center, action revolves around the **Marienplatz**, a large square that's been the heart of Munich since its days as a marketplace and jousting tournament venue in the Middle Ages. Dominating the square is the Gothic **Neues Rathaus**, or New City Hall, home to the city's famed **Glockenspiel**, a toy clock that stages a short performance each day at 11 am and noon year-round and, additionally, at 5 pm in the summer.

Between the alleys just south of the square are **St. Peter's** church and Munich's largest outdoor food market, the **Viktualienmarket**. The market is home to a small summertime beer garden, several quick lunch kiosks, and the city's ornate maypole. Stalls are open Monday through Friday, 7 am to 8 pm, and Saturdays till 4 pm. Farther from the Marienplatz, several small chunks remain of what once was the city's fortifying wall – the best sections are at **Sendlinger Tor** to the southwest and **Isartor** to the southeast. Between the Marienplatz and

Inside the Asamkirche (Andreas Praefcke)

Sendlinger Tor is what must be Germany's most jaw-droppingly ornate interior. For an eyeful, duck inside the tiny **Asamkirche** at Sendlingerstrasse 32.

A Head for Heights

Pack a map and gain some altitude to get an orienting view of Bavaria's most expansive metropolis:

■ My favorite vantage point within the city center is **St. Peter's Church**, where ambitious visitors climb 297 narrow scaffolding steps to the catwalk atop the old tower, or *alter turm*. Built in the 11th century, "Old St. Peter's" is Munich's most beloved church.

The Frauenkirche (Bob Tubbs)

■ Those desiring a less daunting climb can head for the 15th-century **Frauenkirche**, the city's cathedral and signature landmark. Here, just 86 steps and an elevator ride deliver guests to the highest tower top in central Munich – building restrictions dictate that no structure can stand taller than the church's twin onion-domed towers.

■ Faster, higher, stronger... the elevators in the **Olympic Tower** whisk visitors upward at a rate of seven meters per second. Five floors of indoor and outdoor observation decks (including one revolving restaurant) offer far-reaching views from 192 m/630 feet above the valley floor. The tower is open daily from 9 am to 12 pm; €4.

The Emperor's Staircase at the Residenz
(Gryffindor)

Bavaria's ruling families dumped mind-boggling wealth into the construction of their palaces, several of which are now open to the public. In the center, **The Residenz** was home to the Wittelbachs and the seat of Bavarian power for 500 years. The complex's 130 rooms show off a splendid collection of antiques and interior design from the successive eras and include the magnificent, barrel-vaulted Antiquarium Hall. Call ☎ 089 290 671 for more info.

West of the city, **Nymphenburg Palace** was the summer residence of Ludwig I and is home to his kingly pin-up collection, the famed "Gallery of Beauties." The Baroque palace's expansive gardens are worth a stroll as well. It's open daily April through September from 9 am-6 pm, and October through March, 10 am-4 pm. For more information, dial ☎ 089 179 080.

Munich's Museums

■ Thanks in large part to the Wittelsbach royal family's commitment to the creation, preservation, and collection of art, modern Munich's cultural wealth lies in its impressive museums. No fewer than 50 collections vie for attention. Below, we've highlighted a few of the best.

ART

■ The **Old Pinakothek** enjoys international renown for its collection of European paintings dating from the 14th through the 18th centuries. Rembrandt, Rubens, and Leonardo da Vinci are well represented here. It's open Tuesday through Sunday from 10 am-5 pm, Tuesday until 8 pm; ☎ 089 23 80 52 16, www.alte-pinakothek.de; €5.50, free on Sundays.

Old Peasant Woman, Pieter Breugel the Elder (1568)

■ Nearby, the **New Pinakothek** displays 18th and 19th century art, with particular emphases on English landscapes and the French Impressionist, Biedermeier, and Art Nouveau styles. View the collection Wednesday through Monday from 10 am-5 pm, Wednesday until 8 pm; ☎ 089 23 80 51

95, www.neue-pinakothek.de; €5.50, free on Sundays.

■ Newly opened and already immensely popular, the **Pinakothek der Moderne**, is the largest modern art museum in Germany. It shows off contemporary collections across all artistic genres, including paintings, sculpture, design, architecture, and graphics. It's open Tuesday through Sunday from 10 am to 5 pm, Thursday and Friday until 8 pm; ☎ 08923 80 51 18, www.pinakothek-der-moderne.de; €9.

Richard Schur

Josef Stieler, self-portrait (1806)

■ The **Municipal Gallery**, housed in the whimsical old Lenbachhaus villa, displays a fine collection of paintings by Kandinsky, Klee, and other artists of the Blue Rider movement. The museum opens daily except Monday from 10 am-6 pm; ☎ 089 23 33 20 00, www.lenbachhaus.de; €10.

HISTORY

■ The **Münchner Stadtmuseum**, or City Museum, houses an interesting display of cultural history. Features include historical interiors, a rundown of the city's development, and changing special exhibitions. The exhibits are open Tuesday through Sunday from 10 am-6 pm; ☎ 089 23 32 55 86, www.stadtmuseum-online.de; €4, Sundays free.

■ The **Bavarian National Museum** houses historical collections focusing on Bavarian art and artifacts. The museum opens Tuesday through Sunday from 10 am-6 pm, Thursdays until 8 pm; ☎ 089 211 24 01, www.bayerisches-national-museum.de; €3, free on Sunday.

TECHNOLOGY

■ If you're a technology buff, the item topping your don't-miss list should be the **Deutsches Museum**. One of the world's first museums of science and technology (and the largest in the world today), the huge complex occupies an island in the middle of the Isar River and houses a planetarium and an IMAX theater. It's open daily 9 am-5 pm; ☎ 089 21791, www. deutsches-museum.de; €7.50.

■ The **BMW Museum** shows off historical and futuristic propulsion methods, traffic management techniques, and – of course – a dream collection of cars. Look for the Bavarian Motor Works building in the Munich skyline; it's the clover-shaped silver sky-rise designed to resemble a four-cylinder engine. The museum is open Monday through Sunday from 9 am-5 pm, last entry at 4 pm; ☎ 089 382 23 307, www.bmw.com; €3.

■ Looking for something a bit more unusual? Check in at the **Center for Extraordinary Museums**, where a handful of "cultural" collections spotlight things like pedal cars, perfume flasks, Easter bunnies, and "potties." It's open daily, 10 am-6 pm; ☎ 089 290 4121, www.zam-museum.de; €4.

● TOURS

In a city the size of Munich, a short orientation tour can considerably simplify sightseeing logistics. Multiple outfitters oblige: **Panorama Tours**, alternatively known as Stadt-Rundfahrten, offers a varied program of bus and walking tours. Their one-hour city orientation tour departs hourly in an open double-

Germany

decker bus from in front of the Hertie Department Store across from the main train station, ☎ 055 02 89 95, €11.

Mike's Bike Tours offers guided city tours by bike from March through October. The four-hour tours stick to easy bike paths and are suitable for young cyclists; ☎ 0651 42 75, www. mikesbiketours.com.

Radius Tours & Bikes does biking tours and bike rental and adds a good collection of themed walking tours under the banner of Munich Walks. Contact ☎ 089 98 60 15, www. radiusmunich.com or www.munichwalks.com, for current offerings and meeting points.

Finally, **Weisser Stadtvogel** guides a variety of irregularly scheduled tours with interesting themes like "Beer," "National Socialism," and – my favorite – "Hangmen, Whores, and Hags." Contact them at ☎ 089 29 16 97 65, www.weisser-stadtvogel. de, to see what's on.

The Adventures

 Müncheners play like most city-dwellers, cycling, playing, and **walking** in parks and gardens. Visitors wishing to do the same can join locals in several recreation centers: at the **Schlosspark Nymphenburg** behind the palace, along the central banks of the **Isar River**, at the **Olympic Park** (see below), and at the **English Gardens**.

THE OLYMPIC PARK

The focal point of Munich's athletic prowess is the Olympic Park, a rambling sports complex developed in preparation for the XX Olympic Summer Games in 1972. The park has since staged no fewer than 30 world, 12 European, and 84 German athletic championships. Today, it regularly hosts soccer, equestrian, swimming, ice-skating, tennis, volleyball, track, cycling, and concert events.

Recreational athletes, too, enjoy the park's facilities. Several small lakes and streams stud grassy grounds, and the sprawling, silvery angles of the tent roof add a modern artsy touch. Visitors enjoy walking paths, playgrounds, and pedal boat rentals. The complex's swimming, ice, and skating facilities are open for public use, and elevators scale the heights of the Olympic Tower. Tourists enjoy the mini-train tours that depart the tower base every 15 minutes and the themed soccer, architecture, and roof-climbing tours offered from April through October. For more information, contact ☎ 089 30 67 24 14, www.olympiapark-muenchen.de.

The Olympic Park

Bike rental is available at several city outlets, but our favorite is **Radius Touristik**, a British-run operation conveniently located at the main train station from May through October; ☎ 089 98 60 15, www.radiusmunich.com. **DBRent** rents bikes year-round; www.callabike.de.

Several public **swimming** complexes are open for public use. The **Olympia Swimmhalle** at Olympic Park has a 50-m pool, diving boards, and a sauna area; ☎ 089 30 67 21 50. And the traditional **Müllersches Volksbad** boasts lovely Art Nouveau design, ☎ 089 23 61 34 29.

The **Olympic Park's Eissportzentrum** offers **ice-skating** year-round and its Action Area proves a hit for **inline skating** and **skateboarding** from March through October. Skate rental is on-site; dial ☎ 089 30 67 21 50 for more information.

Climbers head for the indoor wall **DAV-Kletteranlage Thalkirchen**, www.kletterzentrum-muenchen.de – or, from April to October, harness up at the Olympic Park for the **Zeltdach Roof Climb** tour. Contact ☎ 089 30 67 24 14, www.olympiapark-muenchen.de for more info.

For more **outdoorsy adventures**, several tour operators run package deals to the Chiemsee, Garmisch-Partenkirchen, and Berchtesgaden recreation areas. Contact **PanoramaTours Gray Line**, ☎ 089 54907560, www.autobusoberbayern.de, for ideas.

Where to Sleep

Munich's most prestigious address is the **Kempinski Hotel Vier Jahreszeiten** (€€€€), a large, luxurious house on Maximilianstrasse, the city's most expensive shopping street; ☎ 089

Kempinski Hotel Vier Jahreszeiten

212 50, www.kempinski-vierjahreszeiten.de.

Suite at the Königshof

The **Königshof** (€€€€) at Karlsplatz and the **Bayerischer Hof** (€€€€) on Promenadeplaz also offer plush, traditional accommodations in the city center. Book the Königshof at ☎ 089 55 13 60, www.koenigshof-muenchen.de; the Bayerischer Hof at ☎ 089 212 00, www.bayerischerhof.de.

Also in the heart of the old town, but somewhat less pricey, is the **Hotel Platzl** (€€€), with its charming Pfistermühle restaurant. It is conveniently located near the Hofbräuhaus and the Marienplatz. Book at ☎ 089 23 70 30, www.platzl.de.

Near Sendlinger Tor, try the cozy **Garni Acanthus** (€€); ☎ 089 23 18 80, www.acanthushotel.de and the **Englischer Garten Garni** has homey villa rooms near the English Gardens; ☎ 089 383 94 10.

Out near the Oktoberfest grounds, try the friendly **Hotel Uhland** (€€), ☎ 08954 33 50; and, in the heart of old town near the Hofbräuhaus, try your luck at the very basic **Hotel Alcron**, ☎ 089 228 35 11, www.hotel-alcron.de.

For budgeting youth, Munich's **HI Youth Hostel** (€) has its own restaurant, bar, beer garden, and disco; ☎ 089 12 00 60, www.haus-internationl.de. **Das Zelt** (€), or The Tent, offers a memorable (and possibly sleepless) night's stay in an enormous communal tent. It's open June through August, and rates include a pad, a blanket, a shower, and breakfast; ☎ 089 141 43 00, www.the-tent.com.

Where to Eat

 With over 500 restaurants, Munich offers something to please all palates. Best among the city's gourmet establishments are **Am Marstall** (€€€), where traditional Bavarian basics get a French gourmet kick; ☎ 089 29 16 55 11. And, just outside the center at Schwabing, the revered Tantris (€€€) serves creative cuisine amid ultra-modern décor; ☎ 089 361 95 90.

For traditional Bavarian dishes, I like the old, ivy-ensconced **Pfiftermühle** (€€) at Pfisterstrasse 4; ☎ 089 23 70 38 65. Also the **Haxenbauer** (€€) at Sparkassenstrasse; ☎ 089 29 16 21 00. Both are near the Hofbräuhaus.

A trio of traditional restaurants clusters at Dreifaltigkeitsplatz, a tiny square just off the Viktualienmarket – each, of course, serves a different brand of beer. Try the **Balentin Stüberl** (€€) for Paulaner; the **Zum Alten Markt** (€€) for Spaten; or the cheery **Bratwurstherzl** (€) for Hacker-Pschorr and fresh Nürnberger bratwurst. Each has outdoor seating in the sum-

Hofbräuhaus

mer. **Beer halls** and most beer gardens serve limited menus of reasonably priced Bavarian food in addition to local beers – see *Munich's Beer Halls* below. For dinner out with entertainment included, the **Welser Kuche** (€€€) at the Feldherrnkeller offers a medieval gourmet dinner each evening from 7 pm to 1 am; ☎ 089 29 65 65, www.welser-kuche.de. And the famed **Hofbräuhaus** (€€€) serves buffet Bavarian alongside a variety of traditional acts; ☎ 089 29 01 36 10, www.hofbraeuhaus.de.

MUNICH'S BEER HALLS

The beer hall on the first floor of the Hofbräuhaus

Munich's beer halls bring the city international fame, and every tourist should visit at least one. Here, guests share tables (but not necessarily conversation), dirndl-clad maids hoist huge loads of beer, and oompa-bands spout traditional tunes with which crowds cheerfully sing along. Each house serves food and its own brand of Bavarian beer, the latter always in a one-liter mug, or *mass* – a quantity quite generous by international standards.

Most visitors head straight for the **Hofbräuhaus** at Platzl, the city's most famous beer hall and the place most likely to be packed with foreign tourists. It's got a big, vaulted hall, a shady fountain garden, and a multilingual staff. On a nearby corner at Talstrasse 7, just east of the Marienplatz, the **Weisses Bräuhaus** has a more reserved atmosphere, serves up delish Bavarian food, and specializes

Weisses Bräuhaus

in white, or *weisses*, wheat beer. Also in the center, at

Augustiner Grossgäststätte

Karlsplatz, the **Augustiner Grossgäststätte** dates from 1328. Today it offers great food, a cheerful little garden and upper terrace, and an elegant painted-and-plastered interior. From early spring through late autumn, Munich's beer-drinking scene expands into the outdoors. Any time the sun shines, head for one of the city's many beer gardens. Best among them are the **Augustiner Keller** west of the main train station at Arnulfstrasse 52; the friendly **Chinesischer Turm** near the pagoda in the English Gardens; and, also in the English Gardens, the classy **Seehaus**, where sunny lakeside seating, good food, and a nearby boat rental make for a pleasant afternoon.

Where to Party

For artsy evening entertainment, Munich's 57 theaters stage a wide range of performances. Music lovers flock here for performances by the city's three orchestras: the **Munich Philharmonic**, the **Bayerischer Rundfunk Symphony Orchestra**, and the **Bavarian State**

Opera. Popular venues include the National Theater, the Residenztheater, the Deutsches Theater, and the freshly re-modeled Münchner Kammerspiele.

✔ For all event tickets, check **München Tickets**, ☎ 089 54 81 81 81, www.muenchenticket.de.

Munich's late-night party places open their doors around mid-night – about the same time the city's beer halls shut down and theaters let out. Bouncers here are notorious for their snobby selectivity, but the following are some places to try. The **Feierwerk** and the **Nachtwerk** are two separate nightclub complexes. Each houses three dance clubs with DJs and live music. See what's on at the Feierwerk at ☎ 089 769 36 00, www.feierwerk.de. Contact the Nachtwerk at ☎ 089 570 83 80. **Kunstpark Ost**, near the Ostbahnhof, is a concert, bar, and disco complex with over 30 outlets and frequent live perfor-mances; ☎ 089 49 00 29 28. For jazz, try **Mr. B's** at Isavorstadt; ☎ 089 53 49 01.

Where to Play

Families enjoy the several **playgrounds** at Olympia Park and the English Gardens and the interactive ex-hibits at the Deutches Museum. Just outside the city center, the **Hellabrunn Zoo** is popular for its 440 species, all housed in naturalistic habitats. Kids enjoy a petting area, an in-frared bat cave, and a jungle tent. The zoo is open daily April to September from 8 am-6 pm and October to March from 9 am-5 pm; ☎ 089 62 50 90; €9; www.zoo-munich.de.

Festivals & Events

After the Carnival parties pass, Munich's breweries stage their **Strong Beer Season** in March. The tradi-tion owes its start to the city's first monks, who cre-ated the especially strong brews for nourishment during the Lenten fasting season. (How will you know a strong beer? Look for beer names with an *-ator* suffix; for example, *Triumphator*, *Maximator*, and *Delicator*.) Other festivals include the **Auer Dulten** markets, the **Summer Festival** at Olympia Park in Au-gust and, of course, the world-renowned **Oktoberfest** in late

September (see *O´zapft is* below). Munich's popular **Christmas Market** centers on the Marienplatz from late November through Christmas Eve.

Three times each year at Mariahilfplatz in the Au District, Munich hosts the **Auer Dulten**, folkloric fairs and markets featuring household gadgets, tableware, flea-market stalls, rides for kids, and lots of food and beer. The **Maidult** takes place from late April through early May; the **Jakobidult**, from late July to early August; and the **Kirchweihdult**, from mid- to late October.

Culture-loving nightowls appreciate the city's Long Night events: **The Long Night of Music** in May, when some 100 venues host a wide range of musical performances from 8 pm to 3 am; and **The Long Night of the Munich Museums** in July. The Bavarian State Ballet hosts **Ballet Week** in late March, and the Bavarian State Opera stages the **Munich Opera Festival** late June through July.

● **O´ZAPFT IS!**

Olympia Loop & Carousel at Oktoberfest (Bernhard J. Scheuvens)

Oktoberfest, the world's largest festival, kicks off with the opening of the first keg and the mayor's pronouncement, "*O´zapft is*" (it's tapped)!

The festival tradition began in 1810, when Bavaria celebrated the wedding of Crown Prince Ludwig and Princess Therese von Sachsen-Hildburghausen, shown at left, in a field named the

In a tent at Oktoberfest

Theresienwiese, or Theresa's meadow, in honor of the bride. Both the fairgrounds and the festival itself are often referred to as the "*Wiesn,*" a shortened version of this name.

From that celebration grew the *Wiesn* of today, an international party featuring carnival rides, hearty traditional food, and lots and lots of beer. Fourteen enormous brewery tents reign over the festival grounds, each serving up one-liter mugs of house-proud brew, a specialty roast dish or two, and enormous pretzels – all within sight and sound of an energetic Bavarian band. Statistically inclined? Each year, approximately six million visitors take part in the festivities. Last year they consumed 1,638,000 gallons of beer, 481,649 roast chickens, and 359,678 sausages.

Upcoming Oktoberfest Dates

The festival runs each year for 16 days, always ending on the first Sunday in October:

2007	22 September-7 October
2008	20 September-5 October
2009	19 September-4 October
2010	18 September-3 October
2011	17 September-3 October

Oktoberfest, Sunday night

The festival grounds are at the Theresienwiese, a 15-minute walk southwest of the main train station. Take subway lines U4 and U5 to Theresienwiese station and then follow the lederhosen-clad crowd to the festival. The brewery tents serve beer from 10 am to 10:30 pm on weekdays and 9 am-10:30 pm on Sundays and holidays; the festival shuts down each night at 11:30 pm. (Want to stay later? Käfers Wiesnschänke and the Wein- und Sektzelt stay open until 1 am – last call for drinks at 12:15 am. After that, the city's bars and dance clubs host "After-Wiesn" parties; look for the advertisements posted around town.)

With in-tent seating for 98,000 available, it's hard to believe but true: Finding a place to sit can be difficult – and *you must be seated to order a beer.* (During the busiest hours in the evening and on weekends, it can get so crowded that security shuts off entry.) Our strategy? Go with a group, stake out a table early, and stay put, sending sightseers off in pairs to explore.

✔ Table reservations for small groups are advised during the festival's busier hours. Reservations must be made in advance through tent-specific hosts, and some tents require pre-booking of meals and beer vouchers. Two favorite tent hosts take on-line reservations in English: **Hippodrome** at www.hippodrom-oktoberfest.de, or the **Hofbräu Festzelt** at http://www.hb-festzelt.de.

Several events highlight the festival calendar. If you're in town, don't miss these:

- The colorful **Grand Entry of the Breweries** takes place at 10:45 am on the first Saturday of the festival. Beer-tent landlords parade through town with their families, staff, and horse-drawn keg wagons en route to the festival grounds and the opening of the festival.

- The **Costume and Marksmen's Parade** runs a seven-km route beginning at 10 am on the first Sunday of the festival. Over 7,000 participants show off brewery floats and wagons, marching bands, and rifle troops – all splendidly costumed in traditional dress.

- The **Concert of the Oktoberfest Bands** sounds off at 11 am on the second Sunday of the festival. Some 400 musicians gather at the festival grounds on the steps beneath the statue *Bavaria* for what must be the loudest oompah-pah-ing known to mankind. (In case of bad weather, catch the outdoor concert the following Sunday.)

Dachau

Population: 39,922
Base Elevation: 480 m/1,574 feet
Tourist town

Dachau prisoners

Those who pass through Dachau come to visit the Dachau Concentration Camp Memorial, or the *KZ-Gedenkstatte Dachau.* They come here to remember and learn – and leave here gripped by the same conviction that's inscribed out front: "Never again."

Approximately 20 km northwest of Munich, Dachau is lodged in the world's memory as the location of Hitler's first concentration camp, a complex opened in 1933 to train Nazi officers and to "process" Jews, Poles, homosexuals, welfare recipients, gypsies, and any others deemed unacceptable by the Nazi regime.

Inside the gates, the main hall exhibits photographs, maps, and models documenting the abuse, exterminations, and scientific experimentation to which Dachau prisoners were subjected. By the time the war ended in 1945, over 206,000 prisoners had been held here, and 32,000 of those had died. To put those numbers into horrifying perspective, however, note that Dachau was merely a work camp and staging area from which prisoners were sent east to die in gas chambers beyond Germany's borders – over a million were killed at Auschwitz alone.

The memorial is open Tuesday through Sunday from 9 am to 5 pm; admission is free. Be forewarned, a visit here is a sobering experience that will disturb children and many adults. For more information, contact ☎ 08131 66 99 70, www.kz-gedenkstaette-dachau.de.

Although most tourists drop in only for a tour of the Dachau memorial, the town itself makes a worthwhile visit. Most notable here is the hilltop **Schloss Dachau**, which began its existence as a me-

Schloss Dachau

dieval fortress and eventually morphed into an expansive country palace for Munich's 16th-century Wittelsbach court. A wooden Renaissance ceiling, a collection of Wittelsbach coats of arms, and a lovely garden are the attractions here. Visit the palace Tuesday through Sunday, April through September from

10 am to 6 pm, and from October through March from 9 am to 4 pm.

 Want to stay? The **Bräuereigästhof Zieglerbräu** has inexpensive rooms in the center next to town hall. This traditional house is proud of its restaurant, a cozy wood-beamed dining room serving hearty traditional food. For more info, contact ☎ 08131 45 43 96, www.gasthof-ziegler-braeu.de.

 Dachau's tourist office is at Konrad Audenauer Strasse 1, ☎ 08131 752 86, www.dachau.info.de. Guides lead tours from in front of the town hall, May through September, Monday, Wednesday, and Saturday at 3 pm.

Chiemsee

Base Elevation: 518 m/1,699 feet

Lake resort

Chiemsee draws holiday-makers from all over Bavaria for its beaches, water recreation, and island castle. At 80 square km (31 square miles), the lake is Germany's largest. It is endearingly known as the "Bavarian Ocean".

Approximately one hour southeast of Munich by car along the lovely A8 autobahn, Chiemsee pleases with a wide range of natural and historical sights and plenty of options for recreation. Bordered to the south by a magnificent stretch of Alps, the region has through history played host to the region's most influential rulers: It was here that King Ludwig I built his elaborate castle, here that Hitler developed his Rastätte Resort, and here that world political leaders convened to hash out Germany's 1948 constitution.

Today, tourists come for the islands, **Herreninsel**, or "men's island," and **Fraueninsel**, or "women's island." Although no discrimination amongst visitors of either gender is made today, the islands took their names from the monastery and convent, which once occupied their shores. On the larger of the two islands sprawls **Schloss Herrenchiemsee**, "Mad" King Ludwig's late 19th-century replica of French King Louis XIV's Versailles.

Schloss Herrenchiemsee (Rainer Zenz)

The smaller of the two inhabited islands, Fraueninsel, is home to a Benedictine convent and a tiny fishing community.

Along the southwestern lakeshore cluster the lake's primary recreational facilities. At both Bauern/Felden and Prien/Stock, rental services offer bikes, boats, windsurfers, and surreys; beer gardens serve up frothy brews; and grass-and-sand beaches beckon to sunbathers. Kids of all ages hop aboard the Chiemseebahn, a steam tramway running an original 1888 locomotive between Prien's main rail station and the lakeshore docks at Stock. In Prien, a large, attractive village, visitors can ogle the elaborate ceiling within the parish church, shop in glossy boutiques, and dine in high style at a wide variety of restaurants, many with outdoor garden seating.

ISLAND-HOPPING BAVARIAN STYLE

While the two- to three-hour drive around the lake is a worthwhile excursion, I prefer a day out by ferryboat. Starting early from the Prien/Stock dock, head for Herreninsel, wander the gardens, take a castle tour, and stop off in a shady beer garden. From Herreninsel, hop a ferry to Fraueninsel. Stroll the fishing village's flower-festooned alleys, hike around the shoreline, take a swim at an island beach, and don't miss a chance to sample the smoked fish at the alley stalls near the northern end of the island. Pottery collectors should seek out the **Insel-Töpferei Klampfleuthner**, a family-run pottery workshop that's been turning its wheels since 1609. Longing for more? Venture around the lake by boat on the "Grosse," or grand tour, or head back to shore and rent a boat of your own.

✔ Book rooms on the islands and sample life here without all the day tourists. Try the simple **Schlosshotel** in the old monastery grounds on Herreninsel or, on Fraueninsel, cozy up at the **Gästhof Zur Linde**. Book the Schlosshotel (€€) at ☎ 08051 90 30, www.schlosshotel-herrenchiemsee.com, and the Gästhof Zur Linde (€€) at ☎ 08054 903 66. Both houses have seasonal closing periods; call for more information.

Fraueninsel

The **Chiemsee Schifffahrt Company** has been operating ferries here for 116 years, and they're quite good at what they do. Most boats converge at Prien/Stock and Herreninsel island and then fan out from there. (Passenger ferries en route to the islands also stop in at Bernau/Felden.) Boats run year-round, although service is most frequent during the June-through-

September high season – check www.chiemsee-schifffahrt.de for more info. Day-trippers choose between several ticket plans including one or more islands, a "grand" round-trip, or single-trip tickets. Those seeking a special night out should consider the themed pleasure cruises taking float during the high season and weekends; features include dancing, jazz, fairy-tales, and specialty dining.

Chiemsee's tourist information center is at the Bernau/Felden recreation area at the lake's southwestern shore. Dial ☎ 08051 965550 or surf www.mychiemsee.de for more information.

◆ Garmisch-Partenkirchen

Population: 28,000
Base elevation: 720 m/2,362 feet
Mountain resort town

At the foot of the Zügspitze, near the border with Austria, Garmisch-Partenkirchen remains Germany's favorite climatic health and recreation resort. With an Olympic history and an encircling ring of mountains, the twin towns offer a bustling ambiance, two quaint pedestrian areas, and a range of outdoor recreation to suit all tastes.

History & Orientation

Garmisch-Partenkirchen and the Werdenfelser Land got its start as an intermediate stop on the Roman trade route between Italy's Brenner Pass and Augsburg to the north. The regions's name, the Werdenfels, derives from the castle now in ruins at the edge of the Kramerspitz. Local citizens enjoyed a prosperous 14th century but lost much during the Thirty Years War. New wealth poured into the region in the mid-19th century, as students, painters, and musicians found inspiration in the surrounding hills. Adventuresome mountaineers, climatic health seekers, and wealthy landlords arrived soon after, and Alpine tourism took hold. The valley became Europe's preeminent winter sports resorts, founding Germany's first ski club in 1905. Bobsledding made its first run here in 1911, and Bavaria's first hockey players took to local ice in the 1920s. The, as the town prepared for the Olympic Winter Games in 1936,

Walking at the foot of the Zügspitze and Alpspitze

Hitler declared the two villages of Garmisch and Partenkirchen a single town.

Today's Garmisch-Partenkirchen spreads out along a Werdenfels valley, encircled by mountains and split by the Partnach and Loisach rivers. Along the southern edge of town, the magnificent Zügspitze and its Wettersteingebirge range forms the border of Austria; the Wank rises to the east; and to the north rests the sunny, peaceful Kramerspitz area. The quieter hamlet of Grainau lies west of town, near the Eibsee at the foot of the Zügspitze.

Ludwigstrasse

The Town

Today, Garmisch-Partenkirchen forms what is politically one town – but culturally two separate centers. Garmisch lies to the west and Partenkirchen to the east, the railroad tracks and Parnach River separating the two. From Garmisch, the Zugspitzstrasse heads west toward the Zügspitze, Reutte, and Füssen; and from Partenkirchen, the Hauptstrasse runs north toward Oberammergau and Munich and south toward Mittenwald and Innsbruck.

In Garmisch, tourism centers on the pedestrian-only stretch of Am Kurpark, the road running between the Kongresshaus and the Marienplatz. The old residential district lies just north, across the Loisach River at Fruhlingstrasse. The somewhat quieter historical and tourist district of Partenkirchen spans Ludwigstrasse, a cobblestone street to the east of, and parallel to, Hauptstrasse.

Getting Here & Around

 Garmisch sits approximately 1½ hours south of Munich and one hour north of Innsbruck, Austria. Both cities have international airports. Garmisch's train station is in the center directly between the two old villages, a 15-minute walk from Partenkirchen's old town, Garmisch's old town, and the Hausbergbahn lift station. Transportation around town is via the local bus system. For taxi service, dial ☎ 00821 16 16.

✔ The **Garmisch-Partenkirchen Visitor's Card** offers overnight guests free access to the bus system and a single entry to the Alpspitze Wellenbad wave pool, the spa gardens, and casino. Other discounts apply as well. Ask for the card on arrival at your hotel.

Mountain transportation includes a total of 38 lifts spanning, from west to east, the Zügspitze, Alpspitze, Kreuzeck, Hausberg, Eckbauer, and Wank areas. Only the Kramerspitz to the north lacks lift service. For more information, contact the Bayerische Zügspitzbahn at ☎ 08821 79 70, www.zugspitze. de.

LIFT PASS PRICE SAMPLES	
Winter	
1-day adult Classic Pass	€31
6-day adult Happy Ski Card	€165
Pedestrian round-trip to Alpspitze	€31
Pedestrian round-trip to Zügspitze	€37
Summer	
Pedestrian round-trip to Alpspitze	€25
Pedestrian round-trip to Zügspitze	€46

Getting More Info

 The main branch of the Garmisch-Partenkirchen Tourist Office is housed near the Kongresshall at Richard Strauss Platz 2. Visitors reserve accommodations, purchase event tickets, arrange guides, and gather brochures and maps. For more info, check in at ☎ 08821 180 700 or www.garmisch-partenkirchen.de.

The most convenient post offices are at the train station and in Garmisch at Marienplatz 8 near the Pfarrkirche St. Martin.

For Internet access in Partenkirchen, try the **Computerhaus** at Ludwigstrasse 69; in Garmisch, head for **Hobi's Internetcafé** – it's got a great bakery, and there's even a small computer station for kids.

The Sights

Traditional painted façade

In Garmisch, shoppers stroll the pedestrian-only **Am Kurparkstrasse**, and history buffs seek out old-world Garmisch along **Frülingstrasse**, where municipal restrictions ensure that the residences appear just as they did 200 years ago. The quaint, cobblestone street parallels the north bank of the Loisach River, just north of Marienplatz and the Pfarrkirch St. Martin. Nearby at Fürstenstrasse, look for the Hungarian soldier in the *Lüftmalerei* window on the façade of the **Bräustubl** restaurant, the town's first *gästhaus*. Beyond the old building façades, duck inside the 11th-century **Alte Kirche**, where meticulous work continues in efforts to unbury newly discovered frescoes from beneath centuries of over-paint.

Across town in Partenkirchen, tourists wander the shops and restaurants along scenic Ludwigstrasse, one of the valley's original Roman roads and a route used by King Ludwig II on his way to the Schachen mountain lodge. Of note are the **Post Hotel**, where King Ludwig stayed; the **Gästhof Frauendorfer**,

Germany

fronted by a fanciful Lüftmalerei of a Bavarian wedding party; and at house 54, Partenkirchen's own **Goldener Dachl**, a miniature copy of Innsbruck's golden roof. Nearby, the **Werdenfelser Heimatmuseum** covers 2,000 years of local history with its folklore and cultural displays. The museum is at Ludwigstrasse 47 in Partenkirchen, open Tuesday through Friday, 10 am-1 pm and 3-6 pm, and Saturday and Sunday, 10 am-1 pm; ☎ 08821 21 34, €2.50.

For those interested in music, the **Richard Strauss Institute** documents the life and work of hometown son Richard Strauss. The museum includes multimedia displays, a musical museum, and a library. It's open Tuesday through Friday from 10 am to 5 pm and Saturday and Sunday, 2-5 pm; ☎ 08821 910 950, www.richard-strauss-insitut.de, €2.50.

The Zügspitze

The Zügspitze, Germany's highest mountain, draws busloads of international tourists to its peak each day. The views from the top are spectacular on a clear day, and the trip up is half the fun. Ride the Bayerische Zügspitzbahn from Garmisch-Partenkirchen station past Grainau to Lake Eibsee. The old track railway, first opened in 1930, ascends up and through the mountain to the Schneefern Glacier and the cozy Sonn Alpin restaurant. From there, the Gletscherbahn cable car makes the quick trip up to the 3,000-m Zügspitze peak.

At the top, visitors can enjoy views across four nations, search out the Austrian-German border cut into the forest far below, and cross into Austria – the Alte Zöllhütte snack stand was once passport control. The scrappy, wooden Münchner Haus is interesting for two reasons: First, because its self-service grill offers a refreshing *mass* of beer; second, because it was built here in 1897, well before the railway was in place. Daredevils will want to make the short, sporty climb up to the *gipfelkreuz*, or peak cross.

After visiting the peak, descend via the Eibseeseilbahn cable car back down to Eibsee. (Before boarding, make sure you're on the right cable car: The Gletscherbahn brought you here; the Eibseeseilbahn will take you back down to the valley; but the *third* cable car will strand you in Ehrwald, Austria, far, far from where you want to be.) The Zügspitzbahn and cable cars run daily except during the two-week fall and spring maintenance periods. For more information, log on to www.zugspitze.de.

The Adventures

● ON FOOT

A 300-km network of **mountain paths** winds around the resort. Valley paths meander along the base of the Wettersteingebirge from Partenkirchen through Garmisch and on to Grainau and the Eibsee. At altitude, the Wank, Eckbauer, Kreuzeck, and Alpspitze area offer opportunities for lift-served hiking, and each area is scattered with inviting mountain restaurants. On the north side of

town, the Kramerspitz does not have lift service but is popular for its easy Plateauweg walk and its scenic Almhütte and St. Martin mountain restaurants.

THE PARTNACH GORGE

The Partnach Gorge (K. Dana)

If you can only take one hike, head for the **Partnachklamm**, or Partnach Gorge, for a fascinating look at the power of water. To reach the gorge, start from the west side of the Olympic Ski Stadium (worth a quick look, particularly if ski-jumping practice is in session) and take the 20-minute walk or horse-drawn carriage ride up the Wildenau Valley to the gorge base. From the base entry booth, walkers navigate the gorge via a narrow gallery path cut into the gorge walls. The gorge is open year-round – and is at its most beautiful in the winter, when enormous icicles add a surreal ambiance to the already spectacular rock formations. To return, walkers can either head back down the gorge or, from the upper end of the gorge, take the steps uphill toward Graseck and back to the ski stadium via the trail or the Eckbauerbahn cable car.

Yet another favorite hike ascends two-three hours from the Partnach Gorge up to **Schachen**, King Ludwig II's private hunting lodge. Royal views extend to the Zügspitze, and the house's upper floor is decked out in splendid Oriental style. Here, in the Turkish room, the eccentric king celebrated special occasions in isolation, joined only by servants dressed in lavish Oriental robes. The lodge and restaurant open in late May or early June (depending on when the snow melts) and close in early October. Guided lodge tours run at 11 am and 1, 2 and 3 pm, €2.

● **IN WATER**

Garmisch's public **swimming complex**, the **Alpspitz Wellenbad**, offers indoor and outdoor pools, wave and children's pools, a whirlpool, and a sauna area. It's open throughout the year; contact ☎ 08821 753 313, www.gw-gap.de, for more information.

Although Garmisch has several lakes to call its own, they are all tiny, each offering little more than a bathing area and some pleasant trails. The best of the local lakes is **Eibsee**, a small azure lake at the foot of the Zügspitze, surrounded by forests, and with both a **bathing area** and a dock renting **row boats**. In the summer, the **Freizeitpark Loisachbad** maintains a **riverside bathing area** and a **Kneipp therapy** trail on the banks of the Loisach River. **Thomas Sprenzel's Wildwasser & Kajakschule** offers **kayaking** instruction and trips, ☎ 00821520 33. **Fly-fishing** is possible from May through September in the **Loisach** and **Partnach rivers**, but completing the required paperwork is time-consuming and expensive. For more information on fishing, contact the **Landratsamt** at Olympiastrasse 10; ☎ 08821 7511.

● **ON WHEELS**

In the summer, **skaters** enjoy the small park near the Ice Sports Center, and a **wheeled toboggan run** thrills kids at Eckbauer. **Mountain biking** is extremely popular, and trails of all levels of difficulty wind up,

around, and through the local mountains. A favorite easy trek runs from Garmisch to Grainau and around the lovely Lake Eibsee, where a restaurant offers refreshments. The tourist office's map *Radln & Mountainbiken* offers additional ideas. For bike rental – in both city and mountain styles – the best place in town is **Trek Bikes** at Rathausplatz 11 in Partenkirchen; ☎ 00821 548 44, www.trekproshop.de.

Paragliders fill the sky

● IN THE AIR

Paragliders leap from several local launch points, including Wank, Hausberg, and the Alpspitz. Want to try? The **Gleitschirmschule Michael Brunner** offers lessons and tandem flights. Contact ☎ 00821 742 60, www.gleitschirmschule-gap.de, for more information. **Climbers** enjoy the **Hochseilgarten ropes course** near Eibsee, and climbing gardens challenge at Breitenau in Garmisch and on the Alpspitze.

● ON SNOW & ICE

Garmisch-Partenkirchen is Germany's premier Alpine sports resort, boasting 118 km of groomed ski runs, 38 lifts, and the hallowed Kandahar piste, site of Germany's only World Cup ski race. In the local area, **skiers** enjoy early- and late-season runs at Zügspitze on the Schneefern Glacier. Beginners head for the Zügspitze plateau and the Eckbauer family area, intermediates enjoy runs of the entire mountain, and advanced skiers head for Kreuzeck and Hausberg and the Kandahar racing run. A funpark and halfpipe entertain **snowboarders** on the Zügspitze plateau.

✔ The **Happy Ski Card** lift pass combines access to 111 lifts and 250 km of runs at 11 resorts in Germany and Austria, including Garmisch-Partenkirchen, Mittenwald, Seefeld, and Ehrwald. Passes can be purchase for a minimum of three days.

Cross-country skiers take to 40 km of loipe in the local area and near Grainau and day-trip to the additional trails winding through the Loisach and Oberammergau valleys. **Specialist Ski School Thomas Schwinghammer**, at the east entrance of the Olympic Ski Stadium, offers Nordic ski instruction in English; ☎ 08821 556 32. **Wintertime walkers** enjoy 100 km of cleared or groomed paths, while **snowshoers** head out from the Alpspitz-Wellenbad or, for a more difficult challenge, from the Wand middle station to the peak and back.

✔ The tourist office sells a good winter trail map with information (in German) entitled *Sport & Wintergaudi*.

Fans of **ice sports** head for the **Olympic Ice Sports Center**, the largest complex of its kind in Europe. Five rinks make space for ice hockey, skating, and both indoor and outdoor curling. To see what's on, contact ☎ 08821 753 291. For **tobogganing**, rent sleds in town and hike up to the two-km Hornschlittenrennen run at Parnachklamm or the popular 1.6-km trail below St. Martin's at the Kramerspitz. Try also the fast four-km run at the Hausbergbahn lift – it's open and lit from 5 to 8 pm, Wednesday and Friday evenings. The bottom of this run is good for kids, too. **Horse-drawn sleighs** await at the ski stadium or by reservation at ☎ 08821 94 29 30.

Sports Services, Outfitters & Guides

■ The **Garmisch-Partenkirchen Ski School** offers multi-lingual lessons from the base of the Hausberg area. Contact ☎ 08821 742 60, www.skischule-gap.de, for more information. The school rents equipment, too.

■ For multi-sport equipment rental, try **Welt des Sports** at Fürstenstrasse 20, and at Marienplatz, **Sport Total.** Ski rental is available at the Hausbergbahn valley station and at on the glacier at the Zugspitzplatt mountain station.

■ The **Wildwasserschule and Bike Verleih Center** at Alpspitzstrasse 16 team up to offer rafting, kayaking, and mountain-bike outings in the summer. In the winter, ski rental and service is available at the same address. Contact ☎ 08821 14 96, www.ww-gap.com, www.bikeverleih.de.

■ The **Werdenfelser Mountain Guides** run a wide range of all-season outings. The bureau offers private guiding services and maintains several mountain huts as well. Contact ☎ 08821 180 744 for more information. Alternatively, meet a representative at the tourist office Monday or Thursday from 4 to 6 pm, between Christmas and Easter and from late May through mid October.

Where to Sleep

 Best among the upscale traditional houses here is the **Hotel Zügspitze** (€€€), a large, cozy chalet brimming with geraniums in summer. The proprietors are most hospitable, and there's an indoor pool and sauna to boot. Book at ☎ 08821 90 10, www.hotel-zugspitze.de.

The creeky, old-world **Reindl's Partenkirchner Hof** (€€€) encompasses three sprawling houses in Partenkirch's center, the first built in 1911. World War II history buffs should consider a stay here, as Hitler used the hotel for a hospital before occupying Americans housed a headquarters here; ☎ 08821 943 870, www.reindls.de.

Both **Clausings Post Hotel** (€€€) and the **Post Hotel Partenkirchen** (€€-€€€) offer traditional accommodations at midrange rates. Clausings Post Hotel is in the center of Garmisch near the Marienplatz, ☎ 08821 70 90, http://www.clausings-posthotel.de; the Post Hotel Partenkirchen, in the center of Partenkirchen's old town at Ludwigstrasse, ☎ 08821 936 30, www.post-hotel.de. Cozy, traditional accommodations are also found at Partenkirchen's **Gästhof Fraundorfer** (€€), home to the town's favorite Bavarian dinner show; ☎ 08821 92 70, www.gasthof-fraundorfer.de.

Gästhof Fraundorfer (K. Dana)

The **Alpina** (€€), on a busy corner in the center of Garmisch at Alpspitzstrasse 12, offers modern chalet accommodations within easy reach of the Garmisch old town and the Hausburgbahn lift. Get more info at ☎ 08821 78 30, http://www.alpina-gap.de.

Finally, conveniently located at the train station, the **Hotel Vier Jahreszeiten** (€-€€) is more cheerful than its low rates and pragmatic locale might convey. Check in at ☎ 08821 91 60, www.vierjahreszeiten.cc.

> ### LODGING FOR US MILITARY
>
> The **Edelweiss Lodge and Resort** (€€) serves US military members and their families. Well located near the Kreuzeckbahn lift and a Zügspitzbahn train station, the recreational resort offers 330 rooms and suites, a conference center, and a wellness center. The slope-side Hausberg Sport Lodge serves skiers, and a full range of regional tours is available. For more information, ☎ 08821 729 81, www.AFRCEurope.com; proper ID required upon reservation.

Where to Eat

 Traditional dining options abound in Garmisch-Partenkirchen. In Garmisch's old residential area, the **Bräustüberl** (€€) at Fürstenstrasse 23 swarms with Bavarian charm, as does the more elegant and modern **Restaurant Alpenhof** (€€€) at the casino on Am Kurpark. Reserve a table at ☎ 08821 590 55, www.alpenhof-garmisch.de. Also in the center near the Kurpark, try the **Hofbräustüberl** (€€) on Chamonixstrasse for an odd mix of Yugoslavian and Bavarian cuisine.

For dinner and entertainment under one roof, the cozy **Gästhof Frauendorfer** (€€) in Partenkirchen stages nightly folklore dinner shows, including an immensely popular Bavarian slap dance. Make reservations at ☎ 08821 92 70, www.gasthof-fraundorfer.de. Nearby, at Ludwigstrasse 58, the **Gästhof**

Werdenfelser Hof (€) often features live music and dance alongside its traditional cuisine; ☎ 08821 36 21, www.werdenfelser-hof.de. If it's a sunny day and you're in the Wank area, hike or drive up past the old Wankbahn to the **Panorama Restaurant** (€€) for outdoor dining, and splendid views of the valley and its surrounding mountains.

Where to Party

Garmisch-Partenkirchen's party scene hinges more on quiet cafés than late-night clubs. That said, the town's youngest, hippest disco is the **Musik Café** on Marienplatz. Nearby, the **Peaches** and **Zum Holzwurm** prove popular as well.

Near city hall, try the popular **Irish Pub** at Rathaus 8, and check in at **John's Club** at Rathaus 7 for cocktails and dancing. The **Spielbank Garmisch-Partenkirchen** casino spins roulette, poker, blackjack, and slot machines daily from 3 pm. It's off the Garmisch pedestrian area at Am Kurpark 10, ☎ 08821 959 90.

Where to Play

In the summer, kids enjoy the **Freizeitpark Loisachbad**, a riverside playground and park on the banks of the Loisach. Additional **playgrounds** are between the Rathaus and Wettersteinstrassein Partenkirchen, at Gartenstrasse in Garmisch, and near the Hausbergbahn mountain station. Cable car and carriage rides, the Alpspitze Wellenbad, and the summer toboggan run at Eckbauer all prove popular, too. The tourist office can help with **babysitting** arrangements, and the office's *Ortsplan* map conveniently marks the outlying walking paths suitable for wheelchairs and strollers.

Festivals & Events

A local tradition, **New Year's Day Ski Jumping** kicks off each January, and the **International Sports Weeks** offer cultural and sporting events for two weeks beginning the day after Christmas and continuing through early January. A variety of **sporting competitions** highlight the winter months – including the World Cup races in late January – and mountain biking competitions take to the trails in summer.

Mid-June brings the **Richard Strauss Festival** in celebration of the composer's birthday. Garmisch hosts its **Folklore Festival** at the end of July; Partenkirchen, in early August. From August through September, the **Culture Summer** festival highlights a wide range of theater, cabaret, fine art, and concert events.

Oberammergau

Population: 4,906

Base Elevation: 850 m/2,788 feet

Tourist village

Best known for its intricately painted facades, its skilled woodworkers, and its long-running passion play, this lovely little village amuses tourists year-round.

In a tight valley just a 20-minute drive north of Garmisch, the village of Oberammergau huddles along the banks of the Ammer River in the shadow of the 1,343-m Kofel peak. The old town center clusters around the beautiful Baroque church, a web of alleys lined with woodcarving workshops, *gästhofs*, and fancifully frescoed façades. Anchoring the east side of town, near the base station of the Laber cable car, are the WellenBerg swimming complex and a NATO officers' school (which, by the way, explains the hodgepodge of military uniforms in town around lunchtime). The two sides of town are connected by both Ludwig Lang Strasse and Am Kreuzweg, streets ideal for drive-by sightings of Lüftmalerei façades.

One of many painted houses in Oberammergau

LÜFTMALEREI

Although the custom of painting house façades was well developed by the 18th century, Oberammergau local Franz Zwinck took the tradition to new heights, developing the art of

Luftmalerei, or "airy painting." The trompe l'oeil technique entertains the eye with false architectural features and fanciful representations of folk tales, historical events, and religious stories. Luftmalerei façades are common throughout Bavaria and the Austrian Tirol and Oberammergau, the tradition's point of origin, positively abounds with fine examples. For a look at Zwinck's original work, head for the Pilatus House at Verlegergasse.

Painting with Little Red Riding Hood (Nicholas Even)

Germany

Although the true joys of Oberammergau are best encountered by simply wandering around, there are some sights of note. First, the **Heimatmuseum Oberammergau**, a reasonable documentation of the history and culture of the village, opens each Satuday from 2 to 6 pm. The museum includes an excellent display of woodcarvings and nativity sets. One of Bavaria's finest examples of Lüftmalerei, the **Pilatushaus** on Verlegergasse also serves as a summertime workshop for local artists – barrel painters, woodcarvers, and potters. Come watch them work May through October, Monday through Saturday from 1 to 6 pm. Want to give woodcarving a try? The town's masters offer several week-long **woodcarving courses** each April and Sep-

tember; contact the tourist office at ☎ 08821 180 700 or www.garmische-partenkirchen.de for more information.

The Oberammergau Passion Play

The Passion Play)

Oberammergau's "Play of the Suffering, Death, and Resurrection of our Lord Jesus Christ" got its start in 1634 after the region was hit hard by both the plague and the Thirty Years War. The villagers vowed to perform this play every 10 years if the village was spared, a bargain the powers-that-be saw fit to oblige.

So, to this day, every 10 years, 2,000 locals participate in the staging of the world-famous Oberammergau Passion Play. The play relives the final five days in the life of Jesus, a story that lasts

Facing page: Oberammergau Valley

six hours on stage. In the months prior to opening night, the mayor declares preparations in effect: Men forgo shaving (what would a passion play be without beards?), women grow their hair, barbers become costumers, and woodcarving shops turn into set-building studios.

If you won't be here in 2010 when the next play is scheduled, you can see the facility, costumes, and photos on a theater tour. The playhouse is open daily in the winter, 10 am-4 pm, and summer, 9:30 am-5 pm. Occasional operas take the stage, too. Check with the tourist office at ☎ 08821 180 700 for more information.

Adventurers head into the hills on the Kolbensattel chairlift and on the Laber cable car. Both operate in the summer, accessing over 100 km of hiking and mountain biking trails. In winter, the former takes you to easy hikes and downhill ski runs; the latter, to an expert off-piste ski descent and the town's favorite paragliding launch site. Oberammergau's loipe are some of the best in Bavaria, and cross-country ski trails wind along the river, past cozy inns to Ettal and, for those with considerable stamina, all the way to Linderhof's castle. Mountain climbers conquer the Kofel, and swimmers enjoy the WellenBerg swimming complex, which offers indoor, outdoor, and children's pools.

Oberammergau is a base from which to explore the sights of the Bavarian Alps. Besides being within easy day-tripping distance of Garmisch, Füssen, and Mittenwald, Oberammergau sits between the **Ettaler Benedictine Abbey** to the east, (www.kloster-ettal.de) and the lovely **Wieskirche** to the north (www.wieskirche.de).

 Want to stay in Oberammergau? I liked the **Hotel Garni Fux** (€-€€) for its variety of simple, homey rooms, its friendly hospitality, and its central locale. Reserve a room or apartment at ☎ 08822 930 93, www.firmafux.de.

 The tourist office is at Eugen Papst Strasse 9a. Contact ☎ 008822 923 10, www.oberammergau.de, for more information.

SCHLOSS LINDERHOF

Some 12 km southwest of Oberammergau along the Alpine road that runs from Graswang toward Reutte and Füssen, nestles what I consider the finest of King Ludwig's castles. Completed in 1878, the castle is small and manageable, easily covered in an hour or two; it's eccentric, with features like a hidden cave grotto, a trap-door dining table, fanciful fountain gardens, and eye-popping Rococo decor; and it's *real* – the only one of the king's castle's that was actually finished and where he actually spent considerable time. Visit the castle April through September, 9 am-6 pm, and October through March, 10 am-4 pm. Open daily; €7, www.linderhof.de.

Füssen

Population: 14,357
Base Elevation: 808 m/2,650 feet
Tourist town
First a stop on the 3rd-century Roman route between Italy, Austria, and Augsburg, Fussen is today a stop on the route of most Bavarian bus tours. The modern draws here are a quaint pedestrian center; nearby lake, mountain, and spa retreats; and, most significantly, a pair of spectacular castles.

First a stop on the third-century Roman route between Italy, Austria, and Augsburg, Füssen is today a stop on the route of most Bavarian bus tours. The modern draws here are a quaint pedestrian center; nearby lake, mountain, and spa retreats; and – most significantly – a pair of famous castles.

Neuschwanstein

Schloss Neuschwanstein remains many tourists' quintessential image of Germany and the Alps. The most ambitious of King Ludwig's palace projects, the fairy-tale castle perches dramatically above the Pöllat Gorge, high on a forested hill near

Füssen. Built between 1869 and 1886, the castle was designed as a fanciful replication of medieval grandeur, but it was never completed and the king was in residence here only a few days.

To reach the castle, follow the road signs to the Königschlosser, or royal castles; park at Höhenschwangau; and make the 25-minute uphill climb or hire one of the waiting horse-drawn carriages. At the top, join thousands of other international visitors for a guided tour. The castle opens daily April through September from 9 am to 6 pm (Thursdays to 8 pm) and October through March from 10 am to 4 pm; ☎ 008362 810 35, www.schlossneuschwanstein.de; €7.

And by the way, do those turrets look familiar? Walt Disney modeled his Disneyland castle and logo after Neuschwanstein.

Höhenschwangau, with Schwansee on the right and Alpsee at left

The "other" castle in town is **Hohenschwangau**, a yellow palace below Neuschwanstein. This was the much more practical summer home of the Wittelsbach royal family, and King Ludwig I spent much of his time here – possibly gazing up the mountain dreaming up the fairytale castle he eventually constructed there.

The 700-year-old **town center** of Füssen is worth a stroll as well. Visitors enjoy shopping in the old town, tours of the Town

Hall **history museum** in the former monastery of St. Mang, views of the exquisite Lüftmalerei in the **Hohe Schloss** courtyard, and visits to the **Lechfall**, a ravine waterfall cut by the River Lech. The Königswinkel region of the Ällgau is known throughout Germany as a low-key **health and recreation center**, and local villages take full advantage of their lakes, rivers, and mountain attractions. Visitors can hop aboard the Tegelberg cable car, rent boats and enjoy ferry rides on Lake Forggensee, and wander the 180-km trail network through local mountains. Ballooning, cycling, and snow- and water-sports keep visitors in town year-round.

LUDWIG² : THE MUSICAL

Fans of musical theater may want to check out this rendition of the tragic life of "mad" fairy-tale king: his early ascent to the throne, his passions for art and technology, and his relationship with Richard Wagner. Performances take the stage north of Füssen in a lakeside Festspielhaus encompassing restaurants, a beer garden, and gardens. Shows play Tuesday through Thursday and Sunday, and backstage tours are available. For reservations, contact ☎ 08362 93 90 70, www.ludwigmusical. com, tickets from €20.

Want to stay? The **Hotel Hirsch** offers lovely accommodations directly in the pedestrian center at Kaiser-Maximilian-Platz 7. All rooms have modern amenities, some with Bavarian antiques and frescoed walls. Reserve at ☎ 08362 939 80, www. hotelhirsch.de.

Hotel Hirsch

The tourist office is at Kaiser-Maximilian-Platz 1; ☎ 08362 938 50, www.fuessen.de.

◆ Berchtesgaden

Population: 8,100

Base elevation: 571 m/1,873 feet

Mountain tourist town

Spectacular natural beauty surrounds Berchtesgaden. Crystal rivers run through steep-peaked valleys, rustic mountain huts offer fresh Alpine milk, and a national park harbors rare flora and fauna. Nonetheless, international bus tours tend to blow through town, affording only a single day to visit Hitler's "Eagle's Nest" and the World War II documentation center. Though these historic sites certainly merit attention. I suggest planning a longer stay.

Berchtesgaden, with the Watzmannmassiv behind it (M. Klüber Fotogafie)

History & Overview

Legend maintains that Berchtesgaden's once ice-locked landscape was first inhabited by fierce dragons and wild beasts – an unruly crowd that was inexplicably scared off when a group of Augustiner monks moved in during the early 12th century. For seven centuries, the archbishops ruled the region from a monastery on the site of today's palace, gaining wealth and power from the harvesting of salt, or "white gold," from local mines. In the early 19th century, rule passed from Napoleon to Austria and then Germany, and Berchtesgaden eventually became a favorite Alpine retreat of the Wittelsbachs, Bavaria's ruling family. In the 20th century, the town caught the fancy of Hitler, who overran the nearby village of Obersalzburg, built his Mt. Kehlstein mountain retreat – and escorted World War II to the Berchtesgaden's doorstep.

Berchtesgaden lies in the Bavarian Alps in the southeastern-most corner of Germany on a politically defined peninsula jutting into central Austria. Shadowed by the 2,713-m Watzmann Mountain, the town enjoys a wealth of natural splendor, including lakes, rivers, dramatic peaks, and a neighboring national park. Several towns are easily reached via the network of valley roads that intersect at Berchtesgaden: **Ramsau** to the west, **Bad-Reichenhall** to the north, **Salzburg** to the northeast, and **Hallein** to the east. Just south of town gleams the lake of **Königsee**, a long narrow stretch of pristine Alpine water – it's covered separately below.

The Town

The modern town of Berchtesgaden sprawls along the B305 valley road between Ramsau ad Hallein, centering on the train station and Königseerstrasse, which heads south to the lake. Above this intersection, Bahnhofstrasse climbs the hillside toward the old town, marked on maps as Markt Berchtesgaden, or "market town" Berchtesgaden. The old center radiates from the modern Kurpark and Alter Friedhof. To the north, a web of shopping streets leads to Marktplatz square and Schlossplatz, the castle complex's quiet courtyard. To the west, a network of old alleys hides a collection of mundane shops and cafés, and Maximilianstrasse traverses the hillside to the south and west.

Getting Here & Around

 Berchtesgaden sits approximately 30 km southwest of Salzburg and 150 km southeast of Munich. Drivers will find the town along Route B305 between Ramsau and Hallein. Parking is difficult here; your best bet for a central spot is the garage under the Kurpark.

Trains pull in to the main station below the center of town, and the regional RVO buses hub there, too. Mountain transportation is limited to the few lifts scattered outside of town at the ski areas – see *Adventures* below. For taxi transfer, dial **Radio Taxi** at ☎ 08652 40 41.

✔ The **Berchtesgaden Holiday Bus Pass** offers five days of unlimited local bus transportation. (A few restrictions apply.) The tourist office, the convention center, and the RVO bus ticket office sell the pass for €15.

Getting More Info

 Berchtesgaden's tourist information center is at Königseerstrasse 2, across the river and road from the main train station. It's open daily except from mid-October through April, when it closes at noon on Saturday and all day Sunday. Get more information at ☎ 08652 96 70, www.berchtesgadener-land.info.

The post office is at Marktplatz 24 in the old town center's pedestrian area.

The Sights

In the old town center, the chief attraction is the **Schloss Adelsheim** castle complex, a combination monastery, palace, church, concert venue, and museum. The castle got its start in the 11th century as a monastery before Bavaria's royal Wittelsbach family came in 1803 and morphed it into the more luxurious palace I see now. In the Schlossplatz courtyard, visitors should note the **war memorial** spanning the western side of the square and should at least take a glance inside the **Stiftskirche**. The castle **museum** itself includes a reasonable collection of art, furnishings, and armour; tours are offered from Easter through mid-October, 10 am-12 pm and 2-4 pm, closed Saturdays; and from mid-October to Easter, Monday through Friday at 11 am and 2 pm. Call ☎ 0852 94 79 80 for more information.

Berchtesgaden's most notorious resident was Adolf Hitler, and most tourists come here to explore this most unfortunate era of the region's history. Hitler's southern headquarters complex grew up around his original **Obersalzburg** vacation home, the Berghaus, just east of town. In the process of expansion, the

Nazi party incorporated or destroyed all of the pre-existing structures, forcing local farmers and their families out of their homes and off their land.

World War II saw extended bombing raids on Obersalzburg, and little of either the original village or Hitler's complex remains. What's left is now the **Dokumentation Obersalzberg**, a museum documenting the Nazi takeover of the Obersalzburg village, the coercion of local citizens, and the construction of the Kehlsteinhaus. Exhibitions include chilling accounts of Nazi tactics and travesties, and visitors are invited to explore part of the massive bunker network tunneled below the Obersalzburg area. The center is open daily, 9 am-5 pm from May through October and Tuesday-Sunday 10 am-3 pm, November through March; ☎ 08652 94 79 60, www.obersalzburg.de.

Kehlsteinhaus (Wolfgang Manousek)

THE EAGLE'S NEST

The Kehlsteinhaus – nicknamed the "Eagle's Nest" – perches at 1,834 m/6,015 feet atop Mt. Kehlstein and enjoys sweeping views of the Berchtesgaden region. The architectural feat was undertaken as a gift for Hitler's for 50th birthday but, after 3,000 laborers completed the task in just 13 months, Hitler didn't much like the place; he claimed it aggravated his vertigo and subsequently held meetings there on just 10 occasions. It was, however, well appreciated by Hitler's mistress, Eva Bräun, who visited much more frequently.

The Kehlsteinhaus was spared bombing during World War II, and its capture became the culminating quest of the 101st US Airborne Division – a story popularized in author Stephen Ambrose's *Band of Brothers*.

Today, the Kehlsteinhaus is open to tourists, who brave the trip up for astounding views from the terrace and refreshments from the dining room. From the Hintereck parking area at Obersalzburg, buses climb the narrow, winding road up the Kehlstein. Passengers alight at the base of an elevator up to the Kehlsteinhaus. The house is open only in summer, mid-May through October; guided tours in English start from the mountaintop at 10:30 am and 11:30 am or from the tourist office at 1:30 pm. Contact ☎ 0852 96 70 for more information.

Dating from 1517, the **Salzbergwerk** salt mine offers fun 90-minute tours through odd salt formations on foot and across an underground lake by raft. To enliven the experience, visitors don old-fashioned miners' overalls and slide down the mineshaft on a pair of parallel banisters. The mine is open daily, May through mid-October, from 9 am to 5 pm, and daily except Sunday, mid-October through April, 12:30 to 3:30 pm. Contact ☎ 08652 600 20, www.salzwerk.de, for more information.

Bertchtesgaden's sights are scattered throughout the region, and **guided tours** can ease the hassle this creates. Best among the tour operators here – particularly for English-language tours – is **Berchtesgaden Mini Bus Tours**. They offer a range of tours, including Obersalzburg, the Eagle's Nest, and the popular *Sound of Music* Tour, which highlights a number of filming locations in Bavaria and Austria. Reservations are required; check in at the tourist office desk or dial ☎ 08652 649 71.

The Adventures

● ON FOOT

While most international visitors consider Berchtesgaden a place of mainly historical interest, German residents come here with recreational pursuits in mind as well. In summer, **hiking** options abound in and around the National Park (see below). For a refreshing, cool stroll, take the bus out to the Kugelmühle, or marble mill, and the base of the Almbach Gorge. It's a 1½-hour walk over 27 bridges to the Theresienklause dam and, from there, a two-hour hike back to Berchtesgaden; gorge entry is €2.50.

● ON WHEELS

Mountain bikers have an extensive trail network; request the tourist office's map, *Mountainbiken Zwischen Bergen und Seen*. Bike rental is available at **M & R Brandner's** at Bergwerkstrasse 52 in Berchtesgaden, ☎ 08652 14 34, and at the Jennerbahn valley station through **Treff-Aktiv** in Königsee, ☎ 08652 667 10. **Drivers** seeking a scenic route can head up the Rossfeld Ring Road. The 16-km road crosses the mountains from Rossfeld to Obersalzberg, with numerous hiking opportunities along the way; €5 toll.

● ON WATER

Swimmers head for the **Watazmann Therme**, a muliple-pool, spa, and waterworks complex at Bergwerkstrasse 54. It's open year-round; ☎ 08652 946 40, www.watzmann-therme.de.

● IN THE AIR

For **ballooning** and **parasailing**, contact the **Outdoor Club** (see *Sports Services* below). Those seeking **mountain-top views** can choose from among several year-round lifts. Most popular are the eight-cabin Obersalzberg cable car departing from Berchtesgaden's center and the Jennerbahn gondola, which climbs from Königsee to 3,320 m/10,890 feet for spectacular lake and mountain views.

LIFT PASS PRICE SAMPLES
Winter
1-day adult pass at Jenner €24
Summer
Pedestrian round-trip to Jenner €20
Pedestrian round-trip to Obersalzberg €10

Facing page: St. Bartholomä church, Berchtesgaden, built in 1134

● ON SNOW & ICE

 In the winter, Berchtesgaden turns ski town, offering a total of 21 regional lifts and 50 km of groomed **downhill runs**. Ski bums beware, however, as lift areas are small and scattered throughout the region. Each lift area operates under separate management (read, "separate lift pass"); and there are few slopes here to challenge any skier with more than early intermediate skills. That said, Berchtesgaden is a view-blessed, low-key place to ski, and its nursery slopes will certainly please beginners. **Cross-country** skiers enjoy a good network of trails, and the **Cross-Country Center Rostwald-Aschauerweiher** offers specialist instruction; contact ☎ 08652 33 66. **Winter walkers** step out on 120 km of groomed hiking trails.

Fans of ice sports can try **curling** on the Berchtesgaden rink at 13:30 pm each Thursday, and daredevils can race by **luge** or **bobsled** down the frozen track at Königsee from October through March. For more information and reservations, contact ☎ 08652 94 78 60, www.rennbob-taxi.de. Berchtesgaden's ice rink opens for **skating** daily when special events aren't occupying the ice; check free skate times at ☎ 08652 614 05. A new **ice-climbing** tower at the Jennerbahn cable car challenges climbers, and the Outdoor Club offers lessons (see *Sports Services* below). Several **toboggan runs** draw speedsters – favorites include a 3.3-km track from the top of the Obersalzberg cable car and, at Ramsau, a 3.2-km run from the Hirscheck cable car down to Gästhaus Schwarzeck.

Sports Services, Outfitters & Guides

■ The **Alpenverein Alpine Association** has a desk at the Kurgarten in the town center at Maximilianstrasse 1. It's open Tuesday, Thursday, and Friday from 3 to 5:30 pm, offering information on the surrounding mountains.

■ The **Bergschule Berchtesgadener Land** has a range of professionally guided mountain and ski outings. Contact the Bergschule at ☎ 08652 53 71.

■ The **Outdoor Club Berchtesgaden** offers ski and mountain guiding in addition to a wide range of outings, such as ballooning, kayaking, rafting, and climbing. For more information, ☎ 08652 977 60, www.outdoor-club.de.

Where to Sleep

Berchtesgaden's hotels haven't modernized much over the years. As a group they're dark, creaky places with reasonable

HOTEL PRICES	
€.....	Up to €80 per night
€€........	€81 to €150
€€€......	€151 to €250
€€€€.......	Over €250

rates and often adorned with of hunting décor. Locations scatter throughout the valley, with few hotels directly in the center. Hotels are outnumbered by small guesthouses, private rooms, and long-stay holiday apartments.

Hotel Vier Jahreszeiten

The old **Hotel Vier Jahreszeiten** (€€-€€€) is the priciest place in town, with a four-star rating, nice views, and a location reasonably close to the old town's pedestrian area. It's at Maximilianstrasse 20; ☎ 08652 95 20, www.berchtesgaden.com/vier-jahreszeiten.

Near the center, try the country-style **Hotel Bavaria** (€€). It's 400 m/ 1,300 feet uphill from the train station, the same downhill from the town center, and offers a selection of accommodations, including family, apartment, and

Hotel Bavaria

romantic whirlpool rooms. Check in at ☎ 0852 966 10, www.
hotelbavaria.net.

The cheery **Wittelsbach** (€€)
sits at Maximilianstrasse 16,
just below old town and the
Kurpark; ☎ 0852 963 80, www.
hotel-wittlesbach.com.

On a sunny hillside directly
above the town center, the budget **Gästehaus Mitterweinfeld**
(€) offers homey, farmhouse
accommodations; contact
☎ 08652 613 74, www.
mitterweinfeld.de.

Hotel Wittelsbach

Where to Eat

Plenty of traditional
food is available in
Berchtesgaden, much
of it served from hotel dining
rooms. In the center just below

RESTAURANT COSTS	
€	Less than €10
€€	€10 to €25
€€€	Over €25

the castle, try the **Gästhof Neuhaus** (€€) for shady seats and
beer-garden fare. Around the corner, the dark, smoky **Brotzeit
Stüberl** (€) serves up traditional plates of salami, cheese, and
bread. The best beer hall in town (and well worth a visit for the
traditional food, too) is the cheery **Bräustüberl
Berchtesgaden** (€) below the old town center at
Bräuhausstrasse 13, ☎ 08652 97 67 24.

The **Echostüberl** (€€), a lakeside *gästhof* with a big terrace, is
worth a drive out to Königsee.

Where to Party

Although Berchtesgaden is a fairly reticent town,
each of its neighborhoods does have a disco. In
Berchtesgaden, try the **Beverly** at the Bahnhof; in
Schönau, head for the **Viva Dance Hall** at Panorama Park; and
in Königsee, cut loose at the **Käser Bar** on Seestrasse 2. Other
evening outlets huddle in the center along Maximilianstrasse –
try the **Pilspub**, the **Sound Café**, or **Heidi's Abend-Café**.

Folk music, and **dancing** are on order at several evening locales. In Berchtesgaden, try the **Gästhof Bräustubl**, the **Gästhof Neuhaus**. In addition, frequent **concerts** take place at the Kurpark and at various venues throughout town; check with the tourist office to see what's playing.

Where to Play

Kids enjoy tours of the **salt mines**, **boat trips** on the lake, **cable car rides**, and the **birds of prey zoo** at Obersalzberg near

the Hintereck car park. In addition, the tourist office can help arrange hiking trips and visits to a local farm. In winter, kids can attend the **ski schools**.

Festivals & Events

The **Christmas season** features several Buttnmandl parades, Klockl singers, and a Christmas market on the Schlossplatz.

Christmas and New Year's shootings – both nonviolent rifle troop salutes – fire away at 11:30 pm on both Christmas and New Year's eves in an effort to scare off the bad spirits lurking at these hours. On January 6th, the **Dreikönigstag**, or Three Kings Singers, go from door to door blessing each house.

Almabtrieb Festival

The **May Pole Celebration** kicks off spring on May first, and June brings the summer solstice and **St. John's Day**, when fires are lit in the mountains. Local residents dress in traditional *tracht* for the **Christmas Shooters Festival** on 14 July and, in August, around 1,000 pilgrims trek from Saalfelden, Austria, to the chapel at St. Bartholomew.

In late September, for **Whitsuntide**, a fun fair comes to the Triftplatz, and around St. Michael's Day, between the middle of September and the end of October, farmers bring their herds down from the Alpine pasture with all the pomp and décor of the Transhumance. This is called the **Almabtrieb Festival**.

Berchtesgaden National Park

Base Elevation: 520-2713 m/1,706-8,899 feet

National Park

A beautiful stretch of pristine wilderness, Berchtesgaden national Park encompasses 210 square km of rugged, high mountain terrain along the border of Austria.

Founded in 1978, the park strives to preserve the course of nature, allowing much of its territory to grow, decay, and burn without intervention wherever possible. Other sections of the park – those inhabited before its formation – are set aside for traditional uses, including the old electric boats on the Königsee and

Looking out at the National Park

the cattle herds grazing on high Alpine fields each summer, for example.

The park's other missions are environmental education and research. To these ends, the park maintains an exhibit in the Nationalpark Haus, and offers guided theme hikes including walk-and-talks about nature, friendship, bird calling, herbs, and geology – as well as walks in the company of a doctor or a priest. The park also supports research efforts toward the understanding and preservation of the region's land, flora, and fauna. Chamois, golden eagles, and marmots now number among the residents here.

Königsee

Adventurers access the park at Hintersee, at Wimbachbrücke, and by boat over the Königsee; from these points of departure, 230 km of hiking, biking, and climbing trails explore the region, many passing by Alpine farmers' huts that serve drinks, snacks, and fresh dairy products. One favorite 2½-hour hike leads from the shore of the Königsee to the Eiskapelle, or "ice chapel." Take the Königsee boat as far as St. Bartholomew, and then follow the trail past the chapel, up through the woods to the avalanche field below the Watzmann. Part of the ice chapel's charm is that it's always changing by season, snowfall, and temperature. If you find the ice cave, don't enter – it's prone to collapse and has, in the past, been the site of tragedy.

The Nationalpark Haus information center is at Fraziskanerplatz 7 in Berchtesgaden. It's open Monday through Saturday from 9 am-5 pm. Other info desks are at St. Bartholomew, Königsee, and Ramsau. Contact ☎ 08652 64343, www.nationalpark-berchtesgaden.de.

Königsee

Base Elevation: 603 m/1,978 feet

Lake resort

The village of Schonau am Königsee sits just a few km south of Berchtesgaden and is oft written off as "just a suburb" of the larger market town. However, there's one little corner of Schonau that rates its own coverage here – a little corner that's one of my favorite places in all of Europe.

At the southern end of the Königseerstrasse lies the tiny neighborhood of **Seefeld**, a lakeside retreat hugely popular with tour-

Seefeld (Tom McCall)

ists, yet still possessed of its natural tranquility. A handful of buildings huddles around the northern shore of the Königsee, or "king's lake," a two-mile swathe of turquoise wedged between steep, forested peaks on all sides. The pristine lake is among the few in Germany to remain undamaged by human use, as its steep walls prohibit excessive development. In addition, early efforts at preservation were successful here, and the Königssee's fleet of ferries continues to use clean electric power.

✔ Tourists understandably adore the Königsee, and crowds overrun the little village during the high summer season. Travelers visiting in the early spring and late fall shoulder seasons, however, will be blessed with a truly tranquil lake – and a scene largely all to themselves.

Driving in, you'll know you've hit town when you reach the parking toll booth and gargantuan lot to the northwest. (Guests not staying the night will have to leave their cars here.) The Jennerbahn lift climbs up the hill just beyond. Walking down Seestrasse toward the lake, visitors will find some interesting rock shops, along with a mix of kitchy souvenir stands, beer gardens, traditional dress outlets, and ice cream stands.

The lakefront road leads past the ferry docks and along the old boat huts to the east and, to the west, along the lakeshore and across a covered bridge to the Od neighborhood, home to the world's first refrigerated bobsled track – a track still in use today as both a training and World Cup competition venue.

Hungry? The **Echostüberl** on the western edge of the lake is, in my estimation, one of the finest little guesthouses in the Alps. The service is friendly, the food is hearty and traditional, and the long, lakeside terrace makes summer dining a treat. (Parents love its proximity to the tiny swimming beach: Envision happy, entertained kids within watching-and-rescuing distance of a beer garden.) In wintertime, dining moves indoors to the cozy, wood-paneled dining room.

Adventures around the Königsee span the seasons. From January through March, skiers come for the Jenner slopes, and sledders rip down the **bobsled** track at 120 km per hour. Visitors can try, too, from October through March. For more info, contact ☎ 08652 94 78 60, www.rennbob-taxi.de; €80.

Summer brings hikers, swimmers, and rowers to the area. Over 100 km of trails wind through the Schönau am Königsee area, and boat tours run year-round – although service is cut considerably during the winter (and occasionally stops altogether when the lake freezes over). Check www.bayerische-seenschifffahrt.de for current schedules.

The Königsee by Boat

A great day on the lake starts with an early departure from the docks in front of the century-old Schiffmeister Hotel. The electrically powered boats move past the tiny isle of Christlieger, then silently cross the deep, glassy lake, passing below sheer cliffs with only the wake waves audible in a scene of sublime beauty. At the far end of the lake, day-trippers can stop to look at the tiny St. Bartholomew Chapel, grab a bite to eat at the local *gästhof*, and head off by foot into the Berchtesgaden National Park.

Want to stay? The rickety old **Hotel Schiffmeister** (€€) remains

 my lodging of choice whenever I'm in the Berchtesgaten area. The 100-year-old hotel fronts the ferry docks at the northernmost end of the lake. The homey furnishings range from antique to just plain old; and the staff is low-key and friendly. Reserve a room at ☎ 08652 963 50.

The nearest full-service tourist information office is down-valley in the town of Schönau; for more information, contact ☎ 08652 1760, www.koenigsee.com.

Italy

(Italia)
Language: Italian
Population: 57,715,625
Phone Country Code: +39
Currency: Euro

Overview & Government

Italy encompasses some 301,255 square km of primarily mountainous terrain. The Alps peer down from the north, and the Appennines run down the

IN THIS CHAPTER

■ People & Culture 4
■ Milan & Northwest Italy 252
■ Venice & Northeast Italy 288

center. Less than one third of the country is plains – the largest portion of that being the Po flats in the north of the country. Major rivers include the Po, Tiber, Arno, and Adige. Italy shares its borders with France to the northwest, Switzerland and Austria to the north, and Slovenia to the northeast. Two tiny states within the country, San Marino and Vatican City, maintain their independence. Italy's boot dips into the Adriatic, Ionian, and Mediterranean seas, kicking the small islands of Sicily and Sardinia.

Italy is a democratic republic of 20 regions; the capital is Rome. Its chief of state is the president, who is elected to a seven-year term. Its head of government is the prime minister, who is appointed by the president and confirmed by parliament. The country enjoys a lively political scene, and some 50 governments have been in place since the establishment of the republic's 1948 constitution. Multiple parties vie for attention, including one of the largest Communist parties in Western Europe.

Ongoing issues concern the social disparity between the wealthy industrialized north and the poor, rural south. Two-thirds of the population now lives in the upper half of the country and the migration continues, as southerners move to the north's large cities in search of work. Further complicating matters, industry has been slow to develop in the south, for reasons of low investment capital and the influence of the Mafia crime

Alpine Italy

LIECHTENSTEIN

SWITZERLAND

AUSTRIA

SLOVENIA

CROATIA

BOSNIA

VENICE & NORTHEAST ITALY

Bolzano

DOLOMITES

Venice

Padova (Padua)

Verona

Bergamo

Brescia

MILAN & NORTHWEST ITALY

Como

Milano

Piacenza

Torino

Monaco

FRANCE

ITALY

Ligurian Sea

Adriatic Sea

N

100 MILES

100 KM

© 2007 HUNTER PUBLISHING, INC

groups. Unemployment rates have steadily declined over the past several years but still remain high at 8.7%.

People & Culture

The population of Italy is 99% Italian, an ethnic mix that includes the Germanic ancestry of the north, the Greeks, Spaniards, and Saracens in the south, and a large influence of Latin and Etruscan cultures in the central regions. Today, although Italian is the official language, other dialects are widely spoken in pocket regions of the Alps and its foothills – languages including German, French, Ladin, and Friulan.

Approximately 83% of the population is Roman Catholic, although only about a quarter of those attend mass regularly. The government eradicated the custom of an official state religion in 1985, and religious education is no longer mandated in public schools. Some 70% of the Italian population resides in urban settings, many of them in the large cities of Rome, Milan, Turin, and Naples. The average population density is approximately 192 persons per square km; however, the population is much sparser in the south than in the industrialized north.

Italy

National Holidays

January 1	New Year's Day
January 6	Epiphany
The 10 days prior to Shrove Tuesday	Carnival (Venice)
47 days prior to Easter	Shrove Tuesday
March-April	Easter
	Easter Monday
April 25	Liberation Day
June 3	Anniversary of the Republic
June 24	St. John's Day
June 29	St. Peter & St. Paul's Day
July 15	St. Rosalia's Day
15 August	Assumption Day
19 September	St. Gennaro's Day

November 1. . . . . All Saints Day
November 4 . World War I Victory Anniversary Day
December 7 . . . . St. Ambrogio's Day
December 8. . . . . Immaculate Conception
December 25. . . . . Christmas Day
December 26 . . . . St. Stephen's Day

TIMELINE	
900-500 BC	Evidence suggests a thriving Etruscan civilization
625 BC	City of Rome is founded
27 BC	Augustus named first emperor of the Roman Empire
395-1200 AD	The Roman Empire splits into numerous city states
1271-1295	17-year-old Marco Polo leaves Venice and returns 24 years later
1350-1600	The Renaissance; Art, music, architecture, and scholarship flourish in the Italian cities of Venice, Florence, and Rome
1796-1814	Italy ruled by Napoleon Bonaparte and the French Empire
1861	King Victor Emmanuel II unifies Italy
1914-1918	World War I; Italy fights with Allies, and at close of war annexes the northeastern Alpine regions of Trentino and Sud Tirol
1922	Rise of dictator Benito Mussolini, "Il Duce"
1939-1945	World War II; Italy aligns with Germany in 1940; Mussolini resigns in 1943 as Italy declares war on Germany; Mussolini imprisoned, then freed by Germans; he is captured and executed by Italians in 1945
1946	Italians vote to end monarchy; democratic republic established
1950-1970	Industrial and economic boom, particularly in the northern cities
1955	Italy joins United Nations
1984	State religion abolished
2001	Mogul Silvio Berlusconi elected Prime Minister; weathers a slew of corruption charges while in office
2006	Italians elect Romano Prodi Prime Minister and Giorgio Napolitano, a former communist, President

For more information, check with the Italian National Tourism Office at www.italiantourism.com.

MARCO POLO

Marco Polo in China

Marco Polo was born in 1254, either in or near Venice, the son of a wealthy merchant explorer. Six years later, young Marco watched his father sail off toward the Orient on a trip that would last nine years. When his father finally returned, he did so with a golden tablet one foot long and three inches wide – a symbolic ticket guaranteeing safe passage by the fearsome Kublai Khan. During his earlier travels, the elder Polo had fascinated the Khan with tales of the Pope and European culture, and the Khan had sent the Polos back to Italy with a letter addressed to the Pope. The letter requested that Pope Clement IV send other westerners who could teach the Chinese about Christianity and European technology. In 1271, the Polos set out for China with 17-year-old Marco, a trip that took 3½ years.

Upon arriving in the Mongol capital, Marco's mastery of languages earned him favor with the Khan. The ruler appointed Marco to his court, and he was sent on missions to China, Burma, and India. During this time, Marco was exposed to many new concepts, such as paper money and multi-class mail delivery. During his 17-year stay in China, he served in a variety of positions, from a seat on the Privy Council to a thug tax collector. He returned to Venice in 1295, 24 years after his departure. What treasure did he bring back from the far-off lands? The *noodle*!

Three years after returning, Captain Marco was captured on his war ship and imprisoned by Genovese. While in prison, he met the writer Rustichello of Pisa. He dictated his book to Rustichello and, upon its release, the book became an immediate bestseller. But few believed the stories were anything more than fiction, and the tome was nicknamed *Il Milione*, or *The Million Lies*. Indeed, much cultural and anthropological evidence suggests that the stories were heavily fabricated. Despite these suspicions, however, the book was popular and remained in print for a century after his death.

Milan & Northwest Italy

The plains of northwestern Italy rise steeply into Alpine terrain. Our coverage spans the westernmost section of the Alps' arch, from the Mediterranean in the south, along the French border to Mont Blanc, and then east along the lakes and the Swiss frontier. Activity here centers on the enormous city of **Milan**, which sprawls out below the Alps and the spectacular scenery surrounding **Lake Como**. Across the plain to the south of Milan, **Turin** bustles with industry – and still bustles from its stint as host of the 2006 Olympic Winter Games. The city's mountain resorts rise to the east, and the **Val d'Aosta** juts off to the northwest. Here, at the foot of Mont Blanc, steep valley walls harbor the Roman town of **Aosta**, the barren peaks of the **Gran Paradiso National Park**, and the delightful mountain resort of **Courmayeur**.

◆ Milan

(Milano)
Population: 1,500,000
Base elevation: 122 m/400 feet
Gateway city

Bustling, hustling, cosmopolitan Milano delights city-folk with its haute couture, a hoard of artistic treasures, and a cultural calendar jam-packed with opera, theater, and concert events. That said, if urbanite frenzy is not your thing, Milan may just get on your nerves.

History & Overview

Milan grew up in the heartland of the Lombardy Plains, populated by Gauls and then conquered by the Romans, who named the city "Mediolanum," or Middle Land. With the growth of Roman trade, Milan became an important center of the Roman Empire, eventually falling to the Goths and coming under Longobard rule. The city rose again in 1176 to defeat Barbarossa and gain its independence as a recognized city-state, an event followed by great growth and prosperity under

Milan & Northwest Italy

N

SWITZERLAND

FRANCE

Courmayeur
S26
Mt Rosa
Aosta
A5
St-Vincent
VAL D'AOSTA
Gran Paradiso
National Park
A32
Stupinigi
A5
Chivasso
Turin
A21
Asti
A6
A4
Biella
143
299
Verbania
Stresa
33
229
S26
Vercelli
Alessandria
S26
S26
A7
Lake Maggiore
Locarno
Varese
A8
Gallarate
A9
32
Novara
Mortara
A7
Pavia
A4
35
Milan
Menaggio
Bellaggio
Lake Como
Como
Lecco
36
Monza
9
Piacenze
A21
38
Bergamo
A4
Treviglio
Crema
415
Chiari
Crema
42
Lake Iseo
Rovato
A21
Cremona

50 MILES
50 KM

© 2007 HUNTER PUBLISHING, INC

the rule of the Visconti and Sforza dynasties – and much of Milan's visible splendor arose from this period.

Today, Milan is the capital of the province that shares its name; and, truth be told, many Italians consider it the capital of all Italy. Its economic influence on the country's finance, fashion, and trade convention industries is unmatched, yet plenty of problems still exist. The population has fled the city center for more comfortable and less expensive housing in the suburbs. But, because the public transportation network inadequately serves these new areas, the exodus at once exacerbates traffic congestion and reduces the tax revenues that might be used to alleviate the problem. All that said, once tourists get settled in the center, they shouldn't feel too much of the crunch.

The Town

The Piazza del Duomo

As the ancient city of Milan expanded, the walls ringing it were moved outward in steps. Although no longer walled, those rings remain discernible on modern maps; the outer rings are made up of streets beginning with the name *Viale*; the inner ring encircles the old city center. The **Piazza del Duomo** lies roughly at the center of this inner ring – and the city's heart beats here. On the outskirts of the inner circle are the Public Gardens and the Stazione Centrale, or central train station, to the northeast. To the northwest stretches the Castello Sforzesco complex; the wide boulevard Corso Sempione continues off toward Malpensa Airport in the northeast.

Getting Here & Around

Visitors arriving by air will fly in to either **Linate International Airport**, seven km east of the center, or **Malpensa International Airport**, 45 km northwest of the center. Malpensa services most intercontinental flights. For more information on either airport, click to www.sea-aeroporti.it. From Malpensa, take the Malpensa Express train to the North Station at Cadorna, just south of the Castello Sforzesco; from Linate, hop a bus or taxi.

Those arriving by **train** should enter the city via the Milano Centrale, Milan Central Station. Some trains, mostly short-distance commuters, use the smaller stations around the outskirts of the center.

For travel in the center, use the city's public transportation network, a reasonably efficient web of **bus** and **subway** lines. Tickets cost €1 per ride and are good for 75 minutes on any line. (They can't, however, be used again once you've left the subway.) For more information, check www.atm-mi.it.

For **taxi** service, call ☎ 02 69 69 or 02 85 85. The city's traffic woes are legendary, and rush-hour jams will send taxi fares soaring. Drivers of private vehicles should use hotel parking or one of the park-and-ride garages near outlying train and subway stations.

✔ The convenient Tourist Day Pass offers 24 or 48 hours of public transportation for €3 and €5.50, respectively. It's a good deal if you'll travel three or more legs each day. Purchase the pass at newsstands, tobacco shops, tourist offices, or from automated ticket machines.

Getting More Info

The main tourist information office is in the Piazza Duomo at Via Marconi 1; ☎ 02 725 243 01, www.milanoinfotourist.com. A second office doles out info from Central Station.

The central post office is at Piazza Cordusio 2, but the post office in the Central Station may be more convenient.

For Internet access, head to Central Station and the **Internet Café Gr@zia** at Piazza Duca d'Aosta 14.

The Sights

The Duomo (Marco Bonavoglia)

Spires jut, buttresses fly, and gargoyles loom all around. Like some ancient stalagmite cluster rising from city-center floor, the Gothic **Duomo** stands proud as Milan's most recognizable landmark. Built over four centuries, beginning in 1386, the cathedral is the third-largest church in the world after St. Peter's and the Seville Cathedral. Visitors shouldn't miss the chance to climb to the roof for a pigeon's-eye view of the city. Surrounding the **Piazza del Duomo**, or cathedral square, are the administrative buildings that were once the seats of the city's religious and civil leaders.

The **Galleria Vittorio Emanuela II** rises behind the church square. Constructed in 1877, the glass-enclosed

Galleria Vittorio Emanuela II

Galleria was among the world's first mega-malls. Today, its arcades are home to a mix of shops and fashionable cafés – all atop a colorful mosaic tile floor.

Sforza Castle

The **Sforza Castle**, or Castello Sforzesco, dominates a lovely park on the northwestern edge of the old center. The fortress was built by the ruling Visconti family in the mid-14th century, then reconstructed by the Sforza family when it took power. Attractions inside include several museums, including a sculpture collection with Michelangelo's *Pietá Rondanini*, which was left unfinished when the artist died. The museum is open Tuesday through Sunday, 9 am-5:30 pm; ☎ 02 884 637 03; €3, free on Friday after 2 pm; www.milanocastello.it.

The **Brera Art Museum**, or the Pinacoteca di Brera, is home to many Italian masterpieces dating from the 14th to the 20th centuries, including Raphael's *Marriage of the Virgin* and Bellini's *Pietá* and *Virgin and Child*. The collection is housed in the Palazzo di Brera, 17th-century palace constructed for Richini. It's at Via Brera 28 and is open Tuesday through Sunday from 8:30 am to 7:30 pm; ☎ 02 72 26 31; €5. Devotees should also see Leonardo da Vinci's *Last Supper*, known in Italian as the *Cenacolo Venciano*. The mural adorns a darkened wall of the **St. Maria delle Grazia Monastery** – travelers must call ahead to book a visit; ☎ 02 894 211 46, €8. For more information on all of Milan's museums, check www.mimu.it.

Opera City

La Scala

Milan and opera harmonize so well that the city's sophisticated audiences have become a veritable testing ground for new works by the world's greatest composers, premiering operas by Rossini, Verdi, Puccini, and Bellini, among others.

The original **Teatro alla Scala**, or La Scala Theater, first opened its curtain in 1778, and since that time has come to rank among the world's finest opera houses – and one of Milan's most treasured institutions. In fact, after much of the city had been bombed during World War II, the theater enjoyed top priority for reconstruction and reopened its stage just a year later in 1946. Today, the freshly renovated interior of the horseshoe-shaped auditorium still gleams in splendid red velvet and gilded carved wood.

Opera buffs should check out **La Scala Theater Museum**; it displays a large collection of artifacts depicting the theater's distinguished history. The theater is just north of the Duomo along the Via Manzoni. For more information on all things La Scala, check in at ☎ 02 88 792 473, www.teatroallascala.org.

Where to Sleep

Interestingly situated in a 15th-century convent, the **Four Seasons** (€€€€) remains our favorite luxury house here. Its

HOTEL PRICES

€..... Up to €80 per night
€€ .... €81 to €150
€€€...... €151 to €250
€€€€....... Over €250

The Four Seasons

peaceful arcades, light beige color schemes, and excellent dining create a perfect place to unwind; ☎ 02 770 88, www.fourseasons.com/milan.

Hotel Spadari al Duomo (€€€-€€€€) rates highly among Milan's art-loving set. The hotel is set in an early 20th-century palazzo and decked out with all manner of modern art, much of it contrived by local artists; ☎ 02 720 023 71, www.spadarihotel.com.

The **Hotel Manzoni** (€€€) enjoys a quiet location near the gardens, tucked off a side street just one block away from the Four Seasons. Inside, the residential décor is homey enough; ☎ 02 760 057 00, www.hotelmanzoni.com.

Room in the Spadari

At a busy location, but a great choice for environmentalists, the **Hotel Ariston** (€€€) is Milan's greenest hostelry. Clean-cut and fresh, the Ariston features lots of natural materials, a meticulous recycling program, a bio-breakfast buffet, and loaner bikes; ☎ 02 720 005 56, www.brerahotels.com.

Hotel London (€€) sits in the center just a short walk from the Piazza Castello and La Scala Theater. Its small lobby features a cozy fire-

Hotel London

Italy

place nook; ☎ 02 720 201 66, www.traveleurope.it/
hotellondon.it.

Where to Eat

Milan offers diners the
same wide-ranging op-
tions as do other cities
of this size.

RESTAURANT COSTS	
€ . . . . Less than €10	
€€ . . . . €10 to €25	
€€€ . . . . Over €25	

The venerable **Cracco Peck**
(€€€) tops the city's charts for gourmet fare. The chef here
specializes in original approaches to Italian cuisine; book a table at ☎ 02 876 774. Also on the upscale list is **Savini** (€€€),
a grand gourmet house first opened in 1867. It's found under
the glass dome of the Galleria Via Emanuele; reserve at ☎ 02
720 034 33.

Literary folks should stop in amid the antique dealers at
Bagutta (€€) at via Bagutta 14. The historic trattoria was once
patronized by a group of writers and publishers that created the
Bagutta Literary Prize there. Tuscan food is on the menu, and
there's summertime seating in the garden; reserve at ☎ 02 760
009 02.

Al Mercante (€€) serves up traditional fare amid the medieval
ambiance of Piazza Mercanti; ☎ 02 805 21 98. At Umbria 80,
the **Trattoria Masuelli** (€€) – also known as the San Marco –
dishes out delish regional specialties amid simple traditional
décor; ☎ 02 551 841 38.

Where to Party

In addition to the highbrow cultural performances
staged at La Scala and the city's many other play-
houses, cosmopolitan Milan offers a predictably
lively and diverse nightlife. For general revelry – bars, cafés,
discos, and such – try the **Brera district** just north of the center.
Lots of good hang-outs line the streets. For a low-key artsy ambiance, try **Jamaica** at Via Brera. For late-night disco action,
head to **La Banque**, near the La Scala – it has a modern interior
and was once actually a bank; the massive weekend-only
Alcatraz; or the always fashionable **Shocking Club** at Porta
Nuova.

For live concerts and shows, try **Binario Zero** at Lambertenghi or the **Magazzini Generali**, an old warehouse on Via Pietrasanta. The **Blues House** posts a solid schedule of live blues performances, and **Zelig** offers cabaret-style entertainment featuring some top names in comedy.

Festivals & Events

 As one of Europe's premier trade fair cities, Milan sees many more convention events than festivals. The city kicks off winter with the **Carnevale Ambrosiano**, a

At the Carnevale Ambrosiano

masked pre-Lenten celebration with a number of related balls and events.

In March, the **Milano-San Remo** cycling races depart, and the **MODIT Fashion Fair** presents designers' new fall fashion lines. April brings the **Fiera dei Fiori**, or the Festival of Flowers, to Via Moscova in an explosion of spring color.

Racing at Monza

The **Festa del Naviglio** market and folklore fest comes to town on the first Sunday in June and, in September, the auto racing world's eyes turn to the **Gran Premio di Monza**. October sees two famed trade events, the **Smau Technology Fair** and the **MODIT Fashion Fair** with its presentations of spring and summer couture. In December the **Oh bej Oh bej Festival** draws market stalls to Sant' Ambrogio on the 7th, and **La Scala** launches its opera, ballet, and theater season.

Lake Como

Base Elevation: 201 m/659 feet
Lake resort

Lake Como

The *Lago di Como* has long been Milan's backyard beach. With mountain walls rising all around, an efficient ferry system, and steeply stacked villages dotting the shore, its enticements are many.

Several lakes glisten along the foothills of the northern Italian Alps. Lining up from west to east are lakes **Orta**, **Maggiore**, **Varese**, **Lugano**, **Como**, **Iseo**, and **Garda** – and many smaller lakes scatter among these. Every one has its own distinct allure, and each draws crowds from the lower Italian plains during the hot summer months. Although the region's attractions could alone fill a book, we'll tease you with just one adventure here.

The narrow, 45-km-long body of water that makes up Lake Como stretches into the Alps in an inverted 'Y' shape, anchored at its southern end by the towns of Como and Lecco and at its northern end by Sorico. Midway up the lake, at the intersection

Bellagio

of the 'Y', rests lovely **Bellagio**. The drive around Lake Como totals 170 km, much of the eastern shore through tunnels. From the town of Como, a nice day-trip can loop by either boat or car around the southwestern leg of the lake. I follow that route below.

The town of **Como** lies at the lake's southwestern tip, approximately 50 km north of Milan. The bustling town boasts a lovely lakefront square, the Piazza Cavour; a 14th- century Gothic church; and a ferryboat hub whence boats zigzag up to Bellagio

Villa d'Este, Cernobbio

and beyond. Traveling north alongside the western shore of the lake, **Cernobbio** is home to the fabulous Villa d'Este, a 16th-century villa that's now the region's most famous hotel – an ideal locale for a memorable lunch. Farther north still is the picturesque village of **Tremezzo**, site of the Villa Carlotta. Lovingly tended gardens srround the 18th-century villa, its beds harboring some 500 species of plants – over 150 types of rhododendrons and azaleas alone. From here, day-trippers should cross by ferry to Bellagio, "pearl of Lake Como." The old village nestles below the northwestern tip of the Punte Spartivento, its villas stacking up the hillside, its cobblestone alleys winding between. Visitors enjoy sweeping lake views and a number of touristy shops, but "sights" here are meager – just two outstanding villas, the Villa Melzi d'Eryl to the south and the Villa Serbelloni to the north.

THE GRAND DAMES OF LAKE COMO

Two famous villa hotels face off across the southwestern leg of Lake Como.

First opened as a hotel in 1873, the neoclassical **Villa Serbelloni** (€€€€) enjoys an enviable position on a lakefront promontory. It's a low-keyplace, but one where marble pillars support coffered ceilings, French tapestries adorn walls, and Persian carpets muffle squeaky wooden floors. The hotel is open from April through mid-Novem-

Villa Serbelloni dining room

ber. For room or restaurant reservations, contact ☎ 031 95 15 29, www.villaserbelloni.it.

Villa d'Este

Across Lake Como at Cernobbio, the **Villa d'Este** (€€€€) is the most famous of the lake district hotels. Built in 1568 by Tolomeo Gallio, Cardinal of Como, the villa changed hands several times before becoming a hotel in 1873. The luxurious villa rests in 25 acres of gardens, fronting the lake and Italy's only floating swimming pool. The cuisine is excellent; the ambiance purely formal. For reservations, contact ☎ 031 34 88 35, www.villadeste.com.

 Want to stay? If you don't wait to shell out the bucks for either of the grand hotels above – or if you simply prefer low-key accommodations – book a room at the

Hotel Florence (€€-€€€) in Bellagio. The 18th-century hotel has dressy rooms, a cozy restaurant, and a vine-strewn terrace with huge lake views. Reserve at ☎ 031 95 0342, www.hotel-florencebellagio.it.

For more information on Lake Como, contact

Hotel Florence terrace

Italy

the tourist office at Piazza Cavour 17; ☎ 031 26 97 12, www.lakecomo.org.

Turin

(Torino)
Population: 908,000
Base Elevation: 240 m/787 feet
Tourist city

Fresh off its stint as host of the XX Winter Olympic Games, Turin sparkles with fresh restorations, new development, and an influx of sports-minded visitors. Although much of the Olympic action took place in the mountains some 100 km east of here, this buzzing city merits a quick stop for its Baroque architecture, its cathedral, and its significance in Italian history.

Turin got its start as a capital of the Taurin, a Celtic tribe, but in the 11th century passed under the control of the House of Savoy for what was to be almost 900 years. The city's heyday came in the early 1700s, when that ruling family erected many of Turin's most magnificent buildings. In the years that followed, the House of Savoy was instrumental in the unification of Italy, patriarch Victor Emmanuel II was named king in 1861, and the family ruled all of Italy until 1946, when the Italian Republic was born.

Today, modern Turin is home to a dynasty of another sort – the Fiat car company thrives here, supporting many of the city's nearly one million residents. The city continues to bask in the memory of its royal heritage, as well, its vast cultural wealth apparent in its rich Baroque architecture and 18th-century monuments. Visitors stroll the 14th-century **Piazza Castello**, nucleus of the old city and home to many cafés, shops, and museums. Several palaces and

The Mole Antonelliana (Kevin Hutchinson)

Duomo di San Giovanni

squares embellish the center, and the 15th-century cathedral, the **Duomo di San Giovanni**, rises to the north. The **Mole Antonelliana** the city's favorite landmark, climbs lacily toward the ski in the east. For a lovely view of the city, ride the elevator to the top.

THE SHROUD OF TURIN

While many cathedrals house religious artifacts, Turin's Duomo di San Giovanni holds claim to Christendom's most notorious relic, The Shroud of Turin. Passed down for centuries through the House of Savoy, the 14.5-foot strip of cloth shows a faint image of the corpse it once wrapped, a corpse believed by many to be the dead body of Christ. Photographic negatives taken in 1898 made the image on the burial cloth clearer, revealing a crown of thorns and wounds to the hands, feet, side, and head.

The shroud officially passed into the hands of the church upon the 1983 death of Umberto II of Savoy, at which point it was carbon-dated by a worldwide team of experts. Disappointingly, they concluded that the cloth was made sometime between the 13th and 14th centuries. Nonetheless, examination continues, and the burial cloth and its mysterious image remains an icon of veneration. The shroud rests in the cathedral but only rarely is it displayed to the public. When it is on display, you'll know it – thousands of pilgrims throng the city.

Italy

Want to stay? The cheery **Hotel Victoria** (€€-€€€) remains the front-runner of the mid-priced houses here. Popular with international visitor, the central city hotel offers reasonable comfort amid considerable

Hotel Victoria

charm, each room individually decorated. Inquire at ☎ 011 561 19 09, www.hotelvictoria-torino.com.

 For more information, check in at the tourist office at the Piazza Castello or contact ☎ 011 53 59 01, www. turismotorino.org.

Torino 2006: Sampling the Sites

Sestriere

Turin played host to the XX Winter Olympic Games in 2006 from 10-26 February. During these 17 days, 2,573 athletes from 80 nations competed in 15 sporting disciplines. More than 1 million spectators, 9,400 journalists, and 18,000 volunteers participated. The games revolved around 13 competition venues and three Olympic Villages, one each in Turin, Setriere, and Bardonecchia. In addition to the sights of the city center, Turin's mountain resorts are worth a look.

The Alpine village of **Sestriere** staged the Alpine Skiing events during the Winter Games. Approximately 100 km west of Turin, Sestriere's sporting facilities are linked with the Milky Way region and currently include 92 lifts and 400 km of runs spanning the border of Italy and France. Although long known as an Alpine eyesore, the village made some aesthetic improvements in preparation for the Olympics, and its new-and-improved façade does to some degree counter its prior reputation. (Its experimental architecture, however, still lacks the charm of the town's more traditional neighbors to the north.) If you're in Sestriere in winter, two event venues merit attention: Mount Sises hosted the Olympic giant slalom course, and the Borgata ran the men's super-G, downhill, and downhill/slalom combined. For more info on Sestriere, contact www.sestriere.it.

Bardonecchia

Snowboarders should head for **Bardonecchia**, 96 km west of Turin, site of the third Olympic Village and host of all Olympic snowboarding events. The small town lies along the French-Italian border and offers access to 23 lifts and 140 km of mostly easy runs. For those wishing to check out some Olympic history, Course 23 was extended for use as the racing run, and a half-pipe was constructed on Course 24. Contact www.comune.bardonecchia.to.it for more info.

◆ Courmayeur

Population: 3,000

Base elevation: 1,224 m/4,015 feet

Mountain resort village

Mont Blanc beckons at the end of the Val d'Aosta, the ancient village of Courmayeur nestling at its foot. Once a roadside rest stop on the Roman map, Courmayeur is today the winter-weekend playground of northeastern Italy's elite. They come to socialize, shop, ski, and dine – but there's a less frivolous crowd here, too. Today, as in days past, Courmayeur welcomes heartier adventurers, those here to conquer mountain summits, trek glacial ice-beds, scale granite walls, climb frozen water-falls, and heli-drop into some of Europe's most extreme wilderness.

History & Orientation

Ascending Mont Blanc, with Courmayeur & the Val d'Aosta below (Krista Dana)

Courmayeur got its start as a thoroughfare along the Roman trans-alpine trade route between the regions that are now Italy and France. After its first church was built around the eighth century, the area saw continued growth and eventually fell under the rule of the House of Savoy. Courmayeur gradually morphed from a 14th-century iron-mining center to an 18th-century spa town, and from there, to a 19th-century mountaineering center. Skiers first took to local slopes in the early 1900s and by mid-century had erected the first lifts, successfully transforming Courmayeur from a summer-only playground to a year-round mountain resort.

Courmayeur nestles at the foot of **Mont Blanc**, Europe's highest mountain. The **Val d'Aosta** stretches southeast toward Milan and Turin, and to the north, **Val Ferret** and **Val Veny** split off at **Entrèves**, running a short distance along the white mountain's southeastern base. To the south, the **Vallée de la Thuile** leads to the resort of **La Thuile** and, in the summer, up and over the **Petit St. Bernard Pass** into the **French Tarantaise**.

The Town

Courmayeur

The village of Courmayeur sprawls along the eastern riverbank of the Dora Baltea. Across the river, the hamlet of Dolonne climbs up the western foothills. Courmayeur centers on the Piazzale Monte Bianco – a busy traffic circle fronting the main valley road, the bus station, and the tourist office. The old center is just up the hill, running north and south along the Via Roma on either side of the old church. This pedestrian zone is home to the valley's most inviting shops, restaurants, and bars. Anchoring the outskirts is the Courmayeur Cable Car to the south, the sports center in Dolonne to the west, and the hamlets of Larzey and La Saxe to the north.

Getting Here & Around

 Those arriving by **air** should fly in to Geneva, 100 km away via the Mont Blanc Tunnel; Turin, 150 km south; or Milan, 190 km east. **Bus** transfers run Saturday and Sunday from Milan's Malpensa Airport; contact ☎ 0165 773 240 for reservations. **Train** travelers can get as far as Pre-St. Didier on rail but must transfer to bus to get to Courmayeur. The main bus station hubs near the tourist office at Piazzale Monte Bianco. For **taxi** service, dial ☎ 0165 842 960.

The Petit St. Bernard Pass road

The quickest **driving** route to Courmayeur is via one of three tunnels that access the valley year-round: the new Val d'Aosta autostrada tunnel from Milan and Turin, the newly reopened Mont Blanc tunnel from Chamonix, France, or the Grand St. Bernard Tunnel from Switzerland. Those wishing to take their time can meander into the valley via three scenic, winding routes: the old road up the valley, which remains open year round; the Grand St. Bernard Pass road from the Swiss Valais; and the Petit St. Bernard Pass road from the French Tarantaise. These final two routes are open during summer only.

Mountain transportation departs for Plan Checrouit from two bases, one at the southern side of town and the other from Entrèves, just up-valley. A new cable car is in the works. Once complete, it will provide access between Dolonne and Plan

Checrouit. The cable car to Punta Helbronner and France departs from the village of La Palud, one hairpin curve before the entrance to the Mont Blanc Tunnel. For more information on Courmayeur's cableways, see www.courmayeur-montblanc. com; for more information on the Mont Blanc Cable Car, go to www.montebianco.com.

LIFT PASS PRICE SAMPLES	
Winter	
1-day adult	€40
6-day adult	€195
Pedestrian round-trip to Helbronner	€35
Summer	
Pedestrian round-trip to Helbronner	€35

Getting More Info

The **Monte Bianco Tourist Information Office** is at the Piazzale Monte Bianco 13, just behind the traffic circle (possibly still a construction zone) when you first enter town. For more info, contact ☎ 0165 842 060, www.aiat-monte-blanco.com.

The post office is near the tourist office at the Piazzale Monte Bianco.

For Internet access, try **Planet Discobar** at the sports center or, in town, the **Bar Tavola Calda Ziggy** at Via Marconi 15.

The Sights

Courmayeur is a resort town with lots of beauty to gaze at but very few "sights" to see. **Mont Blanc** is, of course, the village's primary draw. For more information on how to explore it, see *Adventures* below. Alpine enthusiasts should check out the small **Alpine Museum** at Piazza Henry 2, and all visitors should spend some time exploring the **Via Roma**, the village's oldest street and now its primary entertainment district. Wondering what it might have been like before all the shops set in? Head across the valley to **Dolonne**, where the oft-ignored **Via della Vittoria** retains its old-world residential charm.

Looking out at Mont Blanc from Brevent (Yann Forget)

The Adventures

● MONT BLANC

One Mountain, Two Countries, Six Cableways & a Bus

Both tourists and adventurers come to Courmayeur to experience Mont Blanc – no visitor should miss a trip up. The mountain has much to offer at each of its cableway stages, and travelers can choose among a variety of lift tickets ranging from a quick trip up Mont Frety to a full day's excursion into France. Below, I tell you what's where on Mont Blanc.

The Mont Blanc Cable Car departs from 1,370 m/4,494 feet at La Palud, a village at the head of the valley just north of Entrèves, approximately four km north of Courmayeur. (Local buses make the trip.) The first stage of the Mont Blanc ascent is to Mont Fréty at 2,173 m/7,127 feet. Here, visitors can enjoy a *prosecco* or a hearty meal at the Pavillon Restaurant – or sunbathe in a rented lounge chair on the panoramic terrace. In summer, hikers enjoy several paths, and botanists stroll through the Saussurea Alpine Garden, home to more than 800 species of plants.

From Mont Fréty, a second cable car climbs to Réfuge Torino at 3,375 m/11,070 feet, and a third cable car – this one rather small – ascends to 3,462 m/11,355 feet at Punta Helbronner, the last mountain station on the Italian side of the border. Visitors enjoy the Rock Crystal Museum; marvel at the mountain's jutting needles, or *aiguilles*; or rope up and trek across the glacier with prearranged mountain guides. In winter, experienced skiers and snowboarders venture off-piste from here, down the mountain toward Toula or down the Vallée Blanche into France.

In summer, visitors can opt to cross from Punta Helbronner into France via the Panoramic Mont Blanc Gondola, a triple gondola that dangles its way across the glacial ice and up to the Aiguille du Midi at 3,842 m12,602 feet. The trip takes 30 minutes and covers five km. From there, the magnificent Aiguille Cable Car descends via the Plan de l'Aiguille at 2,137 m/7,000 feet into the outskirts of Chamonix. Buses depart Chamonix for Courmayeur, making the 40-minute trip through the newly reopened Mont Blanc Tunnel. Buses run daily; be sure to check the current schedule before you go.

✔ If you'd rather go with a package deal and a prearranged return bus, inquire at the tourist office about the Trans Mont Blanc Excursion. It currently runs i82 for adults; www.montebianco.com.

● **ON FOOT**

The Courmayeur area enjoys around 300 km of maintained hiking trails, and a good collection of mountain restaurants and refuges offer trailside hospitality. Favorite valley hikes include trails along the Val Ferret, the Val Veny, and Mont Blanc foothills, and numerous trails are easily accessed via the region's summertime cable car service.

One lovely, short walk leads from Arnouva at the end of the Val Ferret road around the Pré de Bard. The two-hour route loops by the Combette Gorge, takes in glacier views, and passes by the cozy Elena, a mountain refuge open mid-June through mid-September. In addition to a good hiking map, pick up the tourist office's brochure, *Mountain Huts and Bivouacs in Aosta Valley,* before you set out.

For more extreme mountaineering action, such as climbing, glacier-trekking, and canyoning, contact the **Courmayeur's Alpine Guides Association** – see *Sports Services* below.

✔ The cable cars in the Courmayeur area close at lunch-time for approximately one to 1½ hours, normally from about 1 pm. But, if you have to wait it out on the mountain, there are in most cases restaurants open at the upper lift stations.

● IN WATER

 In summer, swimmers hop a lift or hike up to the **Alpine swimming pool** at Plan Chercrouit. Here, there are big valley views, a restaurant, and a playground. The pool is open daily from late June through late August, 10:30 am-4:45 pm; entry is €10, or €16 with roundtrip lift ticket. **Canyoning** excursions are organized by the Alpine Guide Association (see *Sports Services* below).

Fishing is technically an option, but the steep rates will make it prohibitive for most. For those wanting to give it a try, the Val Ferret Fishing Club has more information regarding sites, seasons, and regulations. Several hotels and *refugi* sell the pricey permits – a single day permit is €36, and the season runs from May to November. For more information, contact the **Val Ferret Fishing Club** at ☎ 0348 604 65 05, www.valferretfishingclub.com.

● ON WHEELS

 Mountain biking trails wind through each of the local valleys, and steeper technical routes slice down the mountainsides from the upper lift stations. The place to go for more information is M.B. Adventure, a specialist mountain-biking operation in La Salle on the northern side of town. They offer advice, maps, and organized outings, including some rip-roaring biking adventures involving helicopters, rafts, and snowy trails. For more info, contact **M.B. Adventure** at ☎ 0347 241 76 67, www.mbaventure.it. For mountain bike rental in the center, head for **Lo Caraco** at Via Roma 150, ☎ 0165 844 152.

● ON SNOW & ICE

 Courmayeur operates 23 lifts and grooms 100 km of **skiing** runs graded 20% easy, 70% intermediate, and 10% difficult. These numbers deceive, however, as experts find plenty of off-piste activity. The resort is small but offers a nice selection of trails. Beginners enjoy two free lifts, the Chiecco and Tzaly lifts, and intermediates have run of most of the mountain. Advanced skiers and snowboarders head for the long off-piste routes below Crest d'Arp – and venture farther backcountry by helicopter. Both the ski school and the Alpine Guides Association offer off-piste guiding and instruction, including the popular day-trip from Punte Helbronner, down the Vallée Blanche, and into Courmayeur, France.

Helicopter Drops

 The Val d'Aosta is one of Europe's premier heli-skiing and heli-boarding destinations – the region's steep, inaccessible terrain and Italy's laidback laws combine to make it so. A wide range of drops is offered, including extreme excursions to Mont Fortin and less demanding tours to the Pyramides Calcaires. Participants must have advanced skills and be comfortable skiing on off-piste terrain, and a guide or instructor must accompany each group.

For more information and reservations, contact **Mr. Massimo Rey** at ☎ 0338 679 06 36 or the **Alpine Guides Association** in Courmayeur; ☎ 0165 842 064, www.guidecourmayeur.com. Reservations must be confirmed no later than 6:30 pm the evening prior to your excursion.

In addition to skiing and boarding, wintertime visitors **walk** on maintained trails, **ice-skate** at the sports center, and **snow shoe** between cozy mountain huts. **Cross-country skiers** enjoy groomed loipe along the river at Val Ferret, including loops from three to 30 km in length. The Alpine Guides Association runs high-mountain **Alpine treks**, snowshoeing excursions, and **ice climbing** courses (kids can start from age seven). For more information, see *Sports Services* below.

Italy

Sports Services, Outfitters & Guides

The **Courmayeur Alpine Guides Association**, or the Societá delle Guide di Courmayeur, has been leading excursions on rock, dirt, and ice since 1850. Summertime options including glacier treks, free and equipped climbs, and mountaineering courses. In winter, the guides run ski tours all over the region, including popular off-piste runs down the Vallée Blanche in France. For more info, contact ☎ 0165 842 064, www.guidecourmayeur.com.

The **Forum Sports Center** offers a wide range of year-round sporting activities and frequent special events. Its attractions include an ice rink, tennis, indoor golf, ping-pong, video games, a nursery, and even a disco. It's across the river in Dolonne; for more info contact ☎ 0165 844 096, www.sportcourmayeur.com.

The **Monte Bianco Ski School** operates a good range of courses – from first-timer classes to off-piste guided excursions. For more information and reservations, contact ☎ 0165 842 477; www.scuolascimontebianco.com.

Where to Sleep

Courmayeur has a good selection of hotels, although most tend to be pricey for what you get. At the upper end of the luxury scale, I remain a fan of the **Gallia Gran Baita** (€€€-€€€€). Although a long

Gallia Gran Baita

walk from the center, the hotel has a professional staff and an excellent wellness center. The décor is country-cozy fresh, and the views from every balcony are astounding. Inquire at ☎ 0165 844 040, www.sogliahotels.com.

The **Hotel Les Jumeaux** (€€€-€€€€) has a location right at the Courmayeur cable car. The large chalet has nice views from its balconies as well. For more information, check in at ☎ 0165 844 122.

The **Hotel Courmayeur** (€€-€€€) has cozy rooms 200 m/

Les Jumeaux

650 feet from the central cable car – and a fireplace in its lounge. Reserve at ☎ 0165 846 732, www.hotel-courmayeur.com.

The old **Hotel Crampon** (€€) has inviting décor and small rooms just behind the

Hotel Courmayeur

tourist office, a short walk to the center; ☎ 0165 842 385, www.crampon.it.

Italy

HOTEL PRICES	
€	Up to €80 per night
€€	€81 to €150
€€€	€151 to €250
€€€€	Over €250

Hotel Edelweiss (€€) has a great location at the back of old town. Rooms are basic, but each has its own bath, and the private hotel garden makes a fine summer retreat; ☎ 0165 841590, www.albergoedelweiss.it.

In the center of La Palud, approximately four km north of Courmayeur, the **Albergo Delle Funivia** (€) shares a square with the Mont Blanc cable car valley station. The chalet is a simple, homey affair, with residential décor and a restaurant downstairs. Book at ☎ 0165 899 24, www.hotelfunivia.com.

Where to Eat

Courmayeur boasts restaurants of a generally high caliber, a collection well suited to the village's discerning city crowds. At Via Marconi 54, the **Pierre Alexis 1877** (€€€€) does good set

RESTAURANT COSTS	
€	Less than €10
€€	€10 to €25
€€€	Over €25

menus, with creative takes on traditional cuisine. Book a table at ☎ 0165 844 403.

For traditional specialties, try the characteristic **Leone Rosso** (€€). Its stone and wood house is down an ally at 73 Via Roma – look for the red lion sign out front; ☎ 0165 846 726.

Also good, particularly for a summer lunch, is the **Mont Fréty** (€€) at Strada Regionale 21. Garden dining proves a treat, with tables scattered on the lawn around a cheerful little fountain. Pizzas and other traditional dishes fill the menu; ☎ 0165 841 786.

> ✔ If you're looking for a memorable night out and are willing to drive or cab it a bit, head for the **Maison de Filippo** (€€€) in Entrèves, three km up the valley. It's a fixed-price affair, but with a dozen hors d'oeuvres and four courses on the way, you're bound to find something you like. It's popular, so reserve at ☎ 0165 869 797, www.lamaison.com, €40.

For pizza, try **La Terrazza** (€-€€) at Via Circonvallazione 73 or, at Via Roma 86, the cozy **Ancien Casino** (€-€€). I like **Pan Per Focaccia** (€), both for the focaccia and the delish crêpes as well. It sits charmingly on Via Rue Dei Giardini, a tiny passage off Via Roma.

Where to Party

For a town this small, Courmayeur offers a good selection of nightlife. In winter, the evening begins with low-key après-ski in the cafés along the Via Roma. The **Caffe della Posta** at Via Roma 51 draws a casual crowd around the fireplace in its back room; the nearby **Café Bar des Guides** is comfy, too, with sofa chairs and sports on TV. The **Bar Roma** offers drinks and snacks, the **American Bar** gets lively, and the Spanish **Le Prive**, just above, has a good selection of both drinks and *tapas*.

For late-night action, try the **Planet Discobar** in the sports center, **Poppy's** at town center, or **Jimmy's Night Café** at the Hotel Astoria.

Where to Play

Courmayeur provides more **childcare** opportunities than most Italian resorts. The **Plan Checrouit** nursery accepts children from six months of age, the **Kinderheim** at the sports center accepts children from nine months of age, and the tourist office can help arrange **babysitters**. In addition to the winter activities arranged by the **ski school**, families enjoy **organized summer programs** and the area's hiking, biking, and cable car rides. Children love the Plan Checrouit **Alpine swimming pool**, and there's a **playground** there as well.

THE TWO SAINT BERNARDS

Two mountain roads climb out of the Val d'Aosta, each pass confusingly known as the St. Bernard. The Petit St. Bernard heads into France; the Grand St. Bernard climbs into Switzerland.

The road through Petit St. Bernard Pass

The route differentiated as the **Petit** or **Piccolo St. Bernard** – in English the Little St. Bernard – heads southwest toward France and the Tarantaise region. Since ancient times, this road has been a hotly contested strategic trade route through the high Alps; even Hannibal saw it as fit for his elephants.

From just south of Courmayeur, thisroad climbs through La Thuile Valley and out of Italy, passing by the **Cromlech**, or "Hannibal's Circle," an ancient Celtic monument of carefully laid stone that remains an object of much archeological inquiry. The 10th-century **Pilgrim's Hospice** and the **Chanousia** botanical gardens lie farther along. For a lunch break, try the **Bar Ristorante San Bernardo** at 2,200 m/7,216 feet. It has good traditional food, including fondue and raclette. Six simple guest rooms offer accommodations.

Grand St. Bernard Pass (Nolege)

The route called the **Grand St. Bernard**, or the Great St. Bernard, climbs from the town of Aosta north into Switzerland and the region of Valais. While a tunnel keeps the route open throughout the year, the more interesting summer option is the **Col du St. Bernard** mountain road. The pass has long been an important north-south transalpine route – as early as 58 BC, Julius Caesar ordered an army legion over the trail, and the first automobile path opened here in 1905. Aside from the stunning scenery, the route's main attraction is just across the Swiss border. The **Great St. Bernard Hospice** offers Christian hospitality amid some of the Alps' most inhospitable terrain. Since the 11th century, the monks here have sheltered Alpine travelers, on many occasions rescuing stranded walkers with the help of the hospice's enormous dogs, a canine breed we know as the

Great St. Bernard Hospice, 8,200 feet elevation (M. Darbellay)

St. Bernard. Visitors should tour the hospice museum for its fascinating documentation of local history – and, of course, walk through the kennels, summer home of the legendary hospice dogs. Fancy a pup? Plunk down €2,000 to put your name on the waiting list.

It's worth planning lunchtime around a stop at **Praz d'Arc**, up above the tree line on the Italian side of the Grand St. Bernard route. Here, an Alpine dairy offers farm-made cheese, bread, salami, and honey. At the bar inside, requesting piatti misti for the number of people in your party will net you a communal basket of fresh bread and a plate heaped with a mix of cheese and meats. It's all ideally accompanied with a pitcher of red wine and glasses of water from the trough fountain out front.

Aosta

Population: 34,270
Base Elevation: 583 m/1,912 feet
Tourist town

With a 5,000-year history and some of Italy's finest Roman ruins, Aosta deserves more attention than it gets.

Most tourists blow by Aosta town en route to the more famous sights beyond – and I suspect that of those few who do drive in, many leave in frustration after unsuccessfully searching for the

Aosta (Tinelot Wittermans)

old town and/or a place to park. Our advice is this: If at all possible, arrive by train, as the station sits flush against the old town's southern wall. If arriving by car, follow the signs to the

Remnants of ancient walls & tower of Sant'Orso

train station, or *stazione*, where there are several lots nearby.

A bustling town of over 11,000 people, Aosta lies at the foot of Mont Emilius and at the intersection of the Aosta, Grand St. Bernard, and Cogne valleys. Its walled, rectangular old town has a roughly east-west orientation, parallel to the train tracks on the western

Piazza Chanoux

bank of the Torrente Buthier River. The **Piazza Chanoux** and its grand **Municipio** palace comprise the old town's nucleus and the center of the car-free shopping area. From here, cobbled alleys lead off in several directions. Pick up a map from the square's tourist office before you set out; it has detailed information in English.

From the northeast corner of the Municipio on Piazza Chanoux, tourists head down the tiny Via Charrey – past the trash dumpsters along a residential back alley – and, amusingly, stumble upon the magnificent first-century ruins of the **Roman Theater**.

Excavation and preservation work continues (and they're fairly serious about all those posted rules).

South along the town wall is the massive **Porta Pretoria** and, be-

The Roman Theater

yond, the charming **Via Sant Anselmo**, which leads east to the **Roman Arch**. The **Roman Amphitheater** occupies the northeastern corner of town. Farther west along the northern wall are the Renaissance-era **Palazzo Roncas**, the **Regional Museum of Archeology**, and – slightly south – the **Cathedral of the Assunta** with its splendidly ornate central portal.

Portal, Cathedral of the Assunta

 Want to stay? Aosta's central accommodations are less than enticing. A five-minute drive out, however, is the **Hotel Milleluci** (€€-€€€). The renovated farm complex retains its rustic charm yet offers a host of little luxuries, including a lovely freeform pool, a health center, and loads of cozy country charm. Check in at ☎ 0165235278; www.hotelmilleluci.com.

 For more information drop by the tourist office in the old town center at the Piazza Chanoux; ☎ 0165 333 52, www.aiataosta.com.

Gran Paradiso National Park

(Il Parco Nationale del Gran Paradiso)
Base Elevation: 1,891 m/6,202 feet
National Park

Italy's most rugged national park, this reserve draws adventurers year-round. Within the park's bounds, climbers explore rock faces and summit the Gran Paradiso, riders take to equestrian trails, and walkers enjoy routes ranging from a few hours to a few days.

The Gran Paradiso National Park nestles in the northwesternmost corner of Italy, straddling the provincial borders of Aosta

Overview of Gran Paradiso National Park (M. Klüber Fotografie)

and Piemonte and edging the French frontier and La Vanoise National Park just west. At its center, the Gran Paradiso Massif rises 4,061 m/13,172 feet, the highest peak to fall entirely within Italian borders. The region was for centuries an ancient transalpine crossroads and, in the mid-19th century, the land here became the royal hunting grounds of the House of Savoy. The Gran Paradiso National Park was established in 1922 with a royal land grant donated to protect the rapidly disappearing ibex.

✔ **Ibex** are both skittish and fast, so many visitors leave the park without ever spotting one. The best time to view them is during evening hours, when they slow down to graze along the high-Alpine pastures.

In winter, cross-country skiers tour high glacier trails or take to the loipe along the valleys, and snowshoers venture into the woods and up mountain paths. Observant visitors are likely to see ibex, chamois, marmots, and eagles. The park is accessed via the Val d'Aosta and any of three side-valleys, **Valgrisenche** to the west, **Rhemes** in the middle, and **Valsavarenche** to the east.

We prefer to explore the park from the Valsavarenche. The valley centers on the small community of **Degioz**, where the Na-

Capra ibex mother and baby (Roberto Caucino)

tional Park Information Center makes its home. Museum entries here document the predators living inside the park, with particular focus on the lynx. The Valsavarenche offers excellent cross-country and easy downhill skiing in winter; good climbing, hiking, and biking in summer; and a reasonable tourism infrastructure year-round.

 Want to stay? The **Hostellerie du Paradis** (€€) in Valsavarenche offers mountainside accommodations at the park's doorstep. Walking trails depart directly from the hotel, maps and mountain bikes are available, and the food's darn good as well. To inquire, contact ☎ 0165 905 972, www.hostellerieduparadis.it.

 For more information on the park, stop by the Gran Paradis AIAT office at Villaneuv or click on www. granparadiso.net.

Venice & Northeast Italy

Northeastern Italy claims some of the Alps' most majestic terrain. Our coverage spans the region from the Adriatic Sea to the high Alpine terrain along the Austrian frontier. To the south,

Venice glistens at the heart of a large lagoon, rich with ancient architecture and untold mounds of gilded art. The serene city's shimmering waterways, tiny shops, and sidewalk cafés entice the international crowds to linger. From here, the northern plains quickly give way to the southern wall of the Dolomiti Alps.

Farther on, the resort town of Cortina courts a wealthy Italian clientele with upscale hotels and pricey boutiques – but makes room, too, for an international mix of adventuring tourists who come to marvel at the craggy peaks that soar all around. Beyond, the Val Gardena offers a wealth of dramatic hiking, biking, and skiing terrain at the foot of stalwart Sella Massif.

◆ Venice

(Venezia)
Population: 64,076
Base elevation: Sea level
Gateway tourist city

Like a crumbling old dame grieving the lost bloom of her youth, Venice races against the indomitable powers of time, erosion, and pollution; of late, and sadly, vandalism scars her as well. Yet the city once known as *La Serenissima Repubblica*, "the most serene republic," remains elegant, an alluring mix of dilapidation and exotic glamour. Today, as in days past, the name conjures up shimmering visions of palaces reflected in water, narrow webs of cobblestone alleys and squares, and classical music echoed off narrow canal walls.

History & Orientation

Settlers first fled into the Venetian Lagoon some 1,500 years ago, when barbarians attacked the Roman towns of the Veneto. The island settlements soon formed an alliance, their bonds gradually strengthening and culminating in the joint election of their first leader, or *doge*, in 697. Venice's merchants quickly became the world's wealthest, importing the finest spices, fabrics, and wares from the east; fattening the city's coffers; and inspiring young Ventians such as Marco Polo to even greater exploits. With its wealth grew envy, and with envy, enemies; yet Venice protected herself. The Venetians sacked Con-

Venice

1. Piaza San Marco
   (St. Mark's Square)
2. Santa Maria della Salute
3. Accademia Bridge
4. Campo Santa Margherita
5. Rialto Bridge
6. Santa Lucia Ferrovia
   (Train Station)
7. Piazzale Roma
   (Bus stop & parking)
8. Tronchetto (parking)

N

500 METERS
500 YARDS

stantinople in 1204 and, after a 127-year war, won dominance over Genoa, the city's primary competition in Mediterranean trade.

The height of Venetian empirical power peaked during the 15th century, yet her party-town reputation continued and, at one point during the 16th century a local tourist guidebook boasted 11,654 registered prostitutes. So, although Venice's power had faded, her stowed riches carried her grandly through 1791, when the last Venetian *doge* abdicated power to Napoleon. The city was tossed back and forth between Vienna and Italy, finally joining the Kingdom of Italy in 1866.

Tourism grew in the 19th century, yet the city saw a drastic population exodus, as its residents left in search of greater economic opportunity – a trend that continues alarmingly. Today, the city that once claimed over 174,000 residents now has just 64,000.

The Town

The city of Venice is comprised of some 120 islands connected by over 400 bridges, only three of which span the Grand Canal. Six *sestieri,* or districts, make up the city – Cannaregio, San Marco, and Castello to the east of the Grand Canal; Santa Croce, San Polo, and Dorsoduro to the west. Houses are numbered by *sestrieri* rather than streets, a system that newcomers find more hindering than helpful. In fact, most visitors spend their time in Venice dizzyingly disoriented, wandering a tangled maze of dark alleys without the aid of any predominant landmark.

Now, I realize the following orientation method will seem a bit silly; scoff, if you must. But, I've been getting around Venice with it for years, and it might just work for you, too. Picture Venice's *Centro Storico,* or old center, as a whale riding the wave of the Giudecca, the island to its south. The whale's nose points west at the ship dock; its tail forks toward the east with the gardens at its downward tip. Cars and trains enter the city via the spout; the Grand Canal marks a backwards 'S' down the whale's center; and the Dorsorduro district forms its lower fin – at its tip, the Dogana da Mar and the Santa Maria della Salute church. And finally, if our whale had a belly button, the Piazzo San Marco would be it.

Getting Here & Around

 Travelers arriving by air will fly in to the **Marco Polo Airport** on the northern edge of the lagoon, some 13 km by car from Venice. **Buses** make the trip to Piazzale Roma in about 30 minutes. More interesting, however, is transfer by **boat**. Public waterbuses leave the docks just outside the terminal to make the 50-minute trip to the Piazza San Marco, or St. Mark's Square. Bus and boat tickets are sold inside the airport's arrivals terminal.

Trains pull in on the northern edge of the city, and waterbuses depart from the docks just out the station's front doors. As Venice is a traffic-free city, drivers must cross the lagoon bridge and park their cars in the enormous garages at Tronchetto and Piazzale Roma. The slightly more central Piazzale Roma lots are more expensive and fill quickly in high season – I suggest the Tronchetto garage. Both parking areas are well-served by waterbus.

Venice is most efficiently navigated by boat. **Water-taxis** are both the most convenient and most excruciatingly expensive means of travel. (If you're going to splurge, at least bargain a bit.) Public waterbuses, or **vaporetti**, offer a more affordable means of travel, making the rounds through the Grand Canal and to the outer lagoon islands. The Grand Canal *vaporetti* stops most frequented by tourists are Tronchetto and Piazzale Roma for parking; Ferrovia for the train station; Rialto for its bridge and shopping area; Accademia for the museums; and either San Marco Giardinetti or San Zaccaria for St. Mark's Square.

Grand Canal *Vaporetti* Routes

To the Grand Canal, from Tronchetto, Piazzale Roma, or Ferrovia:

Route 1 – the slow boat; stops at every dock.

Route 82 – the boat stops several times, including Rialto, Accademia, and San Zaccaria; also loops via the Giudecca Canal along the southeastern edge of the city.

Route 3 – the express boat; stops only at San Samuele, Accademia, and San Marco; then loops back to Tronchetto.

If you plan to make more than two rides each day on the *vaporetti* waterbuses, purchase a 24-hour (or more) pass. For more information on routes, check www.actv.it.

✔ Many, many books have been written on Venice – and many, many films have been shot here. Thomas Mann's 1971 Death in Venice stirred local sentiment, but our favorite Venice-set saga is the film version of Henry James' novel, The Wings of the Dove.

Getting More Info

 The main tourist office is Piazza San Marco 71, in front of the San Marco Giardinetti waterbus stop. There's a smaller, less useful office in the train station as well. For more information, contact ☎ 041 529 87 11, www.turismovenezia.it.

The main post office is in the Fondaco di Tedeschi on the eastern side of the Rialto Bridge. The train station has a convenient post office, too.

For Internet access, head to the **Net House** on Campo Morosini, near San Stefano, just north of the Accademia Bridge.

The Sights

Venice harbors more tourist "sights" than any city I know. Every alley begs to be explored; every shop, browsed; every church, entered. If you must attempt it in a single day, I suggest a boat ride from the parking and station area down the Grand Canal to Piazza San Marco, and then a walk back via the Rialto Bridge. In any case, you can't see it all. With this in mind, we've narrowed the city's infinite attractions down to several must-see sights.

The Grand Canal

Perhaps the most famous waterway in the world, the **Grand Canal**, or Canale Grande, is Venice's biggest boulevard. The canal winds 3½ km through the city center, clogged the entire way with waterbuses, motorboats, water-taxis, and slow-moving gondolas. (Although water-taxis do offer excellent tours, a more affordable version comes by way of a waterbus ride – preferably in one of the coveted seats at the boat's bow.) Some 200 palaces flank the Grand Canal, most of them built between the 12th and 18th centuries; I won't attempt to describe them all here, but if you're interested, excellent maps and canal guides are available at the kiosks near the station. On the way south, note the locations of the canal's three bridges, the **Ponte Scalzi** near the train station, the famed **Rialto** about midway down the canal, and the wooden **Accademia** just before the canal opens into the basin.

✔ Most tourists go ashore at Vallaresso or Giardinetti, the first stops near Piazza San Marco. I suggest continuing on by boat a bit, in order to get your first view of the square from the water. Stay on the boat as it moves along the San Marco Basin – at least one more stop to San Zaccaria. If you stay aboard to Arsenale or Giardini, you'll have a nice walk back to the square and big views of the Venetian Lagoon.

Italy

Piazza San Marco

St. Mark's Square, or the Piazza San Marco, is Venice's living room, the administrative and religious center of the city. It's the largest open space in the city and the only square to bear the title of *piazza* – other smaller squares are called *campo*, *piazzeta*, or *piazzale*. Cafés and shops line the arcades encircling the square. St. Mark's basilica lies at the eastern end, fronted by the Campanile tower, and flanked by the Palazzo Ducale to the south and the 15th-century clock tower to the north. Visitors shop for souvenirs, climb the Campanile for views, and await the striking of the hour by the clock tower's two Moors.

A TALE OF TWO CAFÉS

Caffeine-consumers unite, and thank Venice for introducing coffee to Europe. In 1640, Venetian ships began importing coffee beans, or *kahve*, from Turkey to be used as medicine, a precursor to Prozac, if you will. Some 80 years later, on the 29th of December in 1720, a Venetian named Floriano Francesconi threw open the doors of Europe's first coffee house: it was called the **Venice Triumphant**, and it sat on St. Mark's Square. The café drew such illustrious visitors as Lord Byron, Goethe, and Charles Dickens. Casanova found the female-friendly coffee house a prime hunting ground. In the decadence of the 18th and early 19th centuries, the whole of St. Mark's Square became a solid ring of cafés – houses of hedonism that saw in one week more intrigues than 10 seasons of *Friends*.

During the Austrian occupation of the 19th century, Austrian soldiers frequented the **Gran Caffé Quadri** on the northern side of the *piazza*. Proud Venetians boycotted the place, sitting and sipping elsewhere around the square. Today, only two of the original cafés remain: **Florian's**, originally the Venice Triumphant, and the once-traitorous **Quadri** across the square. Although tourists are likely to note no difference between the two save the color schemes of the elegant interiors, true Venetians remember where their loyalties lie.

✔ Both cafés host live music on the square during summer evenings, each house dueling for the biggest crowds. It's a delightful, if extravagant, way to while away a Venetian evening.

St. Mark's Basilica, or the Basilica di San Marco, shown on the facing page, is the city's most enduring landmark. First built as a doge's chapel in the ninth century and reconstructed in the 11th, the magnificent church has been gradually adorned with all manner of glorified loot, from the remains of St. Mark (stolen from Alexandria in 828) to the much-touted Four Bronze Horses (swiped from Constantinople in 1204). The exterior of the church puts the "busy" in Byzantine, with five domes, a gaggle of 13th-century carvings, and several splendid mosaics – the one to the right depicts the pilfering of St. Mark's body. Inside, admire the exquisite mosaic floors and pay a nominal fee to see the Pala d'Ora, an altar piece made of 250 gold panels and encrusted with jewels.

The **Doge's Palace**, or the Palazzo Ducale, was the nucleus of Venetian life from its founding in the ninth century. A pale pink, lacey façade fronts the Gothic structure, hiding within a richly ornamented interior that served at once as residence of the *doge* rulers, seat of the government, and home to both the

courts and the prison. The famous Ponte dei Sospiri, or **Bridge of Sighs**, links the palace courts to the prison cells, a place of great horror, indeed. (Although you can walk through it here, the bridge is best seen and photographed from the outside of the palazzo, along the waterfront at Rio di Palazzo della Canonica.) Tours are offered in English; the "Secret Itineraries" tour is particularly recommended. The palace is open daily from 9 am to 5 pm, till 7 pm in summer; ☎ 041 271 59 11; €12.

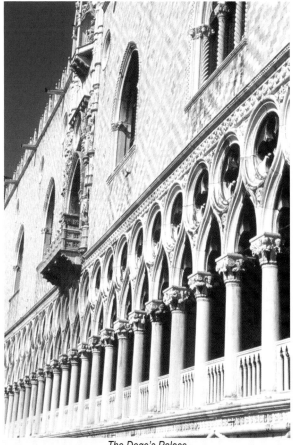

The Doge's Palace

Venice Under Water

Each winter, occasional high tides flood the low-lying areas of Venice, particularly those around the Doge's Palace and St. Mark's Square. On several occasions we've witnessed the piazza under water. It's a tragic yet magical sight, the splendid Basilica seeming to float above a continuous sea.

These high waters, or *acque alte*, have grown more frequent over the years, as Venice sinks and tides rise. The population copes with *acque alte* by erecting elevated wooden walkways, rearranging waterbus docks, and sounding warning sirens. However, none of that stops the floods from hastening the erosion of the city's foundations. So, a massive rescue effort is underway; the installation of huge drainage pipes beneath the city will relieve the flooding – and, unfortunately, make a construction-zone mess of St. Mark's Square over the next several years.

The **Rialto Bridge**, or Ponte Rialto, was the first to span the Grand Canal, a valuable link between the mercantile centers on either side. First constructed as a wooden drawbridge, the stone version that stands today was built in the late 16th cen-

San Marco Square across the Grand Canal

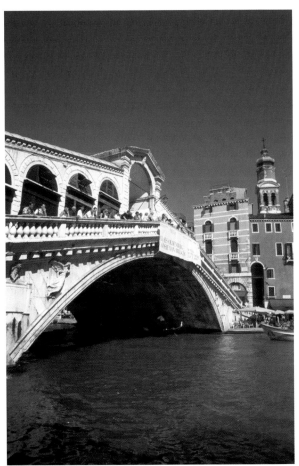

The Rialto Bridge

tury based on a design by Andrea da Ponte. (He beat out Palladio for the gig.) Today the bridge's arcades are home to a collection of expensive touristy shops. The alleys down its steps lead northwest toward Piazzale Roma and the train station and southeast toward Piazza San Marco – this latter route through the city's most exclusive shopping district. Follow the yellow signs to the square (where two *San Marco* signs point in opposite directions, choose one, and you'll get there eventually).

For museum hounds, three museums stand out. The **Gallerie dell'Accademia**, or Accademia Gallery, is the city's most famous museum and home to the globe's most extensive collection of Venetian art. Housed in a former church, the exhibit displays works from the 14th through the 18th centuries, including paintings by Veneziano, Carpaccio, Tintoretto, and Veronese, among many, many others. The museum is open from Tuesday through Sunday, 8:15 am-7:15 pm, Monday from 8:15 am-2 pm; ☎ 041 522 22 47; €6.50.

The nearby **Peggy Guggenheim Collection** invites visitors into the neo-classical Palazzo Venier dei Leoni for a look at one of the world's greatest private collections of modern art. The museum is open 10 am-6 pm daily except Tuesday; ☎ 041 240 54 11; €10.

One *vaparetto* dock north, the Ca' Rezzonico houses the new **Museo del Settecento Veneziano**, or the Museum of 18th-century Venice. The fascinating collection features art and interior design exhibits, all well-displayed within the palace walls. Open 10 am-5 pm Tuesday-Sunday; ☎ 041 522 54 95, www.museicivicineneziani.it; €6.50.

✔ Venice's cramped alleys may well feel a bit claustrophobic, particularly for those travelers now accustomed to panoramic Alpine views and wide, open spaces. If you feel the need to climb something – or just want a big-picture perspective – hop a boat for **Isola di San Giorgio Maggiore**, the island directly across the basin to the south of Piazza San Marco. From there, enjoy wide water views, and ascend the church tower for panoramic lagoon vistas. Although the San Marco Campanile is taller, this tower remains my favorite vantage point in Venice.

The Adventures

Venice's adventures are simple: long wanders through the city, and long boat rides through the lagoon. The most popular outings by boat are gondola rides through the center's narrow canals and waterbus excursions to the outer islands of Murano, Burano, Torcello, and the Lido.

The Gondolas

Gondolas covered with snow

Gondolas have plied Venetian canals since the 11th century. At the height of their use in the 18th century, some 14,000 gondolas rowed through town. Each boat adheres to traditional specifications, constructed using 280 separate parts and eight kinds of wood; each weighs approximately 400 kilograms; and, in adherence with the luxury laws of 1562, each is glossed with seven layers of black lacquer paint. The boats are flat along the bottom and are asymmetrically framed, listing to the right in order to counteract the effect of the gondolier's single oar. Each gondola sports a *forcola*, or oar rest, toward the back; and on the bow, a *fero*, a decorative six-pronged fork symbolizing the six *sestieri* districts of Venice.

Today, the city's 400 remaining gondolas corral at several locations to await tourist fares. Some of the most popular docks are near the Doge's Palace, behind St. Mark's Square at Orseolo, and near the Rialto Bridge. Rides are pricey – expect to pay €80 for a 50-minute evening jaunt, day rates somewhat less. Bargaining is most appropriate.

✔ The city's least expensive gondola rides are via the **traghetti**, stationed at strategic crossing-points along the Grand Canal. Gondoliers oar straight across the canal, ferrying pedestrians for a small fee – at last count, €1.40. When a *traghetto* gondola fills up, passengers stand rather than sit, giving the ride an extra-sporty touch. (Widen your stance for balance. You don't want to swim in this water.)

Lagoon excursions depart by waterbus from the San Zaccaria dock near Piazza San Marco. The island of **Murano** is famed for its ornate glasswork, examples of which can be purchased throughout the city. Visitors can watch master craftsmen at work in shops around the islands, and learn about the history of glassmaking at the **Museum of Glass Art**.

Burano

The island of **Burano** is renowned for is elegant lace, and tourists come here to visit the lace-making school. I love Burano, too, for its brightly painted fishermen's houses, a legacy of the fishing industry that once thrived here. Take time, if you can, for a meal in one of the island's small seafood restaurants.

Nearby, the island of **Torcello** rests peacefully in the northern lagoon. First settled between the fifth and seventh centuries, the island was the birthplace of Venice and was once home to some 20,000 people. Today, fewer than 100 residents remain. Torcello draws tourists for the mosaics inside its elegant cathedral, the **Santa Maria dell'Assunta**, a church built in the seventh century and reconstructed during the 11th.

The Lido, at the eastern edge of the lagoon, is Venice's beachside community. The long, narrow strip stretches between the Adriatic and the Venetian Lagoon, a land bar first popularized around the turn of the 20th century and today cluttered with paid-entry beaches and cabana bars.

Venice Off-Hours

We hope you'll spend a night in Venice. Most of the city's guests – and, indeed, its workers, too – daytrip into the city then flee to the mainland at night in search of less expensive lodging. While it's true that local hotels post outrageous rates, a splurge here buys you a look at the off-hours city that most never see.

■ **Late-night** Venice is quiet – deathly, delightfully so. Wander through the deserted alleyways, stroll along the splashing canals, and sit silently on a bridge a while. A homebound gondola might just pass under, the gondolier singing only for himself.

■ **Nighttime boats** run up the Grand Canal, allowing riders the opportunity for a wee bit of palace-peeping. Although most palaces remain dark, some illuminated interiors tease with glimpses of Murano-glass chandeliers, luxurious draperies, and ornately carved ceilings.

■ **Sunrise** is most spectacular from the banks of the San Marco Basin. The sun climbs up behind the Lido and the Isola di San Giorgio Maggiore, throwing a warm glow over the Gothic arches of the Doge's Palace and the dome of the Santa Maria della Salute church. Photographers gather at the Doge's Palace for that classic gondolas-in-the-foreground shot.

■ The **morning market** sets up on the northwestern side of the Rialto Bridge, its colors, sounds, and smells giving rise to some most memorable moments. Come either by gondola (via the Santa Sofia *traghetti* across the Grand Canal) or on foot. The

Italy

authentic action here takes place beyond the Rialto tourist stalls, so wander north to the covered markets at Campo Battisti and Campo Pescaria, where fresh fish and produce is hauled in each morning by boat.

✔ Tourists and workers flood into the city in the morning and out of the city at night, cramming boats beyond comfortable capacity. If you stay in the city, you have the opportunity to sightsee opposite the current crowd flow. In the evenings, ride south from the station toward San Marco; in the mornings, ride north instead.

Where to Sleep

Venice hotels post notoriously high rates for rooms that are notoriously scruffy. Nonetheless, occupancy and turnover rates in the city are so high that owners understandably claim that there's no good time to renovate. I've looked for hotels with good locations and average rates; rooms facing any type of water will be more expensive.

If you have the cash, there is no better stay in the lagoon than the legendary **Cipriani** (€€€€). The hotel sits in an isolated position at the western edge of the Giudecca, one island south of the old city center. The rooms are luxurious, the views mes-

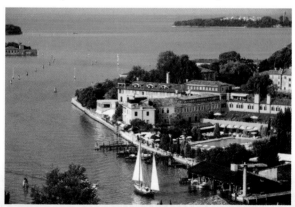

The Cipriani

merizing, and the canal-side garden pool a pleasant retreat. A private motorboat ferries guests between the hotel and St. Mark's Square. Inquire at ☎ 041 520 77 44, www.hotelcipriani. com.

The **Romantik Hotel Metropole** (€€€) fronts the wide basin, just east along the waterfront from St. Mark's Square and flanks a smaller canal to one side. Inside, loads of antiques and homey touches warm fancifully decorated rooms. Reserve at ☎ 041 520 50 44, www.hotelmetropole.com. Also near St. Mark's Square, try the **Flora** (€€-€€€), a small hotel

Terrace at the Metropole

with a fetching little garden and rooms of variable comfort; ☎ 041 520 58 44, www.hotelflora.it.

Near the Fenice Theater, the quaint **La Fenice et des Artistes** (€€-€€€) draws applause from

Room at the Flora

its artsy clientele; ☎ 041 523 23 33, www.fenicehotels.it.

For a waterside view near the Rialto, try the **Locanda Sturion** (€€-€€€). It has Venetian-style rooms up a steep flight of stairs; ☎ 041 523 62 43, www.locandasturion.com.

I've long had a soft spot for the charming **Accademia Villa Maravege** (€€€). It's in Dorsoduro, housed in a small villa with a pleasant canal-side garden; ☎ 041 521 01 88, www. pensioneaccademia.it. Just around the corner, the similarly named **Accademia Bed & Breakfast** (€€) occupies the top two floors of a villa just one lot back from the Grand Canal – a

Italy

few steps from the
Accademia museum
and boat stop. Guests
enter via a locked
courtyard and relax on
a garden terrace with
pleasant views. Some
rooms have a bath,
others share, but all
enjoy the hospitality of
Mr. Luca Bigozzi;

Accademia B&B

☎ 041 522 11 13, www.bbaccademia.com.

Where to Eat

Venetian cuisine, like its lodging, is pricey, yet not
particularly good. But, I do have a few favorites to
share. The best thing going for a romantic summer
night out is **Cip's Club** (€€€), a Hotel Cipriani endeavor. The
restaurant floats atop a barge along the Giudecca, with enormous views of the city and St. Mark's Square stretching out
across the water. Candlelit, tables with white linens provide an
elegant décor. Reserve at ☎ 041 520 77 44; also inquire about
boat transfers.

North of St. Mark's Square, try **Da Arturo** (€€€), a small restaurant with good regional cuisine and a quiet location on a
calle near Campo Manin. Reserve at ☎ 041 528 69 74.

For fish, head to the market area at Rialto and the restaurant **Ai
Mercanti** (€€€). Here, creative seafood specialties highlight
the traditional Venetian tasting menu. Book a table at ☎ 041
523 8269.

For mid-range fare near the Rialto, try my favorite pizzeria,
Aquila Nera (€€), home to a delish arugula pizza. It's been
down a narrow alley off of Campo S. Bartolomeo since 1505.
There's a small terrace in summer and homey décor inside;
☎ 041 522 47 69. Nearby, the **Ristorante Da Mario** (€€) has
traditional cuisine and a large summertime dining terrace;
☎ 041 528 51 47.

Venice has a booming **café culture**, and visitors should spend
a little time just sitting, watching the world go by. At St. Mark's

Square, **Florian's** and **Quadri** are the most famous cafés in town. Cozy little bars dot the shopping streets behind the square, and sidewalk cafés line the Riva along the basin's waterfront. On sunny days, join the good mix of locals and tourists at the cafés along the Zattere.

Where to Party

 As both tourists and workers exit the lagoon *en masse* each evening, Venice sees very little nighttime action. To simply soak up the ambiance of the city, park yourself in a café along the **Riva waterfront** or join the Venetians sitting out at **Campo Santa Margarita**. **Il Doge** has the best gelato there.

In summer, **Florian's** and **Quadri** (see *A Tale of Two Cafés*, above) both host live music outdoors on **St. Mark's Square**, offering an ideal way to spend an evening amid the grandeur of the square. The piazza inspires less formal performances, too; I once watched a group of Austrian tourists break into to splendid, spontaneous song – it turns out they were an off-duty touring choir. **Harry's Dolci** sometimes hosts jazz out on the Giudecca, and **Casanova**, near the station along the Lista di Spagna, has occasional live music as well.

La Fenice

The **Gran Teatro La Fenice** has once again risen from ashes, reopening its curtain in 2003, after a devastating fire in 1996. See what's playing at the opera house at www.teatrolafenice.it.

The **Interpreti Veneziani** ensembles perform several times each week at various venues around the city; if you can catch one of their classical concerts staged in an old church, the ambiance alone is worth the price of a ticket. For more information, check current listings or www.interpretiveneziani.com. The elegant **Palazzo Vendramin Calegari** is home to the city's **casino**. It's along the Grand Canal and can be reached either on foot or by boat. Shuttles leave St. Mark's Square at regular intervals; ☎ 041 529 71 11, www. casinovenezia.it; jacket required.

Where to Play

All of Venice is an adult playground, but children won't find much specifically designed for them. That said, kids enjoy feeding the pigeons at St. Mark's Square, boat rides along the Grand Canal, and trips out to the Lido beaches.

Festivals & Events

Venice is busy all year – but come festival time, the old city packs in tourists by the busload. **Carnivale** is the town's most renowned festival, drawing tourists from around the world during the 10 days prior to Lent, when fabulously costumed revelers adorn bridges, doorways, and squares. (If you want to visit during Carnivale, book far, far in advance.)

Carnivale

On Ascension Sunday, the **Vogalonga**, or "long row," regatta takes oarsmen some 32 km through the lagoon, finishing up on the Grand Canal. The regatta celebrates the doge's historical *Bucintoro* ceremony, when he would row out to the Lido, throw a ring into the Adriatic, and thereby reaffirm Venice's "marriage to the sea."

Summer brings the **Festa del Redentore**. Held on the third Sunday in July, this festival marks the passing of the 1576 plague. A bridge of boats crosses the Giudecca to the church, and fireworks light up the sky.

For the three months of summer during even-numbered years, the **Biennale** brings to Venice the world's largest festival of modern art. Each September, on the first Sunday of the month, the **Regata Storica** on the Grand Canal features a parade of rowers dressed in historic costumes. Finally, the festival season closes on the 21st of November with the **Festa Della Salute**, a celebration marking the passing of the 1630 epidemic of the bubonic plague. Today's festival includes a candlelit procession over the pontoon bridge crossing the Grand Canal to Santa Maria della Salute.

◆ Cortina d'Ampezzo

Population: 6,500

Base elevation: 1,224 m/4,015 feet

Mountain resort town

Cortina draws a glamorous crowd – boutiques gleam, cell phones ring, and socialites strut their ritz and glitz. It's a fascinating display, really, but one that regretfully obscures the greater riches here. So stop. Step back. Pull your eyes away from the pompous parade.

And look up. The scenic splendors *here* are some of the most magnificent of all the Alps. Jagged peaks soar all around, their forested foothills networked with paths, their crags made cozy in hospitable mountain huts.

History & Orientation

Although evidence shows that prehistoric hunters once wandered the Ampezzo Valley, Cortina remained a quiet backwater until access roads brought transalpine travelers its way. In the 1860s the region was discovered by budding mountaineers, wealthy adventure travelers from England and Germany in search of new sites to practice their newfound sport. Their influential accounts popularized tourism in the area. Winter tourism took hold in the early 20th century, and in 1956 Cortina took the world stage as host of the VII Olympic Winter Games. Today, this little town of 6,500 people swells to over 60,000 in high season.

The village of Cortina sits in natural splendor in the basin of the Ampezzo bowl, a valley surrounded by some 23 peaks of over 2,000 m/6,500 feet. The valley rests in the north of the Veneto region and in the province of Belluno. Jutting mountains rise all around, including the Faloria to the east, the Cristallo to the northeast, the Tofana to the northwest, and the Cinque Torri to the west.

✔ Many films have been shot in Cortina and its majestic Dolomites. For a big-screen look at the region, check out the following flicks: the James Bond film *For Your Eyes Only*, Peter Sellers in *The Pink Panther*, Elizabeth Taylor and Henry Fonda in *Ash Wednesday,* and Sylvester Stallone in *Cliffhanger*.

Cortina d'Ampezzo (Dolomito Turismo, www.infodolomiti.it, photo R. Ghedina)

The Town

Cortina centers on its old town, now a pedestrian zone crammed full of expensive boutiques and cafés. The old town flanks a river and fills a rectangular area created by four one-way roads: **Via Franchetti** loops up the hill, **Via Marconi** runs the long leg north, **Via Grohmann** heads downhill to the west, and the main road squares off the area (and goes by changing names including **Via Battisti**, **Via Mercato**, and **Via Olimpia**). This old-town pedestrian area revolves around the **Piazza Venezia** and its lovely church. The main pedestrian drag, **Corso Italia**, runs the length of the center, and several smaller alleys veer off uphill.

Getting Here & Around

 Those traveling by **air** will fly in to the international airports at either **Venice** or **Innsbruck**. Cortina is just 44 km south of the Austrian border, 162 km north of Venice and 156 km south of Innsbruck – about a 2½-hour drive from either city. **Train** travelers arrive at the station in **Calalzo di Cadore**, some 35 km away, and transfer to a connecting bus. **Drivers** will find the center a frustrating place to navigate – and curse the town's lack of parking. Several lots lie below the town along the river.

✔ From December through March, direct buses run between Cortina and the airport at Venice, eradicating the need for a private vehicle or complicated train transfer. The service operates only on Saturdays and Sundays – the start and end days of local hotel package weeks. Reserve a seat on the bus when you book your hotel.

Public **buses** hub at the **Via Marconi** station on the northern edge of the center. Local buses ply through town and well serve the outlying lift bases. Buses are free to lift-pass holders.

Mountain transportation is scattered on the outskirts of town. Only the Faloria cable car departs from the town center. (However, buses run between the lift stations at reasonable intervals.) Lift passes run the gamut from single-lift rides to the winter-only Dolomiti SuperSki Pass, a ticket covering 460 lifts and 1,220 km of runs.

Marmolada 3342 m

Gruppo Sella Gruppe 3152 m

Col d. Puez – Kofel 2723 m

CANAZEI
GRANTITELLO
1446 m

M. Pic
2546 m

Rif. Maria Hütte

Pas Pordoi Joch
2242 m

Rif. C. Razzo Schütz Hütte

Tierser Alpe

Rif. Sass Hütte

Int. Alb./ Passo Sella
Bergasthäuser Sellajoch

Albergo-Zilmer Berggasthof

Rif. Treno
Albergo

Rif. Enter
Albergo

Rif. Molignon
Mahlknecht Hütte

Saltaria

ALPE DI SIUSI SEISERALM

Alberto
Albergo
Gasthof

Gschwendt

Passo Gardena – Grödner Joch
2137 m

Pez Topic
Piz Cir

Cir Piz

Rif. Toni
Comici

O. Sellaronda / Ums Sellamassiv

Plan de Gralba

Bar Ristorante Gianbiers
Restaurant Berggasthof

Monte Piana

Tschapit – Alpe

Pufflatsch 2176 m

1680 m

Puez

Col d. Puez – Kofel 2723 m

2475 m
Rif. Puez Schützhütte

Colfosco

Selva Gardena/Wolkenstein
1563 m

2000 m

1600 m

Vallunga
Langental

Stevia

Rif. Stevia
2311 m

Bar Ristorante Cianves
Restaurant Berggasthof

VAL GARDENA
GRÖDEN

Ortisei/St. Ulrich
1236 m

Baita Juac Hütte

S. Cristina/St. Christina
1428 m

Ninia Sangon Hütte

Selva Gardena/St. Christina

Resciesa/Raschötz

2037 m

Rasciesa / Raschötz

2282 m

Piz Pienes
Regensburger Hütte

Rif. Pieres
Regensburger Hütte

Cauf Fermeda

Baita Daniel Hütte

2392 m

Rif. Malta Hütte

Secëda 2518 m

2004 m

Via Ferrata Sassolungo Mugou

LIFT PASS PRICE SAMPLES	
Winter	
1-day adult local area...................	€37
1-day adult SuperSki....................	€40
6-day adult SuperSki..................	€202
Summer	
Pedestrian round-trip to Cinque Torri.......	€12

Getting More Info

The tourist information office is in the center at Corso Italia. For more information, check ☎ 0436 27 11, www.cortina.dolomiti.org.

The post office is in the center at Largo Post.

The Sights

Sightseeing in Cortina must include a see-and-be-seen stroll along the **Corso Italia**, the main drag of the pedestrian zone shopping area. Over 50 shops clog Cortina's old alleyways, offering antiques, fashion, and jewelry. (Sports shops, on the other hand, are hard to find.)

Tourists should visit Cortina's lovely **parish church** in the center of town, an 18th-century rebuilding of the original 13th-century chapel that once stood here. Inside are several worthwhile frescoes, carvings, and altars. The **bell tower** next door is an 1858 reconstruction of a 12th-century original. Nearby, the **Ciasa de Ra Regoles** houses three small museums, including a collection of modern art, an ethnological display of folkloric art and costumes, and a paleontology exhibit of fossils gleaned from the Do-

lomite region. For more information on the museums, contact
☎ 0436 22 06, www.musei.regole.it.

✔ Several interesting day-trips are possible from Cortina.
DynamicTour does a good range of outings to far-off
destinations such as Venice, Innsbruck and Salzburg –
and even into Germany for visits to King Ludwig's castles and Hitler's Eagle's Nest. See *Sports Services* below, page 320.

The Adventures

● **ON FOOT**

Cortina's network
of footpaths winds
some 300 km
through the local mountains.
Cableways assist **walkers** in
reaching the area's 56 mountain restaurants and *refugi*,
and the Cortina Mountain
Guides organize daily excursions for both families and
more experienced hikers.
The guides also arrange a
wide variety of outings for
climbers, including free-
climbing and trips to the region's excellent *vie ferrate*
(see *Sports Services*, page 320).

Mountain walking (D.G. Bandion)

In addition, the **Parco Naturale Regole d'Ampezzo**, or Natural
Park of the Ampezzo, shelters some 20,000 acres of the
Dolomites just north of Cortina. Strict preservation laws protect
the environment here in order to cultivate a habitat in which the
region's rich flora and fauna can thrive. Visitors wander the park
on over 500 km of trails, along the way spotting chamois, marmots, and even golden eagles. For more information on the
park, contact ☎ 0436 22 06, www.dolomitiparco.com.

WORLD WAR I & CORTINA

From the 16th through the 19th centuries, while under the rule of Austria's Hapsburgs, the region enjoyed a peaceful prosperity. That peace shattered in dramatic fashion, however, when Italy declared war on Austria in 1915 and World War I brought fierce fighting to Cortina's mountains. The Austrian lines stretched along the Stelvio Pass, at Lagazuoi, and across the Valparola Pass. Italian troops fought from Cinque Torri. Over the course of the war, both armies tunneled into the mountains, digging trenches and fortifying their positions.

Today, war-history hounds can tour the **Great War Museum in the Dolomites**, a collection of three preserved sites just west of Cortina, all with explanatory markers in English. Farthest west is the Austrian fort at **Tre Sassi**; for a nominal entry fee, its interior is open for exploration. Above the Valparola Pass to the east tower the **Lagazuoi peak** and its open-air war museum, a collection of galleries, tunnels, and trenches enhanced with exhibits, model figures, and commentaries. The area can be reached on foot or via the Lagazuoi cable car. Nearest to Cortina is the **Cinque Torri**, or "five towers," mountain region. Here, visitors ride a chairlift or hike up to the Italian defense lines, where several easy itineraries lead through entrenchments and artillery emplacements. Look for uniformed soldiers in the woods, and don't miss the fresh pasta at the Refugio Scoiattoli.

● IN WATER

 Watersports in Cortina are limited to **swimming** in the old pool complex, ☎ 0436 86 05 81, and the **whitewater** day-trips arranged by the Cortina Adrenaline center (see *Sports Services* below). Trips include rafting, kayaking, hydro-speeding, and canyoning.

● **ON WHEELS**

Mountain bikers love Cortina for its wide variety of long, looping trails. Easy trails meander along waterways, and intermediate trails head up side-valleys. Advanced riders take to more technical trails. One favorite difficult itinerary takes bikers from Cortina's center up the Faloria cable car, then down a winding path to Rio Gere. From here, a lift mounts the Cristallo, where a long trail speeds from Rifugio Son Forca

Biking Cortina

down to Ospitale. An easy trail loops along the river from there back to Cortina. The tourist office has trail maps, and Due & Due rents gear (see *Sports Services*, page 320).

● **ON SNOW & ICE**

Cortina has 51 lifts and 140 km of local **skiing** runs, which are graded 33% easy, 62% intermediate, and 5% difficult. The groomed trails span five fragmented mountain areas, each served by local buses. In addition, holders of the legendary Dolomiti SuperSki Pass have choice of an enormous area, including 1,220 km of runs and some 460 lifts.

Favorite runs include the secluded trail off the back of the

Ski lift (S. Zardini)

Faloria (Dolomito Turismo, www.infodolomiti.it, photo R. Ghedina)

Faloria area and a long run from the Passo Falzarego and the top of Lagazuoi down to San Cassiano – and even beyond to the Sella Ronda circuit. Along the trail, don't miss a stop at the tiny memorial chapel and a warm-up in the cozy Scontoni Refuge. If you're lucky, teams of ski-joring horses will be waiting to pull you across the run-out. (Buses head back to Cortina from San Cassiano; and the Dolomiti SuperSki Pass is required for lifts beyond Lagazuoi.)

Olympic Trails Tour

The Olympia ski itinerary loops through all of the slopes on which racing competitions were held during the 1956 Olympic Winter Games. The route crosses Tofana, Monte Cristallo, and Monte Faloria, among other areas, and can be accomplished in one or two days. The ski ticket office has maps and information. True followers of the Olympic Torch should also check out the Duca d'Aosta hut, where the torch was stored prior the opening ceremonies; do a lap on Olympic ice at the local rink; and race down the Olympic bobsled track at the Cortina Adrenalin Center (see *Sports Services* below).

Snowboarders take to the new funpark at **Faloria**, and **cross-country skiers** enjoy the new **Fiamesport Nordic Center** in the Fiames neighborhood. A 30-km loop runs between Cortina and Dobbiaco and, from there, loipe (trails) continue into Austria, some 200 km away. **Dog-sledding** is available, as are **high-mountain treks** and **ice-climbing** at no fewer than seven frozen falls. The ice rink, on the northern outskirts of town, offers **skating, hockey**, and **curling**.

● IN THE EXTREME

The **Cortina Adrenaline Center** advertises their odd activities as "everything that doesn't in any way resemble your grandmother's cookies, or a stuffed armchair with you sitting in it...." In addition to popular TaxiBob **bobsled rides** on the Olympic ice track, winter visitors can hop aboard a rubber boat for **snow-rafting** on the ski jump slope; **toboggan** down a moonlit run on a "very aggressive sledge," miner's lamp strapped to their foreheads; or **luge** without breaks down the Olympic ice tube over "the most personal 400 m/1,300 feet of your life." Summer activities include **hydro-speeding, kayaking, rafting**, and **canyoning** on nearby whitewater runs and **wheeled bobsled rides** on the concrete TaxiBob course. For contact info, see *Sports Services* below.

Sports Services, Outfitters & Guides

Dynamic Tours arranges an array of outings and adventures in both summer and winter. For example, the operator coordinates dog-sledding, wine tasting, and day-trip tours to destinations in Italy, Austria, and Bavaria. For more information, stop by the DynamicTour office at the northern end of the Corso Italia; ☎ 0436 23 63, www.dynamictour.it.

The **Gruppo Guide Alpine Cortina**, or the Cortina Mountain Guides, maintains a century-long tradition of education, training, and guiding. In addition to scheduled group outings, the guides lead private excursions, including rock and ice climbing, multi-day treks, and even nature walks. Contact ☎ 0436 86 85 05, www.guidecortina.com.

The **Cortina Adrenaline Center** spikes heart rates with a range of extreme activities you probably won't find at home. See *In the Extreme* above, and contact ☎ 0436 86 08 08, www.adrenalincenter.it.

Where to Sleep

Cortina offers a good range of accommodations, much of it in creaky old buildings, and much of it closing in shoulder season. The

HOTEL PRICES	
€ . . . . . Up to €80 per night	
€€ . . . . €81 to €150	
€€€ . . . . . . €151 to €250	
€€€€ . . . . Over €250	

castle-like **Miramonti Majestic** (€€€€) has long been Cortina's

grand dame. In a forested park setting outside of town, the elegant old house offers formal luxury, an indoor pool, and a private nine-hole golf course. Book at ☎ 0436 86 70 19, www.geturhotels.com.

Miramonti Majestic

For rustic tradition, try the **Hotel de la Poste** (€€€-€€€€), directly in the town center. The large yellow chalet has been welcoming guests since 1835. Reserve at ☎ 0436 86 84 35, www.delaposte.it. Also along the Corso Roma, the **Hotel Aquila** (€€-€€€) offers homey accommodations and a lovely wine bar and

Hotel de la Poste

lounge. Inquire at ☎ 0436 86 73 15, www.aquilacortina.com.

The **Hotel Olimpia** (€€) is a friendly, family-run lodge popular with budget travelers and tour groups. It's directly in the center at Largo delle Poste 37, and some of its rooms offer balconies; ☎ 0436 32 56, www.hotelolimpia.com.

Where to Eat

Diners seeking gourmet cuisine should head to the outskirts of town for several epicurean treats. **Tivoli** (€€€) is the most cele-

RESTAURANT COSTS	
€	Less than €10
€€	€10 to €25
€€€	Over €25

brated gourmet house here, serving regional cuisine with a creative kick. Book a table at ☎ 0436 86 64 00. Nearby **El Toula** (€€€) occupies a ramshackle barn on a northwestern hillside in Ronco; in summer, the terrace and garden are lovely open-air dining rooms. Make reservations at ☎ 0436 33 39.

For grilled meats, head to the rustic **El Zoco** (€€€), a few km up the road toward Dobbiaco; ☎ 0436 86 00 41. (The pumpkin gnocchi here ranks among the best we've tasted.) Also special for regional fare is the **Lago Pianozes** (€€), a chalet situated on a small lake at the base of the Croda da Lago; ☎ 043656 01.

For somewhat less glorified fare in the center of town, head to the reliable **Cinque Torri** (€€), a large restaurant with pizza, pasta, and meat dishes and a terrace overlooking the Largo della Poste; ☎ 0436 86 63 01.

Our favorite pizza place – and that of many others – is the **Porto Rotundo** (€€). It's just off the main square below the church tower; ☎ 0436 86 77 77.

For picnic supplies, the **Da Giacomo** fruit stand, the adjacent **wine shop**, and the **Panifico Alvera** down the block. All three are north of the Café Royal along the Corso Italia.

✔ On Cortina's mountains, several *refugi* offer hearty regional fare amid cozy surroundings. At the top of the Cinque Torri chairlift is the **Scoiattoli** mountain restaurant, where fresh pasta is made in-house – my favorite is a rich ravioli dish, Cansuziei all'Ampezzana – little pasta packages filled with seasoned beets, served in a browned butter sauce, and topped with poppy seeds and parmesan cheese. The hut is open year-round.

Where to Party

 Cortina afternoons begin with coffee and cake in any of the town's many cafés, and evenings commence with a pre-dinner stroll, or *passeggiatta*, along the Corso Roma – a tradition offering ample opportunity for flaunting furs and haute couture fashion. Dinner starts late and runs long, and the best bars don't really get going until well after midnight. Hearty partiers rock on until daylight.

At tea-time, try the **Café Royal** on the Corso Italia, just uphill from the Piazza Venezia, or the **Rubens** at the Corso Italia's northern end. A younger crowd hangs out under the umbrella at the **Cristallino** on the Largo della Poste. The **Hacker-Pschorr Haus** pub just off of Largo della Poste offers good beer and food just across the alley.

Wine bars are a popular afternoon and pre-meal stop, particularly for a glass of sparkling Prosecco wine. I suggest making the rounds. Try the dark, wood-paneled **Enoteca** at Via Mercato 5, the **Bar Becalen** at Via Battisti 22, or the **Villa Sandi** at Largo Poste 1. **L'Osteria** offers a good selection of wine, local ham and bread, and outdoor seating on a garden deck. It's tucked away just off of the Corso Italia.

Later – much, much later – dance through the night at one of the town's five discos. **Ciarlis** is at the site of the old Hyppo bar, Largo Poste 35, and promises to be just as popular. The **VIP Club** draws a lively crowd, and the **Discotecha Belvedere** is often worth the taxi fare out to Pocol.

Where to Play

 In winter, **ski schools** take kids from four years of age, and the new Kinderheim Babypark **nursery** service offers care for children three months to three years of age. It's in the Pocol skiing area and is open daily from 9:30 am to 4:30 pm. During the summer months, children enjoy **walks, bike rides, mini golf,** and any of the several **organized outings** arranged by the local mountain guides. For play areas, try the **park** on the northeast corner of the old town, or head for the **snow playgrounds** at several lift-base huts.

Festivals & Events

 Cortina's festivals and events include many sporting competitions. The winter opens with a festival **Christmas Market** along the Corso Italia. Snowboarding, bobsledding, curling, and sled-dog events punctuate a schedule dominated by ski racing events including the **women's World Cup races** in mid-January and the **Dobbiaco-Cortina cross-country race** in February.

Festival of the Bands (D.G. Bandion)

Summer brings a number of cultural, musical and sporting events, including mountain-bike races and the **Cortina-Dobbiaco Marathon**. The town's traditional folklore festival, the **Feste Campesetri dei Sestrieri**, draws crowds of colorfully costumed locals; the **Festival of the Bands** gathers regional musical groups; and the **Dolomites Golden Cup** shows off vintage cars.

The Val Gardena

(Gröden)

Population (Selva): 2,570

Base Elevation (Selva): 1,563 m/5,127 feet

Mountain resort village

This lovely valley tucks away in the Dolomite mountains smack in the heart of Ladin country. Three villages play host to the many visitors who come year-round hike, bike, board, and ski.

The Val Gardena tucks away in the Dolomites in the heart of Ladin country, 250 km north of Venice and 120 km south of Innsbruck, Austria. The valley runs 25 km from the A22 Autostrada at Chiusa in the west to Selva at its head in the east. The magnificent pillar of the Sella Massif rises just beyond. To its

Ortisei

north, the valley is bordered by the Parco Naturale Puez-Odle; to the south, the Alpe di Siusi and the Sasso Lungo.

Three small villages line the Val Gardena, each confusingly known by two names: **Ortisei** (or St. Ulrich) at 1,236 m/4,054 feet, **Santa Cristina** (or St. Christina) at 428 m/1,404 feet, and **Selva Gardena** (or Wolkenstein) at 1,563 m/5,127 feet. All three serve as reasonable bases from which to explore the valley in both summer and winter. Ortisei is the largest and most developed of the three villages, home to numerous shops, museums, and sporting facilities. Up-valley, Santa Cristina is the smallest hamlet, ideal for families and those looking for a peaceful holiday. Our favorite base, Selva Gardena, lies at the heart of the region's hiking and skiing trails. It has a nice sports center and a good tourism infrastructure.

The valley is known first for its green tourism – the **Sella Massif**, the **Parco Naturale Puez-Odle**, and the **Alps di Suisi** all beckon to hikers, climbers, and skiers. It's known as well for its

Selva Gardena in summer

adherence to traditional customs, including its craftsmanship and woodworking, its colorful festivals, and its Ladin culture and language. (The valley uses three languages: Italian, German, and Ladin.) Visitors interested in learning more about the Ladin culture should visit the **Val Gardena Local Heritage Museum** in Ortisei at Rezia 83; ☎ 0471 79 75 54. Also of cultural note are several churches, including the **Church of St. Giacomo**, reachable by foot from Ortisei. It was first built in the 12th century and is the oldest in the valley today.

> ✔ The **Val Gardena Card** offers summertime access to the entire valley's bus and lifts. Included are the lifts and buses around the Sella Massif, allowing experienced hikers to complete the Sella Ronda loop in approximately eight hours The cards can be purchased at the tourist office; €56 for seven days.

Adventurers set out on foot across the valley's numerous trails, linking paths with summertime lifts along the way. From Selva, climb to ruins of **Wolkenstein Castle**, follow the old line of the Val Gardena Railway on an hour's stroll to **Santa Cristina**, or take on an overnight excursion to one of the natural park's refuges. Mountain guides lead organized and private excursions; ☎ 0471 79 41 33. And climbers check in with Catores, Ortesei's climbing guides; ☎ 0471 79 82 23. In winter, snow sport fans

In the Parco Naturale Puez-Odle

take to the valley's 81 lifts and 175 km of local trails or, purchase the more expensive Dolomiti SuperSki Pass, which opens up 464 lifts and some 1,100 km of groomed runs.

The Sella Ronda Ski Circuit

Selva Gardena sits on the doorstep of the Sella Ronda – and the world's only opportunity to ski on groomed runs *around* an entire mountain. The region's network of lift-linked trails encircles the Sella Ronda group, allowing skiers to circumnavigate the massif like a snow-sporting merry-go-round. Along the way, travelers cross several passes and enter four villages: Selva, Canazei, Arabba, and Corvara.

The 40-km circuit requires stamina rather than any great skill, as the pistes here are mostly intermediate level. The loop can be made in either direction, but the clockwise runs employ fewer draglifts. Some long run-outs create minor issues for snowboarders, and poor snow conditions sometimes interfere along the lower-altitude runs. In any case, start early to allow time to enjoy the mountain huts and spectacular scenery along the way. Done in its entirety – with no lift-line waits and no rest stops – the circuit takes approximately four hours. Inquire at the tourist office for a route map.

Want to stay? The **Hotel Aaritz** (€€-€€€) has a good position near the Ciampinoi chairlift. Its interior warms with lots of wood paneling, elegant arches, and an enormous open fireplace. Inquire at ☎ 0471 79 50 11, www.aaritz.com. Rates vary dramatically by season.

Hotel Aaritz

Each village has its own tourist office. Contact Ortisei at ☎ 0471 79 63 28; Santa Cristina at ☎ 0471 79 30 46; or Selva Gardena at ☎ 0471 79 51 22. All three share a website at www.valgardena.it.

Liechtenstein

(Fürstentum Liechtenstein)
Languages: German, local dialects
Population: 33,525
Phone Country Code: +432
Currency: Swiss Franc (CHF)

History & Government

THE ROYAL FAMILY

Liechtenstein's royal family has resided inside the country's borders only since 1939, when Prince Franz Josef II moved his family into the hillside castle and sent his son, current ruler Prince Hans Adam II, off to be educated at the local school. Today, silvery ladies still whisper over white-wine spritzers regarding his schoolboy antics. One such tale tells of the day that two playground bullies – both girls – pushed the prince to the ground. He responded calmly, as only a young royal could, that when the day came for him to take the throne, all females would be banned from Liechtenstein *forever*. He hasn't yet made good on the threat.

IN THIS CHAPTER

- People & Culture   331
- Vaduz   333

Measuring only 25 km long and six km wide, Liechtenstein squeezes itself between Switzerland to the west and Austria to the east. Half of the principality's territory is mountainous; the other half, pasturelands reclaimed with dikes from the once-unruly Rhine. The principality is divided into two sectors, the Unterland to the south and the Oberland to the north, and a total of 11 communities. The largest communities – **Vaduz**, **Triesen**, **Schaan**, and **Balzers** – line the Rhine at the foot of the mountains toward the south end of the small country. Up the steep mountain road from Triesen are several smaller villages: **Triesenberg**, **Steg**, and **Malbun**.

Liechtenstein

People & Culture

Liechtenstein joined the United Nations in 1990 and the European Economic Area in 1995. Today it enjoys a prosperity founded largely on tourism, wine production, and manufacturing.

✔ Liechtenstein is the largest exporter of dentures in the world. Its other claim to fame is as a self-described "liberal" international banking center.

The banking business has boomed in the past several years, doubling total deposits between 1995 and 2001 and increasing the number of banks here from three to 17. Liechtenstein remains an attractive haven for tax-avoiding businesses (both real and paper), and boasts an unemployment rate of just 1.2%. The country's population is 80% Catholic, 7% Protestant, and 13% of other religious orientations.

National Holidays

January 1	New Year's Day
January 2	Berchtold's Day
January 6	Epiphany
February 2	Candlemas
47 days prior to Easter	Shrove Tuesday
March 19	St. Joseph's Day
Friday before Easter	Good Friday
March/April	Easter; Easter Monday
May 1	Labor Day
10 days before Whit Sunday	Ascension Day
7th Sunday after Easter	Whit Sunday
Monday after Whit Sunday	Whit Monday
Thursday after 8th Sunday after Easter	Corpus Christi
August 15	Assumption Day & National Day
September 8	Nativity of Our Lady
November 1	All Saints Day

Liechtenstein

December 8 . . . . Immaculate Conception
December 25 . . . . Christmas Day
December 26 . . . . St. Stephen's Day
December 31 . . . . New Year's Eve

TIMELINE

5000 BC	First evidence of Raetian and Celtic populations at region's higher elevations
15 BC	Raetia conquered by Romans and declared a Roman province
400 AD	Christianization of region begins
500-800 AD	Decay of Roman Empire and arrival of Alemanni tribes
Middle Ages	Division of Raetia and emergence of counties; plague devastates in 1600s
1699-1719	Acquiring the Lordship of Schellenberg in 1699 and the County of Vaduz in 1712, Prince Johann Adam Andreas of Liechtenstein unifies the territories that would in 1719 become an independent principality of the Holy Roman Empire
1815-1866	Member of German Confederation; acquires independence in 1866
1868	Liechtensteiner Army dissolved; start of neutrality
1914-1918	World War I; Liechtenstein maintains neutrality, but Hapsburg monarchy ends in Austria; Liechtenstein aligns with Switzerland
1921-1923	Liechtenstein adopts constitution in 1921 and, in 1923, the Swiss Franc as official currency
1938-1984	Reign of Prince Franz Josef II; succeeded by Hans-Adam II
1939-1945	World War II; Liechtenstein maintains neutrality
1984	Women granted the right to vote in national elections
1990	Liechtenstein joins United Nations
2000-2002	Blacklisted by the Organization of Economic Cooperation and Development for money laundering
2004	After having secured sweeping authority for his throne in 2003, Prince Adam II passed management of his country's affairs to his son, Prince Alois. Prince Adam II, however, remains the official head of state.

The very helpful Liechtenstein Tourism Office is in Vaduz, Städtle 37; ☎ 239 63 00, www.tourismus.li. The office is open daily from 9 am-12 pm and from 1:30-5 pm in season; from mid-September through mid-April, closed Saturday and Sunday. For more information on Liechtenstein, see www.liechtenstein.li; for more information on the royal family, go to www.fuerstenhaus.li

Vaduz

Population: 4,949
Base elevation: 455 m/1,492 feet
Tourist town

The average tourist blows through Liechtenstein seeking only a glance at its castle and a stamp in his passport. But stay a while; there's really much more to see than that. Concentrated in this compact country are a number of worthwhile attractions – a cheerful town center, a prince's art collection, a royal wine cellar, and an all-season wilderness playground.

The Town

Vaduz center (Carl Rogers)

Although it was probably first settled in the fifth century, Vaduz (or *Faduzes*) is first mentioned in historical texts dating from the 12th century. Today's city, the capital of the country, spreads out along the Rhine Valley between the eastern riverbank and the western foothills of The Alps. One major road, Route 16, runs through Vaduz and the length of Liechtenstein. However, Route 16 is rarely marked as such. Instead, the street signs change names every few blocks: Landstrasse, Herrengasse, Aulestrasse, Heiligkreuz,

Liechtenstein

Austrasse, etc. You get the idea. In the text that follows, we'll re-
fer to Route 16 as the "main road." When you're in town, it's
hard to miss.

Visitors' first stop should be the small pedestrian area at the
town's center. Wander along the Städtle between the art museum, the tourist office, and the many surrounding shops.
Gazing down from the hill above is Liechtenstein's landmark
castle, which, because it's the private residence of the royal
family, is not open to the public.

✔ Liechtenstein's national flag shows two equal horizon-
   tal bars – one blue and one red – with a crown emblem
   in the upper left corner. The royal family's flag, however, shows simply two equal bars – one gold and one
   red. From Vaduz, look up the hill toward the castle: If
   the gold and red flag flies there, the royal family is in
   residence.

Getting Here & Around

 Liechtenstein has no airport. Those traveling by **air**
should fly into Zürich, 110 km west. Liechtenstein
does have some **train** service, but the rail system is
Austrian owned-and-operated, and two issues complicate
travel: first, no international trains depart the country, and travelers must change trains before continuing into Switzerland or
Austria; second, the tracks don't reach to Vaduz. Passengers
headed for the capital must take a bus from the nearest train
station in Schann. (It's easier, really, to disembark at the border
and bus in from Feldkirch, Buchs, or Sargans.) The **bus** terminal is in the town center within easy reach of hotels, the art museum, and the tourist office, and the Liechtenstein Bus Anstalt
(LBA) runs efficient service between all local communities. For
taxi service, try **Castle Taxi** at ☎ 0 423 777 00 77.

Two roads run the length of the country: Route 16, from Balzers
in the south to Feldkirch in the north; and A13, the Swiss Autobahn on the western bank of the Rhine River. A third route, the
mountain road, winds from Route 16 east, through Triesen,
Triesenberg, and Steg to Malbun. Parking can be troublesome
– in the center, try the underground garage below the museum.

Getting More Info

The very efficient Liechtenstein Tourism handles tourist information issues for Vaduz. Drop by Städtle 37 for assistance, or contact ☎ 0 423 239 63 00, www.tourismus.li. The central office is open daily from 9 am-noon and from 1:30-5 pm in season; from mid-September through mid-April, closed Saturday and Sunday.

The post office is in the center near the tourist office.

For Internet access, try the **Telecom Shop** on the main road Austrasse 77.

CURRENCY CONVERSION		
1 CHF	€0.82	€0.65
€1	1.30 CHF	€0.80

The Sights

Schloss Vaduz (Michael Gredenberg)

For a town this tiny, in a country this small, Vaduz has far more than its share of **museums**. Several collections stand out. The **National Art Museum Liechtenstein**, housed in a striking modern building in the center, houses the substantial Collec-

Liechtenstein

tions of the Prince. Exhibits include works by diverse masters, including Rembrandt, Rubens, and Picasso. The museum is open Tuesday through Sunday 10 am to 5 pm and Thursdays until 8 pm; www.kunstmuseum.li, 8 CHF. The **Liechtenstein Landesmuseum** should open its historical collections as we go to press. Check in at ☎ 0 423 236 75 50. Winter-sports fans should visit the **Ski Museum Vaduz**, a lovingly cared-for collection assembled by Noldi Beck. Mr. Beck was equipment manager for Hanni Wenzel, a skier who found herself Liechtenstein's darling after bringing home the gold medal from the 1980 Olympic Winter Games in Lake Placid. His collection is considerable, and his connections apparent.

Liechtenstein Postage Stamps

Philatelists know Liechtenstein for its coveted postage stamps – tiny elegant works of art perfectly suited to this tiny elegant nation. The **Briefmarken Postmuseum** houses a collection of postal stamps that together tell the story of the principality. The museum is upstairs from the tourist office at Stadtle 37 and is open daily, 10 am-12 pm and 1 to 5 pm; ☎ 0 423 236 61 05; free admission.

In the **Hofkellerei des Fürsten von Liechtenstein**, otherwise known as the prince's wine cellars, visitors can sample and purchase local wines. (If you do the first, the latter is customary – even if you just buy one small bottle.) The surrounding vineyard is planted with 9.9 acres of Pinot Noir grapes and, yes, it is actually owned by the royal family; ☎ 0 423 232 10 18, www.hofkellerei.li. A path through the vineyard leads to the Restaurant Torkel (see *Where to Eat* below).

In summer, the **Vaduz City Train** departs the main bus station each day at 4:30 pm for a 30-minute tour of town; www.citytrain.li; 9 CHF. The tourist office also arranges **guided tours** through Vaduz and around Liechtenstein. Regularly scheduled, hour-long walking tours depart Monday through Friday at 2 pm from the bus terminal desk (summer only, 10 CHF). Private guides can be arranged through the tourist office, www.citytrain.li.

Vineyards owned by the Prince of Liechtenstein (Ed Sexton)

✔ Still want that stamp in your passport? Although the border-patrol no longer takes interest in the comings-and-goings of Liechtenstein visitors, the tourist office doles out a souvenir passport stamp for 2 CHF each.

Those seeking outdoor recreation in Vaduz hike, bike, and ride into and along the nearby mountains. **Bikers** and **skaters** enjoy 90 km of posted trails, rolling the length of the nation in an easy stretch along the Rhine. More difficult mountain-biking trails climb at altitude, and the **Dreamteam** offers guided tours; ☎ 423 392 29 92, www.dreamteam.li. The **Bike Garage**, on the main road in Triesen, rents mountain bikes; ☎ 0390 03 09, www.bikegarage.li. **Bernhard and Sabine Tschol** offer a variety of guided, single- and multi-day **horseback rides**; contact ☎ 0392 29 85, www.westerntrekking.li.

While Vaduz is very much a tourist town, Malbun and Steg – its mountain neighbors – are the local centers for **outdoor play**. There, adventurers head into the mountains on a 400-km network of hiking and biking trails and ski on 21 km of groomed runs. For more information, see the entries below for *Malbun* and *Steg*.

An Interesting Deal

Liechtenstein's adventure pass, the **Erlebnispass**, offers free and discounted admission to 21 of the principality's summertime attractions. (The marketing scheme claims you'll "save up to 400%," but I might question that math.) You can, however, save plenty – if you make good use of the card. It sells for 25 CHF (or half that for kids) and is good for two days. Partner attractions include the National Art Museum, the Ski Museum, the chairlift at Malbun, CityTrain Tours, and Liechtenstein Bus. Purchase your card at the tourist office, the post office, partner attractions, or at many hotels. Six-day passes are also available.

Where to Sleep

Fresh and new in 2003, the **Hotel Residence** (€€€) is Liechtenstein's undisputed top choice for business travelers and tourists

HOTEL PRICES	
€	Under 120 CHF
€€	120-225 CHF
€€€	226-375 CHF
€€€€	Over 375 CHF

looking for a friendly staff and modern amenities. The hotel has a town-center locale and rooms outfitted with high-tech gadgets like security doors and flat-screen TVs with integrated Internet access. Its slick, artsy kick ideally suits fans of the art

Hotel Residence

museum just across the street. Reserve at ☎ 0 423 239 20 20, www.residence.li.

The **Gästhof Löwen** (€€€) is the oldest hotel in Liechtenstein; it's been welcoming guests since 1388 and, if practice makes perfect, it certainly has the hang of it now. The back rooms have lovely vineyard views; ☎ 0 423 238 11 44, www.hotel-loewen.li.

Halfway between Vaduz and Malbun – with spectacular views of the Rhine Valley – the **Hotel Restaurant Kulm** (€€) in Triesenberg

Gästhof Löwen

welcomes vacationing families with great food and friendly hospitality; ☎ 0 423 237 79 79, www.hotelkulm.li.

Where to Eat

Liechtenstein has no shortage of expensive restaurants. In a lovely vineyard setting, the romantic **Torkel** (€€€) specializes in freshwater fish dishes; ☎ 0 423 232 44 10, www.torkel.li. The **Hotel Real** (€€€), too, is well-known for its international take on haute cuisine; ☎ 0 423 232 22 22. For re-

Dining room in the Gästhof Löwen

gional specialties and a traditional atmosphere, try the old **Gasthof Löwen** (€€€); ☎ 0 423 238 11 44.

RESTAURANT COSTS	
€	Under 15 CHF
€€	15-37 CHF
€€€	Over 37 CHF

Where to Party

Vaduz is a pretty staid town, and those looking to party may find themselves partying alone. For social lounging, try the piano bar at the **Hotel Löwen**, the less elegant **Crash Bar** in the center, or **B'eat** at Städtle 5.

For a cultural evening out, check what's playing at the **Theater am Kirchplatz** (better-known as TAK). The schedule highlights a variety of performers, several international acts each year, and summer concerts in a mountainside fortress; www.tak.li. The **Kino Movie Theater** is on Aeulestrasse – check the newspaper, or call ☎ 0 423 232 12 18 for current shows.

Where to Play

Each of Liechtenstein's communities maintains a **playground** and swimming center – both popular activities with kids. Favorites include the **Adventure Playground** at Triesen, the **bird park** at Mauren, and the **Vaduz City Train Tour**. Malbun runs a variety of **children's programs** during the summer and a ski kindergarten in winter, and the Vaduz tourist office can make suggestions regarding babysitters.

Festivals & Events

Vaduz starts its year with a town-center **New Year's Eve** party and a festive **Mardi Gras** carnival season. Spring brings a slew of art, film, and music festivals that pack the calendar through summer. Favorites include the **Rhine Park Stadium Film Festival** from late June through mid-July; **Guitar, Jazz, and Classical Music Days** throughout July; and the five-day **Meeting of the Artists** in early August.

If you happen to be in town on the evening of August 15th, you're cordially invited to the castle garden for cocktails with Prince Hans Adam II. Each year, in celebration of **National Day**, the royal family opens its castle grounds to the public for drinks, food, and a fireworks show. It's a fun party, and a rare opportunity to see Liechtensteiners let loose.

Vaduz to Malbun

The trip up to Malbun from Vaduz can, of course, be made in the most direct fashion – going there and back via the steep road from Triesenberg. However, when snow closures don't prevent it, I suggest making a circular tour via the lesser-known castle road just north of Vaduz. North of town along the main road, head up the hill through the vineyards and up past the castle's back door. Continue along the narrow, forested, one-way path to Triesenberg, but beware of emergency vehicles headed *down* this "one-way" uphill road. In Triesenberg, you'll intersect the main drag near the church and can head for Malbun from there. After your mountain visit, continue downhill in the direction of Triesen, turning north on Route 16 to get back to Vaduz.

Malbun (Fbieger)

Malbun

Base Elevation: 1,602 m/5,254 feet

Mountain resort village

Up the mountain 15 km from Vaduz and nestled below the Three Sisters massif, Malbun is Liechtenstein's outdoor playground. Popular in winter with families for its traffic-free center and easy, centralized ski runs – and popular in summer for its cool temperatures and good trail network – this quiet hamlet draws mostly local crowds but is well worth a traveler's look, too.

Malbun grew up in the 1960s after completion of the tunnel and road from Steg. Today's village includes several hotels, a handful of shops, and a cluster of privately owned holiday cabins, all centered on Malbun's original

The Friedenskapelle (FS Sebowsky)

hotel, the brightly painted Alpenhotel Malbuner. Worth a quick look is the **Friedenskapelle** just up the hill at the entrance to town – a stone chapel built in 1945 as a war memorial in pious gratitude for Liechtenstein's avoidance of the war.

The Falknerei Hotel Garni Galina puts on a small **falconry show** that will delight kids and all those fascinated by wildlife. From the hotel's dining terrace, visitors get an intimate look at aerial acrobatics by several of the falconry's 19 birds of prey. Don't stand up during the show – flight paths run within a few feet of spectator tables. The standard show is presented in German, of course, but the handler, Mr. Rot, speaks English well and will answer any questions you have might have about his flock. Catch the 40-minute presentation at 3 pm every day except Monday, from May through October. (6 CHF, drink and snack service additional.)

Winter-season adventurers enjoy a wide range of sports, including ice-skating, ski touring, winter hiking, snowshoeing, tobogganing, and downhill skiing, with six lifts and 21 km of mostly easy pistes. Snowboarders enjoy a funpark, bikers test their skills on snow-scoots, and skaters take to the ice on a natural rink. Cross-country skiers head for Steg, three km down the mountain. For snow sport instruction, contact the **Malbun Skischule** at ☎ 0 423 263 97 70, www.schneesportschule.li. For equipment rentals and sales, contact **Malbun Sport** at ☎ 0 423 263 37 55.

✔ The **Sareiserjoch** moutain restaurant stages raclette dinners every Thursday during winter season. The chairlift from Malbun operates late on these evenings for transport to the inn. Reserve ahead at ☎ 0 423 263 46 86.

In summer, lift-assisted hiking is popular – try the **Fürstin-Gina-Weg**, a view-blessed trail that hugs the Austrian border as far as the Bettlerjoch hut and then drops down through Gritsch for the return to Malbun. Need a more difficult challenge? Step out onto the **Fürstensteig**, a narrow, cliff-hugging trail cut into rock of the Three Sisters massif. Hold on tight – to the cableway *and your soul*. Local lore alleges that the mountains here steal human spirits.

LIFT PASS PRICE SAMPLES	
Winter	
1-day adult pass	41 CHF
6-day adult pass	171 CHF
Round-trip to Sareiserjoch	11 CHF
Summer	
Round-trip to Sareiserjoch	12 CHF

Malbun can be reached by car or hourly bus from Vaduz, Treisenberg, and Steg.

Want to stay? Try the creaky old **Alpenhotel Malbuner** (€€); ☎ 0 423 263 11 81. The **Falknerei Hotel Garni Galina** (€€) offers a falconry show in summer and well-regarded cake specialties year-round; ☎ 0 423 263 34 24, www.galina.li. Reserve accommodations early in winter.

 For more information, check with the Tourist Office Malbun at ☎ 0 423 263 65 77, malbuninfo@liechten-stein.li. For lift openings, check www.bergbahnen.li.

Steg

Steg

Base Elevation: 1,303 m/4,274 feet

Mountain resort village

Too much bustle in Malbun? The tiny hamlet of Steg is merely a handful of pre-World War II alpine farmers' huts, the simple summer residences of the Triesenberger farmers who once brought their herds here in search of greener pastures.

The huts circle around a well-fertilized grazing field and today create a rustic little holiday village for vacationers in search of peace, convenient hiking trails, and fresh dairy products. In winter, the main attractions in Steg are a groomed winter walking trail and Liechtenstein's finest cross-country ski loops, 19 km in all, including a lovely trek along the Valünerbach stream in the shadow of the Kirchlespitz peak. (Check in at the Malbun Tourism Office for an inexpensive loipe pass.)

Barring the road traffic en route to and from Malbun, Steg is an extremely quiet place – the village claims a population of just 50 residents and, by the look of things, even that may be exaggerated. However, buses stop here hourly, and a couple of hotels are on hand. Try the cozy **Hotel Restaurant Steg** (€€), ☎ 0423 263 21 46, or up the mountain, the **Berggästhaus Sücka** (€), ☎ 0 423 263 25 79, www.suecka-erlebnis.li, a remote inn with shared baths, a dormitory, and several private rooms. Treats here include house-produced cheese, milk, butter, and yogurt – goodies that make the hike up worthwhile even for non-guests. In winter, ask about the guesthouse's fondue dinners and nighttime toboggan run.

Steg has no tourist office. Check with the Liechtenstein Tourist Office for more information; ☎ 0 423 239 63 00, www.tourismus.li.

Switzerland

(Schweiz, Suisse, Svizzera)
Languages: German, French, Italian, Romansch
Population: 7,301,994
Phone Country Code: +41
Currency: Swiss Franc (CHF)

HENRI DUNANT

Henri Dunant was born in 1828 to a family with staunch religious, civic, and humanitarian convictions. When he was 26, he began traveling for business and, in 1859, he went to Solferino to discuss a business proposition with the French ruler, Napoleon III. At the time, France and Italy were at war with Austria, and it was during this trip that Dunant witnessed one of the bloodiest battles of the 19th century. The images would haunt him for the rest of his life.

In 1862, Dunant authored a book telling of the carnage at Solferino, *Un Souvenir de Solferino*, or *A Memory of Solferino*. After describing the battle and its aftermath, Dunant used the last third of his book to propose an organization of relief societies to provide care for wartime wounded. The proposal interested Gustave Monyier, a prominent lawyer in Geneva, who then helped Dunant establish *The Permanent International Committee of the Red Cross*. In October of 1863, delegates from 16 nations met and approved the resolutions of the Geneva Committee – the First Geneva Convention. The attending delegates agreed to create private societies in their own territories to complement the work of their military's medical services; workers were to be universally identified by the large red cross on their equipment – a symbol taken from the Swiss flag.

Through the years, the Red Cross flourished; Dunant, however, did not. Focusing his energies on his organization rather than his business, Dunant went bankrupt in 1867. As such, Dunant was no longer welcome in Geneva society groups, and from 1875 to 1895 he lived in relative seclusion. In 1895, Dunant was at last recognized for his contributions with honors and a large monetary award. Dunant died in 1910, having spent almost none of the award money. At his death, as during his life, Dunant gave his wealth to the sick and poor.

The Swiss Confederation spans some 41,293 square km in west-central Europe. Bounding Switzerland are Germany to the north, France to the west, Italy to the south, and Liechtenstein and Austria to the east. Around

IN THIS CHAPTER

- People & Culture — 350
- Geneva & the Valais — 352
- Interlaken & the Jungfrau — 384
- Zürich & Central Switzerland — 415
- The Graubünden Region — 449

70% of Switzerland's terrain is mountainous, much of its land rippling along the Bernese, Rhaetian, and Pennine Alps. The mighty Rhine River drains 68% of the land here, and some 60% is either pastureland or forest.

Switzerland is a federal republic made up of 26 cantons; its capital city is Bern. Its chief of state is the president, who also serves as the head of the government. However, states' rights are of extreme importance here, and the federal administration allows great cantonal autonomy. Many political issues revolve around perceived threats to this autonomy; other ongoing issues include questions of immigration and asylum policy. Switzerland enjoys a high standard of living, with among the world's lowest unemployment, highest income, and longest life expectancy rates. Recent unemployment rates rose to 3.8% – still not bad, given Europe's 8% average.

Alpine Switzerland

N

HUNTER PUBLISHING

GERMANY

AUSTRIA

LIECHTENSTEIN

Vaduz

THE GRAUBUNDEN

Davos

Chur

St. Moritz

CENTRAL

Winter-thur

ZURICH

Baden

Engelberg

Lucerne

Basel

BERN

THE JUNGFRAU

Brienz

Thun

Interlaken

Grindelwald

Lake Neuchâtel

Fribourg

Gstaad

Ascona

Lake Maggiore

Lake Lugano

Lake Como

ITALY

FRANCE

Montreux

Martigny

Zermatt

Lausanne

Lake Léman

GENEVA

GENEVA & THE VALAIS

25 MILES

40 KM

© 2007 HUNTER PUBLISHING, INC.

People & Culture

The Simmental ski area in summer
(Roland Zumbühl)

Switzerland's official name is *Confoederatio Helvetica*, a Latin term that translates as Swiss Confederation – and explains both the "CH" stickers you'll see on cars and the "CHF" abbreviation for the Swiss Franc currency.

The country has three widely spoken official languages, each practiced in the corner of Switzerland nearest its origin – and each with its own slang term for Switzerland: in **German**, *Schweiz*; in **French**, *Suisse*; in **Italian**, *Svizzera*.

✔ Sign postings and publications often include text in all three languages.

The fourth official language is **Romansch**, an ancient dialect practiced today by just one percent of the population. Further befuddling the situation is the common use of both regional dialects and *Schweizerdeutsch*, or Swiss German. However, even with four official languages and a babble of traditional dialects, Swiss communication works out better than you might expect. Public schools enforce rigorous language studies, and thus most Swiss are multilingual. Better still for readers of this guide, more English is spoken here than in any other corner of the Alps.

The Swiss population includes four main ethnic groups: German, French, Italian, and Romansch. Some 65% of the population is German, 18% French, 10% Italian, and 1% Romansch. Most of the population claims to be Christian – 48% Roman

Catholic and 44% Protestant. Six in 10 live in urban settings, with the remaining 40% in smaller villages. Major cities include **Zürich**, **Basel**, and **Geneva**. Switzerland's population density hovers at about 177 persons per square km.

National Holidays

January 1	New Year's Day
January 2	Berchtold's Day
The 6 days prior to Shrove Tuesday	Carnival (Lucerne)
47 days prior to Easter	Shrove Tuesday
Friday before Easter	Good Friday
March/April	Easter; Easter Monday
May 1	Labor Day
10 days prior to Whit Sunday	Ascension Day
7th Sunday after Easter	Whit Sunday
Monday after Whit Sunday	Whit Monday
Thursday after 8th Sunday after Easter	Corpus Christi
August 1	Confederation Day
August 15	Assumption Day
November 1	All Saints Day
December 8	Immaculate Conception
December 25	Christmas Day
December 26	St. Stephen's Day
December 31	St. Sylvester's Day

Switzerland

TIMELINE	
800-58 BC	Celtic tribes thrive in western Europe, including the Helvetians, namesake tribe of the Confoederatio Helvetica, or early Switzerland. (Even today, Swiss car tags read CH, the common abbreviation for Switzerland.)
58 BC-400 AD	Roman Empire under Julius Caesar occupies Swiss territory until around 400 AD
Middle Ages	Rise of the feudal system; Germanic forces end Roman rule

1291-1515 AD	In effort to repel the Hapsburg counts, three Swiss territories (Uri, Schwyz, and Unterwalden) form the first Swiss confederacy; Eventually, they gain far-reaching territories across Switzerland, then abandon expansionist pursuit and declare neutrality
1519-1536	The Reformation begins in Zurich; Zwingli and Calvin import Luther's protestant ethics from Germany
1530-1798	The confederacy of 13 states, led by several ruling families, dominate Switzerland
1798-1815	Revolution and civil war; Occupation by Napoleonic forces and the establishment of a parliamentary republic in 1802; Congress of Vienna sets up 22-canton federation in 1815
1800-1900	Switzerland leads European industrialization, rail development, and tourism
1847-1848	Civil war, Protestant defeating Catholic cantons; Federal state established
1863	Henri Dunant established the Red Cross
1914-1918	World War I; Switzerland maintains neutrality
1918-1933	Inter-war recession
1933-1939	Switzerland provides asylum for Germans fleeing Nazi Regime; concerns rise regarding German threat
1939-1945	World War II; Switzerland maintains neutrality but is later criticized for some wartime policies, including the acceptance of stolen goods and sometimes restrictive asylum policies
1971	Women given right to vote
2001	Switzerland votes against joining the European Union
2002	Switzerland becomes member of the United Nations

For more information, check in with Switzerland's National Tourism Office at www.myswitzerland.com.

Geneva & The Valais

The Valais region encompasses Switzerland's most rugged terrain. Our coverage extends from the gateway city of Geneva to the upper reaches of the Walliser Alps along the Italian frontier. Visitors are apt to enter the region in **Geneva**, a small, cosmopolitan city between the border of France and the western end of Lake Geneva, known in French as *Lac Leman*. The city bustles with the business of international organizations, plays along a garden-lined lakefront, and harbors a pleasant pedestrian old town.

The city of **Lausanne** lies across the lake, drawing visitors for its own pleasant lakefront and the Olympic Games History Museum. Beyond, in the Valais region, protrudes the magnificent **Matterhorn Peak**, with famed **Zermatt** at its foot and secluded **Saas-Fee** just over the hill.

◆ Geneva

(Genève)

Population: 184,758

Base elevation: 374 m/1,227 feet

Gateway city

While Geneva's cuisine, language, and fashion sense reveal its French heritage, the city's people are today a cosmopolitan mix of over 200 nationalities. As home to some 250 international organizations and host to thousands of conventions, trade fairs, and meetings each year, Geneva enjoys a reputation as the world's neutral ground. Over the years, it has also garnered nicknames such as "the world's smallest big city," "city of parks," "city of peace," and even the lofty "capital of human knowledge." Geneva is an ideal gateway to the Alps.

History & Orientation

Geneva got its start under Roman rule, when Julius Caesar passed through in 58 AD and the city came under Rome's rule. Development during the first century focused on the little knoll we know as old town – its central Bourg-de-Four square was in those days a Roman forum. Geneva saw continued growth under the rule of Burgundy, eventually becoming an important market town under the Holy Roman Empire.

In 1536, Jean Calvin moved to town, ushering in the Reformation, founding an academy, and turning Geneva into the "Rome of the Protestants." The 18th century saw an influx of Europe's elite artists, businessmen, and scientists into the city, including rivals Rousseau and Voltaire. Then, after brief occupation under Napoleon's French troops, Geneva joined the Helvetic Confederation on 12 September, 1814.

Switzerland

Geneva's lakefront (AM Aeschlimann)

Geneva rests at the western end of Lake Geneva, or Lac Leman, 75 km long and Switzerland's largest Alpine lake. The Alps rise to the south, the Jura Mountains stretch north, and vineyards roll along the foothills all around. The city is conveniently located within striking distance of several Alpine resorts, including Verbier, Courmayeur in Italy, and Chamonix in France.

The Town

Geneva sprawls out from the western tip of Lake Geneva, at the mouth of the Rhône River. Tourists frequent three districts: the **city center**, the **old town**, and the **Place des Nations**. The city center splits into two sections, the right bank of the Rhône to the north and the left bank to the south. On the right bank clusters the train station and a number of hotels and restaurants; on the left bank, the bulk of the city's business and upscale shopping zones. The hilltop old town sits to the south of the center, and the Place des Nations sits to the north. Here, many international organizations make their homes near the city's pleasant gardens.

Getting Here & Around

 Geneva's international **airport** lies just four km from the city center, and a new railway terminal allows air passengers to transfer to the main **train station** in only six minutes. Trains pull into the Gare Cornavin at the Place de Montbrillant. It's on the right bank, on northern edge of the city center. **Buses** gather around a dwarfed church at the Square du Mont Blanc, just north of the Rhône River mouth, and **trolleys** ply the city streets. For **taxi** service, contact ☎ 022 331 41 33, www.taxi-phone.ch. Traffic conditions are dismal in the city center, and **drivers** are likely to have difficulty both navigating and parking.

✔ If you can take your eyes off the traffic fray for a moment, digital parking signs indicate the number of free spaces in each garage.

Getting More Info

 Check in at the very helpful tourist office at Rue du Mont-Blanc 18 or, at the second office, on the Pont de la Machine bridge. For more information, contact ☎ 022 909 70 00, www.geneva-tourism.ch.

Two post offices are convenient, one at Rue des Gares 16 near the train station, the other at Rue du Mont Blanc 18 next to the tourist office.

For Internet access, head to **Charly's Multimedia Check Point** at Rue de Fribourg 7; it's near the train station off the Rue des Alpes.

The Sights

The **City Center** is home to Geneva's modern rush – shops, businesses and banks dominate. On the left bank, or south side of the river, is the commerce and banking center. Café tables and flowers enhance the **Place Molard**. Between the Rue du Rhône, the Rue de la Confédération, and the Rue du Marché, pricey shops at street level prop up the banks that tower

Place Molard (AM Aeschlimann)

Switzerland

above. But the city center is also the location of Geneva's elegant lakeside, a garden-lined promenade at the mouth of the Rhône River. You can relax along the lakefront, admire the **Jet d'Eau**, and wander north along the right bank toward the **Perle du Lac Park** and the **Botanical Gardens**.

The Jet d'Eau

In 1886, Geneva had a problem. Each night, when the city's craftsmen closed their workshop faucets, the water pressure at the Coulouvrenière Hydraulic Factory rose to alarming levels. An ingenious plan created the solution – a pipe downstream along the Rhône

The Jet d'Eau (AM Aeschlimann)

would empty the excess water pressure. When installed, however, the valve blew with such force that it soon became a tourist attraction. In 1891 the Jet d'Eau was relocated from the Rhône to the Rade, where it now stands.

Today, the fountain is Geneva's most recognizable landmark, hurling 500 gallons of water each second to a height of 140 m/459 feet. The jet reaches speeds of 200 km an hour. Except in times of high winds, it operates from early March through the second Sunday of October, 9:30 am-11:15 pm.

The **Old Town**, or *Vieille Ville*, sits on a knoll behind the city center, comprising the most fetching little corner of the city. Antique

Cathédrale St. Pierre & the Old Town (AM Aeschlimann)

shops, cafés, and art galleries gather around the **Place du Bourg-de-Four**, Geneva's oldest square. The 12th-century **Cathédrale St. Pierre** tops town – climb the tower for far-reaching views over the city, mountains, and lake. Below the cathedral, an **archaeological site** exposes fourth-century ruins and the lifestyle of the Roman era. Around the corner is the 16th-century **Ancien Arsenal**, or old arsenal, and the **Hotel de Ville**, or Town Hall, where the Alabama Room saw the founding of the Red Cross in 1864 and the signing of what we know today as the original Geneva Convention. Nearby the **Maison Tavel**, first built in 12th century, is Geneva's oldest house and home to the **Museum of Old Geneva**; open Tuesday through Sunday 10 am-5 pm; free entry; ☎ 022 418 37 00.

The **Place des Nations** district is home to many of the city's more than 200 international organizations. Best known on the international scene is the Palais des Nations, home of the **United Nation's European Headquarters**. Built in 1936 in exemplary Art Deco style, the massive complex enjoys lovely views and offers tourists a look inside from April through October, daily from 10 am-noon and 2-4 pm; from July through August, daily 10 am-5 pm; from November through March, Monday to Friday from 10 am-noon and 2-4 pm. It's closed the second half of December. Book a tour in any of 15 languages at ☎ 022 917 48 96, www.unog.ch; 10 CHF. Nearby, the **Red**

Switzerland

Cross and Red Crescent Museum offers a wealth of historical documentation in relation to the Geneva-based humanitarian organization; open Wednesday through Monday, 10 am-5 pm; ☎ 022 748 95 25, www.micr.org; 10 CHF.

 Henry James set his classic story of *Daisy Miller* against the backdrop of Geneva's lakeshores. It's a good short read on a sunny day. Mary Shelley's *Frankenstein* was also penned near here – a great spooky story for stormy nights in Old Town.

Several **guided tours** are offered from Geneva Tourism, including a 2½-hour self-guided audio tour through the old town. Recordings rent for 10 CHF, plus a 50 CHF refundable deposit; check in at the tourist office for more info. In the summer, mini-train tram tours chug along three routes: the old town, the lakefront, and the parks and residences district. Each tour runs 30-45 minutes and costs around 8 CHF per person.

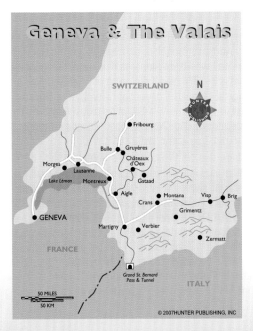

The Adventures

Boat excursions depart the city center's docks for a wide variety of **lake cruises**, including everything from a one-hour harbor tour (12 CHF) to a full-day Lake Geneva loop (80 CHF). Evening and theme cruises are available as well. For more info, check www.cgn.ch or www.swissboat.ch.

Genève Mouette boats run **river cruises** up the Rhône and short **water-taxi transfers** between the lakeside parks. **Boat rentals,** including sail, pedal, and motor models, are offered at Quai Gustave-Ador. Contact **Les Corsaires** at ☎ 022 736 25 66, www.lescoursaires. Miniature electric ships are a hit with kids from April through October.

In the summer, **lake swimmers** enjoy two strips of lakeside land. The first, the Paquis Baths, is little more than a jetty stretching into the lake from the right bank. The second, Genève Plage, has a heated, Olympic-size **swimming pool**, playgrounds, windsurfing, and a restaurant. Several outfitters run **whitewater excursions** to destinations outside the city. Try **Rafting Genève Adventure Center** for kayaking, hydrospeeding, canyoning, and rafting; ☎ 079 213 41 40, www.rafting.ch.

Where to Sleep

 Some 125 hotels welcome Geneva's guests, 14 of them with five full stars – a highly disproportionate percentage, but one highly

HOTEL PRICES	
€	Under 120 CHF
€€	120-225 CHF
€€€	226-375 CHF
€€€€	Over 375 CHF

suited to a town that draws so many high-level visitors to so many high-profile events. Hotel rates tend to be as lofty as the

The Beau Rivage

names of the people paying them, and *the entire town* can book out during popular trade fairs.

Of the five-star palaces here, I like best the **Beau Rivage** (€€€€), a family-run establishment built

Switzerland

in 1865 and still gleaming along the lakefront; ☎ 022 716 60 60, www.beau-rivage.ch.

Single room at Les Amures

In the old town, head for the **Hotel Les Amures** (€€€€€), an intimate townhouse with wood beams and residential decor – elegant but neither stuffy nor pretentious. It's on the square at Rue du Puits St. Pier 1; ☎ 022 310 91 72, www. hotel-les-amures.ch.

The **Tiffany** (€€€) welcomes with bright colors and cheery Art Nouveau décor. It's near Plainpalais at Rue des Marbriers 1; ☎ 022 708 16 16, www.hotel-tiffany.ch.

Where to Eat

With over 1,100 restaurants, 10 of those with Michelin stars, Geneva dines well. Visitors enjoy the international mix of cuisine, French gourmet influences, and wines from the local vineyards – many growing dry white Perlan and Pinot Gris or red Gamay and Pinot Noir.

Dining terrace at Les Amures

Several of the most renowned gourmet houses are slightly out of the center, taking up more attractive residences outside the city. Of the stars here, Chef Philippe Chevrier heads up the **Domaine de Chateauvieux** (€€€), a 16th-century

Domaine de Chateauvieux

stone house in the vicinity of
Satigny Station. The hotel boasts
a menu of seasonal cuisine, a cellar with over 900 wines, and
menus starting at €120; book at
☎ 022 753 15 11, www.chateauvieux.ch.

RESTAURANT COSTS	
€	Under 15 CHF
€€	15-37 CHF
€€€	Over 37 CHF

Joseph Righetto guides the **Hostellerie de la Vendée** (€€€)
on Lacey Hill, offering a choice of two creative menus, each coordinated with wines and encouraging tastings by the glass.
Check in at ☎ 022 792 04 11, www.vendee.ch.

For fish specialties, head for **Le Cigalon** at Thonex (€€€), a
tavern and bistro with a good selection of local wines; ☎ 022
349 97 33.

For traditional Swiss cuisine, try the touristy **Chalet Suisse**
(€€) at the Place du Cirque, ☎ 022 328 58 20, www.
chaletswiss.ch; the **Café Au Petit Châlet** (€€) at Rue de
Berne 17, ☎ 022 732 69 79; or the **Auberge de Saviese** (€€)
at the Rue des Paquis, where warm cheese dishes are served
until midnight, ☎ 022 732 83 30.

Where to Party

Geneva is known for its work ethic, but it does relax –
quietly, elegantly, and above all, with great sophisti-
cation. A typical evening out starts with an aperitif
and a long, expensive meal. Later, some 40 **theaters** stage a
range of **classical music** and **opera** performances, although
on most occasions the most exciting thing to happen after dinner is the distribution of nightcap digestifs. For stage and ticket
information, check in at **Ticket Corner**; ☎ 0848 800 800.

For drinks in Old Town, **Café La Clemence** has a big terrace on
the Bourg de Flour. Later, English-speakers congregate at the
old **Shaker's Club** at Rue Boulangerie 7 or nearby at
Flanagan's Irish Bar. Both are in old town. Several disco venues dot Geneva's outskirts, but for dancing action in the city
center, try **l'Inderdit** or drag-show-driven **Le Loft**; both stay
open until dawn.

Switzerland

Festivals & Events

Best known for massive trade shows and conventions – its **PALEXPO** convention center can seat 6,500 people – Geneva hosts a multitude of annual events. Several renowned trade fairs are open to the public. Check out the **International Motor Show** in March, the **International Exhibition of Inventions** in April, the **Book Fair** in May, and the **Geneva Fair Ideal Home Exhibition** in November. To see what's on at the PALEXPO, check www.palexpo.ch.

Le Bol d'Or (AM Aeschlimann)

Carnivale comes to town during the pre-Lenten season, and **Le Bol d'Or** draws over 500 crews for a prestigious sailing regatta. Geneva's **Musical Summer** takes center stage from June through September, **Swiss National Day** is celebrated at Bastions Park on the 1st of August, and the **Fêtes de Geneve Summer Festival** brings shows, concerts, parades, and food to the city's shoreline in early August. Oddly, Geneva holds the world's largest foreign celebration of **American Independence Day** each 4th of July – fireworks and all. When Christmas rolls around, festivities include a month-long **International Christmas Market** at Fusterie Square, a **Christmas Tree Festival**, and **La Coupe de Noel,** a nippy lake-swimming competition. Finally, in the midst of the holiday season, comes the **Escalade**, Geneva's favorite party.

THE ESCALADE ESCAPADE

The Escalade celebration (Ricardo de la Riva)

In the fall season of 1602, the Duke of Savoy set out to overthrow his ally Geneva. The duke's troops toiled in secret, crafting and hauling wooden ladders with which they planned to scale the city walls. On the night of December 11th, 1602, the army mounted its assault. While many heroic acts transpired that night, one tale tells of the daring deeds of Mère Royaume. Upon spying an invading Savoyard soldier outside her kitchen window, the cook sacrificed her family's dinner, attacking the invaders with a cauldron of boiling stew. With daring acts such as these, Geneva's townsfolk united – and together repelled the traitorous Duke of Savoy.

Four hundred years later, Geneva continues the victory celebration with an annual festival, The Escalade. For one weekend in mid-December, mounted brigades, fife and drum parades, and torchlight marches bring the old quarter to life. Kids trick-or-treat through the local cafés, alarm bells clang, and a bonfire roars in the Cathedral's square. Around the corner at the Ancien Arsenal, shivering revelers line up for a freshly prepared bowl of Mère Royaume's soup.

Lausanne

Population: 128,432
Base Elevation: 375 m/1,230 feet
Tourist City

Castle St-Maire, former seat of the bishops of Lausanne

Although Lausanne figures prominently on few tourist itineraries, its pleasant lakeside location, its connections to the Olympic Movement, and its accessible small-city feel make it a worthwhile stop.

The lake-set, vineyard-ensconced town revolves around Ouchy, a lakeside community bustling with parks, cafés, and the ferry docks. Climbing uphill, visitors shop along the Rue de Bourg, visit the city's 13th-century Gothic cathedral, and wander through the old center around the Place de la Palud and its imposing Town Hall.

Want to stay? Although the **Beau Rivage** (€€€€) down the lakefront is the grandest hotel here, I like the **Château d'Ouchy** (€€-€€€€). The neo-Gothic 19th-century château sits on the lakefront at the site of a 12th-century castle. The hotel has a glassed-in terrace lounge, a good restaurant, and an Internet café. Its deluxe rooms are worth the small jump in price. To book, ☎ 021 616 74 51, www. chateaudouchy.ch.

THE OLYMPIC CAPITAL

Lausanne is the world's Olympic capital – home to the International Olympic Committee, 17 international sporting federations, and the renowned Olympic Museum. This museum, the Musée Olympique, occupies a sprawling modern complex at the Ouchy lakefront. Sculpture-studded parks step down to the water, and views stretch to the mountains beyond. Inside, interactive exhibits depict the history, culture, and art of the Olympic Movement, ranging from equipment of interest to computer and film presentations of the Olympic Games' most memorable moments. The museum is open daily from May through September, 9 am-6 pm; from October through April, closed on Mondays; 15 CHF. For more information, contact ☎ 021 621 65 11, www.museum.olympic.org.

 For more information, contact the Lausanne tourist office at ☎ 021 613 73 73, www.lausanne-tourisme. ch. Offices are at Ouchy and at the central train station.

◆ Zermatt

Population: 5,500

Base elevation: 1,620 m/5,314 feet

Mountain resort town

In southeastern Switzerland next to the border of Italy, Zermatt reclines amid a cluster of 38 4,000-m peaks. Above the town towers the distinctive hook of the Matterhorn crest. But, curi-

Following pages: The Riffelalp chapel (7,300 ft) in the Gornergrat area, with the Weisshorn in the background.

Switzerland

ously, few here pay much attention. In this glamorous, clamorous town, electric taxis tear through the alleys, moving shoppers, sightseers, and skiers at a frantic pace. For this jet-setting clientele, Zermatt isn't a place to relax; it's a place to play, and play *hard*.

History & Orientation

Zermatt was first known as **Pratobornum**, under which name records exist from as early as 1280, and the first use of its current name dates from the 15th century. Its sovereign, the Bishop of Sion, largely ignored the little valley, and by 1691 the three local hamlets voluntarily united under a single village constitution. British climbers discovered the area in the late 18th century, and in 1838, a local surgeon opened the village's first guest house. It was called the Hôtel Mont Cervie, and it accommodated up to three people. Today, this little village of 5,500 can house some 14,000 guests per night.

The Matterhorn

Its very name conjures up fairy-tale images of high-Alpine grandeur. The fascination began early, when British adventurers first discovered the climbing potential of the region's peaks. In 1792, Horace Benedict scaled the Klein Matterhorn and estimated its larger sibling to be 4,501.7 m/14,760 feet high. Thus, the gauntlet was thrown down.

Climbers thronged to the region. And finally, on July 14th, 1865, after seven previous attempts and a 32-hour ascent, Edward Whymper and a party of six others became the first to summit the Matterhorn: Edward Whymper, the two Peter Taugwalders (father and son), Michel Croz, Reverend Charles Hudson, Lord Francis Douglas, and Robert Hadow had made history. However, early in their triumphant descent, one member of the roped party slipped over the North Wall, dragging with him three other climbers. A weak roped snapped, and all four fell to their deaths. Whymper and the Taugwalders returned to Zermatt alone.

The cog-wheel railway to the Gornergrat between Riffelberg and Riffelalp backdropped by the Matterhorn (Franziska Pfenniger)

The Town

Zermatt streches along the Mattervispa River, up the valley toward the imposing Matterhorn. Anchoring its northern end is the train station, where most visitors arrive. Across Bahnhofstrasse, the street running in front of the station, the Gornergrat Railway chugs up the mountainside to the southeast. Bahnhofstrasse, the main road in town, heads south toward the Matterhorn, paralleling the river and its waterside road. The road travels past the church at Platz, and several cross-streets lead east over the river.

Confusingly for visitors, houses are numbered, but street names are rarely used; learn districts and landmarks instead. The Matten district is home to the railway station and the sports fields, and Hinterdorf, Hof, Am Bach, and Oberdorf lie south on the same side of the river. Across the river to the east, on the extreme northern end of town, is Wiesti. Oberhausern,

Steinmatte, and Winkelmatten lie south. At the valley's northern head, the Schluhmatten district is home to the Matterhorn Express cableway stations.

Getting Here & Around

 Travelers arriving by **air** should fly in to either Geneva or Zürich, both approximately 3½ hours away by car. Helicopter transfers are possible for those willing to part with substantial amounts of cash. **Drivers** head up a southern valley from Visp, or park their cars and hop a **train** for the 90-minute ride to Zermatt. (Park-and-ride spaces here are free for Zermatt visitors.) Motorists can drive as far as Täsch, park in paid lots, and catch the train to Zermatt from the new Matterhorn Terminal. Convenient luggage carts are available – they can be taken aboard the train, strapped in for the ride, and deposited on arrival in Zermatt. New arrivals at Zermatt's train station move in a muddle of taxis, carriages, and luggage carts. (Before you pay for an in-town transfer, check with your hotel to see if they offer a complimentary shuttle.)

Once settled, visitors get around town on foot, via electric bus or taxi, or in a horse-drawn carriage. For electric **taxi** service, contact ☎ 027 967 77 77 or 027 12 12. For **horse-drawn carriage** and **sleigh** service – either as a taxi or a round-trip tour – contact **Imboden Werner** at ☎ 079 436 76 12.

LIFT PASS PRICE SAMPLES	
Winter	
1-day all-area	76 CHF
6-day adult	379 CHF
Pedestrian round-trip on Gornergrat Railway	72 CHF
Summer	
1-day Matterhorn ski pass	63 CHF
1-day Matterhorn & Schwarzsee	84 CHF
2-day all-area Panoramic Pass	130 CHF
6-day all-area Zermatt Peak Pass	238 CHF

Mountain transport rises in three main sections: the **Matterhorn Express** from the southern edge of town to Furi, Trockener Steg, Schwarzsee, and the Klein Matterhorn; the **Alpen-Metro train** to Sunnegga from the northeastern corner of town; and the **Gornergratbahn railway** from its base near the main train station to Riffelalp and beyond.

Getting More Info

The excellent tourist office is near the train station at Bahnhofplatz 5. For more information, contact ☎ 027 966 81 00, www.zermatt.ch.

The post office is on Bahnhofstrasse directly in the center.

Zermatt is a well-connected town – some 25 outlets offer Internet access. Check with your hotel, or head for the **Stoked** office or the **Country Bar**. Both are in the center just around the corner from the train station.

The Sights

In town, Zermatt's sights are limited. Visitors stroll and shop along Bahnhofstrasse and through the narrow village lanes, stopping at cafés and perhaps at the church cemetery, where many famous climbers are buried. The most interesting **old lanes** wind just beyond the church and, as well, between Bahnhofstrasse and the river in the Hinterdorf district.

Look, too, for the new Matterhorn Museum, a collection of interactive displays housed in an underground "Zermatlantis."

Several peaks draw tourists as well as sports enthusiasts, but no visitor should miss a trip up to the **Klein Matterhorn Peak**. A glacier grotto sits just below the top lift station; inside the cave, enjoy sculptures and exhibits on glaciers, geology, and climbing sports. For a panoramic view of the Matterhorn, however, no vantage point compares to the top station of the old **Gornergratbahn** across the valley – sunsets are particularly memorable from here.

Switzerland

The town of Zermatt (Christof Sonderegger)

WHAT'S THAT?

One of the Alps' most ambitious construction projects is underway atop the Klein Matterhorn peak. Once complete, Zermatt's newest mountain lodge will be a glass and steel pyramid soaring 384 feet above the mountain's 12,736-foot natural summit. The 30-story-high, suspended structure will house restaurants, shops, multimedia attractions, and hotel rooms, all pressurized to insure the comfort of guests – who, incidentally, will pass through equalization cabins as they enter.

Young ibexes in the Monte Rosa massif (15,000 feet), high above Zermatt (Christof Sonderegger)

The Adventures

● ON FOOT

About 400 km of **hiking** paths wind through the mountains above Zermatt, most areas well-served by cableway or mountain train. The most spectacular of the trails run through the Sunnegga and Rothorn areas, winding around lakes, skirting glaciers, and all within view of the Matterhorn across the valley. One of these, the **Marmot Trail**, leads from mid-mountain Rothorn at Blauherd down to Sunnegga via a path lined with several marmot family groups.

Walkers wanting a closer look at the majestic mountain should try the new **Matterhorn Trail**. It drops from the lift station at Schwarzsee, along the foot of the Matterhorn to Stafel, to the lake at Zmutt, and then down to the lift station at Furi – passing several inviting mountain huts along the way.

✔ Zermatt is one of the few high-mountain resorts to remain open into late fall. Autumn wanders are enhanced with colorful views of blue sky, icy peaks, red pasturelands, and variable green larch trees. When weather conditions allow, footpaths remain open through October.

Switzerland

Zermatt cut its tourism teeth on the earliest mountaineers, and opportunities for **climbing** still abound. Visitors head out with mountain guides to climb rock faces, scale glacier crevasses, and trek to remote mountain huts. Outdoor and indoor climbing walls and an ice-climbing tower are available, the climbing school offers instruction, and an excellent equipped route traverses the Gorner Gorge. For experienced climbers, a number of summits beckon – not least the legendary Matterhorn. Check in with the **Alpin Center Zermatt** to join a group or to hire a private guide. For more info, see *Sports Services* below.

Memorable Moments

Zermatt has a knack for creating fond memories. Check in with the tourist office regarding the following adventures:

■ Fondues under the full moon at the Rothorn restaurant and a moonlit ski run down.

■ Winetasting in the glacier grotto at Klein Matterhorn.

■ Evening snowshoeing to dinner in a mountain hut.

■ Sunrise excursions to the Rothorn, Klein Matterhorn, and Gornergrat.

■ Open-carriage train rides on the Gornergrat Mountain Railway.

■ Fire-and-ice ski descents by torchlight from the Gornergrat.

● ON HORSEBACK

 The **Zermatt Mule Trekking Company** runs mule-trekking excursions varying in length from one hour to several days. Check in at ☎ 027 967 64 59, www. rhone.ch/zermatt-mule-trekking. **Llamas** plod along the Gornergrat at Riffelberg from July to September; www.zermatt-tours.ch. And **horse-drawn carriage** and **sleigh rides** are offered from **Imboden Werner**, ☎ 079 436 76 12.

● ON WHEELS

 Zermatt maintains 80 km of designated **mountain biking** trails but – after much contention between bikers and hikers – now prohibits biking on walking trails not specifically marked "MTB." Four popular trails cross the Gornergrat and Rothorn areas – check with the tourist office for the latest map. For mountain bike rental and instruction, check in with the **Swiss Ski School**; see *Sports Services* below.

● IN THE AIR

 Air Zermatt offers **helicopter rides** around the Matterhorn, **heli-taxi transfers** from several airports, and **heli-skiing drops** to the Theodul Glacier. For more information and reservations, contact ☎ 027 966 86 86. Visitors can also take to the sky with the **Air Born Flight School**. **Tandem paragliding** rides are offered, and the Rothorn is a favorite launch point. For more information, drop by the **Haus Montana**, or contact ☎ 027 967 67 44.

● ON SNOW & ICE

Summer Skiing

Zermatt's Klein Matterhorn boasts the highest summer skiing area in the Alps. Skiers and boarders slide down the Theodulgletscher at Plateau Rosa, which – depending on snow conditions – offers anywhere between 6.2 and 21 km of marked pistes. One cable car and six drag lifts serve the 36-square-km area. When conditions cooperate, the glacier ice opens for skiing from early morning till midday between early July and late October. So then, a perfect summer day in Zermatt: Ski in the morning until the ice gets slushy, enjoy lunch at a mountain restaurant, and hike dry trails in the afternoon.

 In the winter, **skiers** take to 313 km of pistes across Zermatt and connecting Cervinia. Zermatt's 184 km are graded 22% easy, 50% intermediate, and 28%

difficult. Beginners are hard-pressed to find novice runs, and best head for the blues on Gornergrat and Riffelberg. Intermediates enjoy the run of most area slopes, and advanced and expert skiers head off-piste with a guide – or take to the air for some of Europe's best heli-skiing. **Snowboarders** enjoy a growing selection of facilities, including three fun parks, a halfpipe, and a prepared mogul steep. A boarder-cross run and quarter-pipe are at Blauherd, and a new snow park at Rotenboden on the Gornergrat includes a number of obstacles, a kids' corner, an igloo, and a teepee bar. In summer, the Theodul glacier hosts the **Gravity Park**, the biggest snow park in Europe, with a 200-m super-pipe, a halfpipe, and several other obstacles.

✔ Skiers and boarders enjoy the relatively rare opportunity to slide across international borders. Although Cervinia, Italy, is an eyesore of a resort, it is nice to ski over for a lunch of fresh pasta. (I liked the food and the views at **l'Etoile**, mid-mountain.) Beware, however: Not all lift passes access both the Swiss and Italian lifts – check before you follow the Italian flags downhill into Italy. If you get stuck without the right pass, it's an expensive one-way ticket back to the peak.

Cross-country skiers are limited to just nine km of runs, but **winter walkers** enjoy 40 km of groomed hiking paths, including 30 km at the new Swiss Nordic Park in the Rothorn-Schwarzsee area. Fans of ice sports take to two **ice-skating rinks** and 10 **curling rinks**. For **tobogganing**, head to the Gornergrat and the Rotenboden-Riffelberg 20-minute run. For a one-hour **dog-sledding** excursion along the foot of the Matterhorn, dial ☎ 027 967 77 09. In addition, the Alpin Center (see *Sports Services* below) offers a wide range of winter activities, including **snowshoeing**, **ice climbing**, and **ski touring**.

Sports Services, Outfitters & Guides

■ The **Alpin Center Zermatt** consolidates the efforts of some 80 mountain guides who together offer a wide range of mountaineering options for visitors at all levels of ability. Climbing, high-mountain treks, and glacier excursions are on the menu here. Stop by the office at Bahnhofstrasse in the town center from 8:30 am-noon and from 4-7 pm daily. From more info, contact ☎ 027 966 24 60.

■ The **Swiss Ski and Snowboard School** offers on-slope instruction in summer as well as winter. The school also runs mountain biking excursions in summer. For info and reservations, drop by the office on Bahnhofstrasse or contact ☎ 027 966 24 66, www.skischulezermatt.ch.

■ **Stoked** is the town's alternative ski and snowboard school – and I've heard good things. They have a small, energetic team of instructors specializing in off-piste glacier adventures. Stoked runs the Snowflakes Kids Club and organizes some summer activities, too. For more info, stop by Hofmattstrasse 7 or contact ☎ 027 967 70 22, www.stoked.ch.

Where to Sleep

 The **Grand Hotel Zermatterhof** (€€€€€) teams up with Swiss Deluxe Hotel sibling **Mont Cervin** (€€€€€) to offer the plushest accommodation in town. Both are in the center, both boast excellent cuisine, and both share the same rate structure. Book the Zermatterhof at ☎ 027 966 66 00, www.zermatt.ch/zermatterhof; the Mont Cervin at ☎ 027 966 88 88, www.zermatt.ch/montcervin.

Grand Hotel Zermatterhof

Switzerland

The **Hotel Monte Rosa** (€€€€€) was once the Mont Cervie, the village's first hotel, a three-room establishment opened in 1838 by Josef Lauber. Since that day, it's witnessed many his-

Hotel Monte Rosa

torical events, including the backside of guest Edward Whymper as he headed off for the Matterhorn summit. Today, the traditional rooms show individual décor, and all bask in the warmest of Swiss hospitality. Inquire at ☎ 027 966 03 33, www.zermatt.ch/monterosa.

The **Romantik Hotel Julen** (€€€-€€€€) is a family-run affair, an old chalet within sight of the Matterhorn peak. There's a kid-pleasing indoor pool, a garden, and a sauna. Most of the traditional, pine-paneled rooms have balconies. Book at ☎ 027 966 76

Romantik Hotel Julen

00, www.romantikhotels.com/Zermatt.

The **Hotel Post** (€€-€€€) is the town's social center, offering three restaurants, three bars, and a disco all under one roof. The décor is cozy and eccentric, with cartoon characters lining the entry and knickknacks strewn about like something from an Old West tavern. It's comfy enough and very central, but it can

The Kulm Hotel

also be loud – a mix to suit those looking for a party. Book at ☎ 027 967 19 31, www.hotelpost.ch.

For a remote night on the mountain, book the **Kulm Hotel** (€€) at Gornergrat. The fortress-like structure tops the 3,100-m peak at the terminus of the Gornergratbahn Railway. The rooms are Spartan, the views spectacular, and the mood convivial. Rooms share baths, and west-facing rooms are worth the bump in price for their Matterhorn views; ☎ 027 966 64 00.

Where to Eat

With over 100 restaurants in town and some 38 dining outlets on the mountain, Zermatt guests don't go hungry. Many of the best restaurants are in local hotels; most are pricey. For gourmet grub, try the dining rooms at the **Grand Hotel Zermatterhof** (€€€) and the **Monte Cervin** (€€€).

The historical **Whymperstube** (€€€) at the Monte Rosa sets an elegant table with the highest quality regional dishes; ☎ 027 967 22 96.

For traditional cuisine, the rustic **Stockhorn** (€€-€€€) offers good grills and fondues across the river on the east bank; ☎ 027 967 17 47, www.grill-stockhorn.ch. Nearby, the tiny **Grill Restaurant Spycher** (€€-€€€) offers traditional dishes and a specialty flambée. Reserve at ☎ 027 967 2041. In the center, on the square just behind the church, **Chez Gaby** (€€) does grills and Swiss specialities; ☎ 027 967 31 34. The **Restaurant Stadel** (€€), also on the main drag, does the same; ☎ 027 967 35 36.

For less expensive fare, head for the Hotel Post, where the **Pizzeria Broken** (€-€€) spins a good pie, the **Old Spaghetti Factory** (€-€€) does decent pasta, and the **Brown Cow** (€-€€) dishes out sandwiches and snacks. The **Papparela** (€) is popular for both après-ski and its pizzas. Finally, a trip up to the **Restaurant Zum See** makes for a special evening out. A 40-minute walk uphill (or a 15-minute downhill walk from the Furi lift), this little mountain hut serves up gourmet grub amid loads of ambiance. Book a table at ☎ 027 967 20 45, www.zumsee.ch.

Where to Party

Après-ski starts early on the mountain, with skiers dropping down to town via Furi and the **Hennu Stall**, a hut with a big deck, loud music, and a crowd. It's along the trail to town, just under the Matterhorn Express.

In the center, on the east bank of the river, après-ski revelers head for **Papperla** for drinks and pizza. Later, **Murphy's Bar** proves popular, too; it's an Irish Pub with nightly live music. For other options, simply wander down Bahnhofstrasse and shop for an appealing crowd. At the Hotel Post, **Pink** offers live music, **Le Broken** does disco into the wee hours, and **Le Village** pumps a club mix. The **Brown Cow** draws a casual crowd, and the new **Papa Caesar's** chills out in lounge-like surrounds – both of these are also at the Hotel Post. Also on Bahnhofstrasse, **Grampi's** plays multiple roles as a pub, a pizzeria, and a late-night disco.

Behind the Hotel Monte Rosa, the **Pink Elephant** piano bar is a classier affair. The tiny old **Elsie's Place**, on the square across from the church, draws an elegant crowd for snails and cocktails, and the Hotel **Beau-Site** has a mellow piano bar and smoking lounge.

Where to Play

In summer, children head for the **Dwarves' Paradise**, a **playground** near the Blauherd cable station with swings, slides, ropeways, and climbing rocks. The **Kinderparadies** offers daycare programs between mid-June and mid-August for kids three months and older; ☎ 027 967 72 52, www.kinderparadies-zermatt.ch.

A few years back, Zermatt premiered the **Snowflakes Kids' Club**, a winter facility offering a play park and a novice snowboarding arena. Parents appreciate Zermatt's **kids-ski-free** program for kids through nine years of age – those nine-15 years old pay just half of the adult fare. Finally, the tourist office can help arrange **babysitting** services.

Festivals & Events

Zermatt offers so many activities that it's as if there's a festival on year-round. In winter, official events run to winter sports competitions, including the men's **FIS World Cup** races in December and several **freestyle ski-**

ing and boarding events throughout the season – of which the **Triftji Bump Bash** in mid-April is most popular.

In summer, Zermatt welcomes a number of sporting events, including the **Zermatt Open**, an international tennis tournament; the **Zermatt Marathon**; and the **Matterhornlauf**, an uphill foot race from Zermatt to Schwarzsee. The **Folklore Festival** sees the return of traditional customs in mid-August, and fans of classical music should come to town for the **Riffelalp Concerts** in early September.

Saas-Fee

Population: 1,607

Base Elevation: 1,800 m/5,904 feet

Mountain resort village

Although Zermatt is certainly the glamour-girl of the Valais, I have a soft spot for its less conspicuous neighbor, tiny Saas-Fee.

While the village lacks Zermatt's jaw-dropping Matterhorn views, Saas-Fee offers intimate looks at the Feegletscher, or "fairy glacier," and has what is in our opinion a much more romantic ambiance. First developed in the 17th century as a summer farming community, Saas-Fee retains its traditional architecture, including one of the region's finest collections of traditional *stadel*, the farmers' huts built on stone pillars to deter rummaging rodents. Its clientele is largely Swiss and German, with less than one percent of its winter guests arriving from North America.

Saas-Fee lies to the east of Zermatt, on the opposite side of the towering Dom. Like Zermatt, the resort is reached via a climb up the forked valley south of Visp – to reach Saas-Fee, drivers at Stalden take the lft fork toward Saastal instead of the right fork toward Täsch. (Although only a few km apart as-the-crow-flies, the drive between Saas-Fee and Zermatt takes around an hour.) Also like Zermatt, the village of Saas-Fee is technically car-free, served only by a swarm of electric taxi carts. The swarm here, however, is considerably smaller and less menacing. Drivers park in the nine-story cliff-side garage on the village

Switzerland

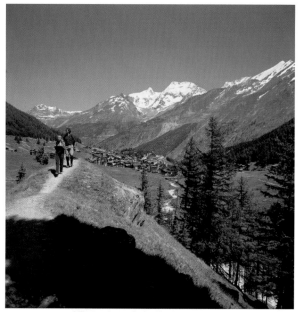

Hikers above Saas-Fee (Lucia Degonda)

edge and, from the garage loading bays, telephone hotels for pickup. (Visitors arriving by train must bus in from Brig or Visp.)

Guests here split into two distinct camps – those who've come for the small-resort exclusivity, and those who've come for the big-mountain recreation. Both camps enjoy the views from the **Allalin**, where the world's highest revolving restaurant, the **Drehrestaurant Metro-Alpin**, does a full rotation each hour. Steps away, adventurers stroll through the largest ice pavilion in the world (the **Mittelallin Eispavillon**), a cave carved out of the glacier and embellished with sculptures and a chapel.

Active visitors enjoy **summer skiing** on top of the glacier each morning and **hiking** and **biking** throughout the region on some 350 km of trails. With 13 nearby peaks towering to 4,000 m/ 13,000 feet and more, Saas-Fee remains an excellent **climbing** base, and even those new to the sport should try the cable-, rope-, and ladder-equipped route through the **Alpine Gorge**. In winter, 140 km of groomed runs offer **skiing** and **snowboarding**

Saas-Fee in winter (Saas-Fee Tourism)

for all levels, and several easy slopes run along the glacial ice, giving even beginning skiers an intimate look at dramatic blue crevasses. In addition, and a particular hit with families, the whole of the Hannig area is reserved for **non-ski** winter activities – a gondola-served mountain where non-skiers enjoy **winter hiking**, **tobogganing**, and **dining** in mountain huts.

✔ For those wanting to explore a bit farther afield, Saas-Fee and Zermatt have partnered up to offer a combined lift pass that gives access to the slopes at both resorts. Plan on a one-hour transfer between the two.

Want to stay? Although this is largely an apartment-stay town, there are several special places from which to choose. Those seeking luxury should plunk down their platinum cards at the **Ferienart Walliserhof** (€€€€), a modern chalet with four restaurants and a fireplace next to its indoor pool; ☎ 027 958 18 00, www.ferienart.

Ferienart Walliserhof

Hotel Dom

ch. Less expensive lodging can be found at the trendy **Hotel Dom** (€€), where fun-loving, kitchy décor draws a young snowboarding crowd to the hotel's popular lounge and basement bar, Popcorn; ☎ 027 957 51 01, www.uniquedom.com.

Those more serious about their sports head for the homey old **Hotel Britannia** (€€), a family-run hostelry with simple rooms – some freshly renovated, others old and dark. All, however, share the same lovely dining room, delicious food, and big terrace views. An excellent base for climbers, the Britannia is run by Jacques and Lori Bigler, who guide walks and are themselves accomplished climbers. Book early at ☎ 027 957 16 16, www.saas-fee.ch/britannia.

The excellent tourist office is at the top of town near the parking garage. For more information, contact ☎ 027 958 18 58, www.saas-fee.ch.

Interlaken & the Jungfrau

Set in the larger area of the Bernese Oberland, the Jungfrau tourist region enjoys the distinction of being Europe's most visited Alpine playground – and its easy to see why. At its center lies Interlaken, a large town encircled by mountains and flanked by two long lakes, the **Thunersee** and the **Brienzersee**. In the town hub, an impressive network of mountain railways, passenger ferries, and cable cars make it easy to explore the surrounding Alpine grandeur. To the south of the town stretches the dramatic **Lauterbrunnen Valley**; the car-free villages of **Mürren** and **Wengen** perch high above. The resort of **Grindelwald** hums with activity, and the majestic mountain trio – the **Eiger**, the **Mönch**, and the **Jungfrau** – soar in the south.

Panoramic view from Beatenberg down to Interlaken, with Wilderswil in the background (Lucia Degonda)

◆ Interlaken

Population: 15,000

Base elevation: 567 m/1,860 feet

Lake & mountain tourist town

At the heart of the Alps lies Switzerland; at the heart of Switzerland lies the Jungfrau region; and at the heart of the Jungfrau lies Interlaken.

Tucked away in what is arguably the most spectacular Alpine scenery in the world, Interlaken enjoys renown for its diversity of outdoor adventures and its role as the Jungfrau region's mountain transportation hub. It's an inviting town – a busy, bustling place with back alleys few tourists take time to explore.

Switzerland

History & Orientation

Interlaken got its start during the 12th century, when a cloister took up residence on the inter-lake land bar that now hoists up the town. Although a worthwhile destination in its own right, the town's tourist industry blossomed due to its convenient location just north of the famous Jungfrau peaks: the Eiger, the Jungfrau, and the Mönch – names, by the way, that translate to the Ogre, the Virgin, and (in between, piously separating the two) the Monk. The valley village of Lauterbrunnen lies directly south of Interlaken, and the resort villages of Grindelwald, Wengen, and Mürren perch in the mountains above. The region's resort villages grow smaller and quieter from east to west. Farthest east, Grindelwald buzzes with big-resort energy; over the hill to the west, Wengen slows down a bit, banning cars from its streets; and across the Lauterbrunnen Valley, the pedestrian-only village of Mürren perches high in splendid isolation.

Interlaken rests on a land bar between Lake Thun, or the Thunersee, and Lake Brienz, or the Brienzersee. However, this is not a lakefront town, per se. The town center clusters directly between the two shorelines, a fair distance from each. The Aare River runs through town between the lakes, and a ship canal forges in from the Thunersee in the west.

The Town

Interlaken has two train stations, pragmatically named the **Ostbahnhof** and the **Westbahnhof**, or the East and West stations. Ferry terminals lie just behind each: Thunersee boats dock behind the West Station; Brienzersee boats dock behind the East Station. The main boulevard, the **Höheweg**, runs from one station to the other paralleling the Aare River. Midway, the **Höhematte Park** offers some semblance of a town center. The town's grandest hotel, the **Victoria Jungfrau**, fronts the park, and the **Metropole Tower** rises at its southwestern corner. A bit farther east, Höheweg briefly intersects the pedestrian zone, which centers on the streets of Jungfraustrasse, Marktgasse, Postgasse, and Neugasse.

Getting Here & Around

 Visitors arriving by **air** should fly in to the international airports at Zürich, 129 km north, or Geneva, 214 km west. Allow 2½ hours driving time from Zürich, and two hours driving time from Geneva. Those arriving by **car** enjoy easy access via the A8 Autobahn from Thun.

Once in town, **buses** run the city streets, and the Post Bus network well covers the surrounding region. **Boats** ply the waters of both the Thunersee and the Brienzersee, but the ferry loops make more sense as recreation than as transportation – see *On the Lakes* below. Mountain trains depart Interlaken Ost station for Mürren, Wengen, Grindelwald, and the Kleine Scheidegg. Mountain transport by railway is covered below under Adventures by Rail.

✔ Guests staying in the Jungfrau region should receive at check-in their **Eiger, Mönch, and Jungfrau Gästekarte**. The card brings a number of small price reductions that together can add up to significant savings.

Getting More Info

 The tourist office is on the corner at Höheweg 37. For more information, contact ☎ 033 826 53 00, www. InterlakenTourism.ch. Radio Berner Oberland broadcasts news in English several times each day, and on TV, the *Panoramic* cable channel serves up tourist information and panoramic live shots from the nearby peaks.

The main post office is at Postplatz near the Interlaken West train station.

For Internet access, head for the **Weltr@um Café** at Rosengarten 5. On Centralstrasse, **Yess** has terminals as well.

The Sights

Although most tourists blow through town en route to the mountains just south, Interlaken itself offers several sights worth seeing – and several back alleys worth strolling. Walkers should wander down Höheweg, into the Kursaal gardens, around the Höhematte Park, and through the small but quaint pedestrian

Interlaken, with the Eiger, Mönch and Jungfrau mountains, seen from the Chienbberg on the road to Beatenberg (Lucia Degonda)

zone along Blumenstrasse, Neugasse, Marktgasse, and Jungfraustrasse.

Just outside of town is Interlaken's newest attraction, the much-awaited **Mystery Park**. This museum and amusement park explores the world's oddest phenomena across seven themes, including ancient writings, the Giza pyramids, Mayan calendars, and outer space. It's open daily, 10 am-6 pm; 48 CHF. For more information, contact ☎ 0848 50 60 70, www.mysterypark.ch.

The Adventures

In addition to the astounding array of outdoor recreation around the surrounding Jungfrau region – see *Grindelwald, Lauterbrunnen, Mürren,* and *Wengen,* listed separately below – Interlaken itself offers a wide range of lake, air, and mountain adventures.

Jungfrau Region

BERN

Langnau

TO LUCERNE

Thun

Niederhorn

Engelberg

Brienz

Meiringen

Titlis

Interlaken

Spiez

A6

Grindelwald

Wilderswil

Wengen

Eiger

Lauterbrunnen

Kleine-Scheidegg

Kandersteg

Mürren

Schilthorn

Jungfrau

Fiesche

ITALY

Sierre

Visp

A9

Simplon
Pass

N

25 MILES

25 KM

© 2007 HUNTER PUBLISHING, INC

● ON FOOT

A vast array of hikes wind throughout the Jungfrau region, with most **walkers** basing themselves in Grindelwald, Wengen, Mürren, or Lauterbrunnen – some of the Alps' most traveled trails are here. **Climbers**, too, like the region. Although most stay at higher altitudes, climbers staying in Interlaken can easily make arrangements with any of the town's adventure outfitters or the guiding specialist school, Swiss Mountain Guides (see *Sports Services*, page 399).

Best among Interlaken's local hikes are those starting from the upper stations of the local mountain trains at Schynige Platte and Heimwehfluh. Experienced hikers should try the six-hour **Faulhorn Trail** from Schynige Platte to First Peak above Grindelwald. The trail goes through and above stunning mountain scenery, passing by the Bachalpsee and two mountain restaurants along the way. Take the Schynige Platte train to start, and return via the First cableway to Grindelwald and then railway back to Interlaken. (The reverse works just as well.)

Interlaken (Broguybro)

● IN WATER

Interlaken loves water – even its name means "between lakes." And, indeed, the town sits between two long lakes on a land bar that was itself under water in ages past. A waterway runs through town center, connecting the two lakes, and snow-capped mountains drip clear water into several Alpine lakes. The Brienzersee sees relatively little recreational action – its banks are steep and its winds calm – but the breezy Thunersee offers a wide range of wet sports.

Swimmers head for **Neuhaus** at the northeastern edge of the Thunersee. Here, a grassy beach, lake-swimming facilities, and sand volleyball courts round out the summer facilities. A restaurant serves up food, and two outfitters offer **sailing**, **windsurfing**, and **pedal boat rentals** in addition to **wakeboarding**, **water-skiing**, and pulls on **tubes and banana-floats**. For more information, contact the sailing school's **Wake Point**, ☎ 033 822 83 30, www.swiss-sail.ch; or the **Hang**

The Brienzersee (Roland Zumbühl)

Loose Surfshop at ☎ 079 023 52 28, www.surfshop-hangloose.ch.

Whitewater sports excursions are offered by several outfitters, most notably **Alpin Raft** – see *Sports Services* below, page 399. In addition, the **Bödelibad** swimming complex offers a 75-ft **indoor pool** year-round and a 150-ft **outdoor pool** in summer. **Lake diving** is offered by a school in the Thunersee village of Gunten – contact the Interlaken tourist office for more information.

Summertime **fishing** is possible without permit from the shores of both the Thunersee and the Brienzersee. Permits for other bodies of water – or for fishing from a boat – are available at the tourist office. The tourist office also stocks info on limits, seasons, and bait regulations; stop by before you cast off. Favorite fishing holes include the Bortsee, the Bachalpsee, and the Lütschine River, all three requiring the extra permit.

On the Lakes

Passenger boats make the rounds on the Thunersee year-round and on the Brienzersee from April to October. Regular service makes possible day-trips to a number of lakeshore destinations, and less frequent lake cruises feature a variety of themes. On the **Brienzersee**, boats run

Switzerland

Waterskiing on the Brienzersee

from behind the Interlaken East train station to docks at Brienz and Iseltwald. Round-trips to Brienz take approximately 2½ hours. The lake is the more attractive of the two and, a less subjective claim to fame, boasts the greatest average depth of all the lakes in Switzerland.

Brienz, on the Brienzersee (Roland Zumbühl)

The **Thunersee** proves more popular for day excursions. Its fleet of 10 boats departs from the docks behind the Interlaken West train station, heading across the large lake to docks including Beatenbucht and the lovely lakeside city of Thun.

The Thunersee (Roland Zumbühl)

The round-trip takes approximately four hours. For more information, contact www.bls.ch.

Children will want to meet the Thunersee's resident dragon, the fabled Ponzo. The large lizard figures prominently in the attractions around **Beatenberg**, a hillside town best reached by fanciful rides on the steam-breathing **Dragon Ship.** From the Beatenbucht boat dock, Ponzo's funicular roars up the mountain to Beatenberg; from there, a gondola rises to the peak of the **Niederhorn**, stopping midway at Vorass for those wishing to roll back down. (Trottibike scooters and mountain bikes are for rent at the valley station and can be carried up.) At the top of the Niederhorn, views, paragliders, trails, and a mountain restaurant delight adventurers of all ages. The Dragon Ship also calls at the Beatushöhlen-Sundlauenen dock and its **Dragon's Den**, a fascinating historical site also known as St. Beatus Caves.

● ON WHEELS

Mountain bikers enjoy some 420 km of marked mountain biking routes in the Jungfrau region. In addition, 360 km of marked biking routes wind around the shores of the Thunersee. From Beatenberg, experienced riders set out on a difficult nine-km loop around the Niederhorn. **Trotti-bike scooters** are for rent at the Mittelstation Vorass

Switzerland

above Beatenberg; ride down via either a six-km or a 12-km trail.

Back in Interlaken, **Daniel's Rentals** rents **motorcycles, jeeps, scooters**, and **bikes**. It's next door to Balmer's Hostel; ☎ 079 286 58 44. **Skaters** and **skateboarders** head for the Interlaken airfield, where a skate park is illuminated until 1 am in good weather. For inline skate rental, try **Eiger Sport** at Bahnhofstrasse 2.

● BIG-MOUNTAIN EXCURSIONS

Chief among Interlaken's attractions are the famed peaks to its south – the Eiger, Mönch, and Jungfrau – and the opportunity to scale them via railway, funicular, and cable car. As the region's hub for mountain transportation, Interlaken offers a convenient base from which to set out exploring. Although expensive, these rail routes are some of the most memorable in Europe, and I hope you'll do at least one. Each can be completed in a half-day if you choose the quickest connections, but I'd recommend lingering awhile in the villages along the way. The following are just two of the region's big-mountain excursions.

The Jungfraujoch (Roland Zumbühl)

The Jungfraujoch, nicknamed The Top of Europe, is the region's classic mountain excursion loop. In fact, when you return home from Switzerland, "Did you go up the Jungfrau?" is probably among the first questions you'll get. The outing departs from

Interlaken's east train station, passes into the **Lauterbrunnen Valley**, then loops up to **Klein Scheidegg** via either **Wengen** or **Grindelwald**. (We think the clockwise, Grindelwlad-first route offers the more dramatic approach, but reasonable people disagree. To see it all, complete the loop on your way back down.) From Klein Scheidegg, the Jungfraujochbahn railway climbs up a tunnel just inside the Eiger's North Face, making two in-mountain stops at viewpoints along the way – viewpoints also used as rescue stations from which to aide stranded climbers. At the top, 3,454 m/11,330 feet up, visitors enjoy panoramic views from the terrace, visits to the Sphinx research center, and wanders through the tunnels and the Ice Palace, a cave carved out of the Aletsch Glacier. In summer, huskies pull sleds, guides lead treks, and skiers, climbers, and sledders play on the glacial ice. It's a spectacular journey that may well produce your trip's most memorable moments. Transportation links operate year-round. Allow at least six hours. www.jungfraujoch.ch.

The Schilthorn (Roland Zumbühl)

The Schilthorn lies across the Lauterbrunnen Valley from the majestic trio, the Eiger, Mönch, and Jungfrau – offering an ideal vantage point from which to view the big-picture panorama. The Schilthorn loop starts with a train ride from Interlaken to **Lauterbrunnen**, continues with a climb via Mountain Railway to Grütschalp and along the cliff to **Mürren**. After visiting the lovely little car-free village, visitors ascend to Piz Gloria on the

Switzerland

Schilthorn summit. Here, views stretch out in all directions, and a revolving restaurant serves meals. Much is made of the mountain station's role in the James Bond flick *On Her Majesty's Secret Service*. Piz Gloria provided the primary set for the film – clips screen today in the mountaintop theater. Adventurers return to the valley via cableway to **Stechelberg**, traveling back to Interlaken by bus. Although it's not as renowned as the Jungfraujoch loop, the Schilthorn is the favorite excursion of many visitors who've done both. They laud its 360° panoramic views, its *007* connections, and its proximity to charming, cliffside Mürren. Transportation links operate year-round except during maintenance closures for a few days in late April and for three weeks late November through early December. Links as far as Mürren operate year-round. Allow at least five hours. www.schilthorn.ch.

✔ The Berner Oberland's Panorama cable channel broadcasts live shots from rotating cameras perched at mountain stations. Although weather conditions can change quickly on the mountain, it's worthwhile to check conditions before you hop the train or lift. These are expensive excursions, and bad weather or low visibility greatly diminishes their worth.

Local Mountain Excursions

Although less glamorous than the Jungfrau and Schilthorn loops, several worthwhile excursions ascend the foothills at Interlaken's doorstep. Perfect for family outings and area orientation rides, these trips are far less expensive than the state-of-the-art, peak-scaling outings above.

Schynige Platte should be your choice if you only have time for one local mountain excursion. The trip starts out with a short train ride from Interlaken East Station to Wilderswil and a transfer to the Schynige cogwheel railway. At the top, views reach out to the Eiger, Mönch, and Jungfrau, and trails head off in several directions. The Schynige Platte Hotel offers dining service on its terrace, and an Alpine garden boasts over 500 species of plants. Transportation links operate from the end of May through mid-October; allow at least three hours.

*Schynige Platte cog railway ascending the
Schynige Platte* (Schynige Platte)

✔ Those traveling with children should request the booklet Tammi & Tomi: The Last Screw, from the valley station of the Schynige Platte train. The book tells the
story behind the local *Teddyland* hoopla, and kids enjoy searching out the story's scenes.

The **Harder Kulm** funicular departs from the northern edge of
town, across the river from Interlaken East train station. In just
eight minutes, visitors rise to sweeping views of the Thunersee,
the Brienzersee, and the Jungfrau rising above in the south. At
the top there's a short walking loop, the Goblin's Path, and at
the bottom, a tree nursery and a small animal park with chamois and marmots – both the nursery and park are free. Transportation links operate May through October; allow at least one
hour.

Visitors ascend **Heimwehfluh** in just five minutes via a nostalgic old funicular, departing a base at the southwestern edge of
town just behind the Interlaken West train station. At the top,
views stretch over the lakes and back to the Jungfrau. Although
more a hill than a mountain, the Heimwehfluh proves popular
with families, who enjoy a large playground, a show model rail-

Switzerland

way, and two summer toboggan runs – one a slide, one on rails. The funicular operates from April through October; allow at least one hour.

● IN THE AIR

During my last visit to Interlaken, I collected a dozen brochures from outfitters offering airborne sports – and I wasn't even looking that hard. The region's favorable wind conditions make flying extremely popular here, and activities range from paragliding jumps to glacier flights. **Bungee-jumpers** leap out of cable cars, off bridges, and into canyon gorges. **Hang-gliding** and **paragliding** excursions are offered by at least 100 outfitters; make arrangements through **Alpin Center** or **Alpin Raft**, both listed below under *Sports Services*. For **ballooning**, contact **Max Michel**, ☎ 031 911 13 08 or the tourist office.

Skydive Switzerland and **Scenic Air** pair up to offer a good range of outings, including **tandem skydiving** from planes and helicopters, **scenic flights**, and **glacier-landing flights**. In addition, they offer **fly-to-ride heli-skiing** and an **airborne ski shuttle** to Zermatt and the Matterhorn. For more info, contact ☎ 033 826 77 17, www.skydiveswitzerland.com, www.scenicair.ch.

> ✔ For a memorable adventure – or perhaps a positive reply to a marriage proposal – **Scenic Air** will lift you high above the region's lakes and mountains, land on ancient glacial ice and, on request, provide a champagne picnic.

● ON SNOW & ICE

Interlaken's rail network makes it a reasonable location from which to explore the region's **skiing and snowboarding** slopes, a network of some 205 km of runs and 45 lifts jointly marketed under the moniker of the Jungfrau TopSki Region. Cooperating ski areas include Grindelwald, Wengen, and Mürren (see separate listings below). The old railways provide much of the transfer service between the areas; they're a quaint but painfully slow way to get around, however, and snow-sport enthusiasts shouldn't plan to visit more than one resort each day. For example, transfer from

Mürren to Kleine Scheidegg above Grindelwald will take you approximately 1½ hours; the trip from Interlaken to above Kleine Scheidegg takes just slightly less. Nonetheless, if you're prepared for the haul, Interlaken makes a good-value base.

For local on-ice sports, head to the **Bödeli** recreation complex. Its artificial rink is open to the public for **ice-skating**, and equipment is for rent. For more information, contact ☎ 033 822 61 63.

Snowshoeing is on the menu at several local adventure outfitters. The local specialist, however, is **Base Camp**; ☎ 033 823 93 23, www.basecamp.ch.

Ice-climbing, glacier trekking, and **high-mountain tours** are offered by several outfitters, in particular the mountaineering specialists at **Swiss Alpine Guides** – see *Sports Services,* below.

● **IN THE EXTREME**

Interlaken caters to its youthful crowd with the Alps' widest selection of extreme sports outfitters – **Alpin Raft**, **Outdoor Interlaken**, and **Alpin Center** are three of the most reputable; contact info for each is listed below under *Sports Services*. With 14 years in the businesss, Alpin Raft offers a good selection of activities and an admirable safety record. The group specializes in **whitewater** activities, including **rafting** on four rivers and **canyoning** at six locales. Its **bungee-jumping** venues include a glacier and a canyon, and its air team offers **sky diving, paragliding**, and **hang gliding**. Outdoor Interlaken offers a similar program.

An affiliate of the Swiss Ski and Snowboard School, Alpin Center focuses on ski instruction and guiding in addition to its all-season offerings. For a rip-roaring good time, call Alpin Center and book an appointment for **zorbing** – a new adventure sport that involves rolling down a hill inside an inflatable transparent ball.

Sports Services, Outfitters & Guides

■ The **Swiss Ski and Snowboard School** offers a wide range of winter sports programs in addition to its **Alpin Center** adventure sports program. For more information, stop by their shop in Wilderswil or contact ☎ 033 838 55 23, www.alpincenter.ch.

Switzerland

■ **Swiss Alpine Guides** runs a selection of adventure sports, but really shines as an all-season mountaineering school. Private guiding, private instruction, and group courses are offered – options cover terrain from rock to ice. Check in at ☎ 33 822 60 00, www.swissAlpineguides.ch.

■ **Alpin Raft** – see *In the Extreme* above; ☎ 033 823 41 00, www.alpinraft.com.

■ **Outdoor Interlaken** – see *In the Extreme* above; ☎ 033 826 77 19, www.outdoor-interlaken.com.

Where to Sleep

Hotel Victoria-Jungfrau (€€€€) is the queen bee in Interlaken, a grand old Belle Époque affair dominating the center and sprawling along the Höhematte Park. It's next to the casino, equidistant from either train station, and equipped with an in-house daycare program. Book

Victoria Jungfrau

at ☎ 033 828 28 28, www.Victoria-jungfrau.ch.

Hotel du Lac

The **Hotel du Lac** (€€€) sits on the waterway between the boat dock and the Interlaken East train station, a good locale for early-morning rail departures into the mountains. Unless you're a huge fan of trains, book a water-view room; ☎ 033 822 29 22, www.bestwestern.ch/dulac-interlaken.

The **Hotel Neuhaus** (€€-€€€) has lakeside rooms and cheery décor on the grassy beach at Thunersee. Also available are family rooms, with two separate sleeping areas. Contact ☎ 033 822 82 82, www.hotel-neuhaus.ch.

Hotel Neuhaus

HOTEL PRICES	
€	Under 120 CHF
€€	120-225 CHF
€€€	226-375 CHF
€€€€	Over 375 CHF

There is no shortage of hostel accommodations. Best among the bunch for my buck is still **Balmer's Herberge** (€), Switzerland's classic youth hostel stay. The central, chalet-style complex is rowdy, energized perhaps by the extreme sports outfitter that books adventure outings – canyoning, rafting, bungee-jumping, ice climbing, ski tours and such – directly at the hostel. Nightly movies, a guest kitchen, a coin laundry, and e-mail access are offered. In summer, out near the autobahn, **Balmer's Tent** (€) bunks overflow guests. Contact Balmer's at ☎ 033 822 19 61, www.balmers.com.

✔ Interlaken offers a good range of budget accommodations, making it an attractive base during the winter season, when rates in the mountain resorts soar.

The best of the summertime **camping** (€) is lakeside at Neuhaus at **Alpenblick**; ☎ 033 823 14 70, www.camping-alpenblick.ch. Or, beautifully set at the foot of a cliff and waterfall, the **Jungfrau** in Lauterbrunnen. The latter rents bungalows as well; ☎ 033 856 20 20, www.camping-jungfrau.ch; open winter, too.

Where to Eat

Great gourmet fare can be found at the **Jungfrau Brasserie** (€€€) in the Victoria Jungfrau Hotel. Its elegant Art Nouveau dining room dishes up creative Swiss specialties; reserve a table at ☎ 033 828 28 28.

Switzerland

Near the Interlaken West train station, at Bahnhofstrasse 4, the inconspicuous **Le Caveau** (€€-€€€) has a small, simple dining room and delicious French and Swiss specialties, including local fish dishes and meat fondue; ☎ 033 823 24 65.

RESTAURANT COSTS	
€ . . . . Under 15 CHF	
€€ . . . . 15-37 CHF	
€€€ . . . . Over 37 CHF	

For reasonably priced Swiss specialties, head for my favorite restaurant in town, the **Loöwen** (€€), on the main pedestrian square at Marktgasse 10; ☎ 033 821 05 05. Across the square, try also the restaurant **Bären** (€€) in the hotel of the same name – I've heard its fondues are excellent; ☎ 033 822 76 76.

Budgeting visitors enjoy the cheerful **PizPaz** (€), where a long list of pizzas and a good corner locale draws a young crowd. It's at Centralplatz; ☎ 033 822 25 33. Try, too, the self-service restaurant in the **Coop** (€) at Interlaken East.

Where to Party

 Much of Interlaken's nightlife is geared to the youthful crowd attracted by its good selection of hostels. First, the ever-popular **Brasserie 17** has live music each Thursday from September through June starting at 9 pm. It's in the Happy Inn at Rosenstrasse 17; ☎ 033 822 32 25. In the pedestrian zone, the **Löwen** on the Marktstrasse serves beer till late and, just around the corner at Postgasse 3, the **Hüsi Pub** is the town's favorite dive bar with DJs, darts, and video games. **Johnny's Club** in the Hotel Carlton draws a local crowd with frequent live music, and the **Black & White** disco gets rowdy late night on Höheweg.

For more elegant evenings, the **Restaurant Shuh** has tea on the menu, a mature crowd at the tables, and a pianist at the keyboard. Check in at Höheweg 56; ☎ 033 822 94 41. The **Interlaken Casino** is located amid the gardens of the Kursaal at Strandbadstrasse 44. It offers slots, roulette, and blackjack; ☎ 033 827 61 00, www.casino-kursaal.ch.

Evening entertainment can be had at Spycher Restaurant's **Folklore Show**, where a dinner, music, and dance production runs daily from May through October; ☎ 033 827 61 00. Also entertaining, the **William Tell Open Air Theatre** stages the classic Swiss tale on a grand scale with some 180 actors and dozens of farm animals. The play runs one or two times each week from mid-June through early September. For more info, contact ☎ 033 822 37 22, www.tellspiele.ch.

Where to Play

 The Jungfrau region offers more to families and children than any other mountain destination I know. In and around Interlaken, kids enjoy family-oriented activities like lake cruises aboard the Dragon Boat, cable car and train rides, year-round snow play, wildlife parks, model railways, hiking, horse-drawn carriage rides, and the new **Mystery Park**. (And the list could go on.) A **children's train** runs through the center during summer, and the **Toy Library Jojo** allows checkout of games and toys; contact ☎ 033 822 87 86 for more information. **Playgrounds** are at Höhematte Park, near the east school, in the Kursaal garden, and on the mountain at Heimwehfluh.

✔ Although most families come to Interlaken to play together, the tourist office can provide current information regarding daytime childcare and babysitting.

Festivals & Events

 Interlaken and the Jungfrau host many popular events, both in the town and in the mountains. As the mountains are easily reached via Interlaken, I include the events of both Interlaken and the mountain resorts here.

The year kicks off in mid-January, when the **FIS World Cup** races hit town for the **Lauberhornrennen** in Wengen. Mürren cuts loose a week later with the **Infernorennen**, a legendary race that is, together with the Kandahar race, one of the two oldest surviving ski events in the world. It was first held in 1928, and today, each year 1,800 amateurs to experts come to town to rip down the 12-km course, one after the other, all day long. Also in mid-January, Grindelwald hosts the **World Snow Festival**, an impressive ice festival during which snow-carvers whittle away at ice blocks, some the size of a small house.

In March, the **Horischlitten Race** sees the racing of traditional long-horned sleds down the Eiger Run. In early April, the region hosts the **Snowpen Air Rock Concert**, an outdoor party on the Kleine Scheidegg slopes – and with an echo off the Eiger, the winter season clangs to a close.

May brings the **World Barbecue Gold Cup** to the Kursaal and Casino park, and June hauls in the **International Trucker and Country Festival**, drawing top names in country music and an appreciative crowd. In mid-August Interlaken celebrates its **Village Festival** with musical entertainment, games, and folklore, and for two weeks between mid- and late August, the **Interlaken Music Festival** offers a wealth of classical music. The summer ends in September with the **International Jungfrau Marathon**, a grueling race from Interlaken up to Wengen and Klein Scheidegg. The course has a vertical climb of 1,525 m/ 5,000 feet and is aptly nicknamed the most beautiful marathon course in the world.

For more information, contact the tourist office on the corner at Höheweg 37; ☎ 033 822 21 21, www.InterlakenTourism.ch.

Lauterbrunnen

Population: 930
Base Elevation: 796 m/2,611 feet
Valley resort village

The Lauterbrunnen Valley stretches from Interlaken south towards Stechelberg, a steep-walled swathe punctuated with new fewer than 72 waterfalls. Its namesake village is a main transit point on the Jungfraujoch rail loop, making this an ideal and relatively inexpensive base for visitors wanting to explore the surrounding mountains.

The Lauterbrunnen Valley stretches from Interlaken south toward Stechelberg. It's a narrow, steep-walled glacier gorge – cliffs rise on both sides, and waterfalls plunge all around. The village of Lauterbrunnen has just 1,000 residents, most of them employed in the tourist industry. They adeptly cater to the busy crowds that pass through or park cars here en route to auto-free Wengen, soaring above in the east, and Mürren, dangling cliff-side to the west. Although few tourists stop here for long, the valley makes a good-value base for accommodations and is itself well worth exploring.

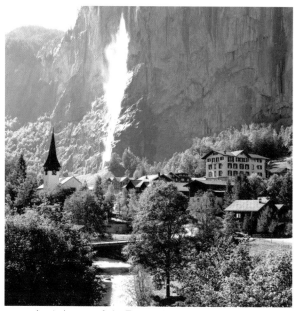

Lauterbrunnen & the Trümmelbach Falls (Lucia Degonda)

Aside from the general attraction of its staggering natural beauty, the Lauterbrunnen Valley's main tourist draw is the spectacular **Trümmelbach Falls**, a collection of 10 glacier waterfalls roaring inside the mountain. An elevator and a network of walkway galleries climb alongside the chutes, where up to 21,000 gallons of water per second drain down from the Eiger, Mönch, and Jungfrau above. The glacial falls are the only accessible subterranean waterfalls in Europe. Trümmelbach is open from April through November from 9 am-5 pm; for more info, dial ☎ 033 855 32 32. Two other waterfalls in the valley are worth seeking out as well. The **Staubbachfall** drops some 300 m/1,000 feet from a cliff near Mürren and, at the end of the valley, the **Sefinenfall** plunges straight to the valley floor.

 Want to stay? Lauterbrunnen has a nice selection of good-value accommodations. I liked the **Hotel Schützen** (€€), a chalet property squeezed between the main road and the valley wall. Rooms are dark and simple, but most have balconies. There's a pleasant terrace restaurant and big views of the Jungfrau and waterfall. In winter, the ski run from Mürren empties out right behind the hotel (although poor snow conditions frequently close the route). Book at ☎ 033 855 20 32, www.hotelschuetzen.com.

 Lauterbrunnen's busy tourist information office is just across from the train station. Inquire at ☎ 033 856 85 68, www.wengen-muerren.ch.

Grindelwald

Population: 3,800

Base Elevation: 1,050 m/3,444 feet

Mountain resort town

This likeable resort lies at the center of the Jungfraujoch rail loop – an excursion so popular that the village and its main thoroughfare jostle with day-trippers year-round. That said, even throngs of tourists can't distract from the surrounding natural beauty here.

The busy resort of Grindelwald sprawls out in a wide valley 25 km southeast of Interlaken. The 3,970-m North Face of the Eiger and the 3,701-m Wetterhorn dominate the valley from above. The Jungfrau and the Mönch tower just behind, glaciers lap at the valley floor, and mountain rail- and cableways chug in all directions.

LIFT PASS PRICE SAMPLES	
Winter	
1-day Grindelwald & Wengen	57 CHF
6-day Grindelwald & Wengen	265 CHF
6-day Jungfrau region	295 CHF
Jungfrau supplement with 3-day or more pass	52 CHF
Pedestrian:	
Round-trip to First	50 CHF
Round-trip Jungfraujoch	154 CHF

*A postal bus at the Obere Grindelwald glacier
near Grindelwald (Lucia Degonda)*

For all this hustle and bustle, however, Grindelwald's mountain transportation network moves at a sluggish pace. Old mountain trains crawl up toward the Eiger and Kleine Scheidegg, and in winter the cableways to First and Männlichen often back up with crowds. That said, Grindelwald remains one of the best hiking bases in the Alps, with 300 km of hiking trails winding through the area in summer – and a whopping 80 km are groomed for winter walking as well. Mountain bikers ride on 160 km of marked routes, and all manner of extreme adventures can be arranged. Check in with the tourist office for more info. The year-round sports center offers an enormous indoor swimming pool, wellness facilities, curling rinks, and an indoor ice rink and stadium. In winter, skiers and snowboarders head for the First area above town or hop a train to the Kleine Scheidegg at the foot of the Eigerwand and Jungfrau. Non-skiers, too, enjoy winter activities – a wide range of fun including some 57 km of tobogganing runs.

Switzerland

Top Tobogganing

Sledding on the 15-km Faulhorn,
Europe's longest sled run (Christof Sonderegger)

Grindelwald and its surroundings offer some of the most expansive sledding runs in the Alps. It also boasts the **world's longest sledding run**, a 15-km trail from First down to Grindelwald via Faulhorn and Bussalp. Other trails include the 4½-km **Speed Run** from Bussalp to Weidli and the groomed **Eiger Run** from near the Wengernalp Railway down to Grindelwald Grund. Just like ski runs, sledding runs here are graded with easy, intermediate, and advanced designations. Toboggan rentals are available; several runs are illuminated for nighttime sledding. Several mountain huts offer atmospheric fondue evenings – followed, of course, by a high-speed slide back to the village. Check with the tourist office to see what's on.

 Want to stay? Grindelwald has all manner of accommodations; I recommend finding a hotel off the main road and a room with an Eiger view. For rustic luxury in the center, try the **Schweizerhof** (€€€€), a sprawling old chalet just above the train station. The rooms are simple and cozy; the food is gourmet. Reserve at ☎ 033 853 22 02, www. hotel-schweizerhof.com.

Above the village, 100 m/328 feet above the First cableway valley station, the **Hotel Bodmi** (€€-€€€) is a modern chalet offering family-run accommodations and big views. The hotel sits near the ski school in winter and in a pasture in summer; apartments are available here, too. Contact ☎ 033 853 12 20, www.bodmi.ch.

✔ Those here solely to ski or hike will appreciate the isolation of Klein Scheidegg – a cluster of hotels dwarfed at the foot of the Eiger Wall. Consider the historical **Scheidegg Hotel**, a creaky old house at the base of the Jungfraujoch railway; ☎ 033 855 12 12, www.scheidegg-hotels.ch.

 For more information, check with Grindelwald Tourismus. It's in the sports center; ☎ 033 854 12 12, www.grindelwald.com.

Wengen

Population: 1,405

Base Elevation: 1,274 m/4,179 feet

Mountain resort village

Perched across the Lauterbrunnen Valley from Mürren, car-free Wengen is above all a quiet place for a restful holiday. In summer, trails head off in all directions; in winter, ski runs wind down to town from the below the Eiger Wall.

Over the Männlichen from Grindelwald, and around the corner from the Jungfrau, Mönch, and Eiger, the village of Wengen is the Jungfrau region's high-altitude middle ground. The car-free village sits at 1,274 m/4,178 feet, some 400 m/1,300 feet above the Lauterbrunnen Valley floor. (Visitors should park cars in the garage at Lauterbrunnen and ride the train up to the village.) Particularly popular with British families, the resort offers an ambiance quieter than that of Grindelwald and an infrastructure somewhat more developed than that of tiny Mürren.

A new cable car plies to the Männlichen Peak directly from the center of town, and the Jungfraujoch train route comes through town, too; both operate year-round. Kids enjoy a big outdoor swimming pool in summer and village-center nursery slopes in winter. Parents appreciate the sport center's childcare center,

which accepts children from 18 months of age. Several hotels offer public use of their indoor pools, and there's outdoor ice skating and curling in the winter.

LIFT PASS PRICE SAMPLES	
Winter	
1-day Grindelwald & Wengen	57 CHF
6-day Grindelwald & Wengen	265 CHF
6-day Jungfrau region	295 CHF
Jungfrau supplement with 3-day+ pass	52 CHF
Pedestrian:	
Loop via Männlichen & Kleine Scheidegg	51 CHF
Round-trip to Jungfraujoch	154 CHF

Want to stay? A five-minute walk south of the center, the **Hotel Hirschen** (€€-€€€€) is a homey old chalet with basic rooms and a good location at the foot of the home run in winter and at the head of the hiking trails in summer. It's known more for its food than its rooms – the restaurant serves up grilled and meat fondue specialties and hosts a weekly barbeque in summer. Contact ☎ 033 855 15 44, www.hirschen-wengen.ch.

Wengen's information office is in the center along the main pedestrian drag. Head around the corner to your left as you exit the train station. For more info, contact ☎ 033 855 14 14, www.wengen-muerren.ch.

◆ Mürren

Population: 350

Base Elevation: 1,650 m/5,412 feet

Mountain resort village

Spectacular, magnificent, astounding, and extraordinary; one tends towards superlatives when describing the village of Mürren. Allow us just a few. . .

Set splendidly – *impossibly* – on the precipice of a 2,600-foot cliff, the tiny village of Mürren glories in Alpine tradition, its car-

Facing page: Wengen and the Lauterbrunnen valley

free alleys winding among rustic old chalets, its balconies strewn with flowers or tucked under thick duvets of snow. It's the place I run to for a romantic weekend, a tranquil retreat amid the Alps' most majestic terrain. In short, I'm an unabashed fan.

Mürren owes its allure to three attributes. First, its location is unmatched for sheer beauty. The resort runs steeply up the hillside along the ledge of a granite wall, gazing east across the Lauterbrunnen Valley toward an in-your-face panorama of the Eiger, Mönch, and Jungfrau peaks. Second, the village bans cars from its narrow alleys, allowing access only via rail from Lauterbrunnen or cableway from Stechelberg – ditch your car in a lot at either base. Mürren's 500 residents and its visitors alike move about on foot and by train and cableway. In winter, toboggans prove the most efficient means of transport – rent yours on arrival from the local sporting goods store. Third, the village enforces strict architectural codes. While several of its hotels are grand old remnants of the Belle Epoque boom, its homes are rustic wooden chalets, with most façades stacked with firewood in winter and bursting with flowers in summer.

✔ Much of the James Bond flick *On Her Majesty's Secret Service* was filmed on location on Mürren's Schilthorn Mountain and inside Piz Gloria, its futuristic lift terminal. The resort milks the association for all it's worth, offering 007-deals on everything from breakfast to souvenir pins. As kitschy as it sounds, the rotating restaurant's *007* Breakfast is a darn nice way to start the day. Inquire at your hotel for reservations.

Mürren sits at the foot of the **Schilthorn**, a 2,970-m/9,742-foot peak that's popular with day-tripping tourists year-round. In summer, hiking trails head up from the village toward the peak, down toward the hamlet of Gimmelwald, and on to the Lauterbrunnen floor. In winter, skiers enjoy access to the Jungfrau's TopSki network – although in practice Mürren is a long haul by lift and rail to the other included resorts. The local pistes have a good variety of runs, and several mountain huts

Facing page: Cable car ascends the Schilthorn (in the distance), above Mürren (Switzerland Tourism)

offer atmospheric dining and après-ski. In town, visitors swim in the sports center's indoor pool, stroll cleared walking trails, and ice-skate on a large outdoor rink. For dinner, don't miss the traditional Swiss specialties served up on the back porch of the ramshackle old **Stägerstübli**; ☎ 033 855 13 16.

Lift Pass Price Samples

Winter

1-day Mürren	57 CHF
6-day Mürren	250 CHF
6-day Jungfrau region	295 CHF
Jungfrau supplement with 3+ -day pass	52 CHF

Pedestrian:

Round-trip to Schilthorn	66 CHF
Round-trip to Jungfraujoch	174 CHF

 Want to stay? Like many others, we're impressed with the hospitality of the **Hotel Alpenruh** (€€€), a chalet hotel with big balconies, big views, and a convenient location near the upper station of the Stechelberg cable car, the lift by which visitors enter town. For more info, check ☎ 033 856 88 00, www.alpenruh-muerren.ch.

At the opposite end of the village, across from the railway station, the **Eiger Guesthouse** (€-€€) offers a solid budget option, and the excellent bar downstairs draws a friendly and young British clientele. To reserve, contact ☎ 033 856 54 60, www.eigerguesthouse.com.

✔ Overnight guests enjoy characteristic events at several mountain huts. The **Bergrestaurant Winteregg** offers an Alpine Breakfast with folk music each Sunday during summer. In the winter, the hut has fondue and grill evening every Saturday. For more info or reservations, dial ☎ 033 855 18 93. The **Allmendhübel** does weekly fondue nights as well – guests can tote toboggans up on the funicular and sled home by moonlight. Contact ☎ 033 855 25 12 for reservations.

Restaurant Allmendhübel, above Mürren, with the Eiger, Moench and Jungfrau peaks in the background (Christof Sonderegger)

For more information, stop in at the tourist information office in the sports center or contact ☎ 033 856 86 86, www.wengen-muerren.ch.

Zürich & Central Switzerland

Although not normally a fan of urban chaos, I am always delighted with the city of Zürich. Long a bastion of conservative Swiss norms, the metropolis thumps today with an emerging artistic beat. Set on the northern edge of the Alps, the lakeside town has a large, well-preserved old town and an impressive wealth of art and architecture. Well-connected links head north to spectacular Rheinfall. To the south, at one point of the spidery Vierwaldstättersee, the city of Lucerne draws tourists year-round for its lovely lakeside old town and its easy access to the nearby mountain recreation areas, including the famed Titlis Peak above Engelberg.

© 2007 HUNTER PUBLISHING, INC

◆ Zürich

Population: 363,000

Base elevation: 409 m/1,342 feet

Gateway tourist city

Zürich's marketing slogan, "Live it, Love it," sums up the city's newfound lust for life. Once a stronghold of religious piety, then a bastion of world finance, the Zürich of today has let down its counter-cultural hair. Ready for the excitement of a city break? Join pleasure-seeking weekenders from all over Europe as they flock to Zürich for shopping, dining, art, theater, and a thumping underground nightlife.

History & Orientation

The area around Zürich was first settled by the Romans, who built a customs post here around 15 BC and christened it "Turicum." By the 10th century the town was fortified and, in 1218, declared a free imperial city. During the 14th century, Rudolf Brun brought power to the craftsman guild houses – many of which are still in operation – and the city signed on to the Swiss Confederation. A new wave of cultural change came in 1523, when local preacher Huldrych Zwingli shepherded the Reformation into Switzerland, and the city's Grossmünster Church became a haven for students and dissident Catholics from all over Europe. Based largely on the discipline, individualism, and work ethic instilled by Zwingli and his "pray and work" motto, Zürich built its wealth and, in the 19th and 20th centuries, emerged as an economic leader in industry, insurance, and banking. It is only recently that the city has indulged a more hedonistic bent.

The city of Zürich nestles among the wooded, rolling hills of central Switzerland and sprawls along the banks of the Limmat River and the northern shore of Lake Zürich – in German, the *Zürichsee*. Although it's Switzerland's largest city, although it's sometimes raucous, and although it's always expensive, vibrant Zürich enjoys what independent researchers recently deemed "the highest quality of life in the world."

The Town

Most of Zürich's sights lie south of the Hauptbahnhof train station on a triangular peninsula bordered by the Sihl and Limmat rivers and the lakeshore. **Bahnhofstrasse**, the wide boulevard running from the station down to the Bürkliplatz docks, is the home of Zürich's famed banks and boutique shops, while the quaint **old town** and **Schipfe** district tuck away along cobblestone alleys between Bahnhofstrasse and the western bank of the Limmat River. Just across the river, the trendy **Niederdorf**, or "**Dörfli**," district stretches south toward the lake in a delightful web of hip shops, seedy bars, and popular streetside cafés.

Switzerland

Zürich, view of the river Limmat and the Old Town, with Lake Zürich and the Central Swiss Alps in the background (Christof Sonderegger)

Farther south, lakeside parks and promenades line both the eastern and western shores of **Lake Zürich**. Heading south on the western shore, visitors will find **Mythenquai**; down the eastern shore, the **Utoquai** and the parks at **Zürichhorn**.

Getting Here & Around

Air travelers will arrive at the international airport, just 10 minutes by rail from the city center. The airport offers the services of 152 airlines, making it Switzerland's largest. Zürich is a major **rail** hub, as well – 95% of Swiss rail destinations are reachable with no more than one transfer. Drivers will find the city a challenge, as both navigation and parking are difficult. Once a parking spot is secured, most will be happier moving about on foot.

First and foremost, Zürich is a city of pedestrians. The compact center is easily accessed on foot, and walking, biking, and riding trams prove the most efficient and enjoyable means of travel. Better still, the extensive public transportation network proves surprisingly economical. **Bikes** are loaned here free of charge – just show an ID and place a deposit at the train station

– and inexpensive **tram** passes are offered by the trip, day, or week.

✔ For active visitors, the **Zürich Card** can be a bargain. Cardholders enjoy unlimited use of all public transport in the greater Zürich area – including trains, buses, trams, boats, and funiculars. Also included is admission to 43 of the city's museums, welcome drinks at selected restaurants, and substantial discounts on several city tours and attractions. Cards can be purchased for either 24 or 72 hours (15 CHF and 30 CHF respectively) at the Hauptbahnhof tourist office, at your hotel, or at the Bürkliplatz boat docks.

Although ferries do ply up and down the Limmat and between several lakeside villages, most tourists in Zürich board boats for purely recreational reasons. Check out the wide array of boat tours available at the Bürkliplatz docks, or hop aboard a riverboat at any Limmat landing.

Getting More Info

 The tourist information office is in the main train station at the northern end of Bahnhofstrasse. The often-crowded office doles out loads of brochures, makes hotel reservations, and sells the popular Zürich Card. The office is open in the winter from 8:30 am-7 pm Monday through Saturday, 9 am-6:30 pm Sunday; in the summer from 8 am-8:30 pm Monday through Saturday, 8:30 am-6:30 pm Sunday. For more information, dial ☎ 044 215 40 00, www.zuerich.ch.

The main post office, *Sihlpost*, is at Käsernenstrasse 95/97, just around the corner at the southwest end of the train station. It's open Monday through Friday from 6:30 am-10:30 pm and on Saturday from 6:30 am-10 pm. A second branch is in the Hauptbahnhof near the southern entrance of the station.

Several cafés offer Internet access and other business services, the best of which is the aptly dubbed **Internet Café** at Uraniastrasse 3, a five-minute walk southeast of the main train station. Other options include **Cybergate Star** on Bahnhofplatz and **Quanta** at Limmatquai 94.

View from the Quaibrücke of Zurich's most prominent churches on either side of the Limmat river: Fraumünster and St. Peter at left, Grossmünster at right (Bruno Meier)

The Sights

A pedestrian's paradise, Zürich is best toured on foot. That said, and although it has its share of attractions, the city is loved more for its pulsing ambience than its circuit of "sights." So relax and wander. Instead of setting out to look *at* something, set out to simply look *around*.

✔ Zürich gurgles with the sound of water. Its cobbled squares have more than 1,100 ornamental fountains, all of which – according to locals – bubble with pure, potable H_2O. Take a drink, not a dip, as bathing in fountain waters is generally frowned upon.

The city's central districts are well worth a wander, and visitors should note a few of the old city's most recognizable landmarks. Built in the 12th century, the **Grossmünster Cathedral** dominates the eastern bank of the Limmat River. The church is historically significant as the base of the Swiss Reformation movement instigated by Huldrych Zwingli. Visitors can climb the church tower for magnificent city views from mid-March through October, 9:15 am-5 pm, November through mid-March, 10 am-5 pm; Sundays in afternoon only. Facing off from across the river is the **Fraumünster**, a 13th-century church built on the sight of a much older convent. One of Zürich's artistic highlights, the lovely structure is graced with five enormous stained-glass windows, created in 1967 by then 80-year-old Mark Chagall. View the interior Monday through Saturday from 10 am-4 pm. Nearby, at the end of the oh-so-quaint Augustinergasse, the tower of **St. Peters Kirche** claims the largest clock face in Europe – a monster timepiece spanning 8.7 m/28 feet. Just north up the alley, **Lindenhof Park** offers a pleasant place to relax amid shaded city views.

Zürich's Museums

With over 50 museums to choose from, Zürich offers collections ranging from art and design to history and industry. Two of the best are the Zürich Art Museum and the Swiss National Museum:

■ The **Zürich Art Musuem**, or Kunsthaus Zürich, has an outstanding collection of Italian and Dutch paintings from the 17th and 18th centuries and a good schedule of rotating and temporary exhibits. It's high on the east bank at Am Heimplatz 1 and open Tuesday through Thursday, 10 am-9 pm, and Friday through Sunday, 10 am-5 pm; ☎ 044 253 84 84.

■ **Swiss National Museum**, or Schweizerisches Landesmuseum, occupies a modern replica of a Höhenzollen castle. Inside, the enormous collection includes displays of ancient and religious art, historical Swiss costumes, traditional interior design, and military history. The imposing grounds include a large, water-bounded park between the Limmat and Sihl rivers. The museum is just north of the Hauptbahnhof and is open Tuesday through Sunday from 10 am-5 pm; ☎ 044 218 65 11.

Switzerland

Zürich's **shopping** districts stretch north to south, from the train station toward the lake, in three distinct swathes. So, take your pick: chic, hip, or charm? **Bahnhofstrasse** is Switzerland's most famous upscale shopping street. Lined with banks, boutiques, and exquisite chocolate shops, lime-tree- and Lamborghini-lined Bahnhofstrasse should please even the most discriminating couture-hound.

East of Bahnhofstrasse, on the western bank of the Limmat River, is Zürich's quaint old town and riverside **Schipfe** district. Here, a maze of steep cobbled alleyways winds through historical houses occupied now by antique shops, book dealers, and specialty art, liquor, and tobacco outlets. Those shoppers with trendier tastes should head for the east bank of the Limmat and the gritty **Dörfli** district. A dining, drinking, and (table-) dancing hotspot after dark, Dörfli draws a young, artsy crowd during the day. Shops here peddle inexpensive clothing, costume jewelry, lingerie, and tattoos.

Also worth shoppers' notice is the Swiss Handicrafts Store, or **Schweizer Heimatwerk**. With a branch in each of the shopping districts, it offers high-quality crafts from all over Switzerland. Stop in at the Hauptbahnhof, on the river at Rudolf Brun-Brücke, in old town at Rennweg, or at Bahnhofstrasse 2.

Want to see more? The tourist office offers **guided city tours** by foot, bus, boat, and trolley. Two-hour walking tours depart daily from Easter through October at 3 pm from the Hauptbahnhof tourist office (adults 20 CHF, children 13. 50 CHF).

The Adventures

Zürich plays more to city pleasures than to outdoor adventures, but locals do enjoy boating, swimming, and hiking. **Boat tours**, many including meal service, depart from Bürkliplatz at the southern end of Bahnhofstrasse. Ferries, too, depart here and make round-trip runs around the lake. **Boat rentals** are offered just to the west of Bürkliplatz and down either lakeshore at Mythenquai, ☎ 01 201 65 10, or Utoquai, ☎ 01 251 32 23. Lake **swimming** is popular at several locales. Try the grassy beaches along the lakeshore or the pools at both Mythenquai, ☎ 01 201 38 89, and Utoquai, ☎ 01 251 61 51. Great days out

Cycling near Horw on Lake Lucerne (Christof Sonderegger)

can include a combination of these activities. Hop a ferry from Bürkliplatz to either Mythenquai or Utoquai – both have ferry docks – and spend a sunny day boating, swimming, and people-watching.

Hiking trails wind through the forested hills south and west of Zürich. Trains depart the main station every half-hour for the 20-minute ride to Uetliberg, just west of the city. A viewing platform offers the area's best views, and hiking trails fan out into the forest. One scenic route, the *Planetenweg* (approximately 1½ hours), leads from Uetliberg across the Albisgrat ridge to Felsenegg – watch for the to-scale planet markers along the way – and returns to Zürich via cableway to Adliswil and then by railway to Zürich. Ask at the tourist office for maps and more information.

Where to Sleep

The **Hotel Widder** (€€€€), Rennweg 7, is our favorite high-end choice in Zürich. The property includes eight historic townhouses in the heart of old town, each decorated in crisp, modern style.

HOTEL PRICES	
€	Under 120 CHF
€€	120-225 CHF
€€€	226-375 CHF
€€€€	Over 375 CHF

Hotel Widder

The restaurant is popular for its elegant Swiss cuisine; the bar for its live jazz. Book at ☎ 044 224 25 26, www.widderhotel.ch.

Nearby, the cheery, charming **Zum Kindli** (€€€) brings suitable Laura

Zum Kindli

Ashley florals to an ideal townhouse location in Zürich's old town; ☎ 043 888 76 76, www.kindli.ch.

Romantik Hotel Florhof

On the eastern hillside near the art museum and university, the **Romantik Hotel Florhof** (€€€) has bright rooms, home boutique décor, and a pleasant garden terrace; ☎ 044 261 44 70, www.florhof.ch.

The Hotel Hirschen (€€-€€€) is housed in a trio of half-timbered houses, the oldest dating from the 13th Century. A massive renovation a few years back installed small, commercial rooms that

Hotel Hirschen (second from left)

are rather boring but comfortable enough. The real attractions here, however, are location – it's smack in the heart of the Dörfli district – and a barrel-vaulted, candlelit wine cave with great wine, cheese, bread, and sausage. If you end up there, plan on staying a while. Book at 043 268 33 33, www.hirschen-zuerich.ch .

Hotel Limmatblick (€€), on the bustling east bank of the river near Dörfli, offers 16 small, artsy rooms with an eye on the Dadaist art movement. The tram hub is steps away, river views are available, and the Dada Bar downstairs often books live music. Dial ☎ 01 254 6000, www.limmatblick.ch.

The best of the budget accommodations here is the **Biber Hotel** (€), also known as the City Backpacker, with a community kitchen, Internet service, and super-cheap dorms. It's in the heart of the party-hearty Dörfli district, and no curfew is imposed. Reserve at ☎ 01 251 9015, www.city-backpacker.ch. Party-minded accommodations are also offered in Zürich West at **Hotel Limmat**, where simple rooms round out the services and the city's largest dance club, Club X-TRA. The hotel-disco is in Zürich West at Limmatstrasse 118. Reserve rooms with bath (€€) or without (€) at ☎ 01 448 15 95, www.x-tra.ch.

Where to Eat

Dining out is one of Zürich's chief pleasures, and visitors will find all manner of cuisine at all price levels. Over 1,700 restau-

RESTAURANT COSTS	
€ . . . . Under 15 CHF	
€€. . . . . 15-37 CHF	
€€€ . . . . Over 37 CHF	

rants serve central Zürich, and a whopping 400 of these offer terrace or garden dining. For traditional Swiss cuisine, try **Adler's Swiss Church** (€€) in old town, ☎ 044 266 96 66. **Churrasco** (€€) is popular for its Argentinean grill and garden-style dining; ☎ 044 221 11 44. On Bahnhofstrasse at Paradplatz, **Bierhalle Kropf** (€€) is worth a stop for its restaurant's oh-so-elegant setting – and the beer's good, too. Just up the road at Bahnhofstrasse 21, **Sprüngli** offers the city's finest chocolates and, in the café, a tempting selection of snacks.

Switzerland

✔ For a Swiss-flavored night out, hop a train and make the 20-minute trip to **Uetliberg**. Sweeping city views and a feast of Neuchâtel fondue await. Tuesday through Saturday, adults 49 CHF, children 25 CHF. Book your train and dinner package at the tourist office.

Where to Party

 Leisure travelers come from around Europe to take part in Zürich's emerging nightlife and performing arts scene. The **Tonalle** hosts world-class philharmonic concerts, the **Opera House** ranks among Europe's best, and the **Maag Music Hall** features first-run musical events. The legendary **Schauspielhaus Theater** is now supplemented by the Schiffsbau entertainment complex in burgeoning Zürich West, where one-time industrial plants have been transformed into some of the trendiest hotspots on the continent. Movie theaters thrive throughout the city and, in summer, films play on giant outdoor screens along the lakeshore.

Over 300 of the city's **nightclubs** now stay open past midnight – by far the largest number in any Swiss city. Dance clubs and bars run the gamut from haughty to hip-hop, from ritzy to rave, and with every imaginable thing in between. So, what's your pleasure? Check the *ZüriTipp Events Guide* and the tourist office's *City Guide Zürich* to see what's on.

Where to Play

 Families should head for the tourist office and request the *Kids Agenda,* a compilation of fun and games including playgrounds, museums, theaters, and other kid-friendly activities. Our favorite playground? Try the park just below Lindenhof and just behind Schipfe.

The **Zürich Zoo**, on the Zürichberg just east of town, draws families for its forested paths and natural animal habitats. The park is easily reached via Tram #6 and is open daily from 8 am-6 pm, March through October, and from 8 am-5 pm, November through February; ☎ 01 254 25 00, www.zoo.ch; adults 18 CHF, children 9 CHF. Other out-of-town jaunts popular with young travelers include the **Sihlwald Nature Center**, south of Zürich near the Silwald train station, and the **Wildpark**

Langenberg, a wild animal park that's a 20-minute hike from the Wildpark-Höfli train station.

Festivals & Events

 Zürich hosts an ever-growing number of festivals, events, and sporting competitions throughout the year. The year kicks off with **CSI Showjumping** in February, and April brings the **Sechselauten Spring Festival**, during which costumed guild members ride through town, ushering out winter and ringing in summer with the burning of a stuffed snowman.

Summer brings the **Swiss Inline Cup**, the largest inline marathon in the

The Sechselauten Spring Festival (Philipp Giegel)

world; the Zürich Festival, a celebration of opera, music, and theater; and the **August Street Parade**, for which over a million costumed partiers take to Zürich's streets. The **Summer Theater Spectacle** hosts international performers on the Landiwiese stage and, in November, the always popular **Expovina** showcases wine-tasting on board Lake Zürich boats. During the Christmas season, Zürich hosts Europe's largest indoor **Christmas**

The August Street Parade (Stephan Engler)

Switzerland

Market in the lobby of its main train station and, on December 31st, rings in the New Year with an enormous fireworks display.

Rheinfall

The Rheinfall with Laufen Castle above (Christof Sonderegger)

Base Elevation: 410 m/1,345 feet

Tourist sight

Conveniently located along a major tourist thoroughfare, Europe's largest waterfall delights crowd with thundering torrents, a deafening roar, up-close viewing platforms, and refreshingly misty boat rides.

Rheinfall lies 50 km north of Zürich, on the border of Germany near Schaffhausen. At 150 m/492 feet wide and 23 m/75 feet high, the falls pump an average of 21,000 cubic feet of water per second – a sight certainly worth the short drive. Although they can be viewed from either side, the falls are most spectacular from Schloss Laufen, a hillside medieval castle. Short paths lead to the Känzeli and Fishnetz platforms, both misty vantage points from which to view the raging waves. Boat rides, cliff climbs, and restaurant dining are available, and souvenir stands abound. Access to the falls is open daily.

✔ If you happen to be in Schaffhausen on August 1st, don't miss the Swiss National Day celebration. Check out the historical city tours, hillside bonfires, and evening fireworks over the falls.

 Want to stay? The Rheinfall tourist office is in town at Industriestrasse 39. For more information, check ☎ 052 672 74 55, www.rheinfall.ch.

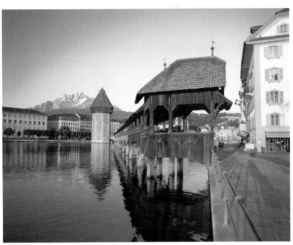

Northern walkup to the covered bridge (Kapellbrücke) with the ancient Water Tower and Mt. Pilatus the background (Christof Sonderegger)

◆ Lucerne

(Luzern)
Population: 61,000
Base elevation: 436 m/1,430 feet
Lake & mountain tourist city

Nicknamed "The City of Lights" and regarded as the cultural capital of Switzerland, Lucerne draws tourist crowds year-round for its lovely lakeside location, its wealth of recreational activities, and its treasure-trove of historical buildings, towers, and bridges.

Switzerland

History & Orientation

First founded as a Roman settlement and eventually home to an eighth-century monastery, Lucerne – or in German, *Luzern* – grew into a market center and was officially founded in 1178. During a brief annexation under Austrian Hapsburg rule, the fledging city pledged adherance to the Oath of Eternal Alliance – a pact that would prove the cornerstone of the modern Swiss Confederation. Lucerne's Catholic patrician class enjoyed expansive rule through the 19th century, and the material perks of that dominance are evident even today in the cultural wealth of the old city center. Thus, although the political capital was eventually set in Bern, and although financial control of the nation most definitely rests in Zürich, Lucerne remains without question Switzerland's premier tourist city.

THE TALE OF WILLIAM TELL

Long lodged in the memories of Swiss nationals and foreign tourists alike is the fetching tale of William Tell. Under the rule of the Austrian Hapsburgs, local villagers were forced to bow to the governor's pole-mounted hat. As the story goes, the heroically rebellious Tell refused and was thus, as punishment, forced to shoot an apple off of his own son's head. An expert marksman – with two arrows in his quiver – Tell succeeded in his task. However, upon being queried regarding his intent for the second arrow, he admitted that, had the first gone astray and injured the boy, the second arrow was meant for revenge.

His now doubly offended oppressor packed Tell off to the dungeon, a trip entailing a boat ride across a stormy lake. However, as Tell was also an expert oarsman, he thrillingly lept ashore near Rütli, darted around the lake to meet the misguided boat, and sent that second arrow flying through the governor's heart. Thus, whether myth or memory, William Tell remains an icon of the Swiss ideal: a cooperative but fiercely independent individual forced to bow to no other man's hat.

The city of Lucerne clusters at the mouth of the Ruess River along the northwestern edge of Lake Lucerne, known in German as the *Vierwaldstättersee*. Pastoral villages and jutting mountain cliffs surround the sprawling body of water, and glorious peaks rise all around: Mt. Pilatus, the Stanserhorn, and Mt. Titlis to the south, and the Klewenalp, Mt. Rigi, and Bürgenstock to the north and east. Picturesque throughout the year, the region draws a steady stream of tourism for its architectural treasures, its cultural events, and its spectacular natural surroundings.

The Town

Many visitors will first become familiar with the newly built area around the train station and boat docks, both on the southern riverbank next to the lake. Adjacent at Europaplatz, the Culture and Congress Center's jutting roof reflects the lights, crowds, and water below, creating a surreal scene that has quickly become a landmark as recognizable as the city's famed Kappelbrücke.

Such ultra-modern architecture stands in stark contrast to the charms of the old city center just north across the bridge, where cobblestone streets wind around medieval houses among eight remaining towers of the 15th-century City Wall, or *Museggmauer*. Moving east along the lakeshore, follow the promenade to the quay's old hotel row and, eventually, to the Lido Park and the Swiss Transportation Museum. Alternatively, climb north along Löwenstrasse up from the promenade to the Gletschergarten and the Dying Lion Monument.

Getting Here & Around

 International travelers arriving by **air** should fly into the airport at Zürich, which lies 55 km northeast of Lucerne, or approximately one hour by car or rail. **Trains** depart hourly between Lucerne and Interlaken and the transportation hubs of Zürich, Bern, and Geneva. Lucerne is also the departure point for Swiss Federal Railway's popular William Tell Express, a picturesque route by boat across the lake, then by train across the mountains south toward the southern lakes and Italy. Regional **buses** depart from in front of the train station.

Ferries serve the local lakeshores year-round, but service is minimal during the winter months. Boats leave from the docks conveniently located just in front of the train station and bus depot. Guests using multiple modes of transportation for day-trips or excursions should note the many money-saving combination passes.

Ferries on Lake Lucerne (Franziska Pfenniger)

For **drivers**, parking is tight and expensive in this pedestrian-oriented town. However, most hotels offer parking, and several multi-story garages are on hand. The Bahnhof garage is the most convenient large garage near the old city center's sights.

✔ The free **Lucerne Visitor's Card**, or Gästekarte, brings all manner of discounts on sightseeing, activities, and transportation. Your hotel can issue and validate a card upon your arrival.

Getting More Info

i The tourist information office is in the main train station at 3 Bahnhofstrasse; ☎ 041 227 17 17, www.luzern.org. The well-stocked center offers stacks of brochure information and the services of a friendly and knowledgeable staff. Guided tours and some transportation passes are sold here.

The post office sits just across the street from the train station at the corner of Bahnhofstrasse and Bahnhofplatz. It's open Monday through Friday, 7:30 am-6:30 pm, and Saturday, 8 am-noon.

Internet access is offered at the tourist office and in many hotel lobbies.

The Sights

Most tourists come to Lucerne for its medieval **Old Town**, a centuries-old center of shops, restaurants, and romantic architecture. The most instantly recognizable landmark here is the **Kappelbrücke**, a kinked bridge over the Ruess River that's well known for its Wasserturm tower, cycle of paintings, and the 1993 fire that destroyed much of it. The bridge structure has since been rebuilt as an exact replica of the original, the paintings painstakingly recreated and recently mounted along the bridge. (Look, too, for the visible line between the old and new wood.) Follow the swans downstream to the 17th-century **Speuerbrücke** for a look at what is now the city's oldest covered bridge. Note, too, the morbid cycle of paintings here, including Megliger's disturbing *Dance of Death*. On the north side of the river, wander the old city streets and squares, now a pedestrianized haven of shops, restaurants, and hotels, and climb the Schirmer, Zyt, and Mannli Towers of the old **City Wall**.

Strolling out of the old town and along the lake's northern shore, walkers enjoy a long gravel path scattered with snack carts and park benches and fronting Lucerne's most elegant old hotels. A detour up Löwenstrasse leads to second cluster of city sights.

Most notable here are the imposing twin towers of the **Hofkirche** and the poignant **Löwendenkmal**, or "The Dying Lion of Lucerne," a carved stone memorial to the Swiss soldiers who died in Paris

The Lion Monument by Thorwaldsen
(Luzern Tourismus AG)

Switzerland

in 1792 while defending the French King. Just beyond, the **Gletschergarten** provides an interesting look at the city's ancient geology, as well as a much more frivolous maze of mirrors. It's open daily from 9 am to 6 pm; ☎ 041 410 43 40, www.gletschergarten.ch.

Lucerne boasts an impressive collection of museums. Most noticeable is the ultra-modern Culture and Congress Center, alternatively known as the KKL, and its top-floor **Museum of Art**, which specializes in exhibitions of international contemporary art. It's next door to the train station at Europaplatz 1; ☎ 041 226 78 78, www.kunstmuseumluzern.ch.

The **Rosengart Donation**, Pilatusstrasse 10, displays a rich collection of works by Klee, Picasso, Monet, Matisse, Miro, and Cezanne. For more info, dial ☎ 041 220 16 60 or see www.rosengart.ch. Also donated by the Rosengart family are the works displayed at the **Picasso Museum**, an intimate collection of drawings and photos featuring the work, life, and loves of the legendary artist during the final 20 years of his life. The collection is housed in the Am-Rhyn-Haus at 21 Furngasse; ☎ 041 410 17 73.

For music buffs, the **Richard Wagner Museum** pays homage to that famed composer at the site of his local residence, Villa Tribschen, the house in which he wrote *Siegfried-Idyll* for his longtime love, Cosima. It's located on the southern shore of the lake at Wagnerweg 27; ☎ 041 360 23 70.

The **Swiss Transportation Museum**, or Verkehrshaus der Schweiz, sees more annual visitors than any other museum in Switzerland, and new arrivals will quickly understand why. The largely interactive museum is a huge hit with kids – and therefore a huge hit with parents, too. Major attractions include a full-sized planetarium, helium balloon rides, laser shows, and an IMAX theater. Multimedia displays on boat, rail, and aviation travel educate and entertain, and a 240-square-yard aerial photograph of Switzerland allows even the least adventuresome visitor to go home bragging, "I walked across Switzerland!" The museum is located at Lidostrasse 5, on the northern lakeshore approximately 1½ km from the town center. Ferries dock nearby. The museum is open daily from 10 am to 6 pm, closed Christmas day; ☎ 0848 85 20 20, www.verkehrshaus. org.

The tourist office arranges **guided factory tours** to several local sites. Favorites include a brewery, an alphorn factory, a dairy, a glass factory, and a refuse incineration plant. (Okay, so this last one might not belong on our list of "favorites," but it is worth a mention.) The tourist office also gives **guided walking tours** through the city center daily from May through October and on Wednesdays and Saturdays from November through April. Walking tours depart at 9:45 am, take two hours, and cost 18 CHF per person.

The Adventures

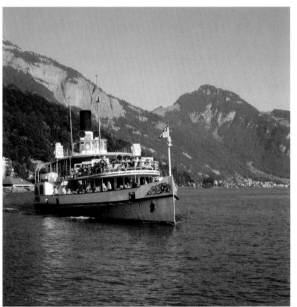

Unterwalden, *a paddle steamer of the Lake Lucerne Shipping Company SGV, near Vitznau* (D. Brawand)

Adventures around Lucerne come in three categories: lake outings, mountain outings, and combinations of the two. Visitors in search of **lake outings** can enjoy any number of boat tours –

more than 20 ferries and tour boats ply the local waters. At the northwest shore near the old city center, **SNG** rents paddleboats, arranges watersports, and offers lake tours and boat taxi service. Dial ☎ 041 210 36 37, www.sng.ch. The city's main ferry service, however, is the **Lake Lucerne Navigation Company**, or Schiffahrtsgesellschaft Vierwaldstättersee, Switzerland's largest ferry operation. The company operates year-round service to all corners of Lake Lucerne, but boats run less frequently during the winter months. Tourists particularly enjoy the themed lake cruises here, which typically include some kind of sustenance such as fondue, cake, or a buffet meal. For more information, dial ☎ 041 367 67 67, www.lakelucerne.ch, or check with the information kiosk just across from the train station.

Weggis on Lake Lucerne with Mt. Pilatus in the background (Doris Brawand)

Mountain outings around Lucerne take day-trippers to several surrounding peaks for hiking, biking, skiing, and view-laden relaxation. Combination boat, train, and cable car passes make transportation a breeze. (The tourist office can help with routing and ticket arrangements.) Popular mountain outings include **Mt. Pilatus**, or "Dragon Mountain," where a cogwheel railway, gondola, and cable car will tug you up to several nice trails, a mid-mountain summer toboggan run, and soaring views from the silvery mountaintop lodge. Another is **Stanserhorn**, with its old funicular, marmots, and rotating restaurant. And there is also **Klewenalp**, where playgrounds, mountain-bike rentals, a petting zoo, and a rock-climbing garden please family members of all ages. Specialist mountain-bikers enjoy a difficult circular run here from Buochs up to Stafel, a 3½-hour trek covering almost 19 miles.

At **Mt. Rigi**, home to Europe's first mountain railway, adventurers enjoy wintertime sledding and skiing and, in summer, some of the region's best mountain hiking – try the two-hour Seeweg route from Kaltbad along the cliffs to Unterstetten and Hinterbergen. To the south, jutting out over the lake is the **Bürgenstock**, a peaceful mountain peninsula overlooking five lakes.

Finally, don't miss the resort of Engelberg and its **Mt. Titlis**, where the world's first revolving cable car, the Titlis-Rotair, totes visitors up to year-round glacier fun, including skiing, boarding, snow-biking, tubing, and sledding. For more info, see this guide's *Engelberg* chapter; call ☎ 041 639 50 60, or see www.titlis.ch.

Hiking, biking, and **skating** trails circle Lake Lucerne and web around the region's peaks – several of the best are mentioned above. Maps and route information are available at the tourist office. The local ferry operator provides specialized sporting tours that include round-trip transportation between Lucerne and recommended hiking, biking, and skiing destinations. Bikes can accompany riders on any train, most boats, and some buses, normally for small extra fees.

Walking the Swiss Path

Seven hundred years after signing the 1291 pact that unified the first three Swiss cantons, Switzerland celebrated the anniversary by – what else – developing a new trail: the *Weg der Schweiz*, or Swiss Path. True to meticulous Swiss ways, the trail is divided into 26 sections, each representative of a Swiss canton, and each length proportionate to the population of the represented canton. The trail begins at Rütli Meadow, the site on which the Oath of Eternal Alliance was signed, and circles 35 km around the Urnersee to Brunnen. Plan two days to walk the entire trail, or walk shorter sections between ferry boat docks. Any area tourist office will have more information and maps.

Swimming options include the floating pools at Spitteler Quay and the grassy beaches at both Lido and Seepark. The **Dietschiberg golf** course offers public play on 18 holes from April through November. The course is the oldest in central Switzerland, with big, mature trees and big, sweeping views of the city, lake, and mountains. Call ☎ 041 420 97 86 or see www.golfclubluzern.ch.

✔ Travelers seeking more outlandish adventures should check with **Outventure**, an extreme sports operator that arranges guided outings around Lucerne and Engelberg. Adventurers can climb waterfalls, bungee-jump out of cable cars, and overnight in a self-built igloo. Find your Alpine adventure at www.outventure.ch or call ☎ 041 611 14 42.

Where to Sleep

The city's three most elegant old hotels line up shoulder to shoulder along the promenade on the northern lakeshore of Lake Lucerne. Exuding old-world splendor from its aging pores, the sprawling **Hotel Schweizerhof** (€€€€) opened in

Facing page: The Bürgenstock peninsula in Lake Lucerne, seen from Vitznau (Max Schmid)

1845 and is now a national architectural landmark. Reserve at ☎ 041 410 04 10, www.schweizerhof-luzern.ch. The **Palace Hotel** (€€€€) boasts lovely décor, a new spa, and a calendar brimming with cultural events; ☎ 041 416 16 16, www.palace-luzern.ch. The

Palace Hotel

Grand Hotel National (€€€€) trades on superb wellness facilities and an excellent, if pricey, Thai restaurant. Book the National at ☎ 041 419 09 09, www.national-luzern.ch.

At the opposite extreme of five-star ambiance gleams **The Hotel**

Palace Hotel

(€€€€), a wonderfully modern, minimalist operation sporting scenes from great movies on its guestroom ceilings; ☎ 041 226 86 86, www.the-hotel.ch.

The **Romantik Hotel Wilden Mann** (€€€) rests just across the river from Lucerne's charming old town. Lovingly decorated, mix-and-matched guestrooms

The Hotel

complement antique-laden public areas and a cozy Swiss *stübe* restaurant with outdoor service in summer; ☎ 041 210 16 66.

Facing page: The Rütli Meadow above Lake Lucerne, where the Swiss Confederation was founded (Christof Sonderegger)

Switzerland

Just across from the train station, the **Waldstätterhof** (€€€), ☎ 041 2 271 271, www.waldstaetterhof.ch, offers courtyard parking and recently refurbished rooms with bright, modern décor.

The **Schiff** (€€) and **Des Alpes** (€€) share similar positions in the heart of old town on the northern bank of the Ruess River. Both have simple décor and some rooms with lake-and-mountain views. Book the Schiff at ☎ 041 418 52 52, www.hotel-schiff-luzern.ch; the Des Alpes at ☎ 041 410 58 25, www.desalpes-luzern.ch.

For lofty mountain lodging on Pilatus Peak, take the train up to the simple **Pilatus-Kulm** (€€); ☎ 041 670 12 55, www.pilatus.com.

Where to Eat

 Lucerne boasts a nice collection of restaurants, many of which are geared toward the city's ever-present tourist crowds. The **Stadtkeller** (€€€ with show), in the old town, has long been popular for its traditional Swiss cuisine and a folklore performance featuring alphorn blowing, flag twirling, and yodeling. Dial ☎ 041 410 47 33 for lunch and dinner reservations.

Novelty dining floats lakeside at the **Schiffsrestaurant** (€€), a converted old paddle steamer with expensive food and extensive views – the ambiance of the deck-top bar is certainly worth the price of a drink.

Good for gourmet dining is **Grottino 13/13**. Featured here is a cozy, casual atmosphere, rustic décor, and a superb menu that is each night chosen by the chef. ☎ 041 361 1313 to reserve a table.

In the center, try **Opus**, a delightful wine bar and terrace restaurant on the southern bank of the Ruess River near the Spreuerbrücke. Nearby, cheery **Sebastian's** (€€€) serves excellent seafood at the corner of Rütligasse and Pfistergasse.

Mr. Pickwick's Pub (€€), just in front of the Kappelbrücke, features English-style pub food and a great selection of beer. Next door, the **Rathaus Brauerei** serves up local brews.

Deep in the maze of old town at Eingasse 15, **Spycher** (€€) offers an interesting selection of Swiss and Oriental specialties – but don't let the odd mix scare you away; this friendly house serves up some of the city's best fondue. Dial ☎ 041 412 37 37 for reservations. Finally, try the **Wirsthaus Taube** (€€) for local specialties at good prices.

Where to Party

 Sedel is a prison-themed, graffiti-festooned concert venue and disco near Emmenbrücke and the youth hostel, home base for much of this club's rowdy clientele. Alternative rock is the favorite here. Dial ☎ 041 420 63 10 to see what's on.

At Seidenhofstrasse 5, ☎ 041 227 66 66, the medieval **Adagio** draws more mature crowds with a mix of music and a more expensive selection of drinks, while **The Loft**, at Haldenstrasse 21, ☎ 041 410 92 44, thumps to a disco beat amid slick modern décor. Looking for more options? Check out Lucerne's bar guide at barfuehrer-luzern.ch.

The **Casino Lucerne** occupies an enviable lakeside lot on the northern edge of town at Haldenstrasse 6, ☎ 041 418 56 56. Live entertainment – in both Vegas and Swiss styles – and an elegant dining room supplement a fanciful gaming room with roulette, poker, blackjack, craps and slot machines. The casino is open daily from noon to 4 am for those at least 20 years of age.

Where to Play

 Families enjoy the playground, petting zoo, and activities atop **Klewenalp**, and several lakeside paths offer family-friendly strolls – particularly enjoyable when combined with a round-trip boat ride. Childcare services are available in the old town at **Kinderparadies**, Hertensteinstrasse 40, ☎ 041 410 44 15. On the sixth floor of the Hotel Waldstätterhof, the **Kinderstube** offers play time for kids 2½ years and older, Tuesday through Friday from 2-5 pm; ☎ 041 210 35 04. The tourist office can provide additional information regarding babysitting.

Festivals & Events

Numerous music festivals highlight calendar, including the well-regarded **Luzern Festival**, a seasonal series of performances by eminent musicians. Check the tourist office to see who's in town.

Carnival in Lucerne (Christof Sonderegger)

From the end of February through early March bizarrely costumed revelers and musicians take to the streets in celebration of **Carnival,** a party renowned throughout Europe.

In late June, the colorful **Old Town Festival** is a traditional tourist favorite and, in early August, a spectacular fireworks show lights up the lake during **Seenachtsfest**.

◆ Engelberg

Population: 3,500

Base Elevation: 1,050 m/3,440 feet

Mountain resort town

While most tourists base themselves in Lucerne and make quick trips up to see the famed Titlis peak before running back to the city, Engelberg's outdoor attractions will for many adventurers merit the opposite arrangement.

Engelberg (Franziska Pfenniger)

Engelberg's founding dates to 1120 A.D., when a group of monks built the first of what would be three monasteries on a site in the upper valley. Through the Middle Ages, the group ruled the surrounding area with an iron religious hand – power granted by the Pope and ungoverned by the Swiss Federation. So, they had a good thing going for several hundred years. But, a rotten run of luck struck in the 18th Century, beginning with a fire in 1729 that destroyed the monastery in its entirety. The place was rebuilt in the Baroque grandeur still standing today, but its glory days came to a quick end when Napolean's armies

446 Zürich & Central Switzerland

turned up on Switzerland's doorstep in 1798. Since then, the monastery has lived a quieter life running a school, library, and dairy operation.

Today, the town of Engelberg clusters at the foot of the Brunni peak, on the northern bank of the Engleberger Aa River. It sits approximately 34 km south of Lucerne, 19 km down the Engelbergertal from the Stans Sud exit of the A2 autobahn. (The trip takes just over an hour by train or about an hour by car.) Architecture runs an odd mix of old-world grandeur, traditional Swiss chalets, and modern apartment blocks.

If the architecture offends the eye, however, the setting certainly will not – lofty peak rise all around. Three mountain recreation areas enclose the steep-walled valley. The sunny **Brunni** area is a multi-use mountain geared toward family fun. Hiking, biking, and skiing trails are well maintained, and winter and summer tobogganing runs are on offer. The Ristis lift station caters to kids, who enjoy a petting zoo, playland, and both summer and winter toboggan runs. At 3,238 m/10,620 feet, the

The Mt. Titlis cable car (Franziska Pfenniger)

Titlis is Engelberg's highest lift-equipped peak, and its Titlis-Rotair rotating cable car is the prime destination of most valley visitors. The bulk of the area's winter and summer activities are here, along with a nice collection of mountain restaurants. Several small lakes tuck back behind the nearby Jochpass. Finally, **Fürenalp** remains the smallest and least known of the local mountains, a boon to those looking to lose high-season crowds. Good trails, big views, and a handful of rustic huts make this small peak a place worth lingering. For more info on mountain recreation activities, contact the Brunni at ☎ 041 639 60 60, www.brunni.ch; Fürenalp at ☎ 041 637 20 94, www.fuerenalp.ch; and Titlis at ☎ 041 639 50 60, www.titlis.ch.

Mt. Titlis Cable-Car Excursion

Rising from 1,020 to 3,020 m/3,345-9,905 feet, the **Mt. Titlis** cable-car route whisks visitors up to the Titlis peak in three stages: a gondola, a cable car, and finally, the world's first revolving cablecar, the Titlis-Rotair. The entire trip takes about 45 minutes one-way. At the top, visitors can wander through an ice cave bored 150 m/492 feet through the glacier and, from the viewing platform, can ogle Alps as far as the eye can see. Here, snow fun is on hand year-round at the Glacier and Freestyle Park, with skiing, boarding, biking, tubing, and sledding on the glacier ice. (The Titlis peak protrudes into Swiss Air Force airspace, so fighter-jet fans should keep watch for F/A-18s dogfighting in the clouds above and thundering through the valleys below.) For more info on the Titlis-Rotair and Mt. Titlis activities, call ☎ 041 639 50 60 or see www.titlis.ch .

Visitors can peek inside local cultural landmarks at the **Engelberg Monastery** and the **Show Cheese Factory** – both open their doors to guests. The latter has a café and shop stocking locally produced cheeses, breads, and gift items. Highly sterile cheese-making demonstrations are staged from behind a wall of glass. The showroom is open daily from 9am-5pm, www.schaukaeserei-engelberg.ch, ☎ 041 638 08 88.

Switzerland

AUTHOR'S CHOICE Finally, for those visitors craving an adrenaline rush, we highly recommend **Outventure.** One of Europe's best adventure outfitters, this wild bunch operates out of nearby Stansstad and serves both the Lucerne and Engelberg areas. Whether bungee-jumping from cable cars, abseiling waterfalls, or braving all-night igloo outings, travelers seeking outlandish Alpine activities will find themselves in safe – if not by all estimations *sane* – hands. Check out Outventure at www.outventure.ch, call ☎ 041 611 14 42, or contact the Engelberg-Titlis Tourist Office.

 Want to stay? In the center, the quaint **Hotel Engelberg** (€€-€€€), ☎ 041 639 79 79, www. hotel-engelberg.ch, fronts a cobbled, pedestrian section of Dorfstrasse. Its balconies spew flowers in the summer, and the center's sights and shopping are all nearby. For budgeting travelers, the monstrous

Hotel Engelberg

Hotel Bellevue houses both dorms (€) and rooms (€€) in a lovely if decrepit old mansion. Its grand lobby and expansive lounge belie the simple accommodations above. The Bellevue welcomes a young clientele and, as the hotel is a base of the Schiller Hotel Management School, guests can expect fairly hospitable housemates. At street level, the Yucatan Bar claims the largest beer consumption in central Switzerland – a claim you'll not dispute after witnessing its après-ski crowd any sunny weekend winter afternoon. Call ☎ 041 639 68 68 or see www. bellevue-engelberg.ch.

i The very helpful Engelberg-Titlis Tourist Office is located in the center of town at Klosterstrasse 3. Visitors can buy lift passes, reserve accommodations, purchase event tickets, and gather brochures and maps. In fact, the office serves as a clearinghouse for most outdoor activities in town – stop by or look them up to see what they can do for you: ☎ 041 639 77 77 or www.engelberg.ch.

The Graubünden Region

Tucked away in the easternmost corner of Switzerland, the Graubünden region is home to world-class cosmopolitan resorts and many tiny, traditional villages. The area first hit the tourism map in the early 1900s as a climatic health resort, and tuberculosis patients came from all around Europe to breathe its clean, dry air. A century later, the region has successfully morphed into a thriving Alpine center. Here, we spotlight St. Moritz, a glitzy hillside town that draws fur-clad crowds to its elegant boutiques and hotels. Nearby Silvaplana proves particularly popular with wind- and water-sport enthusiasts, while the Swiss National Park preserves some of Switzerland's most pristine wilderness. For adventurers, then, the Graubünden

Switzerland

Region harbors an excellent network of hiking, biking, and skiing trails; and for culture-hounds, much of its historical Romansch culture remains intact.

◆ St. Moritz

Population: 5,084
Base elevation: 1,768 m/5.799 feet
Lake & mountain resort town

We choose St. Moritz as our main Graubünden base for its international fame and its comprehensive array of outdoor activities. This is not a quaint Alpine village, nor is it the place for those seeking a wilderness retreat. It is, however, an ideal destination for celebrity hounds and fashion fanatics – and all those who believe a morning hike merits an afternoon massage and seven-course evening meal.

History & Orientation

First discovered by the Celts some 3,000 years ago, St. Moritz and its mineral springs have long drawn summer visitors from across Europe. With an illustrious guest list, including Paracelsus, Hermann Hesse, Friedrich Nietzsche, and Thomas Mann, this old spa town remains a much-ballyhooed summer destination for the world's rich and famous.

It wasn't until 1834 that out-of-towners first stayed the winter, but the idea caught on quickly, and in 1864 the village's first wintertime hotel welcomed a group of trend-setting British vacationers. Since then, St. Moritz has become one of the globe's premier winter destinations and a pioneer in resort marketing – its latest ploys include pricey St. Moritz brands of coffee, mineral water, and music compilation CDs.

St. Moritz sits near the border of Italy in the southeastern corner of the Graubünden region. The town nestles in the famed Engadine Valley, a high-altitude expanse stretching 94 km along the Inn River. St. Moritz rests at an altitude of 1,800 m/ 5,900 feet, and the relatively small difference in height between the valley floor and the surrounding peaks deceives the eye. Although these mountains don't look so imposing, their heights

St. Moritz, with Muottas Muragl in the background (Lucia Degonda)

hover around 4,000 m/13,000 feet and justify the area's nick-name, "The Rooftop of Europe."

Blessed with a stable, high-Alpine climate, St. Moritz boasts an average of 322 sunny days each year. Five major mountain peaks and 25 lakes scatter throughout the area, making this one of the Alps' most attractive natural playgrounds. The snow and ice here have hosted two Olympic Winter Games – in 1928 and 1948 – and over three dozen World Championship competitions. In February of 2003, St. Moritz once again made history as host of the Alpine Skiing World Championships.

The Town

So, its natural surroundings are exquisite; its history, distin-guished; and its patrons, oh-so-refined. Even so, the town of St. Moritz remains a visually unappealing place. Its block-style ar-chitecture huddles around the western side of St. Moritz Lake (or in Romansch, "Lej da Murezzan"), an oblong body of water fed by the Inn River. St. Moritz-Dorf climbs up the hillside to the north, while St. Moritz-Bad – Dorf's poorer urban sister – sprawls out to the southwest.

St. Moritz Bad does appeal to budgeting travelers – although few frugal travelers dare set foot in St. Moritz at all. Hotel rates

Switzerland

in Bad are generally less lofty than in Dorf, iron-rich spring waters bubble up in a public spa, and a large network of trails draws equestrians and cross-country skiers.

However, it is St. Moritz-Dorf that steals the show in the Engadine Valley, and so it is St. Moritz-Dorf I spotlight here. From the lakeshore and train station on the valley floor, multi-story hotel blocks step up the hillside toward the Corviglia ski slopes above. The town centers on Piazza da Scuola, a bustling square framed by the main shopping, dining, and promenading streets of Via Maestra and Via Viglia. Development scatters from this congested center out toward the Olympic Center to the east, St. Moritz-Bad to the southeast, and down to the lake below.

Dorf's terraced streets house a diverse but uniformly upscale collection of designer boutiques, gourmet restaurants, and posh hotels. The village's atmosphere smacks of exclusivity, its elegance attracts an illustrious clientele, and its social calendar includes some of Europe's most lavish affairs. This high-altitude attitude does, however, come at stratospheric cost: Prices here are the highest in the Alps. Like most mountain resorts, St. Moritz more or less shuts down between seasons – from late April through May and in November.

Getting Here & Around

 St. Moritz lies approximately 200 km, or a three-hour drive, from either Milan or Zürich. International arrivals can **fly** into either Zürich or Geneva and make connections either by plane or helicopter to the Samedan Airport just outside St. Moritz. Trains connect St. Moritz to the rest of Europe via Chur to the north and Tirano, Italy, to the south. The St. Moritz train station sits between the lakeshore and St. Moritz-Dorf.

The train station serves as hub for the Post **bus**, which services the Graubünden region, as well as the local Engadin bus, which makes rounds through St. Moritz. The regional train company is the **Rhaetian Railway** (☎ 081 833 59 12). For taxi service, try **Taxi Zentrale** at ☎ 081 833 11 12.

Year-round lift service offers far-reaching views and access to the area's outstanding mountain restaurants. Highly recommended is a trip by foot or lift up to the Corviglia area behind St. Moritz. After transferring at Corviglia from the funicular to a cable car, guests climb to Piz Nair, the black mountain. On the way, look for the 2003 World Cup ski racing start platform – and just below, the world's steepest downhill start, a free-fall drop on which skiers reached speeds of up to 130 km an hour in the first seven seconds of the race.

LIFT PASS PRICE SAMPLES	
Winter	
1-day adult for St. Moritz area	57 CHF
6-day adult all-area pass	265 CHF
Summer	
Pedestrian round-trip to Piz Nair	32 CHF
6-day adult all-area pass	111 CHF

Getting More Info

The St. Moritz Tourist Board is in the heart of the pedestrian old town at Via Maestra 12. Contact ☎ 081 837 33 33, www.stmoritz.com for more information.

The post office is on Via Serias just below the Badrutt's Palace Hotel.

For public Internet access, try the **American Bar** or **Bobby's Pub** in the Galeria shopping center. The **Bibliothek** has computers as well.

The Sights

St. Moritz activities focus less on sightseeing than on shopping, spectacle, and sport. Visitors enjoy **shopping** on the Via Serlas and Via Maestra for goodies from Armani, Bulgari, and Prada, and gift shops sell local crafts, woodcarvings, and chocolates. A few overpriced sporting goods outfitters are on hand to remind visitors that they are, after all, in the mountains.

St. Moritz is a favorite venue for refined spectator sports such as polo, sailing, equestrian competitions, classic car rallies, and greyhound racing. Such events take place throughout the year – check with the tourist office to see what's on. Also popular are the many concerts staged year-round in local gardens, hotels, spas, forests, churches, and squares. Many feature world-renowned musicians, and many are free of charge.

Worth an uphill stroll is a visit to the village's own version of the **Leaning Tower**. The 12th-century structure, once the bell tower of the now-demolished St. Mauritius Church, stands 33 m/108 feet and leans 5½ degrees. A handful of small museums rounds out the sightseeing options here. The **Engadine Museum** houses a worthwhile collection of cultural and historical displays in one of the valley's few remaining traditional buildings (Via dal Bagn 39; ☎ 081 833 43 33). Just up the hill, the **Segantini Museum** honors Giovanni Segantini, an artist famed for his poignant depictions of Alpine life. Segantini spent his last years in the Engadine Valley, and this museum boasts the world's largest collection of his work; Via Somplaz 30, ☎ 081 833 44 54.

The Adventures

Recreation opportunities are immense. Major lift systems congregate in the Corviglia area directly above St. Moritz and sprawl out across Diavolezza, Corvatsch, Pontresina, and Muottas Muragl. The lift system operates year-round, serving skiers in winter and hikers in summer. The lake offers a playground for both summer water sports and winter ice recreation, and walking trails are maintained throughout the year.

● ON FOOT

Some 500 km of well-marked trails wind throughout the Engadin region, and various outfitters offer a total of 600 guided mountain excursions – many of them with themes such as minerals, game, botany, glaciers, or flora and fauna. Trams and cable cars run year-round to the peaks of Piz Nair, Corvatsch, and Lagalb, and all are excellent bases from which to begin hikes among mountain restaurants. The hiking and walking terrain varies from easy to extreme, so everyone will find suitable trails.

Piz Nair soars above St. Moritz, making it a tempting destination for all. Athletic visitors set out for the 3½-hour hike, but less ambitious walkers can take the funicular and cable car to reach the same viewpoint. The Pass Suvretta route takes walkers off the back side of the Piz Nair peak – reached by either lift or the hike above – over to the Pass Suvretta, and down into the Engadine Valley. The four-hour route transverses bleak, high-Alpine pastures, passes Lac Suvretta, follows a meandering stream, and finally arrives back in St. Moritz Dorf.

✔ Shirley Temple's movie classic *Heidi* was filmed in this region, and a 1790s-era hut from the original set has been moved here. A flat, kid-friendly flower trail leads from the Chantarella funicular station to the hut and, from there, down to St. Moritz via a forested path sign-posted with the fairy-tale of *Schellen-Ursli.* The whole loop takes less than two hours.

Canyoning, climbing, and mountaineering activities are all available, too. See the *Sports Outfitters* box below for contact information.

● **ON HORSEBACK**

For those interested in traveling by hoof, **St. Moritz Stables** offers year-round equestrian services. Es-tablished almost 100 years ago, the lakeside center offers equestrian training, maintains bridle paths, and guides trail rides. Full-day rides into the Roseg Valley include a picnic and magnificent mountain scenery; ☎ 081 833 57 33.

● **IN WATER**

St. Moritz is best known for its healing waters. The **St. Moritz Spa Centre** trades on its historical reputation and a long list of spa treatments. Visitors can relax with beauty treatments, mud baths, massages, peat packs, and various baths spiked with additives such as carbonic acid. Make reservations at ☎ 081 833 30 62.

Kite- and wind-surfers love the Engadine during the month of August, when Maloja winds bring clear skies and cool breezes to the lakes of Silvaplana and St. Moritz. World-class events and regattas – including the colorful Windsurfing Marathon in July – dot the summer social calendar. A sailing club, ☎ 081 833 40 56, and a rowing club, ☎ 081 837 33 88, offer instruction and boat rentals. **Whitewater rafting** excursions are operated by **St. Moritz Experience** (see *Sports Outfitters* below). Half-

and full-day trips run along the Scuol-Giarsun and the Pontresina-Samedan stretches of the Inn River.

The **Cantonal Fisch-Farming Institution** (☎ 081 833 67 52) licenses visitors for **fishing** during the May-September season. The Engadine mountain lakes are home to perch and various trout species, but the privilege of fishing here does not come cheap. Licenses cost 46 CHF for a day; 132 CHF for a week and 220 CHF for 15 days.

● ON WHEELS

No fewer than six outfitters rent **mountain bikes** and equipment. The most convenient may be the rental service located in the train station, but our fave remains the specialist shop **Bike Side** at ☎ 081 833 05 55. A good route? The **Poschiavo Trail** offers a mild downhill grade suitable for all mountain bikers. The 22-km trail starts atop Lagalb – take the cable car up from Diavolezza – and descends 2,893 m into Poschiavo. The train and tourist offices offer a package deal including round-trip train transport, bike transfer, cable car ticket, and lunch at the Punschlaver Teller.

Mountain bikers at Suvretta Pass, above St. Moritz, with Piz Tschierva and Piz Bernina in the background (Robert Boesch)

A popular destination for **inline skating**, St. Moritz caters to skaters with a five-km circuit at Samedan Airfield and an 8.6-km route from La Punt to S-chanf. Additional trails wind through the relatively flat St. Moritz-Bad. The Engadin Inline Marathon clogs the main road from Maloja to S-chanf each June. Thousands of skaters turn out for the 42-km race, the world's original inline distance event. For rental information, contact **Samedan Tourismus** at ☎ 081 851 11 60, www.samedan.ch.

● IN THE AIR

Paragliders and **hang gliders** take off from the mountain station at Corviglia. Regularly scheduled flights launch each hour from 10 am to 4 pm, and flights from other locations can be arranged.

✔ Want to try it? Put yourself in the hands of a pro. **Heinz Zwyssig** has been flying since 1976 as a paragliding instructor and guide, and was captain of the Swiss national team for eight years. For more info, contact Mr. Zwyssig at ☎ 079 353 21 59, www.luftarena.ch; 230 CHF per flight.

● ON SNOW & ICE

The **ski slopes** around St. Moritz are some of the most extensive in Switzerland, with 60 lifts servicing 350 km of flatteringly rated runs. Officially rated 16% easy, 71% intermediate, and 13% difficult, the runs cater to intermediate-level skiers (many of whom will feel comfortable on the area's "difficult" runs, too). This is St. Moritz, after all, and *looking* good on the slopes is much more important than *being* good on the slopes. Advanced skiers in search of greater challenge should hire a guide and/or a helicopter and head off-piste. Several local guiding services offer heli-skiing and backcountry treks.

Although certainly not the most obvious **snowboarding** destination, snobby St. Moritz has bent its rigid ways a bit to include some good facilities for boarders. There's a halfpipe and fun-park in Corviglia and two more fun-parks at Corvatsch. The runs are wide, and the off-piste snow is deep. The Wave Division, ☎ 081 830 01 01, of the **Swiss Ski School** offers specialized instruction and guiding.

St. Moritz is one of the world's premier destinations for **cross-country skiing**. Over 150 km of prepared trails wind along the valley floor around St. Moritz Dorf and at Pontresina. The

*Snowboarding in the Corniglia region
above St. Moritz (Christof Sonderegger)*

Swiss Cross-Country Ski School, ☎ 081 833 62 33, offers instruction in skating and classic techniques from December through April. The Cross-Country Ski Marathon takes place each March, with 12,000 participants mob trails to make the 42-km trek over and around the Upper Engadine lakes.

Many St. Moritz trails are groomed for **winter walking**, and the tourist office offers walking maps. **Philosophers' Way** stretches out along the Muottas Muragl plateau. Placards with quotes from renowned philosophers punctuate the two-km trail. The mountain views are mesmerizing, and the thoughts are worth pondering. **Segantini Path** memorializes local artists. The peaceful, wooded trail winds two km from Hotel Soldanella to Suvretta.

Horse-drawn sleighs slide through the Staz forest and over the valley's frozen lakes. Sleighs can be hired next to the Catholic church in St. Moritz Bad. A new **toboggan run** winds from Muottas to Punt Muragl, dropping 700 m/2,296 feet over four km. Sliders can rent sleds at the bottom of the Muottas funicular.

To pick up the pace a bit, try the **Olympic Bob Run**, the world's only natural bobsled run. Since its opening in 1890, the track has hosted more than 30 World Championships. The track is open to novices from late December through early March – two riders pair up in each four-man sled with a driver and a brakeman. Rides are not cheap but do include a photo, pin, and certificate; ☎ 081 833 31 17. Need something more? Check out the Cresta Run (see *In the Extreme* below).

The new **St. Moritz Ice Arena** offers open-air skating and organized hockey games from July through April; ☎ 081 833 50 30. The **Al Parc Curling Center** tops a natural ice arena near the Kulm Hotel. Private and group instruction for new and experienced curling fans is available from late December through early March; ☎ 081 833 45 88.

● **IN THE EXTREME**

The **Cresta Run** clings tight to its reputation as the most testosterone-charged activity in the Alps. Male club members – for those are the only kind – belly-down onto skeleton toboggans and rip headfirst through a tube of natural ice at speeds of up to 140 km per hour. The British-founded tradition is over 100 years old. Steep club initiation fees entitle member males to five runs during the season, from late December to March. If you have the head to try it, wear a helmet. Inquire at ☎ 081 833 31 17.

Sports Services, Outfitters & Guides

■ **St. Moritz Experience** guides lead touring over the Morteratsch Glacier, canyoning in a nearby gorge, high-mountain trekking, and multi-sport days, including climbing, abseiling, rap jumping, hydrospeeding, tubing, sailing, mountain biking and more. Teens can meet like-minded friends while on teen-only treks. With activities geared toward adrenaline-craving youth, these trips are hipper than a video arcade and a pocket full of quarters. Contact ☎ 081 833 77 14; www.stmoritz-experience.ch.

■ The **Schweizer Bergsteigerschule,** or Swiss Mountaineering School, just down the road in Pontresina, is the largest such school in Switzerland. The guides here take a more technical approach to year-round tours and instruction. The

Switzerland

group runs multi- and single-day guided adventures on foot, rope, ski, and snowshoe. Check in at ☎ 081 838 83 33, www.bergsteiger-pontresina.ch.

■ **Engadin Adventure** in nearby Scuol is associated with the Swiss Outdoor Association, offering rafting, biking, and various day tours. Contact ☎ 081 861 14 16, www.engadin-adventure.ch.

■ Two ski schools together offer one of largest instructor forces in the Alps, and many hotels staff in-house teams. (With all the money that passes through St. Moritz, there's a huge demand for private instruction.) The **Swiss Ski School** is the time-honored leader here, ☎ 081 830 01 01, but we've heard better things about **Suvretta Snowsports**, ☎ 081 836 36 00.

Where to Sleep

Over half the hotels here rate four or five stars, so there's a lot to choose from in the splurge category. Rates across all categories

HOTEL PRICES	
€	Under 120 CHF
€€	120-225 CHF
€€€	226-375 CHF
€€€€	Over 375 CHF

skyrocket in winter. Forerunners in the center of town include the elegant old **Hotel Kulm** (€€€€; see *The House that*

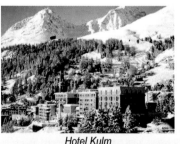

Badrutt Built below); ☎ 081 836 80 00, www.kulmhotel-stmoritz.ch; and a monstrous 1896 reproduction of a Gothic fortress, **Badrutt's Palace Hotel** (€€€€); ☎ 081 837 10 00, http://www.badruttspalace.com.

Hotel Kulm

The House that Badrutt Built

Badrutt's Palace Hotel

In 1856, hospitality pioneer Johannes Badrutt upgraded a local pension into St. Moritz's first hotel, the Hotel Külm. Later, he became the first to suspect that this spa-town's summer guests might like the resort in winter, too. He invited a privileged few Englishmen to be his guests at the Külm for the winter of 1864, and winter tourism was born.

The Badrutt family went on to expand the Hotel Kulm, adding recreation facilities such as curling and ice-skating rinks, and to open the huge Badrutt's Palace Hotel (above) in 1896. Today, thousands of travelers visit St. Moritz each winter – and some of them pay upwards of €2,000 a night to sleep here, in the house that Badrutt built.

Terrace at Hotel Schweizerhof

For slightly less grand surroundings, try the elegant old **Hotel Schweizerhof** (€€€). Its friendly staff, central location, historical interior, and upper, lake-view rooms make this a memorable stay; ☎ 081 837 07 07, www.schweizerhofstmoritz.ch.

Switzerland

Hotel Languard

Also in the center, the small **Languard** (€€€) tucks away next door to the Kulm, mixing antique and modern furnishings. There is no restaurant on the premises, but the breakfast room offers one of the best lake views in town; ☎ 081 833 31 37, www.languard-stmoritz.ch.

Not pretty, but near the center, the **Hotel Soldanella** (€€) has decent accommodations on the western edge of Dorf, near the museums and the Segantini Weg path; ☎ 081 830 85 00, www.hotel-soldanella.ch.

For a quiet, rural location across the lake, try the **Landhotel Meierei** (€€-€€€). It's a lovely walk of reasonable distance into town, and the restaurant and terrace are favorite stops for lakeside strollers; ☎ 081 833 20 60, www.hotel-meierei.ch.

In Bad, the **youth hostel** (€) sports modern comfort in both dorm and room accommodations; ☎ 081 833 69 48, www.youthhostel.ch.

Where to Eat

St. Moritz has no shortage of gourmet dining rooms – 20 restaurants in the area rate a Gault Millau "gourmet" standard, in total earn-

RESTAURANT COSTS	
€	Under 15 CHF
€€	15-37 CHF
€€€	Over 37 CHF

ing a whopping 298 points. **Jöhri's Talvo** (€€€), in a 17th-century house in Champfer, tops the gourmet rankings here with its seafood specialties; ☎ 081 833 44 55. **Jorimann's Refugium** (€€€) runs a close second with creative takes on regional specialties; ☎ 081 833 30 00. Our favorite, however, is **Chesa Veglia** (€€-€€€), a rustic old house in the center with a lovely terrace, traditional fare, and wood-fired pizzas. It's well run by Badrutt's Palace Hotel; reserve at ☎ 081 837 28 00.

On the mountain, the cozy **El Paradiso** (€€) perches on the slopes of the Corviglia area. Its food is traditional, the views from its pillow-padded terrace chairs are astounding, and its atmosphere is as convivial as mountain restaurants come.

Finally, for wood-fired pizzas, try the Schweizerhof's mountain hut, **Acla Clavadatsch** (€€); ☎ 081 833 55 30.

Where to Party

As with local restaurants, most of the town's 20+ bars and discos are hotel-run. All nightclubs are expensive. At Badrutt's Palace, stylishly clad guests lounge at the **Renaissance** and at the **Mexican Bar**, and the **Hotel Schweizerhof** offers three separate bars, including rooms for country-western music, sing-along piano tunes, and dancing. The glamorous **St. Moritz Casino** is housed at the Kempinski Grand Hotel des Bains in Bad. It's open 8 pm-4 am daily, with slots, roulette, black jack, and stud poker.

For a younger crowd, the **American Bar** and **Bobby's Pub** at the Galeria center both chill with a hip casual beat from après-ski on. The cozy, informal bars offer Internet access, too. For an outdoor in-town après-ski party, try the **Roo Bar** at the Hotel Hauser. Later, dance your way to the **Prince** on Via Maistra or, in the Hotel Steffani, the **Vivai Dance Club**.

Where to Play

The **Kids' Club** at the Hotel Schweizerhof offers hotel-based **childcare** and children's activities. Non-guest families are accommodated on a space-available basis daily from 9:30 am to 5:30 pm. (Badrutt's Palace and the Kempinski Grand both offer in-house childcare for guests.) The best **playgrounds** are at the school just above the Segelhaus sailing center in Dorf and at the end of Via Tegliatscha in Bad.

Festivals & Events

St. Moritz schedules almost 300 special events each year. Sporting events range from serious competitions, such as World Cup ski races, to mass spectacles, such as inline skating, windsurfing, and cross-country ski marathons. Cultural events, too, crowd the Engadine calendar, and each year the town offers over 200 free indoor and outdoor concerts.

Switzerland

Horse racing on the frozen lake (Christof Sonderegger)

During the winter season, the lake provides a frozen stage for a number of time-honored events – events as patrician as they are unusual. The on-snow and on-ice competitions include **horse jumping**, **polo**, and **golf** played with red balls. The February **horse races** include betting opportunities, a **skijoring race**, and the most elegant **parties** of the social season.

March brings the **Gourmet Festival**, a **Music Festival**, and **Chalandamarz**, a celebration of youth and spring. Summertime features include a well-regarded **Opera Festival** and, in July and August, the **Engadiner Concert Weeks**.

THE GLACIER EXPRESS

Several scenic train routes pass through St. Moritz, and the Engadine Swiss make much of this skillfully engineered network. The Glacier Express is the most famed of all Swiss rail routes. The train links the western Alps to the eastern Alps, running from St. Moritz to Zermatt via Chur. Travelers view glaciers, peaks, and waterfalls through panoramic windows as the train passes through 91 tunnels and viaducts and over 291 bridges during the 7½-hour trip. The cost from St. Moritz to Zermatt is 215 CHF first class, 129 CHF second class. Reserve through travel agents, at any Swiss train station or check www.glacierexpress.ch. If you go on a standard train, be sure to book a table in the old-fashioned dining car, where good food is topped off with wine served in glassware angled to offset the train's steep climb.

The Glacier Express on the Landwasser Viaduct, just before Filisur
(swiss-image.ch)

Silvaplana

Population: 952
Base Elevation: 1,815 m/5,953 feet
Lake & mountain resort village

It's often discounted as an insignificant suburb of St. Moritz. But for those seeking some distance from that high-society set, Silvaplana is an ideal base from which to explore the natural wonders it shares with its more glorified neighbor.

It's quieter here, and less expensive, and the traditional village center is much more in tune with what most visitors to the Swiss Alps might expect. Silvaplana is also much more sports-minded than well-manicured Moritz. So, for adventurers looking to get their hands dirty, this is the better base.

Just six km upstream from St. Moritz, on the western shore of Lake Silvaplana, the village of Silvaplana guards the Julier Pass. The small village huddles across a busy road from its namesake lake. (Lake Silvaplana is just one of four lakes in the Upper Engadine chain derived from a single ancient lake.) A land bar connects the village center to Surlej, the small hamlet at the base of the Corvatsch cable car and slopes.

In summer, Silvaplana is first and foremost a place of pilgrimage for lovers of windy watersports. Kitesurfing, sailing, windsurfing, and paragliding thrive here on afternoon thermals

Switzerland

Silvaplana and the Upper Engadine Lakes,
seen from the Lake Hahnen region, with Piz Polaschin in the
background (Christof Sonderegger)

whipped up by the Maloja Winds. In addition, hiking, biking, climbing, and fishing supplement summertime snowsports at Corvatsch.

CORVATSCH

Atop the cable car route up Corvatsch at 3,303 m/ 10,833 feet, snow-play is available year-round. Visitors can snowshoe or air-board on the icy slopes, check out the inside of a glacier, and dine in the Engadine's highest restaurant. If you go, don't miss the dizzying panorama from the upper viewing terrace. For more information check ☎ 081 838 73 73, www.corvatsch.ch.

In winter, guests enjoy access to the same ski runs and uplift system that have made St. Moritz famous – 60 lifts and 350 km of runs in all. The local runs, at Corvatsch and Furtschellas, are mostly easy intermediate trails, and other winter sports beckon as well. Cross-country skiing, dog-sledding, ice-skating, snowshoeing, and kite-skiing are all available here. Each Friday, floodlights brighten the Corvatsch slopes for a nighttime ski and snowboard party.

 Want to stay? I like the simple, central, fun-loving **Ferienhotel Julier Palace** (€€); ☎ 081 828 96 44, www.julierpalace.com. The Camping Silvaplana **campground** boasts an enviable lakeshore locale next door to the sport center. It's not luxurious, but it's ideal for budgeting guests here to play on the lake; ☎ 081 828 84 92.

 The tourist office is on the main village road next to the post office. Its helpful staff offers schedules, maps, postcards, brochures, and lift tickets and can make suggestions regarding the wide choice of sports outfitters and schools. Contact ☎ 081 838 60 00, www.silvaplana.ch.

Ibexes, Graubünden's heraldic animal, in the Swiss National Park, Val Mueschauns - Fuorcla Val Sassa (Bernard van Dierendonck)

The Swiss National Park

(Parc Naziunal Svizzer)

Base Elevation: 1,400 m/4,592 feet

National Park

The Swiss National Park is Switzerland's only national park and the nation's largest nature reserve, a pristine wilderness drawing visitors for its trails, its wildlife, and its excellent educational efforts.

Switzerland

Established in 1914, the park sits along the border of Italy and on the eastern doorstep of Zernez, 35 km northeast of St. Moritz and just over the Flüela Pass from Davos. Entry is free, and the gates remain open from June through October.

The park dedicates its efforts and its substantial wealth of territory to the preservation of nature and its processes. Human interaction is minimized: Fires are left to burn unopposed, only one road crosses the grounds, and strict stay-on-the-path don't-pick don't-feed regulations are meticulously enforced. The results of this management are extraordinary, and visitors hiking the pristine, rugged terrain enjoy frequent sightings of red deer, chamois, ibex, bearded vultures, and, of course, those ever-amusing marmots.

The best way to explore the park is, of course, on foot. A great introductory hike is the popular nature trail from Il Fuorn. Enriching the circular path are signposts describing ecology and wildlife of the area – in English and for kids, too.

✔ The four-hour loop is painstakingly documented in the *Along the Nature Trail* guidebook. However, for those with kids – or for those adults who'd like a lighter look at the park's flora and fauna – I recommend the children's version of the guide. Both books are available at the Park House.

 Want to stay? In the middle of the park on the main road, the **Hotel il Fuorn** (€€) offers simple accommodations and a restaurant with regional and trout specialties. Inquire at ☎ 081 856 12 26, www.ilfuorn.ch. In Zernez, the **Hotel Bar-Post** (€€) has been housing travelers since 1905. It's smack in the center of the small village, just 500 m/1,600 feet from the National Park information house. Dial ☎ 081 851 55 00, www.baer-post.ch.

 For more information, check in at the Nationalparkhaus (National Park House), along the main road on the eastern outskirts of Zernez. The center houses an information desk, a gift shop, a small museum, and a theater with an interesting 15-minute video. (The staff will screen the English version on request.) The park house is open daily from June through October, 8:30 am to 6 pm. Inquire at ☎ 081 856 13 78, www.nationalpark.ch.

Language Primer

English	German	French	Italian
Basics			
Hello	Guten Tag/Gruss Gott	Bonjour/Salut	Buongiorno/Ciao
Good evening	Guten abend	Bonsoir	Buona sera
Goodbye	Auf Wiedersehen/Tschuss	Au revoir/Salut	Arrivederci/Ciao
Yes	Ja	Oui	Si
No	Nein	Non	No
It's OK	Alles gut	Ca marche/Tres bien	Va bene
Please	Bitte	S'il vous plait	Per favore
Thank you	Danke	Merci	Grazie
You're welcome	Bitte	Je vous en prie	Prego
Excuse me	Entschuldigung	Excusez-moi	Mi scusi
I don't understand	Ich verstehe nicht	Je ne comprends pas	Non capisco
Help	Hilfe	Au secours	Aiuto
I'm lost	Ich habe mich verlaufen	Je suis perdu(e)	Mi sono perso (persa)
Left	Links	Gauche	Sinestra
Right	Recht	Droite	Destra
Straight	Geradeaus	Tout droit	Sempre diritto
North	Nord	Nord	Nord
South	Sud	Sud	Sud
East	Ost	Est	Este
West	West	Ouest	Ovest
Signs			
Open	Offen	Ouvert	Aperto
Closed	Geschlossen	Fermé	Chiuso
Entrance	Eingang	Entrée	Ingresso/Entrata
Exit	Ausgang	Sortie	Uscita
Forbidden	Vorboten	Interdit	Vietato
Toilets	Toiletten	Toilettes	Bagni
Women	Damen	Femmes	Donne/Signore
Men	Herren	Hommes	Uomini/Signori
Questions			
Do you speak English?	Sprechen Sie Englisch?	Parlez-vous anglais?	Parle inglese?

How much is...	Wieviel kostet...	Combien coute?	Quanto costa.
Where is...	Wo ist...	Ou est...	Dove...
When...	Wann...	A quelle heure...	Quando...
I'd like...	Ich mochte...	Je voudrais...	Vorrei...
Meetings			
My name is...	Ich heisse...	Je m'appelle...	Mi chiamo...
What is your name?	Wie heissen Sie?	Comment appelez-vous?	Como si chiama?
I come from...	Ich komme aus ..	Je viens de...	Vengo da...
Where are you from?	Woher kommen Sie?	Vous venez d'ou?	Da dove viene?
Sleeping			
Hotel/guesthouse	Hotel/Pension/Gastehaus	Hotel	Albergo/Pensione
Youth hostel	Jungendheberge	Auberge de jeunesse	Ostello
Camping place	Campingplatz	Camping	Campeggio
Night	Nacht	Nuit	Notte
Single room	Einzelzimmer	Chambre simple	Camera singola
Double room	Doppelzimeer	Chambre double	Camera doppia
Dorm room	Schlafsaal	Dortoir	Dormitorio
Eating			
Breakfast	Fruhstuck	Petit-déjeuner	Prima colazione
Lunch	Mittagessen	Déjeuner	Pranzo/Colazione
Dinner	Abendessen	Diner	Cena
Menu	Spiesekarte	Menu	Menu/Liste
Restaurant	Restaurant/Gaststatte	Restaurant	Ristorante
Supermarket	Supermarkt	Supermarché	Supermercato
Market	Markt	Marché	Mercato
Bakery	Backerei	Boulangerie	Panetteria
Traveling			
Ticket	Karte	Billet	Biglietto
One-way	Eizelkarte	Aller simple	Sola andata
Round-trip	Ruckfahrkarte	Aller retour	Andata e ritorno
Bus	Bus	Bus	Autobus
Stop	Haltestelle	Arrêt	Fermata
Train	Bahn	Train	Treno

Train station	Bahnhof	Gare	Stazione
Boat	Boot	Bâteau	Barca
Cable car	Luftseilbahn	Télépherique	Funicolare
Chair lift	Sesselbahn	Telesiege	Seggiovia
Days			
Monday	Montag	Lundi	Lunedi
Tuesday	Dienstag	Mardi	Martedi
Wednesday	Mittwoch	Mercredi	Mercoledi
Thursday	Donnerstag	Jeudi	Giovedi
Friday	Freitag	Vendredi	Venerdi
Saturday	Samstag	Samedi	Sabato
Sunday	Sonntag	Dimanche	Domenica
Times			
Today	Heute	Aujourd'hui	Oggi
Tomorrow	Morgen	Demain	Domani
Morning	Morgen	Matin	Mattina
Noon	Mittag	Midi	Mezzogiorno
Afternoon	Nachmittag	Après-midi	Pomeriggio
Evening	Abend	Soir	Sera
Numbers			
0	Null	Zero	Zero
1	Ein	Un	Uno
2	Zwei	Deux	Due
3	Drei	Trois	Tre
4	Vier	Quatre	Quattro
5	Funf	Cinq	Cinque
6	Sechs	Six	Sei
7	Sieben	Sept	Sette
8	Acht	Huit	Otto
9	Neun	Neuf	Nove
10	Zehn	Dix	Dieci
11	Elf	Onze	Undici
12	Zwolf	Douze	Dodici
13	Dreizehn	Treize	Tredici
14	Vierzehn	Quatorze	Quattordici
15	Funfzehn	Quinze	Quindici
16	Sechzehn	Seize	Sedici
17	Siebzehn	Dix-sept	Diciassette

18	Achtzehn	Dix-huit	Diciotto
19	Neunzehn	Dix-neuf	Diciannove
20	Zwanzig	Vingt	Venti
21	Einundzwanzig	Vingt et un	Ventuno
30	Dreizig	Trente	Trenta
40	Vierzig	Quarante	Quaranta
50	Funfzig	Cinquante	Cinquanta
60	Sechszig	Soixante	Sessanta
70	Siebzig	Septante (Soixante-dix)	Settanta
80	Aachtzig	Huitante (Quatre-vingt)	Ottanta
90	Neunzig	Nonante (Quatre-vingt-dix)	Novanta
100	Hundert	Cent	Cento
1,000	Tausand	Mille	Mille
1,000,000	Eine Million	Un million	Un milione

Index

Accommodations, 28-29; Argentiêre, France, 173; Berchtesgaden, Germany, 239-240; Bregenz, Austria, 70; Chamonix, France, 167-168; Chiemsee, Germany, 204; Cortina, Italy, 321-322; Courmayeur, Italy, 278-279; Dachau, Germany, 202; Engelberg, Switzerland, 448; Feldkirch, Austria, 73; Füssen, Germany, 230; Garmisch-Partenkirchen, Germany, 218-219; Geneva, Switzerland, 359-360; Gran Paradiso, Italy, 288; Grindelwald, Switzerland, 408-409; Innsbruck, Austria, 86-87; Interlaken, Switzerland, 400-401; Ischgl, Austria, 64; Kitzbühel, Austria, 113-114; Klein Scheidegg, Switzerland, 409; Königsee, Germany, 246; Krimml, Austria, 150-151; Lake Como, 264-266; Lauterbrunnen, Switzerland, 405-406; lodging tips, 28-29; Lucerne, Switzerland, 439, 441-442; Malbun, Liechtenstein, 343-344; Mayrhofen, Austria, 103-104; Milan, Italy, 259-260; Munich, Germany, 192-193; Mürren, Switzerland, 414; Neustift, Austria, 99-100; Oberammergau, Germany, 226; Obergurgl, Austria, 97; Ortisei, Italy, 328; Ouchy, Switzerland, 364-365; Rheinfall, Switzerland, 429; Saas-Fee, Switzerland, 383-384; St. Anton, Austria, 51-52; St. Christoph, Austria, 58; St. Johann, Austria, 119; St. Moritz, Switzerland, 460-462; Salzburg, Austria, 137-138; Salzkammergut, Austria, 143; Santa Cristina, Italy, 328; Seefeld, Austria, 92; Selva Gardena, Italy, 328; Silvaplana, Switzerland, 467; Silvretta Hochalpenstrasse, Austria, 65; Sölden, Austria, 97; Söll, Austria, 122-123; Steg, Liechtenstein, 345; Swiss National Park, 468; Turin, Italy, 268; for US military in Germany, 219; Vaduz, Liechtenstein, 338-339; Val Gardena, Italy, 328; Venice, Italy, 306-308; Wengen, Switzerland, 411; Zell am See, Austria, 147; Zermatt, Switzerland, 377-379; Zürich, Switzerland, 423-425

Acute mountain sickness, 35

Airports, 22

Alpine flowers, 13-15

Alps: climate, 10-11; fauna, 15-20; flora, 12-15; getting to, 21-22; glaciers, 9-10; Pick-An-Adventure, 4, 7-8; Pick-A-Theme, 4-5; Pick-A-Vibe, 4, 6; prehistory, 8-10

Alps di Suisi, Italy, 325

Aosta, Italy, 283-286

Argentiêre, France, 172-173; accommodations, 173; adventures, 164, 173; Argentiêre Guest Card, 173; information, 173

Arlberg, Austria, 41-73; Arlberg Ski Pass, 60; Bregenz, 65-71; Feldkirch, 71-73; Ischgl, 61-64; Lech, 58-61; map, 42; St. Anton, 43-55; St. Christoph, 56-58; Silvretta Hochalpenstrasse, 65

Austria, 37-151; Arlberg, 41-73; information, 41; Innsbruck and the Tyrol, 73-104; Kitzbühel, 104-123; map, 38; national holidays, 39; people and culture, 37-41; Salzburg region, 123-143; timeline, 39-40; Zell am See and Kaprun, 144-151

Avalanches, 35

Bad Ischl, Austria, 142

Ballooning: Berchtesgaden, Germany, 236; Chamonix, France, 164; Kitzbühel, Austria, 111; St. Johann, Austria, 118

Bardonecchia, Italy, 269

Bavarian Alps, 180

Beatenberg, Switzerland, 393

Bellagio, Italy, 263

Berchtesgaden, Germany, 231-246; accommodations, 239-240; adventures, 235-239; with children, 241; dining, 240; Eagle's Nest, 234-235; festivals and events, 241-242; history and overview, 231-232; information, 233; Obersalzburg, 233-234; outfitters and guides, 238-239; sights, 233-235; the town, 232; transportation, 232-233; where to party, 240-241

Berchtesgaden National Park, Germany, 16, 242-244; hiking, 236, 242-243

Bicycling, see Mountain biking

Bobsledding: Berchtesgaden, Germany, 238; Cortina, Italy, 320; Igls, Austria, 83-84; Königsee, Germany, 245; St. Moritz, Switzerland, 458-459

Bregenz, Austria, 65-71; accommodations, 70; information, 70-71; Lake Constance/Bodensee, 66, 69, 70; map, 42; old town, 69-70

Brienzersee, Switzerland, 391-392

Brotherhood of St. Christoph, Austria, 57-58

Bürgenstock, Switzerland, 437

Buses, 26

Camping, Silvaplana, Switzerland, 467

Canyoning: Cortina, Italy, 320; Courmayeur, Italy, 275, 276; Geneva, Switzerland, 359; Interlaken, Switzerland, 399; St. Johann, Austria, 118

Cernobbio, Italy, 264

CH (Switzerland); CHF (Swiss francs), 27, 28, 335

Chamonix, France, 157-171; accommodations, 167-168; adventures, 163-167; Carte d'Hôte Guest Card, 160; with children, 170; dining, 168-169; festivals and events, 170-171; history and orientation, 157-158; information, 160; L'Aiguille du Midi, 161; Mont Blanc, 158, 163; outfitters and guides, 166-167; sights, 160-162; the town, 158-

159; transportation, 159-160; Vallée Blanche, 165-166; where to party, 169, Germany, 202-205

Children: Berchtesgaden, Germany, 241; Chamonix, France, 170; Cortina, Italy, 323; Courmayeur, Italy, 281; Garmisch-Partenkirchen, Germany, 220; Hochsöll, Austria, 119; Innsbruck, Austria, 89; Interlaken, Switzerland, 403; Kitzbühel, Austria, 115; Krimml, Austria, 150; Lech, Austria, 59-60; Lucerne, Switzerland, 443; Munich, Germany, 196; St. Anton, Austria, 54; St. Moritz, Switzerland, 463; Vaduz, Liechtenstein, 340; Venice, Italy, 310; Zermatt, Switzerland, 380; Zürich, Switzerland, 426-427

Climate, 10-11

Climbing: acute mountain sickness, 35; Arlberg Track, Austria, 47; avalanches, 35; Chamonix, France, 163; Corvatsch, Switzerland, 466; Courmayeur, Italy, 275; Garmisch-Partenkirchen, Germany, 216; Interlaken and Jungfrau area, Switzerland, 389; Mont Blanc, France, 163; Oberammergau, Germany, 226; Ortesei, Italy, 326; St. Johann, Austria, 118; Zermatt, Switzerland, 374, 376-377

Col des Montets scenic drive, France/Switzerland, 174

Como, Italy, 263-264

Cortina d'Ampezzo, Italy, 311-328; accommodations, 321-322; adventures, 316-321; with children, 323; dining, 322; festivals and events, 324; history and orientation, 311-312; information, 315; map, 314; outfitters and guides, 320-321; sights, 315-316; the town, 312-313; transportation, 313-315; where to party, 323; and World War I, 317

Corvatsch, Switzerland, 465-467

Courmayeur, Italy, 270-288; accommodations, 278-279; adventures, 274-278; with children, 281; dining, 279-280; history and orientation, 270-271; information, 273; Mont

Blanc, 274-275; outfitters and guides, 278; sights, 273; the town, 271-272; transportation, 272-273; where to party, 280

Cross-country skiing, see Skiing

Curling: Berchtesgaden, Germany, 238; Cortina, Italy, 320; Garmisch-Partenkirchen, Germany, 217; Kitzbühel, Austria, 112; St. Anton, Austria, 50; St. Moritz, Switzerland, 459; Zell am See, Austria, 146; Zermatt, Switzerland, 376

Currency, 27-28

Dachau concentration camp, Germany, 200-202

Degioz, Italy, 287-288

Dining, 29-32; Berchtesgaden, Germany, 240; Chamonix, France, 168-169; Cortina, Italy, 322; Courmayeur, Italy, 279-280; Garmisch-Partenkirchen, Germany, 219-220; Geneva, Switzerland, 360-361; Innsbruck, Austria, 87-88; Interlaken, Switzerland, 401-402; Jochdohle, Austria, 99; Kitzbühel, Austria, 114; Königsee, Germany, 245; Lucerne, Switzerland, 442-443; Milan, Italy, 260; Munich, Germany, 193-194; Mürren, Switzerland, 414; St. Anton, Austria, 52-53; St. Christoph, Austria, 57; St. Moritz, Switzerland, 462-463; Salzburg, Austria, 138; Schilthorn, Switzerland, 396; tips, 31-32; Vaduz, Liechtenstein, 339-340; Venice, Italy, 308-309; Zermatt, Switzerland, 379; Zürich, Switzerland, 425-426

Dog-sledding: Chamonix, France, 166; Cortina, Italy, 320; Corvatsch, Switzerland, 466; Zermatt, Switzerland

Dolomites, 376, Italy, 316, 317, 324

Dolonne, Italy, 273

Driving, 22-25; car rentals, 23; gasoline lingo, 23; international road signs, 24-25; parking, 25; tips, 23

Dunant, Henri, 347-348

Eibsee, Germany, 213

Eiger, Switzerland, 394

Electricity, 33-34

Engelberg, Switzerland, 444-449; Cheese Factory, 447; Monastery, 447

Ettaler Benedictine Abbey, Germany, 226

Europa Sports Region, Austria, 144

Extreme sports: Cortina, Italy, 317, 320-321; Engelberg, Switzerland, 448; Interlaken, Switzerland, 398-400; Lucerne, Switzerland, 439; Ötzal, Austria, 96; St. Moritz, Switzerland, 459

Falconry, Malbun, Liechtenstein, 342

Fauna, 15-20; ibex, 287

Feldkirch, Austria, 71-73

Fishing: Corvatsch, Switzerland, 466; Courmayeur, Italy, 276; Garmisch-Partenkirchen, Germany, 213; Interlaken, Switzerland, 391; St. Moritz, Switzerland, 456; Seefeld, Austria, 91; Zell am See, Austria, 146

Flora, 12-15; Alpine flowers, 13-15; vegetation belts, 12-13

France, 153-174; map, 152; Mont Blanc region, 156-174; national holidays, 154-155; people and culture, 154-156; timeline, 155-156

Frostbite, 34-35

Füssen, Germany, 227-230

Garmisch-Partenkirchen, Germany, 205-230; accommodations, 218-219; adventures, 211-217; with children, 220; dining, 219-220; festivals and events, 220-221; history and orientation, 205-206; information, 208-209; outfitters and guides, 217; sights, 209-211; the towns, 207; transportation, 207-208; where to party, 220; Zügspitze, 210-211

Geneva, Switzerland, 352-363; accommodations, 359-360; adventures, 359; dining, 360-361; festivals and events, 362-363; history and orientation, 353-354; information, 355; map, 358; sights, 355-358; the town, 354; transportation, 354-355; where to party, 361

Geneva Convention, first, 347

Gerlos Pass scenic drive, Austria, 104

Germany, 175-246; Berchtesgaden, 231-246; Garmisch-Partenkirchen, 205-230; map, 177; Munich & Bavarian Alps, 180-204; national holidays, 178; people and culture, 176-179; timeline, 179

Glacier Express, Switzerland, 464

Glaciers, 9-10; Aletsch, Switzerland, 395; Corvatsch, Switzerland, 466; Courmayeur, Italy, 275; Interlaken, Switzerland, 398, 399; Kitzsteinhorn, Austria, 146; Mer de Glace, France, 161, 166; Pasterze, Austria, 148; Theodul, Switzerland, 376

Glacier skiing: Hintertux, Austria, 102; Saas-Fee, Switzerland, 383; Sölden, Austria, 95; Stubai, Austria, 99; Vallée Blanche, France, 165-166

Golf: Kitzbühel, Austria, 109; Seefeld, Austria, 91

Gran Paradiso National Park, Italy, 16, 286-288

Graubünden area, Switzerland, 449-450

Grindelwald, Switzerland, 395, 406-409, 411

Grossglockner Hochalpenstrasse, Austria, 148-149

Halstatt, Austria, 142

Hannibal, 153

Hannibal re-enactment, Sölden, Austria, 95

Health and safety: acute mountain sickness, 35; avalanches, 35; frostbite, 34-35; insurance, 34; skiing, 50; sunburn, 34

Heidi (film), 455

Helicopter flights: Chaminox, France, 164; Zermatt, Switzerland, 375

Help signals, 35

Hiking: acute mountain sickness, 35; Argentiêre, France, 173; avalanches, 35; Berchtesgaden, Germany, 236, 242-243; Chamonix, France, 163; Corvatsch, Switzerland, 466; Courmayeur, Italy, 275; Engelberg, Switzerland, 446; Garmisch-Partenkirchen, Germany, 211-213; Grindelwald, Switzerland, 407; help signals, 35; Höhe Tauern National Park, Austria, 148; Innsbruck, Austria, 82-83, 85, 86; Interlaken and Jungfrau area, Switzerland, 389; Ischgl, Austria, 63; Kitzbühel, Austria, 109, 112; Königsee, Germany, 245; Lech, Austria, 61; Lucerne, Switzerland, 436, 437; Malbun, Liechtenstein, 343; Oberammergau, Germany, 226; Saas-Fee, Switzerland, 382; St. Anton, Austria, 47; St. Johann, Austria, 118; St. Moritz, Switzerland, 454-455; Salzburg, Austria, 135; Seefeld, Austria, 91; Smugglers' Run, Austrian-Swiss border, 64; Söll, Austria, 119-120; Swiss Path, 439; Val Gardena, Italy, 325-326; Zell am See, Austria, 146; Zermatt, Switzerland, 373; Zürich, Switzerland, 423

Hintertux Glacier, Austria, 102

Hoch-Innsbruck Hungerburg, Austria, 84

Hochsöll, Austria, 119-120

Höhensalzburg Fortress, Austria, 131

Höhe Tauern National Park, Austria, 16, 144, 147, 148-149

Horseback riding: Kitzbühel, Austria, 109; St. Moritz, Switzerland, 455; Seefeld, Austria, 91; Zermatt, Switzerland (mule and llama trekking), 374

Horse-drawn sleigh rides: Garmisch-Partenkirchen, Germany, 217; St. Anton, Austria, 50; St. Moritz, Switzerland, 458-459; Zermatt, Switzerland, 370, 374

Ice-skating: Berchtesgaden, Germany, 238; Chamonix, France, 166; Cortina, Italy, 320; Courmayeur, Italy, 277; Garmisch-Partenkirchen, Germany, 216-217; Interlaken, Switzerland, 399; Kitzbühel, Austria, 112; Malbun, Liechtenstein, 343; Munich, Germany, 191; St. Anton, Austria, 50; St. Moritz, Switzerland, 459; Seefeld, Austria, 91; Zell am See, Austria, 146; Zermatt, Switzerland, 376

Igls, Austria, 84-85; bobsled run, 83-84

Information sources, 35-36

Innsbruck, Austria, 73-104; accommodations, 86-87; adventures, 82-86; Azamer Lizum, 86; Bergisel Ski Jump, 79-80; with children, 89; dining, 87-88; festivals and events, 89-90; history and overview, 75; Igls, 84-85; information, 77; Innsbruck Card deals, 77; map, 74; Mutterer Alm, 85; Nordpark-Seegrube, 84; sights, 77-81; Swarovski Crystal World, 81; the town, 76; transportation, 76-77; where to party, 88-89; zoo, 16, 79

Interlaken, Switzerland, 384-404; accommodations, 400-401; adventures, 388-400; with children, 403; dining, 401-402; festivals and events, 403-404; history and orientation, 386; information, 387, 404; outfitters and guides, 399-400; sights, 387-388; the town, 386; transportation, 387; where to party, 402-403

Internet service, 33

Ischgl, Austria, 61-64

Italy, 247-328; map, 248; Milan and Northwest, 252-288; national holidays, 249-250; overview and government, 247; people and culture, 249-250; timeline, 250; Venice and Northeast, 288-328

Jochdohle, Austria's highest restaurant, 99

Jungfrau region, Switzerland, 384-386; with children, 403; excursion, 394-395; festivals and events, 403-404; hiking, 389; lift passes, 411; map, 389; Wengen, 409, 411; see also Interlaken

Kaprun, Austria, 144-151

Kayaking: Cortina, Italy, 320; Garmisch-Partenkirchen, Germany, 213; Geneva, Switzerland, 359

Kitzbühel, Austria, 104-123; accommodations, 113-114; adventures, 109-112; with children, 115; dining, 114; festivals and events, 115-116; Hahnenkamm Ski Race, 116; history and overview, 104-105; information, 107; outfitters and guides, 112; sights, 107-109; the town, 105-106; transportation, 106; where to party, 114-115; zoo, 108

Klein Scheidegg, Switzerland, 395, 407, 409

Klewenalp, Switzerland, 437, 443

Kneipp water trails: Garmisch-Partenkirchen, Germany, 213; Hexenwasser, Söll, Austria, 121; Igls, Austria, 85

Königsee, Germany, 243-246

Krimml, Austria, 149-151

Krimmler Falls, Austria, 104, 149-150

Ladin culture, Italy, 326

L'Aiguille du Midi, France, 161

Lake Como, Italy, 262-266

Lake Constance (Bodensee), 66, 69, 70

Lake excursions: Chiemsee, Germany, 204-205; Geneva, Switzerland, 359; Interlaken, Switzerland, 391-393; Königsee, Germany, 243-244, 246; Lake Constance/Bodensee, Austria, 70; Lucerne, Switzerland, 435-436; Zürich, Switzerland, 422

Lake Geneva, Switzerland, 359

Lake Lucerne, Switzerland, 431, 435-436

Lake Silvaplana, Switzerland, 465

Lake Zurich, Switzerland, 418, 422

Landeck Castle, Austria, 56

Language, 32-33; basics, 469-472; gasoline for your car, 23

Lausanne, Switzerland, 364-365

Lauterbrunnen, Switzerland, 395, 404-406

La Vanoise National Park, France, 16

Lech, Austria, 58-61

Liechtenstein, 329-345; currency (Swiss francs: CHF), 27, 28, 335; Erlebnispass, 338; falconry, 342; history and government, 329; information, 333; map, 330; national holidays, 331-332; people and culture, 331-333; postage stamps, 336; sights, 335-338; timeline, 332; Vaduz, 333-345

Lucerne, Switzerland, 429-444; accommodations, 439, 441-442; adventures, 435-439; with children, 443; dining, 442-443; festivals and events, 444; history and orientation, 430-431; information, 432-433; Lucerne Visitor's Card, 432; sights, 433-435; the town, 431; transportation, 431-432; where to party, 443

Ludwig II, king of Bavaria, 175-176; the musical, 230; Schloss Herrenchiemsee, 202; Schloss Linderhof, 227; Schloss Neuschwanstein, 228-229

Luge, see Bobsledding

Malbun, Liechtenstein, 338, 341, 342-344

Maps: Arlberg and Bregenz, Austria, 42; Austrian Alpine regions, 38; Central Switzerland, 416; Cortina, Italy, 314; French Alpine region, 152; Geneva and Valais region, Switzerland, 358; German Alpine region, 177; Graubünden area, Switzerland, 449; Innsbruck and

Tyrol region, Austria, 74; Italian Alpine region, 248; Jungfrau, Switzerland, 389; Liechtenstein, 330; Milan and Northwest Italy, 253; Salzburg, Austria, 126; Swiss Alpine regions, 349; Venice, Italy, 291; Venice and Northeast Italy, 289

Maria Theresa, Queen, 40-41

Matterhorn, Switzerland, 368-369, 373

Mayrhofen, Austria, 102-104

Mer de Glace, France, 161, 166

Metric equivalents, 36

Milan, Italy, 252-266; accommodations, 259-260; dining, 260; festivals and events, 261-262; history and overview, 252-254; information, 255-256; La Scala Opera, 258; map, 253; sights, 256-258; the town, 254-255; transportation, 255; where to party, 260-261

Mittelallin Eispavillon, Switzerland, 382

Mönch, Switzerland, 394

Mondsee, Austria, 141

Mont Blanc, France, 158; ascent, 163

Mont Blanc region, France, 156-174; Argentière, 172-173; Chamonix, 157-171; and Courmayeur, Italy, 271, 273, 274-275; L'Aiguille du Midi, 161; La Route des Grandes Alpes, 171-172; Le Col des Montets, 174; Mer de Glace, 161, 166

Mountain biking: Argentière, France, 173; Berchtesgaden, Germany, 236; Chamonix, France, 164; Cortina, Italy, 318; Corvatsch, Switzerland, 466; Courmayeur, Italy, 276; Engelberg, Switzerland, 446; Garmisch-Partenkirchen, Germany, 213, 215; Innsbruck, Austria, 82, 85; Interlaken, Switzerland, 393-394; Ischgl, Austria, 62-63; Kitzbühel, Austria, 110; Lucerne, Switzerland, 436, 437; Niederhorn, Switzerland, 393; Saas-Fee, Switzerland, 382; St.

Anton, Austria, 48; St. Johann, Austria, 118; St. Moritz, Switzerland, 456; Salzburg, Austria, 135; Seefeld, Austria, 91; Smugglers' Run, Austrian-Swiss border, 64; Vaduz, Liechtenstein, 337-338; Zell am See, Austria, 146; Zermatt, Switzerland, 375

Mount Pilatus, Switzerland, 437

Mount Rigi, Switzerland, 437

Mount Titlis, Switzerland, 437, 447

Mozart, Wolfgang Amadeus, Salzburg sites, Austria, 132-134

Munich, Germany, 180-205; accommodations, 192-193; adventures, 190-192; beer halls, 194-195; with children, 196; Dachau concentration camp, 200-202; dining, 193-194; history and orientation, 180-181; information, 183-184; München Welcome Card, 183; Oktoberfest, 196-200; Olympic Park, 190-191; sights, 184-191; the town, 181-182; transportation, 182-183; where to party, 195-196

Mürren, Switzerland, 395, 411-415

Neuschwanstein castle, Germany, 228-229

Neustift, Austria, 98-100

Niederhorn, Switzerland, 393

Oberammergau, Germany, 221-227; accommodations, 226; adventures, 226; information, 226; Lüftmalerei (painting house façades), 222-223; passion play, 225-226; Schloss Linderhof, 227; woodcarving, 223, 225

Obergurgl, Austria, 92, 96-97

Oberlech, Austria, 59

Oktoberfest, Munich, Germany, 196-200

Olympic sites: Cortina, Italy, 319; Igls, Austria (bobsled), 83-84; Innsbruck, Austria (ski jump), 80; Munich, Germany, 190-191; Olympic headquarters, Lausanne, Switzerland, 365; St. Moritz, Switzer-

land (bobsled), 458-459; Turin, Italy, 268-269

Ortisei (St. Ulrich), Italy, 325, 326, 328

Ötzal region, Austria, 92-97; extreme sports, 96; Ötzal Card, 92; scenic drive, 97; Stuibenfalls, 93

Ötzi, Neolithic Man 94

Ouchy, Switzerland, 364-365

Parachuting, Chamonix, France, 164

Paragliding: Chamonix, France, 164; Garmisch-Partenkirchen, Germany, 216; Interlaken, Switzerland, 398, 399; Kitzbühel, Austria, 111; St. Anton, Austria, 48; St. Johann, Austria, 118; St. Moritz, Switzerland, 457; Salzburg, Austria, 135; Silvaplana, Switzerland, 465; Zermatt, Switzerland, 375

Parasailing, Berchtesgaden, Germany, 236

Parco Naturale Puez-Odle, Italy, 325, 326

Parco Naturale Regole d'Ampezzo, Italy, 316

Partnach Gorge, Germany, 212-213

Passports, 22

Pasterze Glacier, Austria, 148-149

Polo, Marco, 251

Rafting: Cortina, Italy, 320; Geneva, Switzerland, 359; Innsbruck, Austria, 83; St. Johann, Austria, 118; St. Moritz, Switzerland, 455

Rail Europe, 26

Rheinfall, Switzerland, 428-429

Rossfeld Ring Road scenic drive, Germany, 236

Route des Grandes Alpes, France / Switzerland (scenic drive), 171-172

Saas-Fee, Switzerland, 381-384

Sailer, Tony, 108

Sailing: Interlaken, Switzerland, 390; Silvaplana, Switzerland, 465

St. Anton am Arlberg, Austria, 43-55; accommodations, *51-52;* adventures, *47-51;* with children, *54;* dining, *52-53;* festivals and events, *55;* history and overview, *43-44;* information, *46;* outfitters and guides, *51;* sights, *46-47;* the town, *44-45;* transportation, *45;* where to party, *53-54*

St. Bernard Pass, 281-283

St. Christoph, Austria, 56-58

St. Johann, Austria, 116-119

St. Moritz, Switzerland, 450-464; accommodations, *460-462;* adventures, *454-460;* with children, *463;* dining, *462-463;* festivals and events, *463-464;* Glacier Express, *464;* history and orientation, *450-451;* information, *453;* outfitters and guides, *459-460;* sights, *453-454;* the town, *451-452;* transportation, *452-453;* where to party, *463*

St. Wolfgang, Austria, 142

Salzbergwerk salt mine, Germany, 235

Salzburg, Austria, 123-143; accommodations, *137-138;* adventures, *135-137;* dining, *138;* festivals and events, *140;* history and overview, *123-125;* information, *128;* map, *126;* Mozart sites, *132-134;* Salzburg Card, *128;* sights, *128-135;* Sound of Music and Von Trapp family, *129-131;* the town, *127;* transportation, *127-128;* where to party, *139;* zoo, *135*

Salzkammergut, Austria, 140-143

Salzkammergut Erlebnis-Card, 143

Santa Cristina, Italy, 325, 326, 328

Schilthorn, Switzerland, 395-396, 412, 414

Schynige Platte, Switzerland, 396-397

Seefeld, Austria, 90-92

Seefeld, Germany, 244-245

Selva Gardena (Wolkenstein), Italy, 325, 326, 327-328

Sestriere, Italy, 269

Shroud of Turin, 267

Silvaplana, Switzerland, 465-467

Silvretta Hochalpenstrasse, Austria, 65

Skateboarding and inline skating: Interlaken, Switzerland, *394;* Munich, Germany, *191-192;* St. Moritz, Switzerland, *456-457*

Skiing: Argentiére, France, *173;* Arlberg Ski Pass, Austria, *60;* avalanches, *35;* Berchtesgaden, Germany, *236, 238;* Chamonix, France, *164-166;* Cortina, Italy, *318-320;* Corvatsch, Switzerland, *466-467;* Courmayeur, Italy, *276-277;* Engelberg, Switzerland, *446;* frostbite, *34-35;* Garmisch-Partenkirchen, Germany, *216;* on glaciers, see Glacier skiing; Gran Paradiso, Italy, *287;* Grindelwald, Switzerland, *407;* Hintertux Glacier, Austria, *102;* Innsbruck, Austria, *83, 85, 86;* Interlaken, Switzerland, *398-399;* Ischgl, Austria, *63-64;* Kitzbühel, Austria, *111-112;* Königsee, Germany, *245;* Lech and Zurs, Austria, *60;* Lucerne, Switzerland, *436;* Malbun, Liechtenstein, *343;* Oberammergau, Germany, *226;* rescue insurance, *34;* Saas-Fee, Switzerland, *382-383;* safety, *50;* St. Anton, Austria, *48-51;* St. Johann, Austria, *118;* St. Moritz, Switzerland, *457-458;* Salzburg, Austria, *135-137;* Seefeld, Austria, *91;* Sella Ronda Ski Circuit, Italy, *327-328;* Smugglers' Run, Austrian-Swiss border, *64;* Sölden, Austria, *95;* Söll, Austria, *122;* Steg, Liechtenstein, *343, 344;* Stubai Glacier, Austria, *99;* Zell am See, Austria, *146;* Zermatt, Switzerland (summer and winter), *375-376*

Ski Jump, Innsbruck, Austria, 79-80

Snowboarding, see Skiing

Snowshoeing: Chamonix, France, *166;* Corvatsch, Switzerland, *466;* Courmayeur, Italy, *277;* Garmisch-Partenkirchen, Germany, *216;* Interlaken, Switzerland, *399;*

*Malbun, Liechtenstein, 343;
Zermatt, Switzerland, 376*
Sölden, Austria, 92, 95, 97
Söll, Austria, 119-123
Spas: Bad Ischl, Austria, 142; St.
  Moritz, Switzerland, 455
Stanserhorn, Switzerland, 437
Steg, Liechtenstein, 338, 343, 344-
  345
Stubai Glacier, Austria, 99
Stubaital region, Austria, 98-100;
  Stubaital Card, 98
Stuben, Austria, 59
Stuibenfalls, Austria, 93
Sunburn, 34
Swarovski Crystal, Austria, 81
Swimming: Berchtesgaden, Ger-
  many, 236; Chamonix, France,
  164; Cortina, Italy, 317;
  Courmayeur, Italy, 276; Garmisch-
  Partenkirchen, Germany, 213;
  Geneva, Switzerland, 359; Grin-
  delwald, Switzerland, 407; Inter-
  laken, Switzerland, 390-391;
  Kitzbühel, Austria, 110; Königsee,
  Germany, 245; Lucerne, Switzer-
  land, 439; Munich, Germany, 191;
  Oberammergau, Germany, 226;
  St. Anton, Austria, 48; Söll, Austria,
  122; Zell am See, Austria, 146;
  Zürich, Switzerland, 422
Swiss National Park, Switzerland,
  16, 467-468
Switzerland, 347-468; currency
  (CHF), 27, 28; Geneva and Valais
  region, 352-365; Graubünden region, 449-450; Interlaken and
  Jungfrau, 384-415; Lucerne, 429-
  444; map, 349; national holidays,
  351; overview, 348, 350; Panorama cable channel mountain
  conditions, 396; people and culture, 350-352; St. Moritz, 450-464;
  Swiss National Park, 467-468;
  timeline, 351-352; Zermatt, 365-
  381; Zurich and Central, 415-428

Telephone, 33; emergency number,
  34
Tell, William, 430

Tennis, Kitzbühel, Austria, 109
Thunersee, Switzerland, 391-393
Time zone, 33
Timmelsjoch Hochalpenstrasse sce-
  nic drive, Ötzal, Austria, 97
Tobogganing: Berchtesgaden, Ger-
  many, 238; Cortina, Italy, 320;
  Garmisch-Partenkirchen, Ger-
  many, 213; Grindelwald, Switzer-
  land, 407-408; Innsbruck, Austria,
  83; Kitzbühel, Austria, 112;
  Malbun, Liechtenstein, 343;
  Neustrift, Austria, 99; Saas-Fee,
  Switzerland, 383; St. Anton, Austria, 50; St. Moritz, Switzerland,
  458; Zermatt, Switzerland, 376
Trains, 26; car-carrying, 27; Glacier
  Express, 464; mountain, 26-27
Transportation, 21-27; buses, 26; cable cars and mountain trains, 26-
  27; driving, 22-25; getting around,
  22-25; getting here, 21-22; trains,
  26
Trapp family and Sound of Music,
  Austria, 129-131
Travel basics, 20-27; accommodations, 28-29; currency, 27-28; dining, 29-32; electricity, 33-34; emergency number, 34; health and
  safety, 34-35; Internet service, 33;
  metric, 36; passports, 22; telephone, 33; time zone, 33; transportation, 21-27; when to go, 20-21
Tremezzo, Italy, 264
Trümmelbach Falls, Switzerland,
  405
Trunsee, Austria, 142
Turin, Italy, 266-269
Tyrol region, Austria, 73; Innsbruck,
  73-104; Kitzbühel, 104-123; map,
  74; Salzburg, 123-143; Zell am
  See and Kaprun, 144-151
Untersberg, Austria, 135-136

Vaduz, Liechtenstein, 333-345; accommodations, 338-339; adventures, 337-338; with children, 340;
  dining, 339-340; festivals and
  events, 340-341; information, 335;

the town, 333-334; transportation, 334; where to party, 340

Valais region, Switzerland, 352-353; map, 358

Val d'Aosta, Italy, 277, 281

Val Gardena, Italy, 324-328; Val Gardena Card, 326

Valluga summit, Austria, 47

Venice, Italy, 288-311; accommodations, 306-308; adventures, 302-306; Burano, 304; with children, 310; dining, 308-309; festivals and events, 310-311; gondolas, 303; history and orientation, 290-292; information, 294; Lido, 305; maps, 289, 291; Murano, 304; off-hours, 305-306; sights, 294-302; Torcello, 304; the town, 292-293; transportation, 293-294; where to party, 309-310

Water trails, see Kneipp water trails

Wengen, Switzerland, 395, 409-411, 415

Windsurfing: Interlaken, Switzerland, 390; St. Moritz, Switzerland, 455; Silvaplana, Switzerland, 465; Zell am See, Austria, 146

Zell am See, Austria, 144-151

Zell am Ziller, Austria, 104

Zellersee, Austria, 146-147

Zermatt, Switzerland, 365-381; accommodations, 377-379; adventures, 373-377; with children, 380; dining, 379; festivals and events, 380-381; history and orientation, 368; information, 371; the Matterhorn, 368-369, 373; memorable moments, 374; outfitters and guides, 376-377; sights, 371-372; the town, 369-370; transportation, 370; where to party, 379-380

Zillertal region, Austria, 100-104; Zillertal Card, 100; outfitters, 102-103

Zoos: Innsbruck, Austria, 16, 79; Kitzbühel, Austria, 108; Salzburg, Austria, 135; Zürich, Switzerland, 426-427

Zug, Austria, 59

Zügspitze, Germany's highest mountain, 210-211

Zürich, Switzerland, 415-428; accommodations, 423-425; adventures, 422-423; with children, 426-427; dining, 425-426; festivals and events, 427-428; history and orientation, 417; information, 419; sights, 420-422; the town, 417-418; transportation, 418-419; where to party, 426; zoo, 426-427; Zürich Card, 419